Maritime Challenges and Priorities in Asia

Maritime issues are particularly important for Asian countries, where there is a high reliance on shipping routes for international trade, many difficult disputes over maritime boundaries, and the prospect of increasing tensions where maritime power might play a significant role. This book uses contributions by 18 experts to build a comprehensive survey of the maritime issues affecting Asia. It discusses the issues overall, goes on to examine the issues from the perspective of each of 14 key countries, and concludes by assessing the prospects for resolving common problems in order to preserve good order at sea.

Joshua H. Ho is an adjunct senior fellow at the S. Rajaratnam School of International Studies, Nanyang Technological University, Singapore.

Sam Bateman is a professorial research fellow at the Australian National Centre for Ocean Resources & Security at the University of Wollongong, Australia.

Routledge security in Asia Pacific series

Series Editors

Leszek Buszynski

International University of Japan

and

William Tow

Australian National University

Security issues have become more prominent in the Asia Pacific region because of the presence of global players, rising great powers, and confident middle powers, which intersect in complicated ways. This series puts forward important new work on key security issues in the region. It embraces the roles of the major actors, their defense policies and postures, and their security interaction over the key issues of the region. It includes coverage of the United States, China, Japan, Russia, and the Koreas, as well as the middle powers of ASEAN and South Asia. It also covers issues relating to environmental and economic security, as well as transnational actors and regional groupings.

1 **Bush and Asia**
America's evolving relations with East Asia
Edited by Mark Beeson

2 **Japan, Australia and Asia-Pacific Security**
Edited by Brad Williams and Andrew Newman

3 **Regional Cooperation and Its Enemies in Northeast Asia**
The impact of domestic forces
Edited by Edward Friedman and Sung Chull Kim

4 **Energy Security in Asia**
Edited by Michael Wesley

5 **Australia as an Asia Pacific Regional Power**
Friendships in flux?
Edited by Brendan Taylor

6 **Securing Southeast Asia**
The politics of security sector reform
Mark Beeson and Alex J. Bellamy

7 **Pakistan's Nuclear Weapons**
Bhumitra Chakma

8 **Human Security in East Asia**
Challenges for collaborative action
Edited by Sorpong Peou

9 **Security and International Politics in the South China Sea**
Towards a co-operative management regime
Edited by Sam Bateman & Ralf Emmers

10 **Japan's Peace-Building Diplomacy in Asia**
Seeking a more active political role
Lam Peng Er

11 **Geopolitics and Maritime Territorial Disputes in East Asia**
Ralf Emmers

12 **North Korea's Military-Diplomatic Campaigns, 1966–2008**
Narushige Michishita

13 **Political Change, Democratic Transitions and Security in Southeast Asia**
Mely Caballero-Anthony

14 **American Sanctions in the Asia-Pacific**
Brendan Taylor

15 **Southeast Asia and the Rise of Chinese and Indian Naval Power**
Between rising naval powers
Edited by Sam Bateman and Joshua H. Ho

16 **Human Security in Southeast Asia**
Yukiko Nishikawa

17 **ASEAN and the Institutionalization of East Asia**
Ralf Emmers

18 **India as an Asia Pacific Power**
David Brewster

19 **ASEAN Regionalism**
Cooperation, values and institutionalisation
Christopher B. Roberts

20 **Nuclear Power and Energy Security in Asia**
Edited by Rajesh Basrur and Koh Swee Lean Collin

21 **Maritime Challenges and Priorities in Asia**
Implications for regional security
Edited by Joshua H. Ho and Sam Bateman

Maritime Challenges and Priorities in Asia

Implications for regional security

Edited by
Joshua H. Ho and Sam Bateman

Routledge
Taylor & Francis Group
LONDON AND NEW YORK

First published 2012
by Routledge
2 Park Square, Milton Park, Abingdon, Oxfordshire OX14 4RN

Simultaneously published in the USA and Canada
by Routledge
711 Third Avenue, New York, NY 10017

First issued in paperback 2014

Routledge is an imprint of the Taylor & Francis Group, an informa business

British Library Cataloguing in Publication Data
A catalogue record for this book is available from the British Library

Library of Congress Cataloging in Publication Data
Maritime challenges and priorities in Asia: implications for regional security/edited by Joshua H. Ho and Sam Bateman.
p. cm. – (Routledge security in Asia Pacific series; 21)
Includes bibliographical references and index.
1. Sea-power–Asia. 2. Marine resources–Asia. 3. National security–Asia. I. Ho, Joshua. II. Bateman, W. S. G. (Walter Samuel Grono) III. Series: Routledge security in Asia Pacific series; 21.
VA620.M368 2012
359′.03095–dc23 2011052685

ISBN 13: 978-0-415-51699-0 (hbk)
ISBN 13: 978-1-138-81668-8 (pbk)

Typeset in Times New Roman
by Wearset Ltd, Boldon, Tyne and Wear

Contents

Illustrations

Figures

Tables

Editors

Sam Bateman retired from the RAN as a commodore and is now Professorial Research Fellow at the Australian National Centre for Ocean Resources & Security (ANCORS) at the University of Wollongong, and Senior Fellow in the Maritime Security Programme at the S. Rajaratnam School of International Studies (RSIS) at the Nanyang Technological University in Singapore. He was awarded a PhD from the University of New South Wales in 2001 for his dissertation on "The Strategic and Political Aspects of the Law of the Sea in East Asian Seas." He has written extensively on defence and maritime issues in Australia, the Asia-Pacific, and the Indian Ocean, including a report for the Australian Strategic Policy Institute (ASPI), *Sea Change: Advancing Australia's Ocean Interests*, released in March 2009, and a policy paper for RSIS on *Good Order at Sea in Southeast Asia – Policy Recommendations,* released in April 2009. Recent co-edited publications include *Security and International Politics in the South China Sea: Towards a Cooperative Management Regime* (Routledge, 2008) and the *Lloyd's MIU Handbook of Maritime Security* (Auerbach Publications, 2008).

Joshua H. Ho is Adjunct Senior Fellow at the S. Rajaratnam School of International Studies in Singapore. He has an MA from Cambridge University, UK on an SAF (Overseas) Scholarship, and also holds a MSc (Management) (Distinction) from the Naval Postgraduate School in California, where he was awarded the Graduate School of Business and Public Policy Faculty award for Excellence in Management, which is awarded to the top student in the faculty. He is also a Fellow of the Cambridge Commonwealth Society, an Associate Member of the United States Naval Institute, and a member of the International Institute for Strategic Studies. Joshua was a serving Naval Officer with 25 years of service and held the rank of lieutenant colonel. He has held various shipboard and staff appointments including the command of a missile gunboat and stints in the Naval Operations, Plans, and Personnel Departments and the Future Systems Directorate, MINDEF. He has also held concurrent appointments of Honorary Aide de Camp to the President, Secretary to the Naval Staff Meeting, and Secretary to the Policy and Strategy Meeting, MINDEF. He has edited or co-edited five volumes: *Best of Times,*

Worst of Times: Maritime Security in the Asia-Pacific; *The Evolving Maritime Balance of Power in the Asia-Pacific: Maritime Doctrines and Nuclear Weapons at Sea*; *Globalization and Defence in the Asia-Pacific: Arms Across Asia*; *Realising Safe and Secure Seas for All* and *Southeast Asia*; and *The Rise of Chinese and Indian Naval Power: Between Rising Naval Powers*. He has also published in local and overseas journals such as *Asian Survey*, *Australian Army Journal*, *Contemporary Southeast Asia*, *Defence Studies*, *Journal of the Australian Naval Institute*, *Maritime Affairs*, *The Korean Journal of Defense Analyses*, *Australian Journal of Maritime and Ocean Affairs*, *Marine Policy*, *Military Technology*, *Ocean Development*, *International Law*, *Pointer*, and *Security Challenges*, as well as having contributed numerous chapters to books. He has also taught professional courses at the Home Team Academy and at the Singapore Armed Forces Military Institute (SAFTI-MI).

Contributors

Mohd Nizam Basiron is a research fellow at the Centre for Maritime Security and Environment at the Maritime Institute of Malaysia (MIMA).

Hasjim Djalal is a member of the Indonesian Maritime Council, senior advisor to the Indonesian Minister for Maritime Affairs and Fisheries and to Indonesian Naval Chief of Staff, and lectures at universities and other higher learning institutions in Indonesia.

Wang Dong is an assistant professor in the School of International Studies at Peking University, where he teaches both graduate and undergraduate courses in "International Relations Theories," "American Foreign Policy," and "Chinese Foreign Policy."

Wilfried A. Herrmann is Vice-chairman of the board and Executive Director of the Human Development Forum Foundation in Bangkok.

Tetsuo Kotani is a special research fellow at the Okazaki Institute. His areas of specialization include the US–Japan alliance, security affairs in the Asia-Pacific, and maritime security.

James Kraska is Professor of International Law and Howard S. Levie Chair of Operational Law (January 2010) at the US Naval War College, and Guest Investigator at the Marine Policy Center, Woods Hole Oceanographic Institution.

Seokwoo Lee is Professor of International Law and Director of the Inha International Ocean Law Centre at Inha University in Korea.

Maung Aung Myoe teaches Southeast Asian Politics and International Relations at the International University of Japan.

Joanna Mossop is a senior lecturer in Law at the Victoria University of Wellington in New Zealand.

Nguyen Hong Thao is Professor of International Law, International Organizations, and Environmental Law at the National University of Hanoi in Vietnam.

Prabhakaran Paleri is the former Director General of the Indian Coast Guard. He is currently a professor and heads the newly started School of Management Studies at the National Institute of Technology Calicut (NITC) in India, as well as being a freelance strategy analyst.

Mary Ann Palma is a research fellow at the Australian National Centre for Ocean Resources & Security (ANCORS) at the University of Wollongong in Australia, where she lectures for the Master of Maritime Policy programme and conducts research on international fisheries law and policy, ocean policy, and maritime security.

Geoffrey Till is Professor of Maritime Studies at the Joint Services Command and Staff College and a member of the Defence Studies Department, part of the War Studies Group of King's College London. He is also Director of the Corbett Centre for Maritime Policy Studies.

Robin Warner is a senior research fellow at the Australian National Centre for Ocean Resources & Security at the University of Wollongong in Australia, and the recipient of an Australian Research Council Postdoctoral Fellowship for 2010–2012.

Jiang Xin is a research assistant at the Center for Northeast Asian Strategic Studies, Peking University.

Yee Cheok Hong is Group Director (Policy and Planning) at the Maritime and Port Authority of Singapore.

Introduction

Joshua H. Ho

Concept of the edited volume

Good order at sea ensures the safety and security of shipping, and permits countries to pursue their maritime interests and develop their marine resources in accordance with agreed principles of international law.[1] Threats to good order at sea include piracy and armed robbery against ships, maritime terrorism, illicit trafficking in drugs and arms, people smuggling, pollution, illegal fishing, marine natural hazards and inter-state maritime conflict.

Asia is a distinctively maritime region. The relative lack of land-based transport infrastructure, both within and between countries, as well as its geographical nature, means that shipping plays an extremely important role in the region. The region sits astride key "choke points" for shipping between the Indian and Pacific Oceans, which are economically and strategically important to the economies of North-East Asia, the United States and the emerging maritime powers of Asia. Many countries see themselves as stakeholders in good order at sea in Asia, but it ultimately depends on the actions of regional countries to ensure it.

Most regional countries have extensive maritime interests. Most of these have trans-boundary and regional dimensions that should facilitate cooperation. Regional cooperation is essential to the maintenance of good order at sea, but at present this is underdeveloped in Asia. Particular problems that inhibit cooperation include inadequate resources, poor coordination between national agencies and the lack of maritime boundaries in parts of the region, as well as a concern that cooperation may involve some loss of sovereignty or independence. For similar reasons, key international conventions that help establish good order at sea, and a range of new international measures to enhance security at sea, such as the Long Range Identification and Tracking (LRIT) system for ships and the Ship Security Alert System, are not effective in the region at present.

The Association of Southeast Asian nations (ASEAN) and the ASEAN Regional Forum (ARF) have taken some initiatives to enhance regional maritime cooperation, but the process could be speeded up, including both "top-down" initiatives that might come out of the ARF and ASEAN and "bottom-up" steps using existing processes as "building blocks" to further the process of cooperation.

Aim of the edited volume

With this concept in mind, a conference was organised by RSIS in Singapore in January 2010 to examine ways to improve good order at sea by inviting various regional experts to present papers from the perspective of their own country. The conference did this by first examining the challenges and different priorities that regional countries placed on maritime affairs through presentations made by experts from each regional country. Subsequently, by acknowledging these interests, the conference proceeded to examine areas of collaboration and cooperation that could be feasible. These areas of collaboration should address the interests of most countries and not undermine the core interests of any particular country. Of course, not all countries share the same interests, and mapping these individual interests and priorities can also facilitate bilateral cooperation as long as it doesn't undermine the collective interests of the entire group. The identification of areas of collaboration was done via brainstorming sessions using Geoffrey Till's four historic attributes of the sea as a framing device.[2]

The first breakout session on the sea as a medium of dominion looked at ways the region can deal with the threats of maritime terrorism and conflict in the maritime domain. The second breakout session on the sea as resource looked at ways for sustainable harvesting of the resources of the sea, which included sustainable fishing, sustainable mining of energy resources, protection of the marine environment, delimitation of maritime zones and other ocean management issues. The third breakout session on the sea as a medium of transportation and exchange examined ways to improve safety of navigation in key sea-lanes and included addressing the issue of piracy and armed robbery, ship tracking and identification, ship security alert systems and the illegal trafficking in drugs, arms and humans. The fourth breakout session focused on the kinds of regional institutions required to deal with maritime challenges and looked at the suitability of bilateral or multilateral arrangements.

What follows is a summary of each chapter in the edited volume.

Part I – Overview of maritime challenges in Asia

Managing good order at sea in the Asia-Pacific

Sam Bateman begins by defining "good order at sea" as the need to ensure the safety and security of shipping, and to permit countries to pursue their maritime interests and develop their marine resources in an ecologically sustainable and peaceful manner in accordance with international law. He highlights that cooperation between countries is necessary to ensure good order at sea. Bateman outlines the major threats to good order at sea as: marine pollution that originates from sea-based or land-based sources; piracy and sea robbery; the illegal movement of people and goods; illegal, unreported and unregulated (IUU) fishing; climate change that will likely affect many people directly or indirectly, through the loss of fish stocks and marine habitats or an increased prevalence of natural disasters; lack of maritime boundaries between neighbouring states that could lead to a breakdown in bilateral ties; maritime terrorism; proliferation of WMD; potential causes of conflict at sea, for example the Korean Peninsula, across the Taiwan Strait or over disputed territories; and increased naval defence spending that creates an environment of increased military activity, which is potentially destabilizing.

He notes that managing good order at sea requires consideration of oceans management, which includes arrangements for managing the various uses of the sea and its living resources, protection of the marine environment and maritime security. A comprehensive approach to maritime security that includes measures for protecting sovereignty, preventing illegal activity at sea, protecting SLOCs (i.e., Sea Lines of Communication), maritime safety, search and rescue, and mitigating marine natural hazards is also necessary. Bateman concludes that countries in the Asia-Pacific region have an enormous interest in ensuring that new threats and risks in the oceans are addressed, and that focus must be on achieving real outcomes and not just talk. On Track II level initiatives, he mentions the establishment of a study group by the Council for Security Cooperation in the Asia-Pacific to investigate the implications of naval enhancements in the region; however, he notes that Track I level efforts like the ARF also need to address these issues.

The historic attributes of the sea and maritime developments in the Asia-Pacific

Geoffrey Till begins by quoting Alfred Thayer Mahan: "Control of the sea by maritime commerce and naval supremacy means predominate influence in the world ... [and] is the chief among the merely material elements in the power and prosperity of nations." He then summarizes the four interconnected attributes of the sea in human history.

The sea as a resource

The sea has been crucial to the development of world civilization. Mankind still harvests 20 per cent of its daily protein intake from the sea, and more recently oil and gas extraction from the maritime environment has also been economically crucial. Competition for valuable sea resources has always played an important part in human history. There is a fear that the gross energy shortages that some analysts expect in the future could become a significant source of instability and conflict in the Asia-Pacific.

The sea as a medium of transport and exchange

Water transport was initially very localized but as marine technology improved, local and regional transport systems linked up to form a "system of systems" that spanned the world, allowing colonizations and the exchange of goods to occur. Geoffrey notes that today cargo ships and their cargoes are agents of connection, with an important role in globalization.

The sea as a medium for information and the spread of ideas

Through interactions in the maritime domain, ideas and cultures have been spread both consciously and unconsciously. For centuries, the waterfront was a source of the latest information about one's country as well as the wider world, similar to the role of the Internet today.

The sea as a medium for dominion

Most societies have been subject to attacks from forces by sea. The sea provides both a means for defence and attack and, not surprisingly, peer competition has been the main driver behind naval development. Globally, strong economic performance has also led to high levels of naval construction, and as the Asia-Pacific region continues to see high gross domestic product growth levels, it is expected that naval expenditures may exceed those in the West, excluding the United States.

Carriage capacity of the Straits of Malacca and Singapore

Yee Cheok Hong outlines the Maritime and Port Authority of Singapore's simulation study on the Carriage Capacity of the Strait of Malacca and Singapore (SoMS). As global trade has been projected to increase by 44 per cent by 2020 and to double by 2031, the computer simulation has been used to systematically determine the current level of traffic and assess the carriage capacity of the SoMS, which is being evaluated on the basis of efficiency and safety of navigation within the straits.

Three objectives of the simulation highlighted in the chapter are: (1) to evaluate the carriage capacity of the SoMS, taking into account the historical volume and pattern of maritime traffic in the area, as well as existing navigational routes and rules employed in the area; (2) to identify the narrow or choke points and possible congestion areas in the SoMS in terms of carriage capacity; and (3) to examine possible measures that could enhance carriage capacity while maintaining navigational safety in the SoMS.

Yee explains that two separate models were built: one for the Singapore Strait, which required a more detailed investigation as it is the narrower of the two straits; and another for the Strait of Malacca, which has a much less detailed traffic record. The total number of vessels above 300 gross tonnes transiting and calling at port for the year 2007 was 257,000. In the absence of complete data for the Strait of Malacca, an approximation of 126,000 was used, based on known traffic for the Singapore Strait and available information for the Strait of Malacca.

The preliminary results of the study show that when the traffic level increases in the Singapore Strait there is a corresponding increase in travel time. When traffic is doubled from the base year of 2007, not only does travel time rise by 13 per cent, increasing a seven-hour transit through the

Singapore Strait to nearly eight hours, the number of interactions between vessels also increased from one interaction every ten nautical miles, to 15 every ten nautical miles. However, this increase in interactions is not uniform throughout the length of the Strait. Preliminary results for the Malacca Strait suggest that as the traffic level increases, there is no significant change in travel time, even with a five-fold increase in volume scenario. When traffic is increased three times, each vessel is predicted to have about five interactions for every 100 nautical miles, an increase from the base year in which each vessel would encounter three interactions per 100 nautical miles. This implies that the Malacca Strait can sustain traffic up to five times the current level, assuming that traffic numbers and patterns used in the model for the Malacca Strait are reasonably close to reality and that all technology, processes and operations remain the same as those of today. In contrast, for the Singapore Strait, there is a gradual increase in the vessel travel time and number of interactions per mile travelled as the traffic volume is increased by up to 75 per cent over the base year level, beyond which the increase becomes more pronounced.

In conclusion, Yee mentions that the capacity of the SoMS can be further increased with improved traffic management measures and technological advances. He also notes that if traffic volume and pattern details obtained for the Malacca Strait were as comprehensive as the data used for the Singapore Strait, the model could be adjusted, generating new, more reliable results.

Part II – Maritime challenges and priorities in Southeast Asia

Indonesia's maritime challenges and priorities

For Hasjim Djalal, the first challenge Indonesia needs to tackle is identifying its national boundaries. These boundaries include airspace, land and maritime boundaries. Although there have been many agreements dating back to the colonial period, locating these boundaries has proven to be a challenging task and has led to a number of territorial disputes. Being an archipelagic nation, Indonesia has a complicated maritime boundary, which generates many maritime zones. These zones include internal waters, archipelagic waters and territorial sea, the contiguous zone, the exclusive economic zone (EEZ) and the continental shelf.

Indonesia has so far been unable to demarcate its internal waters as stipulated under the United Nations Convention on the Law of the Sea (UNCLOS), but has fixed its archipelagic waters. There are also problems with delimiting territorial sea. The delimitation negotiations with Malaysia, Singapore, Vietnam, Australia and Papua New Guinea have shown some success, though progress with the Philippines is slow. The next problem is the contiguous zone of 12 nautical miles. Currently, no discussion has taken place between Indonesia and its neighbours on how to exercise their rights in the overlapping contiguous zones. With a large EEZ, Indonesia faces the challenge of delimiting its EEZ boundaries with all of its neighbours except Australia, although the agreement has yet to be ratified by both sides. With regard to the continental shelf, Indonesia has made gains with its neighbours, like Malaysia, Vietnam and the Philippines, but there is still a lot of work to be done on the submission for the extended continental shelf beyond the 200 nautical miles EEZ.

Besides the various maritime zones, Indonesia also has several interests in the high seas. The first is the management of resources that include fisheries and the seabed resources. The second is cooperation with its neighbours in semi-enclosed seas, like the South China Sea, the Celebes Sea, the Arafura Sea, the Timor Sea and possibly the Andaman Sea.

The maritime zones also pose other challenges. The first is related to national unity and integrity: as it is a large and diverse archipelagic country, unsound policies can lead to internal conflict. The second challenge is to eliminate IUU fishing, as Indonesia loses more than US$2 billion a year as a result of illegal fishing. The third challenge is the rampant illegal smuggling of natural resources, like logs, which costs Indonesia US$3 billion a year. Smuggling has not only increased but now encompasses endangered and protected animals. The fourth challenge is to determine the passage of shipping through the archipelago. Although archipelagic sea-lanes have been designated, there has been no stipulation of the extent to which shipping can deviate from these lanes. Other challenges include law enforcement within Indonesia as well as cross-boundary law enforcement, which require bilateral or multilateral cooperation. But perhaps the greatest challenge is to balance the national interests of Indonesia and the interests of the user states, as these do not always coincide.

Malaysia's maritime challenges and priorities

Mohd Nizam Basiron discusses and analyses Malaysia's maritime challenges and opportunities by examining each of the seas and the issues that they pose to the country's policy makers and managers, as well as the crosscutting issues that affect the governance of Malaysia's maritime realm. First, the challenges posed by the Straits of Malacca to Malaysia's policy makers and managers stem partly from its multiple uses as straits for international navigation, a fertile fishing ground and an important location for social and economic activities such as tourism. To address these challenges, Malaysia has implemented various safety of navigation tools and helped to put in place the Malacca Straits Patrols.

Second, Nizam mentions that the South China Sea is important to Malaysia for geopolitical, ecological and economic reasons. Almost all of Malaysia's offshore hydrocarbon resources are located in this area and the South China Sea is site of the second most important fisheries for Malaysia. It is also an area of ecological and environmental significance to Malaysia. Unlike the Strait of Malacca, Malaysia's challenges in the South China Sea are more geopolitical and environmental in nature. Signing of the Declaration on the Conduct of Parties in the South China Sea and bilateral negotiations, regional cooperation and national actions, and stricter enforcement activities are helpful in resolving these disputes.

Third, the Gulf of Thailand is probably the least problematic of Malaysia's sea areas and illustrates the possibility of cooperation even in areas where maritime boundary delimitation has not been completed. Malaysia has two joint development areas in the Gulf of Thailand with Thailand and Vietnam, respectively.

Fourth, the challenges posed by Sulu Sea are mainly non-traditional maritime security issues, including smuggling and human trafficking, movement of transient populations, kidnapping by separatist or terrorist groups and use of destructive fishing methods. To tackle these challenges, Malaysia has implemented integrated security measures under Operation *Pasir* and will continue to enforce these measures.

Fifth, the Sulawesi Sea was for Malaysia an area where traditional maritime security concerns predominates, as the maritime boundary delimitation with Indonesia is still unresolved and naval tension is high. In addition, Nizam mentions that Malaysia has maritime boundaries with Indonesia, Singapore, Thailand, Vietnam, Brunei and the Philippines and has signed various agreements to delimit the boundaries. However, its undelimited maritime boundaries still pose a challenge for maintaining sovereignty and control over parts of Malaysia's maritime realm and the development of its resources. Therefore, Nizam concludes that Malaysia needs to urgently address a myriad of maritime challenges that could affect the sustainability of its maritime resources and its security as a maritime nation.

Myanmar's maritime challenges and priorities

Maung Aung Myoe starts with an introduction of Myanmar's maritime boundaries. The most serious maritime security issue for Myanmar, according to him, is the maritime boundary dispute with Bangladesh. The dispute, which involves an area containing a huge reserve of oil and gas, could potentially escalate into a major armed conflict. Despite eight rounds of talks from 1974 to 1986 – two at a ministerial level and the others at a technical level – the issue remains unresolved, with both Myanmar and Bangladesh disagreeing on the delimitation of territorial seas. The most problematic aspect of the Myanmar–Bangladesh boundary issue was the maritime boundary that covers the territorial seas, EEZ and the continental shelf. Evidently, Myanmar had adhered to the principle of equidistance or the true median line throughout the numerous rounds of talks. However, Bangladesh vacillated from the principle of equality (during the first three rounds of talks) to the equitable principle that included a friendship line followed by a return to the application of the1982 UNCLOS and principle of equality. By 2008, Bangladesh came up with a new proposal based on equality and proportionality. The proposed line would be 180 degrees from the most eastward points of the baseline, taking more than 18,000sq. km away from Myanmar. The case was brought to the United Nations in 2009 for final arbitration.

Next, the dispute between Myanmar and Thailand regarding the ownership of three islands located at the mouth of the Pakchan River was outlined. During the negotiations between Myanmar and Thailand on delimitation of the territorial sea boundary, the Continental Shelf and EEZ from 1977 to 1980, both agreed that the ownership of the three islands would be settled on the basis of historical evidence. Myanmar attempted to reclaim ownership with historical evidence dating as far back as the 1800s. Thailand also produced evidence that identified the three islands as belonging to Thailand. In 1997, an amendment was made by the United Kingdom Hydrographic Office (UKHO) to Admiralty Chart No. 216 that placed the three islands on Myanmar's side, which was met with protest from Thailand. Subsequently, UKHO informed both countries that the future Admiralty Chart No. 216 would exclude the Approximate Boundary Line until an agreement was met. Maung Aung Myoe concludes the chapter with a brief discussion on non-traditional security, such as the decline in mangrove habitats, illegal fishing and unregulated exploitation of marine resources.

Maintaining good order at sea: maritime challenges and priorities in the Philippines

Mary Ann Palma starts by providing the geographical context of the Philippines so as to locate the maritime challenges it faces, which mainly consist of illegal activities in the maritime domain. Philippine's maritime interests include coastal protection, management of offshore marine resources and activities, navigation and marine transportation, law enforcement, and national defence and security.

Preservation of marine biodiversity is a challenge, in particular the need to balance the extraction of petroleum with marine conservation activities. Maritime traffic also poses a challenge for conservation. For the Philippines to be able to conserve its marine resources while promoting its marine activities, it has adopted a number of laws and policies, one of which is the Philippine National Marine Policy of 1994. The concept of maritime security espoused by the National Marine Policy is very similar to the concept of "good order at sea."

The threats to Philippine maritime security are in the realm of transnational crime, such as the trade of illicit drugs and the illegal trafficking of arms and people. Factors that contribute to the proliferation of these illegal activities include poverty and a lack of adequate enforcement compounded by a long and unguarded coastline. Moreover, deficiencies in laws and regulations, for example regarding labour policies and banking systems, add to the problem. In some areas, political instability has contributed to the lack of good order and corruption is an endemic problem. There are also other concerns like territorial and jurisdictional boundaries and the kidnapping of Filipino seafarers in the Gulf of Aden, as well as maritime accidents and disasters. In terms of maritime jurisdiction, there is a new Archipelagic Baselines Law governing maritime boundaries. However, there is currently a petition to the Supreme Court to repeal this law.

There is inter-agency cooperation to address illegal activities on both land and sea. The Philippines has extensively cooperated with international organizations and other states in regional, as well as sub-regional, settings. Palma concludes by stating some of the issues that the Philippines will have to consider in the future, and these include trafficking of human organs, controlling access to genetic resources, upholding the rights of fish workers and the implementation of relevant international agreements, as well as the possibility of setting up a regional LRIT centre.

Singapore's maritime interests

Joshua H. Ho first describes the emergence of Singapore as an entrepot port in the modern era through the vision and actions of Sir Stamford Raffles. With the opening of the Suez Canal, Singapore became more important as a hub port due to its strategic location sitting astride the sea-lanes of the East and the West. Joshua explains the three factors that came together to make Singapore so important as a hub port: location, free trade and a primary producing hinterland covering modern Malaysian and Indonesia. Its importance continues today, as Singapore has become the world's top container port, the world's top bunkering port, the world's third largest oil-refining centre, a thriving international centre for shipbuilding, ship repairs and conversions, and a regional cruise centre. Because of the importance of the sea to Singapore's well-being, it has adopted a comprehensive approach to maritime security, and developed an integrated response that is meant to promote Singapore's maritime interests.

Joshua goes on to elaborate that Singapore's maritime interests can be defined as minimizing disruption to shipping and port activities and ensuring open, safe and secure access to sea lanes through active policy prescription in the areas of maritime safety, security, environmental protection and international law.

Measures that have been taken to enhance maritime safety include the provision of adequate navigation aids and the provision of search and rescue services. Measures to enhance maritime security include the protection of critical maritime infrastructure, defending access to sea-lanes and delimiting maritime boundaries. Measures to enhance marine environmental protection include the implementation of legislative measures and the development of contingency plans.

However, the comprehensive definition of maritime security adopted by Singapore puts a premium on inter-agency coordination at both national and regional levels. Various inter-agency coordinating mechanisms have been implemented at the national level by the littoral countries. In terms of inter-agency coordination at the regional level, three cooperative regimes stand out: the Cooperative Mechanism (CM), the Malacca Straits Patrols (MSP) and the Regional Cooperation Agreement on Combating Piracy and Armed Robbery against Ships in Asia (ReCAAP) Information Sharing Centre (ISC).

Joshua concludes by saying that the creation of a stable maritime regime in the region is important because countries in the region share significant maritime interests. These interests will increasingly intersect as the use of the sea increases in the future due to burgeoning maritime traffic as a result of the robust economies of the Asia-Pacific region. However, to govern maritime cooperation three principles will have to be foremost: that littoral states have the primary role in addressing maritime security issues; that other stakeholders have important roles to play; and that consultation should be pursued and the rule of international law be observed in the implementation of any new initiatives.

Thailand's maritime challenges and priorities

Wilfried A Herrmann highlights the objectives of the Thai Navy, which are to protect territorial integrity and sea-based resources, fight illegal fishing, prevent illicit drug smuggling and prevent human trafficking. He then proceeds to explain that the Royal Thai Navy's strategic pillars include cooperative security building, collective national defence and maintaining internal security through the Internal Security Act 2008. The Royal Thai Navy's main role in defence military operations is to defend the territorial integrity of its 1,500 km of coastline and its attendant claims for EEZ and extended continental shelf. Seeing that Thailand has two sea borders, it makes sense to have two fleets, but the Thais have not been able to achieve that despite ambitions to do so. In military operations other than war (MOOTW), the navy conducts disaster relief operations to support the country's development, protects against illegal fishing, fights illicit drug and arms smuggling, and tackles the human trafficking and refugee problem.

Thailand is a transit land for illegal traffickers and refugees heading south to countries like Australia, but there has been cooperation in dealing with this issue. The Royal Thai Navy also has a role in international affairs assistance, in particular in ASEAN maritime cooperation, in ReCAAP cooperation and support and in disaster relief operations.

The Thai Navy has plans to procure offshore patrol vessels and submarines, as well as to develop amphibious capabilities. In conclusion, Wilfried A. Herrmann states that the Thai Navy is a littoral navy with sufficient assets, as the country is not confronted by many serious challenges. However, there is a need to modernize its command, control, communications, computers and information (C4I) infrastructure and the surface fleet, although budgetary constraints and the economic downturn could dampen those ambitions.

Good order at sea: challenges and priorities of Vietnam

Nguyen Hong Thao highlights three main challenges for Vietnam: the maritime delimitation and settlement of maritime disputes; the depletion of fish stocks; and the development of the marine transport system.

The first challenge for Vietnam is to settle the delimitation of maritime zones with opposite and adjacent states in the South China Sea. Any unresolved disputes concerning the EEZ and continental shelf could hinder resource development and enforcement against illegal fishing. Previously concluded disputes include the Agreement on Maritime Delimitation with Thailand involving the Bac Bo (Tonkin) Gulf in August 1997, the agreement on the delineation of continental shelves with Indonesia in June 2003, and the agreement with Malaysia on joint petroleum exploitation in the overlapping area in 1992.

Any unsettled disputes have evidently affected the whole region, for example, the Paracels and Spratlys, which underscore the importance of good order and security at sea. Other examples include the two major events involving Chinese patrol ships and the US ocean surveillance vessel USNS *Impeccable* in March 2009, and the collision of a Chinese submarine with the sonar cable of the USS *John McCain* in June 2009, due to differing interpretations of the rights and duties in an EEZ.

The second challenge for Vietnam is the depletion of fish stocks compounded by other problems, such as pollution and the destruction of coral reefs and marine habitat. Vietnam's priorities cover illegal fishing and anti-armed robbery of the fishermen in the disputed areas. Such problems arise due to the blurred EEZ boundaries and underdeveloped fishing cooperative management in South-East Asia. To combat these challenges, initiatives based on regional fishing management cooperation in South-East Asia should be set up. The 2001 UN Agreement on the conservation and the management of straddling fish stocks and highly migratory fish stocks must be ratified.

The last challenge is the development of the marine transportation sector, which covers petroleum activities and international maritime transportation along the coast of Vietnam. It is important to focus on these activities as they give rise to problems such as marine pollution, marine accident, piracy, terrorism and illegal trafficking, among others.

Part III – Maritime challenges and priorities in Northeast Asia

China's maritime security: priorities and challenges

Wang Dong and Jiang Xin mention that although China's maritime interest has expanded over the last two decades, its maritime strategy seems to have lagged far behind. An examination of China's maritime security discourses, both scholarly and policy, in the last two decades reveals that four areas of issues related to maritime security have been raised that reflect China's maritime priorities and challenges. The first is the debate over sea power (*haiquan*) and China's maritime strategy. Wang Dong and Jiang Xin mention that there are three ways of interpreting sea power: the legalistic interpretation, the defensive realism-oriented interpretation and the offensive realism-oriented one. The majority of the public support the first interpretation. Interestingly, a considerable number of scholars hold the defensive realist-oriented discourse. However, this could easily metamorphosize into a more offensive realist-oriented one.

The second area relates to maritime disputes in the East China Sea and the South China Sea. Competition for maritime energy resources, nationalistic sentiments among the claimants, the strategic importance of the disputed areas, and the different interpretations of legal principles, as well as the US involvement have all complicated the issues in the South China Sea. With regard to East China Sea disputes, Chinese scholars admit the weakness of Chinese strategy and policy, and propose improving strategic study and planning. Some scholars suggest developing an effective regime to coordinate each party's actions. With regard to South China Sea disputes, scholars have also put forth constructive proposals, including the establishment of a multilateral "Spratly Islands Development Authority."

The third area relates to China's emerging interest in combating piracy and maritime terrorism. China has increasingly participated in the counter piracy and maritime terrorism campaign in recent years. However, one challenge for China is to find an appropriate way to take part in the institutional build-up of a counter-piracy regime in South China Sea and Malacca Straits.

The fourth and final area relates to maritime governance of other non-traditional security issues. In contrast to its slow progress in resolving boundary disputes and countering piracy incidents, China has achieved a higher level of cooperation with ASEAN countries in non-traditional security issues, including people smuggling, illegal drugs trafficking and arms smuggling. Wang Dong and Jiang Xin conclude by saying that China needs to go beyond the concept of *haiquan* and develop a comprehensive maritime strategy that will pave the way for a peaceful rise of China in the twenty-first century.

Japan's maritime challenges and priorities

Tetsuo Kotani mentions that the 2008 Japan Coast Guard (JCG) annual report carried a feature article on the dramatically changing missions of the JCG. Its core missions – marine environmental protection, marine surveys, rescue, law enforcement and navigation safety – remain intact, but, for example, heavily armed, high-speed North Korean spy boats running wild in Japanese waters, growing tension over maritime interests and threats from terrorism and proliferation have all have made the role of the JCG more important in the protection of Japan's sovereignty and sea borders. The JCG has also come to play a greater role in countering the increased number of piracy incidents in the distant waters of South-East Asia. In addition, it has initiated many bilateral and multilateral mechanisms for ensuring good order at sea.

Likewise, Tetsuo mentions that the Japan Maritime Self-Defense Force (JMSDF) has adapted itself to the changing maritime environment. Beyond its traditional region of operation up to 1,000 nautical miles from home, the JMSDF has maintained its presence in the Indian Ocean to support the coalition maritime interdiction operations and began counter-piracy operation in the Gulf of Aden with JCG officers aboard. It has also intensified interactions with navies of other like-minded nations, such as India and Australia. On the other hand, the 2009 Defence White Paper showed concern over Chinese naval activities in and around Japanese waters, indicating that the role of the JMSDF will become more important to meet Chinese naval expansion in the Western Pacific.

Japan faces those old and new maritime challenges in the Western Pacific and Northern Indian Oceans—from the Sea of Japan, the Philippine Sea and the East and South China Seas to the Straits of Malacca and Singapore, the Andaman Sea, the Bay of Bengal, the Arabian Sea and the Persian Gulf. Japan enacted the Basic Act on Ocean Policy in 2007 and formulated the Basic Plan on Ocean Policy and other related measures to meet those challenges. The chapter first examines how Japan has met challenges within its vast sea borders. It then reviews Japan's efforts to secure its long and vital sea-lanes. Lastly, it analyzes the implications of the Basic Act of Ocean Policy for Japan's efforts to maintain good order at sea.

Korea's maritime challenges and priorities

Seokwoo Lee mentions that the sea plays an important role for South Korea's economy and security and, thus, that making good order at sea is a vital priority for the country. Of particular economic concern are issues such as piracy and armed robbery against ships, and the depletion of fish stocks. South Korea has joined various bilateral, regional and international cooperation agreements to address these issues. Moreover, South Korea has territorial disputes with Japan over the Dokdo/Takeshima Islets and with China over the Ieodo/Suyan Rock, which has so far led to little progress in maritime boundary delimitation negotiations between South Korea and these two countries.

Seokwoo continues by saying that in terms of security, South Korea is technically still at war with North Korea, since hostilities during the Korean War were only halted by an armistice agreement in 1953. In particular, the issue of North Korea's nuclear weapons programme, as well as the unresolved dispute over sea boundaries between the two countries in the West Sea present serious challenges to peace and stability on the Korean Peninsula. After naval skirmishes in the West Sea in 1999, 2002 and 2009, tensions have escalated recently following the sinking of a South Korean Navy corvette, the ROKS *Cheonan*, in March 2010. Additionally, South Korea's participation in the Proliferation Security Initiative (PSI) has been met with verbal threats of war by North Korea.

In summary, the first part of the chapter discusses some of the maritime challenges facing South Korea, with a particular focus on issues such as piracy and armed robbery against ships, depletion of fish stocks, the PSI, and the recent conflict over the sinking of the *Cheonan*. The second part of the chapter indicates the status of territorial disputes and delimitation issues between South Korea and its neighbours, followed by a brief summary of South Korea's maritime priorities going forward.

In conclusion, Seokwoo reiterates that recent skirmishes in the Yellow Sea area between South and North Korea have reshuffled the maritime priorities of South Korea, as North Korean issues overwhelm other important priorities. He suggests that the South Korean government should set up guidelines for maritime security as it is surrounded by neighbours with which it has unresolved territorial and maritime boundary issues. South Korea has to prepare not only for bilateral disputes, but also for bilateral disputes from a multilateral perspective.

Part IV – Maritime challenges and priorities for the rest of the Indo-Pacific

America's maritime challenges and priorities: the Asian dimension

Taking a theoretical approach to the history of Ocean Law, James Kraska elaborates on America's perspective on the Law of the Sea. One hundred years before the Treaty of Westphalia, Europe was consumed with religious wars. It was hoped that the maritime domain would provide access to the riches of India and China, while avoiding the Ottoman Empire. Intending to reserve the maritime domain for themselves, Spain and Portugal signed the Treaty of Tordesillas. By controlling maritime access to the New World and exporting vast amounts of wealth, Spain rose to become a pre-eminent power and was able to fund its occupation of the Netherlands. Unable to compete with the Spanish on land, the Dutch turned to the sea instead, and established their sea power. As the predominance of sea power rose, it facilitated legitimate globalization and the multiplier effect of creating wealth through trade, rather than merely extracting and importing it from the New World.

Due to its history of establishment and geographical nature, the US has always looked "with one eye on the frontier and one eye on the oceans." The US fought its first four wars over maritime security and the freedom of the sea, and challenged Portugal and Spain's lock on the oceans. Kraska notes that there were two paths of jurisprudence generally followed by nations: the more liberal common law system, with Dutch and Anglo-Saxon origins, and the more heavily regulated system based on the Napoleonic code. The US normally follows the more liberal path, and with regard to Asia is at odds with the heavily regulated view. The challenge for the US is to navigate between the two competing paradigms in the Asia-Pacific.

Australia's maritime challenges and priorities: recent developments and future prospects

Robin Warner begins by noting that Australia is extremely reliant on the sea for communication, security, resources and future development, but is still in the early stages of realizing the potential of the sea. The scope of her presentation covered three areas of challenges: defining Australia's maritime jurisdiction; protecting Australia's national interests at sea; and understanding the oceans and their relationship to global climate.

Warner notes that Australia has reached an advanced stage in defining its maritime boundaries and has negotiated delimitation agreements or joint resource development agreements with each of its neighbours. Australia's extended continental shelf contains living and non-living resources including sedentary species, marine genetic resources, seabed oil and gas, and seabed minerals. She emphasizes that the exploitation of these resources must take into account established shipping routes, conservation of marine biodiversity, location of submarine cables and pipelines, and the presence of equipment related to marine scientific research.

The challenges Australia faces in protecting its national interests at sea range from preventing potential aggressors from crossing Australia's maritime approaches and deterring criminal activity in Australia's offshore zones, to supporting regional and global security initiatives that help maintain freedom of use and access to the ocean. Australia's 2009 Defence White Paper announced plans for a significant naval force modernization. The ability of Australia's maritime surveillance and enforcement resources to respond to illegal activity will be enhanced through a proposed consolidation of maritime law enforcement powers in a Commonwealth Statute, which will integrate the legal mechanisms contained in 35 separate pieces of Commonwealth legislation. Australia has also been active within other regional and global initiatives, including the Australia–France Cooperative Maritime Surveillance and Enforcement treaties and operations in the Southern Ocean, reinvigorating the Bali Process on People Smuggling, Trafficking in Persons and Related Transnational Crime, and counter piracy operations off the Horn of Africa.

Australia is addressing the emerging challenge of harnessing the oceans to combat climate change by identifying ocean-based energy sources, such as wind, tidal, wave, ocean currents and ocean thermal gradient energy, as well as investigating the potential for using the ocean's capacity to absorb greenhouse gases. In conclusion, she remarks that a reassessment of Australia's Oceans Policy is required to address the addition of substantial new areas of maritime jurisdiction, the presence of ongoing threats to resources and border security, and necessary investments in ocean-based technologies to combat climate change.

Maritime challenges and priorities in Asia: an Indian perspective

Prabhakaran Paleri mentions that the maritime challenges that India faces are similar to those faced by other nations. Perhaps one of the more pressing challenges is trafficking in wildlife. In addition, history shows that India has always faced challenges at and from the sea in the form of colonial invasion, illegal immigration, rampant smuggling leading to a parallel economy, large-scale human smuggling in the post-independence period, insurgencies and terrorist support chains, espionage and intelligence gathering, and the carrying out of crimes at sea.

He notes that the economy of India is gaining influence amid the backdrop of a wider Asian economic renaissance. Because of this, there were tremendous opportunities for India–ASEAN trade, most of which will traverse by sea, making the sea an important domain for both India and ASEAN, thus increasing maritime cooperation between India and ASEAN. Besides cooperation with external partners, India has other maritime challenges to contend with due to its extensive coastline.

To deal with its domestic challenges, Indian has in place many maritime forces and agencies, and part of the challenge is to optimize and enable coordination between these agencies due to the overlapping nature of some of the challenges. Of the agencies, the primary ones are the navy and the coast guard. The navy is certainly crucial in preventing war and the coast guard is essential to law enforcement and services at sea. The Indian government therefore needs a clearer understanding of its maritime interests to optimize the forces for maximum operational effectiveness. With clear and understandable objectives, India will be better prepared to face its maritime challenges.

In conclusion, Prabhakaran states that the maritime challenges in Asia are real and present, and collectively add a new dimension to the overall challenges that each of the nations face. If the political establishments fail to appreciate maritime challenges as part of the overall challenges, the decisions made by national governments can go awry. As such, the solution requires Asia to act as a collective entity and put aside internal differences, and in this regard, India can be a strong and dependable partner.

New Zealand's maritime challenges and opportunities

Joanna Mossop presents the challenges faced by New Zealand, which are created by distance, awareness and governance. First, because of New Zealand's distance from its neighbours, it has the benefit of claiming maritime zones unimpeded by other countries. For instance, New Zealand has control over a significant amount of resources; the EEZ (claimed in 1977) led to growth in the fishing industry; distance from its neighbours also offered security from traditional and non-traditional threats such as warfare, piracy, illegal migrants and refugees. However, since the deregulation of the shipping sector, which had allowed foreign vessels to undertake coastal shipping, New Zealand has been overly reliant on international shipping. This could result in negative economic outcomes, should international shipping firms halt their services. In addition, there is a growing concern regarding "carbon miles" clocked by New Zealand exporters to faraway continents, for example Europe, which was frowned upon by climate lobbyists. Next is the issue of New Zealand's vulnerability to infrastructure failures. Any disruption to submarine cables, whether deliberate or accidental, could potentially devastate the economy.

Another challenge is the lack of awareness of New Zealand's maritime domain that could trigger a host of other challenges. For one, there are not enough vessels dedicated to surveillance and enforcement. During an assessment by the Maritime Patrol Review (MPR) in 2001, it was found that there was not only a very limited level of patrolling of EEZ by military or civilian agencies but also a lack of cooperation between the two, and even within different branches of the New Zealand Defence Force (NZDF). The next issue is the standard of scientific knowledge about New Zealand's marine environment. Only approximately 13–20 per cent of the maritime zones have been mapped in detail. With the increase in exploration for oil and gas, ocean energy production and deep-sea aquaculture, an understanding of the marine environment is important.

The last challenge for New Zealand is the fragmented oceans governance framework. A number of government agencies with a wide array of separate legislation have resulted in a divergence of prioritization, leading to poor regulation of ocean use. A national Ocean Policy was initiated in 2000 to address the problems of oceans governance with a legislative and administrative framework. However, due to the foreshore and seabed controversy, the initiative was suspended in 2003.

Recent developments

Since the papers for this volume were received in final form from their authors, there have been two major developments in the region that are not recognized in the relevant chapters. The first of these developments was in May 2011 when Thailand ratified UNCLOS, and the second was in March 2012 when the International Tribunal on the Law of the Sea (ITLOS) gave its decision on the maritime boundary dispute in the Bay of Bengal between Bangladesh and Myanmar.

When Thailand ratified UNCLOS, it made the following statement:

> The Government of the Kingdom of Thailand understands that, in the exclusive economic zone, enjoyment of the freedom of navigation in accordance with relevant provisions of the Convention excludes any non-peaceful use without the consent of the coastal State, in particular, military exercises or other activities which may affect the rights or interests of the coastal State; and it also excludes the threat or use of force against the territorial integrity, political independence, peace or security of the coastal State.[3]

This declaration is very similar to China's restrictive view regarding military activities in an EEZ. The fact that Thailand made this statement despite reportedly diplomatic interventions by the United States highlights the challenge to the region posed by differing interpretations in the region of a state's rights and duties in the EEZ.

The Bangladesh–Myanmar case was the first maritime boundary dispute to go before ITLOS. As is often the case with international settlement of maritime boundary disputes, there was no outright "winner" or "loser" with the ITLOS judgment.[4] The Tribunal decided on an adjusted equidistant line as the boundary between the two countries. This was rather more in favour of Bangladesh than a median or equidistant line between the boundaries proposed by each of the two countries would have been. Nevertheless, it still gave over half as much more of the "relevant area" to Myanmar than to Bangladesh.

In strategic terms, the ITLOS judgment is a positive development for the region. It resolves a major source of tension in the Bay of Bengal, and shows that, with political will, maritime disputes can be settled peacefully.

In addition to these two specific developments, the situation in the South China Sea has continued to be highly volatile. This is a clear demonstration that maritime security priorities and perceptions of regional countries are subject to continuous change. Or as my co-editor, Sam Bateman, argues in the conclusion to this volume, uncertainty is a key feature of the regional maritime security environment, and the prospect of inter-state conflict at sea remains the greatest maritime concern faced by the region.

Notes

1 Sam Bateman, Joshua H. Ho and Jane Chan, *Good Order at Sea in Southeast Asia* (Singapore: RSIS Policy Paper, May 2009).
2 Geoffrey Till, *Seapower: A Guide for the Twenty-First Century* (Second Edition) (Abingdon and New York: Routledge, 2009), pp. 23–33.
3 United Nations, Statement by Thailand on Ratifying UNCLOS, 25 May 2011, C.N.291.2011.TREATIES-4 (Depositary Notification), http://treaties.un.org/doc/Publication/CN/2011/CN.291.2011-Eng.pdf (15 December 2011).
4 Sam Bateman, "Solving Maritime Disputes: The Bangladesh-Myanmar Way", *RSIS Commentary 048/2012*, 20 March 2012.

Part I

Overview of maritime challenges in Asia

1 Managing good order at sea in the Asia-Pacific

Sam Bateman

The RSIS Policy Paper *Good Order at Sea in Southeast Asia – Policy Recommendations* described good order at sea as follows:

> Good order at sea ensures the safety and security of shipping and permits countries to pursue their maritime interests and develop their marine resources in an ecologically sustainable and peaceful manner in accordance with international law. A lack of good order at sea is evident if there is illegal activity at sea or inadequate arrangements for the safety and security of shipping.[1]

The paper went on to note that at present we lack good order at sea in South-East Asia. Problems in regional waters include piracy and armed robbery against ships, the threat of maritime terrorism, illicit trafficking in drugs and arms, people smuggling, pollution, illegal fishing, and marine natural hazards, such as tsunamis and cyclones. The inability to maintain good order at sea is due to factors such as inadequate resources, ineffective national legislation, poor coordination between national agencies, and a shortage of trained personnel. The lack of maritime boundaries in parts of the region complicates the situation by creating a barrier to effective cooperation between neighbouring countries.

This chapter considers good order at sea in the broader Asia-Pacific region, which comprises the following sub-regions: South-East Asia, North-East Asia, the South Pacific, and the Eastern Indian Ocean. It is only in the South Pacific that a satisfactory level of good order at sea has been achieved, with an effective system of regional arrangements covering activities such as fisheries, shipping, maritime security, marine scientific research, and marine environmental protection. This system has been possible because of the strong common interests of the small Pacific island countries in oceans and fisheries management and the establishment of an effective regional organisation, the Pacific Islands Forum, which provides political "top cover" for functional cooperation on ocean-related issues.

Threats to good order

Marine pollution

Marine pollution originates either from sea-based sources, including ships and offshore oil and gas installations, or from land-based sources, such as run-offs from rivers, illegal dumping, storm-water, and sewage. The massive oil leak from the West Atlas oil rig in the Timor Sea between August and November 2009 highlighted the serious threat to the marine environment posed by an accident involving an offshore installation. Over 400,000 litres of oil spilt into the sea threatening the livelihood of fishermen in eastern Indonesia.[2] More recently, the oil leak in the Gulf of Mexico has provided a dramatic demonstration of the risks posed by offshore oil and gas installations, particularly as drilling takes place in deeper and deeper waters.

About 77 per cent of pollution arises from land-based activities.[3] Land-based marine pollution (LBMP) is becoming more serious in many parts of the region due to coastal development, greater numbers of people living near the coast, and the lack of effective regimes for dealing with LBMP. A 2002 United Nations Environment Programme (UNEP) report showed that the coasts of southern Asia face a greater threat than anywhere else in the world from the discharge of untreated sewage.[4] About 40 per cent of the world's population lives within 60 km of the coast. In southern Asia, 825 million people lack sanitation, putting them at a higher risk of sewage-related diseases and even death.

Marine pollution is a major threat to the fishing industry, coastal tourism, and fragile marine habitats. Arrangements for managing marine pollution include Partnerships in Environmental Management for the Seas of East Asia (PEMSEA) and the South Pacific Regional Environment Programme (SPREP). Ship-based marine pollution is an increasing problem in some parts of the region, including the Malacca Strait and the South China Sea, due to increased shipping traffic and the lack of effective monitoring and surveillance systems.

Piracy and armed robbery

Piracy and armed robbery against ships are major maritime security problems for Asia. Attacks by Somali pirates off the Horn of Africa and far out into the Arabian Sea attract most attention, but incidents continue in South and South-East Asia, particularly in the southern part of the South China Sea near Mangkai and the Anambas islands. The number of actual and attempted attacks in South-East Asian waters increased from 68 in 2009 to 113 in 2010, mainly due to increased attacks in the South China Sea and in and around ports in Indonesia.[5] Vessels laid up at anchor in the eastern approaches to the Singapore Strait have also been robbed. The downturn in international shipping as a consequence of the global financial crisis may be a significant cause of this upsurge in attacks in South-East Asian waters.[6]

The measures taken by regional countries against piracy and sea robbery, both at sea and onshore have largely been effective, including the establishment of the Regional Cooperation Agreement on Combating Piracy and Armed Robbery against Ships in Asia (ReCAAP). However, greater attention to security is now required in the southern part of the South China Sea. Security in ports and anchorages in some countries and general policing against maritime crimes could also be improved. While incidents of piracy and armed robbery will continue to occur in the region, particularly in ports, anchorages, and port approaches, the consequences of the threat are negligible.

Trafficking and smuggling

The sea is the main medium for the illegal movement of people and goods because larger shipments can be carried, covert transhipment may be possible at sea, and maritime borders may be more porous than land and air borders. Illegal trafficking in arms, drugs, and people are all evident to some extent in the region. These are all transnational crimes requiring cooperation between regional countries to deal with them.

Human smuggling by sea is an increasing problem in parts of the region. South Asia and Northeast Africa are major points of origin for refugees and asylum seekers in the Indian Ocean region, while many victims also originate from South-East Asia, particularly women and children.[7]

Natural disasters

Marine natural hazards are those arising through tropical storms, climate change, tsunamis, and other severe oceanic conditions. According to the Asian Disaster Reduction Centre, Asia is the most disaster-affected area in the world.[8] The vulnerability of the Asia-Pacific region to marine natural disasters was demonstrated by the tragic tsunami in the North-East Indian Ocean on Boxing Day 2004, cyclone *Nargis* in Myanmar in May 2008, the tsunami that struck Tonga and Samoa on 20 September 2009, and the massive floods in Pakistan during 2010. Maritime natural hazards that could lead to natural disaster include climatic hazards (cyclones, tropical storms, floods, and sea level changes); geological hazards (earthquakes, volcanic eruptions, and tsunamis); and biological hazards (marine pest infestations and pollution).

In 2007, Geosciences Australia undertook a hazard risk assessment of the Asia-Pacific region for AusAID.[9] This covered earthquakes, volcanic eruption, tsunami, cyclone, flood, and wildfire hazards. It concluded that the unexpected eruption of a dormant volcano was the most dangerous threat. As well as catastrophic damage from fall-outs of ash, such an event could also cause tsunamis. The assessment noted that the northern part of the Bay of Bengal was the most dangerous area for large tsunamis, and that by individual country Indonesia has the highest population threatened by tsunamis, followed by Bangladesh and India.

Illegal, unregulated, and unreported (IUU) fishing

IUU fishing has become a serious problem in the region.[10] Clashes between different groups of fishers and alleged illegal fishermen and maritime law enforcement forces occur regularly in the region, including in the South China Sea, parts of the Indonesian archipelago, and in the west off Thailand and Myanmar.[11] Generally these incidents have negligible consequences, but they can assume a more serious dimension when they occur in areas of disputed sovereignty where clashes or armed "stand-offs" might occur between law enforcement units of neighbouring countries. The risks of fisheries incidents may also increase in the future as regional fish stocks continue to decline and fishermen have to move further afield to obtain worthwhile catches.[12]

Cooperation against IUU fishing largely depends on the existence of an effective regional fisheries management organisation (RFMO), but this is not the case in some parts of the region, particularly in the Indian Ocean. A recent performance review of the Indian Ocean Tuna Commission (IOTC), the main RFMO for the Indian Ocean Region, identified serious gaps and weaknesses in the organisation.[13] It found that the commission's principles for fisheries management were out-dated, lacking concepts such as the precautionary approach and an ecosystem-based approach, and that there was considerable uncertainty in the data submitted to the commission and the quality of stock assessments. Under-reporting of catches is a significant element of IUU fishing.

The lack of maritime boundaries

Agreed geographical limits to maritime jurisdiction are important for good order at sea. However, there are widespread areas of the region, in South-East Asia and North-East Asia in particular, where maritime boundaries have not been agreed between neighbouring states, most notably in the South China Sea. Other areas include the northern Malacca Strait, where there is no exclusive economic zone (EEZ) boundary between Malaysia and Indonesia; the eastern approaches to the Singapore Strait, where sovereignty over key features is divided between Malaysia and Singapore;[14] and the Ambalat region to the East of Borneo.

In early November 2008, Bangladesh and Myanmar naval vessels were in a stand-off in an area off the Bay of Bengal claimed by both countries, where possible hydrocarbon reserves are believed to exist but no maritime boundaries have been agreed.[15] In May 2009, tensions flared again between Malaysia and Indonesia in the Ambalat area with the Indonesian Navy nearly firing upon a Malaysian patrol boat that had allegedly intruded into "Indonesian maritime territory".[16] Boundary clashes occur regularly between North and South Korea, and incidents have also occurred recently in the East China Sea between China and Japan.

While the consequences of these incidents are normally negligible, there is always the risk of misunderstandings that could lead to more serious consequences and the breakdown of bilateral relations. It is important that bilateral agreements and Avoidance of Incident at Sea (INCSEA) arrangements are in place to mitigate the risks of an incident escalating into a more serious situation.

Climate change

As a result of climate change, ocean temperatures will rise markedly, ocean circulation patterns may change, and sea levels will rise. These changes could have compounding effects on the rate of climate change. Ocean circulation plays a major role in determining the regional impact of climate change, which will affect many people through the loss of marine habitats and fish stocks, and the increased prevalence of natural disasters. The higher frequency of "extreme weather events" will have a major impact on coastal, low-lying areas like Bangladesh. According to Robert Kaplan, due to sea level rise, "Bangladesh is the most likely spot on the planet for the greatest humanitarian catastrophe in history".[17]

Climate change will affect the physical conditions of the oceans and regional seas, including temperature, strength of currents, and sea levels, and these impacts are becoming increasingly evident.[18] Ocean acidification is a major problem that will have a very serious impact on coral reef systems.[19] Changes in ocean conditions as a consequence of global warming could have compounding effects on the rate of climate change. The impact of climate change on marine, coastal, estuarine, and freshwater ecosystems will likely affect many people directly or indirectly through the loss of fish stocks and marine habitats and the increased prevalence of natural disasters, such as floods and cyclones.

There is a close link between climate change and food security. Food security is a major threat to regional security. It has two connections with the maritime environment. The first is the direct impact of declining fish stocks and the loss of marine habitats on subsistence fishing and access to seafood at a reasonable price. The second is the indirect impact arising from the consequences of food shortages. This could manifest itself in increased migration flows. This would serve to reinforce flows already occurring more directly as a consequence of climate change. All indications are that climate change will occur and the consequences for the region are significant.

Maritime terrorism

The vulnerability of the maritime sector to attack by terrorists has been of concern due to the economic importance of the sector; the incidence of piracy and sea robbery in parts of the region; and the presence of terrorist groups with either a history of attacking maritime targets or suggestions of an intent to launch such attacks. There are many possible scenarios.[20] Shipping containers are a particular area of concern due to their potential use for shipping terrorist materials or weapon of mass destruction (WMD).

Terrorist attacks have occurred on ferries in South-East Asia, and these vessels, and potentially cruise liners, continue to be vulnerable to attack. The most notorious ferry attack was that on the *SuperFerry 14*, which sank in February 2004 near Manila after a bomb explosion and fire on board with 116 people either killed or missing. Other attacks on ferries in South-East Asia include the February 2000 bombing of the Philippine ferry *Our Lady Mediatrix*, which killed 40 people, and the December 2001 bombing of the Indonesian ferry *Kailifornia*, which killed ten.[21] With passenger ships and ferries, it is not so much the bomb that might do the damage but rather the fire and panic that can follow an explosion with so many people in a relatively confined area.[22]

More serious maritime terrorist attacks could include attacks on port infrastructure that close a major port or an attack or threat of an attack leading to closure of a major regional waterway. It is physically impossible to block either the Malacca or Singapore Strait, but some possible threats, such as sea mining or a small boat suicide attack, could lead to the re-routing of commercial shipping traffic away from these waterways. The more catastrophic scenarios involve possible attacks on liquefied natural gas (LNG) or liquefied petroleum gas (LPG) tankers, through planting devices on board or by the use of a tanker as a mobile weapon to strike secondary targets. Such attacks seem improbable due to the technical complexities involved, and the opportunity and expertise required for such an attack. Although such a scenario is unlikely, its potential is given focus due to the catastrophic results such an attack might produce.

Proliferation of WMD

The proliferation of WMD and their delivery systems is regarded by the international community as one of the greatest threats to international peace and security.[23] This focus has been highlighted by recent developments in North Korea. The Proliferation Security Initiative (PSI) is the main instrument for preventing the transport of WMD and related materials by sea.

The United States has encountered problems in the region, particularly in East Asia, with implementing the PSI and its procedures for intercepting vessels at sea. Only two Asian countries (i.e. Japan and Singapore) are full members of the PSI, and Asian countries that are key to the successful implementation of the initiative, notably China, India, and Indonesia, have deferred active involvement despite pressure from the United States.[24]

With the extensive counter-proliferation regimes now in place, the threat of a WMD attack in the region is unlikely although the consequences might be catastrophic. Without strong adherence to the regimes, the risks of a WMD incident could increase. Terrorist groups have actively sought WMD capability, and while the development of an effective weapon is well beyond the capability of existing regional groups, this could change in the future, particularly as relevant technologies might become more readily available. As proliferation of WMD and related materials may well occur by sea, adherence in the region to relevant international regimes is important, particularly the International Convention for the Suppression of Unlawful Acts against the Safety of Maritime Navigation (SUA Convention) and its 2005 Protocol.[25]

Conflict at sea

Several potential causes of conflict at sea exist in the region, including on the Korean Peninsula, across the Taiwan Strait, or over disputed territories, such as the Takeshima/Tokdo islands, the Senkaku/Diaoyu islands, or in the South China Sea. This conflict may be bilateral or could involve a coalition of forces. Overall the probability of conflict in one of these areas appears to be diminishing with considerable improvement, for example, in cross-strait relations between China and Taiwan.[26] North Korea is an obvious exception, with its nuclear tests and missile launchings in May – June 2009 and the sinking of the South Korean frigate *Cheonan* in March 2010 leading to a serious downturn in regional relations.

The Takeshima/Tokdo dispute has ongoing potential to affect stability in North-East Asia:[27] Japan feels threatened by North Korea with its ballistic missiles, WMD, and special forces, and by China with its nuclear capabilities and modernising military forces; and Russia is emerging again as a potential major military power in the region and has an unresolved sovereignty dispute with Japan over the Kuril islands.

The most serious form of conflict at sea would be that involving the major regional naval powers: China, India, Japan, Russia, and the United States. The US Director of National Intelligence recently predicted that the world faces a growing risk of conflict over the next 20 to 30 years.[28] He referred to the transfer of wealth and power from West to East, the possibility of strategic rivalries revolving around trade, demographics, access to natural resources, investment and technological innovation, and the probability that China and India will be seeking greater strategic influence. Undoubtedly, how relations between these emerging powers develop in the future will have a major impact on maritime security in South-East Asia. Similar concerns pervaded the 2009 Australian Defence White Paper that noted how "Shows of force by rising powers are likely to become more common as their military capabilities expand".[29]

Increased naval spending

The trend in the region towards higher defence spending is one development that could threaten good order at sea. Over the six years from 2002 to 2008, China's defence budget grew by a massive 11.6 per cent per annum in real terms; South Korea's rose by 5.9 per cent per annum; India's by 2.5 per cent per annum; and ASEAN's (Association of Southeast Asian Nations) by 3.4 per cent per annum.[30] Much of this increased spending was on naval capabilities. While some will argue that these capabilities contribute to good order at sea, this chapter takes the opposite view. Higher defence spending creates an environment of increased military activity that is potentially destabilising, with greater numbers of aircraft, warships, submarines, and armoured vehicles. In a speech at the 2009 Shangri-La Dialogue, Singapore's Deputy Prime Minister and Defence Minister, Teo Chee Hean, highlighted the need for regional countries to have greater transparency of military acquisitions, strategic intent, and security concerns.[31]

The situation in the maritime environment is of particular concern with more ships, submarines, and maritime aircraft operating in relatively confined regional waters, some areas of which include sovereignty disputes and unresolved maritime boundaries. Increased military activity at sea increases the risk of an unfortunate incident occurring between naval forces, particularly one involving a submarine. Defence spending also has a high opportunity cost by diverting resources from important programmes for economic development, social improvement, environmental management, and poverty alleviation.

China is often seen as the trigger for a regional naval arms race.[32] There may be grounds for this belief. China's naval force expansion plans may be an explanation for the acquisition of new missile destroyers by South Korea and Japan.[33] China's submarine base on Hainan may well have spurred an "arms race" type reaction from India. Despite India's social problems at home and its internal security difficulties, India's justification for increased defence spending, certainly for its naval spending, is based on assessments of China's larger defence budget and its alleged intentions in the Indian Ocean. China's developments are said to be the most pressing motivation for India seeking greater military power and working hard to close the gap with China by spending heavily on modern weapons.[34]

Management arrangements

Managing good order at sea in the Asia-Pacific region requires consideration of the arrangements for:

- *Oceans management* (or *governance*), including arrangements for managing the various uses of the sea, the sustainable use of its living resources, and the protection of the marine environment. These processes should be integrated as far as possible, recognising the inter-related nature of the various uses of the sea.[35]
- *Maritime security*, taking a comprehensive approach to security and including measures for protecting sovereignty, preventing illegal activity at sea, protecting sea lines of communication (SLOCs), maritime safety, search and rescue, and for mitigating marine natural hazards.

Maritime cooperation is fundamental to the management of the oceans and regional seas, including the exploitation of marine resources and many aspects of maritime security. Part IX of the 1982 UN Convention on the Law of the Sea (UNCLOS) requires states bordering an enclosed or semi-enclosed sea to cooperate with each other. This process of cooperation is institutionalised in the Regional Seas Programme of the UNEP. This provides a framework for regional consultation on the comprehensive and integrated management of marine and coastal areas, including the development of action plans to handle the problems of the marine environment, but in practice it has only had marginal success so far. Regional seas programmes in the Asia-Pacific region include the Coordinating Body on the Seas of East Asia (COBSEA), the SPREP, and the Northwest Pacific Action Plan (NOWPAP).

Regional institutions and networks that address ocean-related issues and maritime security include the ASEAN, the ASEAN Regional Forum (ARF), the ASEAN Defence Ministers Meetings plus Eight, Asia-Pacific Economic Cooperation (APEC), PEMSEA, COBSEA, and the Council for Security Cooperation in the Asia Pacific (CSCAP), as well as various RFMOs. Other regional institutions include ReCAAP, the Western Pacific Naval Symposium (WPNS) and the Heads of Asian Coast Guards meetings.

APEC

APEC is the major regional organization with interests in both oceans management and maritime security. It manages these interests through working groups and special task groups in various fields, including fisheries and transport security. As APEC membership is through "economies" rather than countries, the forum has the advantage of including Taiwan in its activities. As Taiwan has extensive maritime interests, such as shipping and fishing, its inclusion in APEC is important for oceans management in particular. The first APEC Ocean-related Ministerial Meeting was held in Seoul in April 2002. Ministers endorsed the Seoul Oceans Declaration that includes recommendations on marine environmental protection and integrated coastal management and lays the direction for future work by the Marine Resource Conservation Working Group (MRCWG), established by APEC to facilitate domestic and regional policies and programs leading to the sustainability of marine and coastal environments in the APEC region.

Based on the commitments made in the Seoul Oceans Declaration, the Bali Plan of Action was adopted in 2005 to provide practical and specific implementing strategies to work Towards Healthy Oceans and Coasts for the Sustainable Growth and Prosperity of the Asia-Pacific Community. The three main goals of the Bali Plan of Action are: (1) to ensure the sustainable management of the marine environment and its resources; (2) to provide for sustainable economic benefits from the oceans; and (3) to enable sustainable development of coastal communities. Under each goal are specific commitments and actions to be undertaken by APEC member states, individually or collectively, to implement the Bali Plan of Action.

APEC has also been active in developing both regional energy security and regional responses to the threat of maritime terrorism. The Secure Trade in the Asia-Pacific Region (STAR) initiative developed by APEC provides for a range of measures both to protect trade in the region against the threat of terrorism and for energy security, including the security of SLOCs. The Sydney Declaration resulting from the September 2007 APEC meetings in Sydney draws explicit links between energy security, global warming, and the Asia-Pacific's capacity for continued development and economic growth.[36]

ASEAN and the ARF

In recent years, maritime security has been high on the agenda of both ASEAN and the ARF. ASEAN held a workshop in Batam in September 2007 on the establishment of an ASEAN Maritime Forum. This would exchange ideas not only on maritime security issues, but also on other broad, cross-cutting issues, such as protection of the marine environment, illegal fishing, smuggling, and maritime transportation. However, this forum has not met yet.

The ARF has agreed to establish an ARF Inter-Sessional Meeting (ISM) on Maritime Security to provide an annual platform for the discussion of maritime security issues, including increasing cooperation and capacity-building, as well as specific concerns, such as piracy and armed robbery against ships, and the smuggling of goods and persons. The first meeting of the ISM was held in Surabaya in March 2009, and the second in Wellington, New Zealand in March 2010. The third meeting is to be held in Tokyo in February 2011 at which an action plan for the group will be agreed. In other developments, the ASEAN Defence Ministers Meeting Plus Eight has agreed to establish a Maritime Security Expert Working Group, and the ARF is to hold a workshop on UNCLOS in Manila in March 2011.

The World Ocean Conference (WOC)

In May 2009, the WOC was held in Manado, North Sulawesi, to discuss the relationship between climate change and ocean management.[37] The WOC was a global forum attended by thousands of delegates representing governments, industries, academia, non-governmental organizations, and the media from 70 countries. It discussed the importance of the oceans in determining world climate systems, as well as adverse impacts of climate change on ocean resources and ecosystems. It examined measures by which states can manage their activities to adapt to effects of climate change.

Key outputs of the WOC included the Manado Ocean Declaration. This emphasized the commitment of nations to address impacts of climate change on small islands, coastal areas, and communities depending on marine resources. It includes action statements on issues such as management and sustainable use of marine living resources and coastal ecosystems; integrated coastal and ocean management; reduction of pollution from sea- and land-based sources; marine scientific research; and integrated ocean and observation systems. By convening the WOC, Indonesia cemented its position as the leading ASEAN nation on ocean affairs. It has also become a principal player in oceans management at the global level.

Looking to the future

As a vast maritime region, Asia-Pacific has an enormous interest in ensuring that new threats and risks in the oceans are addressed. The WOC set a high benchmark for future international management of the oceans and addressing links with climate change. The problems involved deserve much greater attention in the region than they have received hitherto. The focus must be on achieving real outcomes rather than just talking. Unfortunately, arrangements for oceans management and maritime security in the Asia-Pacific region continue to be inhibited by sensitivities to cooperative arrangements that might impact on sovereignty and the lack of maritime boundaries in parts of the region. Levels of cooperation to ensure good order at sea are generally below what is necessary.

Regional waters are likely to see increased numbers of surface warships, submarines, and maritime aircraft in the years ahead. While these developments may be in response to a feeling of increased maritime insecurity that seems to justify higher defence spending, the developments themselves also have the potential to add to insecurity in the region. Regional forums, such as the ARF and Shangri-La Dialogue, will be challenged in the future to address these spiralling naval force developments. Furthermore, some of the new capabilities, particularly submarines, are not well suited to processes of cooperation and confidence building that might be considered.

Mitigation of the risks involved requires more attention to preventive diplomacy and maritime confidence and security building measures, including INCSEA agreements;[38] greater transparency with regard to naval operations and exercises; and possible limitations on the employment and acquisition of particular naval capabilities. Greater research is required into the implications of increased regional defence spending (particularly spending on maritime capabilities), the risks of particular scenarios, and measures that might be taken to mitigate the risks. At the Track Two level, CSCAP has taken the positive step of establishing a study group to investigate the implications of naval enhancements in the region. However, Track One should also be prepared to address these issues. It is to be hoped that the Maritime Security Experts Working Group established by the ASEAN Defence Ministers plus Eight and the ARF ISM on Maritime Security will do so.

Notes

1 Sam Bateman, Joshua H. Ho, and Jane Chan, *Good Order at Sea in Southeast Asia*, (Singapore: S. Rajaratnam School of International Studies (RSIS) Policy Paper, May 2009), p. 4.

2 See "Indonesia hit by Timor Sea spill", *Channel News Asia*, 2 November 2009, www.channelnewsasia.com/stories/afp_asiapacific/print/1015344/1/.html.

3 Maritime transport accounts for about 12 per cent of pollution, sea dumping for 10 per cent, and oil exploration and production for 1 per cent. Edgar Gold, *Gard Handbook on Protection of the Marine Environment*, 3rd edn (Arendal: Gard, 2006), Figure 1.1, p. 58.

4 See www.unep.org/cpi/briefs/Brief3Oct.doc; and Alex Kirby, "UN maps most polluted coasts", *BBC News*, 2 October 2002, http://news.bbc.co.uk/2/hi/science/nature/2293621.stm.

5 International Maritime Bureau (IMB), "Piracy and Armed Robbery Against Ships", Annual Report, 1 January–31 December 2010, Table 1, p. 5.

6 Sam Bateman, "Increased Risks at Sea? Global Shipping Downturn and Maritime Security", *RSIS Commentary 100/2009*, 9 October 2009.
7 Centre for Non-Traditional Security Studies, "Transnational Organised Crime in Southeast Asia: Threat assessment", *NTS Alert*, July 2010, (Singapore: RSIS) Issue 1, p. 6.
8 See www.adrc.or.jp/publications/databook/DB2006_e.html.
9 Alanna Simpson, Phil Cummins, Trevor Dhu, Jonathan Griffin, and John Schneider, "Assessing natural disaster risk in the Asia-Pacific region – Supporting international development through natural hazard risk research", *AUSGEO News*, Issue 90, June 2008, pp. 1–8.
10 N. Ghosh, "Trawling the seas for catastrophe", *The Straits Times*, 30 May 2009, p. C17.
11 John Butcher, *The Closing of the Frontier: A History of the Marine Fisheries of Southeast Asia* c.*1850–2000* (Singapore: Institute of Southeast Asian Studies, 2004), pp. 229–232.
12 M.J. Williams and Choo Poh Sze "Fish Wars: Science is Shaping a New Peace Agenda", *Maritime Studies 116*, January/February 2001, pp. 1–10.
13 Appendix V – Executive Summary from the Report of the IOTC Performance Review Panel, "Report of the Thirteenth Session of the Indian Ocean Tuna Commission", Bali, Indonesia, 30 March–3 April 2009, www.iotc.org/files/proceedings/2009/s/IOTC-2009-S13-R[E].pdf.
14 On 23 May 2007, the International Court of Justice (ICJ) awarded sovereignty over Pedra Branca/Pulau Batu Puteh to Singapore, and sovereignty over Middle Rocks, lying 0.6 nautical miles to the south of Pedra Branca, to Malaysia. Pedra Branca lies approximately 24 nautical miles east of Singapore, 7.7 nautical miles south of Malaysia and 7.6 nautical miles north of the Indonesia's Bintan Island. A complete set of maritime boundaries in the area will require the agreement of Indonesia, Malaysia, and Singapore.
15 "Myanmar brings warships to explore Bangladesh waters", *Daily Star*, 3 November 2008, www.thedailystar.net/pf_story.php?=61625.
16 "KL – Jakarta tensions rekindled at Ambalat", *The Straits Times*, 30 May 2009, p. C10.
17 Robert D. Kaplan, *Monsoon – The Indian Ocean and the Future of American Power* (New York: Random House, 2010), p. 140.
18 United Nations, "Oceans and the Law of the Sea", Report of the Secretary-General, UN doc. A/63/63, 10 March 2008, p. 89, http://daccessdds.un.org/doc/UNDOC/GEN/N08/266/26/PDF/N0826626.pdf?OpenElement.
19 Ghosh, "Trawling the seas for catastrophe", p. C16.
20 Sam Bateman, "Maritime Terrorism: Issues for the Asia-Pacific", *Security Challenges*, 2006, Vol. 2, No. 3, October, pp. 77–92.
21 John F. Bradford, "The Growing Prospects for Maritime Security Cooperation in Southeast Asia", *Naval War College Review*, 2005, Summer, Vol. 58, No. 3, pp. 63–86.
22 Bateman, S. "Ferry Safety: A Neglected Aspect of Maritime Security?", *IDSS Commentaries 31/2006*, Institute of Defence and Strategic Studies, Singapore, 3 May 2006.
23 Australian Government, *Weapons of Mass Destruction – Australia's Role in Fighting Proliferation – Practical Responses to New Challenges* (Canberra: Department of Foreign Affairs and Trade, 2005).
24 Mark J. Valencia, "The Proliferation Security Initiative: Making Waves in Asia", *Adelphi Paper 376*, October 2005.
25 Robert C. Beckman, "The 1988 SUA Convention and 2005 SUA Protocol: Tools to Combat Piracy, Armed Robbery, and Maritime Terrorism", in R. Herbert-Burns, S. Bateman, and P. Lehr. (eds), *Lloyd's MIU Handbook of Maritime Security* (Boca Raton: Auerbach Publications, 2008), pp. 187–200.

26 B. Glosserman, and B. Glaser, "Another step toward better cross-Strait ties", *PacNet Newsletter No. 58*, Centre for Strategic and International Studies, Washington, DC, 4 November 2008, www.csis.org/index.php?option=com_csis_pubs&task=view&id=5114.

27 Kim Pil-kyu, "Dokdo Issue May Affect Stability in Northeast Asia", *Korea Times*, 11 August 2008, www.koreatimes.co.kr/www/news/include/print.asp?newsIdx=29120; and Ralf Emmers, "Japan-Korea Relations and the Tokdo/Takeshima Dispute: The Interplay of Nationalism and Natural Resources", *RSIS Working Paper no. 212*, 10 November 2010.

28 "World faces growing risk of conflict: US intelligence chief", *AFP*, 1 November 2008, http://afp.google.com/article/ALeqM5iaFFPjfOQh91-YIHDaU00cL5ayQ.

29 Australian Government, *Defending Australia in the Asia-Pacific Century: Force 2030*, Defence White Paper (Canberra: Department of Defence, 2009), p. 22.

30 Based on data from the Commonwealth of Australia, *Defence Economic Trends in the Asia Pacific 2008* (Canberra: Defence Intelligence Organisation), p. 33. www.defence.gov.au/dio/documents/DET_08.pdf.

31 N. Yong, "Calls for transparency in security", *The Straits Times*, 1 June 2009, p. 1.

32 R. Spencer, "China's military ambition fuels Asian arms race", *Telegraph*, 13 September 2008, www.telegraph.co.uk/news/worldnews/asia/china/2827473/Chinas-military-ambition-fuels-Asian-arms-race.html.

33 P. Burnell and A. Denwood, "Perils of a new Pacific arms race", *BBC News*, 14 August, http://news.bbc.co.uk/go/pr/pr/fr/-/asia-pacific/6937293.stm.

34 A. Giridharadas, "India is projecting its military power", *International Herald Tribune*, 22 September 2008, www.iht.com/bin/printfriendly.php?id=16364183.

35 The traditional approach to oceans governance and the management of maritime interests was a *sectoral* one, with each ocean use (i.e. fishing, shipping, mining, tourism, etc.) basically "doing its own thing". However, recognition of the *interconnectedness* of ocean systems has led to the idea of *integrated oceans management*. Bilian Cicin-Sain and Robert W. Knecht, *Integrated Coastal and Ocean Management – Concepts and Practices* (Washington, DC: Island Press, 1998).

36 Michael Wesley, *Power plays – Energy and Australia's Security* (Canberra: Australian Strategic Policy Institute, October 2007), p. 34.

37 Sam Bateman and Mary Ann Palma, "Coming to the Rescue of the Oceans – the Climate Change Imperative", *RSIS Commentary 80/2009*, 17 August 2009.

38 Kwa Chong Guan, "ASEAN's Next Challenge: Preventing Incidents at Sea", *RSIS Commentary 76/2009*, 30 July 2009.

2 The historic attributes of the sea and maritime developments in the Asia-Pacific

Geoffrey Till

After a lifetime of investigation, Alfred Thayer Mahan famously concluded:

> Control of the sea by maritime commerce and naval supremacy means predominant influence in the world ... [and] is the chief among the merely material elements in the power and prosperity of nations.[1]

The sea, he thought, had this great historic effect because its control conferred upon those nations able to exert it such huge economic and strategic advantages that they would prosper in peace and prevail in war. These advantages flowed in large measure from the four basic interconnecting attributes of the sea:

- the sea as a resource
- the sea as a means of transportation and exchange
- the sea as a medium for information and the spread of ideas
- the sea as a medium for dominion.

There are important issues of risk in and between all of these, which could threaten their sustainability and/or worsen their consequences for the Asia-Pacific. Managing these risks offers real choices and dilemmas for the naval planners of the region. Let us briefly explore each of these and consider their implications.[2]

The sea as a resource

All around the world, tens of thousands of years ago, mankind began gathering food from the sea, first in the form of shellfish, and then fish. From earliest Mesolithic times, accordingly, the sea and the estuaries were seen as an unlimited food resource to those with the technology and courage to pursue and exploit it in the open sea. It was indeed a global phenomenon. As a source of resources, the sea was crucial to the development of world civilisation – and it remains crucial, since mankind still harvests some 20 per cent of its daily protein from the oceans. More recently, other marine resources (especially oil and gas) have become economically crucial too. Indeed, demand for all these things shows definite signs of outstripping supply. Inevitably, this tends to increase the competitive element in mankind's exploitation of this attribute of the sea. Sadly, acute competition for scarce or valuable sea resources has always played an important and often destructive part in human history.

Nowhere in the world is this more strikingly true than in the Asia-Pacific, where disputed jurisdictions over such places as the South and East China Seas derive in significant measure from optimistic anticipations about the resources of those disputed areas. The risks that arise from this are legion, and are a factor in the design and deployment of the region's navies. Moreover there is the wider fear that the kind of gross energy shortages that some expect in the decades to come could become a significant source of instability and conflict in the Asia-Pacific as it may well be elsewhere.

The sea as a medium of transportation and exchange

The size of fish skeletons to be found in some of mankind's oldest settlements attests to the fact that those resources were sufficiently rich to tempt ancient people surprisingly far out to sea, and to begin to recognise it as an area across which they could safely travel and so transport their goods – and indeed themselves. Initially, such water transport was very localised, then regional and, later still, as marine technology improved and experience grew, these regional transportation systems linked up to form a system of systems that spanned the world. Technological innovations through the industrial era, especially the advent of steam power, tended to make the connections tighter. The invention of the container has further revolutionised the process. Indeed,

> [i]t is no exaggeration to say that the shipping container may have transformed the world, and our daily lives, as fundamentally as any of the other more glamorous or complex inventions of the last 100 years, the internet included.[3]

The arrival in a European port of a container ship like the *Emma Maersk*, nearly 400 metres long, stacked 200 feet high with containers carrying 45,000 tonnes of goods, probably mainly from China, which its owners expect to be turned around in 24 hours, illustrates the sheer scale of this revolution. By most estimates, over 95 per cent of the world's trade by volume is conducted by sea, and that volume has expanded hugely over the past 30 years or so, from 2.6 billion tons of goods in 1970 to 7.12 billion tons in 2005. In 2005, the world merchant fleet grew by 7.2 per cent over the 2004 total to 960 million deadweight tons.[4] Nor, despite the recent recession, does there appear to be much doubt amongst experts that the increase in the world's population and its growing aspirations will require such long-term trends to continue, at least while the resources required to sustain them are available.

Its supporters argue that sea-based trade sustains globalisation and is the high road to peace and prosperity. Indeed, the whole concept of globalisation is profoundly maritime. Low and decreasing sea-borne freight rates mean that the shipping costs of a $700 TV set from China to Europe is no more than about $10. This helps keeps American and European costs of living and rates of inflation down; encourages China and the rest of Asia to industrialise (thereby raising the living standards of its people); makes possible the kind of distributed manufacture of goods that gives everyone a stake in the prosperity and stability of their neighbours;[5] and provides an expanding market for the commodities of places like Africa. Sea-borne commerce therefore produces a tight, mutually dependent, cooperative community of industrial production and consumption.

This would seem to be particularly salient for the Asia-Pacific region, an area which many would argue is in the process of transforming its place in the wider world to the extent of turning this into the 'Asian Century'.[6] But such a development, for good or ill, is completely dependent on, and indeed an incentive for, regional peace and the continued security of shipping. This unavoidable fact may well encourage a sense of common purpose and common interest amongst the nations of the Asia-Pacific in the development and, if necessary, the defence of the system against anything which might threaten it – threats that might range from extreme weather events at one end of the scale to attack by states or groups hostile to the workings or the values of the system. And indeed Mahan reminded us that a global sea-based trading system *is* acutely vulnerable to a range of such threats.

This, together with the vast increase in rapidity of communication, has multiplied and strengthened the bonds knitting together the interests of nations to one another, until the whole now forms an articulated system not only of prodigious size and activity, but of excessive sensitiveness, unequalled in former ages.[7]

In consequence, he urged the establishment of a community of interests and righteous ideals to defend the system.[8] Dependence on sea-based transport, in short, can be a source of weakness as well as of strength and exemplifies, in Mahan's words, the 'commercial interest of the sea powers in the preservation of peace'.[9] In turn this provides added incentives for cooperative mechanisms in the maritime domain.

The importance of all this helps to explain why the Asia-Pacific is seeing such a renaissance in its maritime power, in comparison with the rest of the world. However, given the burgeoning size of the populations of the Asia-Pacific and their expanding human aspirations this is a *necessary* renaissance and, to repeat the point, is one that depends absolutely on continued security at sea. An increasingly prosperous Asia-Pacific, in short, has an ever-increasing stake in the maintenance of safe and timely shipping and good order at sea.

The sea as a medium for information and the spread of ideas

Trade involves talking. It is about the conscious or unconscious exchange of ideas and information as well as goods. Through their maritime interactions, the Mesolithic Europeans picked up ideas about how to construct burial chambers, how to decorate pots and doubtless about much more that has left no specific trace. Sea transportation, maritime trade and the exchange of ideas and information have from earliest times appeared inseparable.

Sometimes this exchange of information and values is conscious and deliberate. Early explorers discovered new hitherto unknown crops and brought them home. In this way potatoes, tobacco, bananas, coffee, tea and so forth arrived in Europe. Maritime traders from South-East Asia and the Indian Ocean area brought early-maturing rice, sugar cane, jasmine, cotton, pumpkin, cabbage and so on to early China. These all produced green revolutions and major markets. China imported its first sweet potatoes in 1593 and now produces 80 per cent of the world crop.[10] Religious people have gone further and recognised the sea as a means by which they could communicate their ideas to the unenlightened; the sea in consequence has played a significant part in the spread of most of the world's major religions, not least in the Asia-Pacific.

People went not just to spread information but to obtain it as well. The urge to explore, to find out what was over the far horizon and sometimes to reach a better place, is part and parcel of mankind's relationship with the sea. It is about the association of the sea with freedom of travel, open horizons, enquiry, discovery and the pursuit of knowledge and progress, contrasting with the 'ignorant, fearful and foolish' who so limited their destinies by trying to insulate themselves from such maritime endeavour.[11] From this comes the urge for maritime exploration, partly in a spirit of high-minded scientific enquiry and partly for commercial and strategic interests.

As a result, for many centuries, the waterfront was the place where people went for the latest news and information about their own region and the wider world beyond. In this sense, it served much the same function as the Internet does now. Arguably, since electronic means of communicating ideas are so much faster, this historic attribute of the sea is less important now than it was.

To some extent, however this might seem more than counter-balanced by two things. First, to a significant degree the electronic system depends on the web of fibre-optic cables that now straddle the world, many of which lie on the sea bottom and represent a source of vulnerability, especially in the world's choke points.

Second, and more substantially, there is mankind's developing need to understand more about the sea itself. The sea perfectly illustrates the paradox that we do not know what we do not know, and the more we know the more we realise how true that is. Most obviously, as the Australians have pointed out, marine biotechnology is a developing field and since marine biological diversity is so much greater than its terrestrial equivalent it 'represents a vast, relatively untapped source of potential new materials, compounds and organisms'.[12] The need to protect this invaluable storehouse of future knowledge from present, unknowing damage reinforces the drive towards more regulation and environmental protection.

The more we know about the sea, the better able we are to exploit its benefits sustainably. This is an obvious explanation for the burgeoning growth of interest in oceanographic research, since oceanographic knowledge could easily prove crucial to our future. The ocean floor, for example, is covered with the results of volcanic activity, much of it violent and continuous. This is associated with earthquake activity and movement of the tectonic plates forming the continents, and produces huge molten lava lakes under a thin mobile canopy of frozen solidified volcanic rock. Harnessing the tremendous energy to be found in these volcanic magma chambers and exploiting the unimaginably rich minerals they produce through undersea vents could be the key to global survival in generations to come.

Here, much could be at stake for the Asia-Pacific, but much remains uncertain. In consequence, the risks here are literally incalculable; we cannot know what is at risk.

Before moving on to the fourth and last historic attribute of the sea, we should perhaps pause in order to reflect on one common conclusion to be drawn from this cursory survey of the importance of marine resources, transportation and communication. They can be seen as the foundation of the world's trading system, which in turn underpins globalisation that was referred to earlier.[13] Given its centrality to the peace and prosperity of the world, a major preoccupation of the world's navies would accordingly be to 'defend the system' by what they do both at and from the sea to protect trade and, even more importantly, the conditions for trade. The maintenance of good order at sea or, as it is increasingly known, Maritime Security is a precondition for all of this – as a recent G8 meeting for the first time explicitly recognised[14] – and has therefore become an increasing preoccupation of the world's navies. This preoccupation has been manifested by collaborative naval ventures into the defence of the system ranging from the counter-narcotics campaign in the Caribbean and Gulf of Mexico to the anti-piracy operations off Somalia in which the navies of Asia have for the first time become involved.

For naval planners this poses something of a dilemma for maritime security operations mandate forms of maritime situational awareness and types of platforms and procedures that do not necessarily match those associated with the more traditional state-on-state roles which have dominated naval development to date.[15] Choices about priority arise accordingly between the high-intensity requirements of state-on-state functions and the lower-intensity requirements for the maintenance of good order at and from the sea. These increasingly apply to the navies of the Asia-Pacific as the economic growth of the region continues.

The sea as a medium for dominion

The fact that so many coastal communities were, and indeed still are, fortified shows that the sea can be a source of vulnerability to marauders from afar and, at the same time, a springboard for aggressive maritime endeavour. In Europe and the Near East, the Phoenicians, Greeks and Romans demonstrated all too clearly that the sea is a strategic high road, a medium by which one group of people can come to dominate the affairs of another. Later Europeans, initially the Portuguese and the Spanish followed soon after by the Dutch, the French, the British and most others to some degree, came by sea to North and South America, the Indian Ocean and the Pacific, in tiny numbers overthrowing (often with extreme savagery) huge empires such as the Aztecs and the Incas. The Portuguese are an especially good example of what the Greeks call a 'thalassocracy', i.e. an empire founded on mastery of the sea. The Portuguese first fought their way into a new area and then had to protect their investments there. Their soldiers were never sufficiently numerous to engage in major continental campaigns, so their 160-year empire in the Indian Ocean rested on a few garrisons in strategic places and on superior naval forces. When others, especially the Dutch and the English, began to accumulate greater levels of naval force, Portuguese dominion went into decline.

For better or worse, the Europeans created new empires and changed the world. And they did it by sea. To make it all possible, they developed navies and a strategy, a set of concepts of how to use them from which all of the classic functions of sea-power derived: assuring sea control; projecting power ashore in peace and war; attacking and defending trade, directly and indirectly; and maintaining good order at sea. Although the Europeans provide perhaps the clearest example of the sea as a means of dominion, they are far from unique. The Islamic world around the Indian Ocean shows other example of the way in which traders are followed by missionaries and soldiers, and empires result. The Oman sea-based empire of the seventeenth to nineteenth centuries is another later example of the same kind of thing. Nor, historically, was the rest of the Asia-Pacific immune to such endeavours and to the consequences of maritime rivalry; indeed, naval conflict played a crucial role in the region's wars, both internally and externally.[16]

This has particular resonance in the Asia-Pacific now, because although the Asia-Pacific has indeed so far proved to be a region of stability, national tensions have not disappeared. The emergence of China as a potential peer competitor to the United States, the related concerns of China's regional neighbours (not least Japan and South Korea), enduring difficulties over Taiwan, the consequences of the nuclearisation of North Korea, continuing tensions between India and Pakistan, and a host of maritime disputes about jurisdiction throughout the region could all spark conflict.[17]

For this reason, it is hardly surprising that conceptions of sea control continue to be framed by peer competition and the activities and plans of other navies rather than countering the non-traditional activities of asymmetric adversaries, such as pirates, terrorists, and drugs and people smugglers, despite the focus on this in the current news. The sinking of the South Korean corvette *Cheonan*,[18] reportedly by the North Koreans, is a stark reminder of the extent to which traditional state-on-state rivalries still underlie naval development in the Asia-Pacific, as elsewhere. This preoccupation is reflected in the continued acquisition of such high-intensity capabilities as anti-submarine warfare (especially of the blue-water kind), anti-air warfare, ballistic missile defence and the development or maintenance of sea-based strategic deterrent forces – all of which tend to make most sense when planners have relatively sophisticated conventional adversaries in mind. Well over 70 per cent of the Asia-Pacific's projected naval spending over the next 20 years will be taken up by submarines, destroyers, frigates and amphibious warfare vessels.[19] By contrast, the percentage of the projected total spend taken up by the kind of auxiliaries, OPVs and patrol craft associated with the maintenance of good order at sea is comparatively small, at around 7 per cent. This does not however necessarily increase the prospect of interstate conflict, because countries such as China, South Korea and Japan seem to be shifting the pattern of their acquisitions away from specific naval conflict scenarios (such as with, in order, Taiwan, North Korea and the Soviet Union) and towards more balanced portfolios in their fleet development.

More globally, the strong economic performance of many countries of the Asia-Pacific region has produced high levels of gross domestic product that historically have tended to correlate closely with high levels of naval construction. The perhaps natural result has been a substantial growth in naval spending throughout the area. For the first time in several hundred years, naval spending in the Asia-Pacific (less the United States) is expected over the next decade to be greater than in the West (less the United States).[20] This could prove a truly momentous development, both in its implications for the near and long-term stability of the Asia-Pacific region and for the world's strategic architecture later in the twenty-first century. Arguably, naval growth in the area correspondingly produces a greater need for transparency in naval acquisition and employment, and for a renewed focus on a slew of other such confidence-building measures, lest an arms dynamic turns into a potentially destabilising regional arms race.

Conclusions

This survey of the approaches being taken by the countries of the Asia-Pacific region towards the sea as a resource and as a means of transportation, communication and dominion does not admit of easy conclusions. But this volume is partly about maritime risk and how naval planners and policy-makers in the region are setting about managing and prioritising the various sea-based risks they face. To what extent, for example, should naval planners prepare for conventional naval conflict, rather than the maintenance of good order at sea, or humanitarian assistance and disaster relief? How should the risks at sea and on land that threaten trade and the conditions for trade be prioritized? How varied are, and should be, the responses to such questions amongst countries in different parts of the Asia-Pacific region?

The fact that one can reasonably ask such questions perhaps reflects the fact that globalisation is not, whatever the Manchester School might have said, simply a synonym for global peace because economic rationality is far from being the only, or often even the main, motivation of human behaviour. As Sir Christopher Meyer (a former UK Ambassador to the United States) recently so trenchantly argued in *The Times*, 'the Georgian crisis showed that even in Europe, history did not end with the close of the Cold War'. Ethnic and nationalist rivalry, he said, 'is as old as sin, and as inextinguishable'. Globalisation and interdependence were supposed to have swept aside those ancient feuds and rivalries. Theories of the postmodern state now abound. Tony Blair preached how national interest would be trumped by the spread of 'global values'. This, Meyer concluded, not mincing his words, 'is self-evident rubbish'.[21]

Moreover, there is also is a competitive edge to globalisation. The Manchester School argued that international trade was of mutual benefit, but they never said it would be of *equal* benefit.[22] Accordingly, individual nations still have strong incentives to improve their place *within* the global system, relative to their neighbours. Hence, the contemporary relevance of Sir Walter Raleigh's famous and much quoted observation: 'Whosoever commands the sea, commands the trade. Whosoever commands the trade of the world commands the riches of the World, and consequently the world itself'.[23] While these days few would express the point quite so bluntly, such views inform those naval planners, in the Asia-Pacific as elsewhere, who conclude that prudence dictates them to keep their powder dry against the re-emergence, rather like Dracula when the sun goes down, of the older, bleaker, harsher world of traditional national rivalry. Such residual and traditional feelings explain why the patterns of naval rise and fall in the Asia-Pacific are attended with anxiety both within and outside the region, even in the age of globalisation.

Notes

1 Cited in William E. Livezey, *Mahan on Sea Power* (Norman, OK: University of Oklahoma Press, 1981), pp. 281–282.

2 The first part of this chapter is based on Chapter 1 of my *Seapower: A Guide for the 21st Century*, 2nd edn (London: Routledge, 2009).

3 Oliver Burkman, 'The Shipping News', *Guardian*, 27 January 2007. See also Marc Levinson, *The Box: How the Shipping Container Made the World Smaller and the World Economy Bigger* (Princeton: Princeton University Press, 2006), especially pp. 264–278.

4 UN Conference on Trade and Development, *Review of Maritime Transport 2006* (New York: United Nations, 2006), pp. 5, x.

5 Facts and arguments of this sort may be found in 'Shipping and World Trade' reports available at www.shippingfacts.com and the OECD's report, Directorate for Science, Technology and Industry Maritime Transport Committee, *The Role of Changing Transport costs and Technology in Industrial Relocation*, OECD document DSTI/DOT/MTC(2005)5/REV1 (Paris: OECD, 9 May 2005).

6 For an elegant exposition of this theme, see Kishore Mahbubani, *The New Asia Hemisphere* (New York: Public Affairs, 2008).

7 Alfred Thayer Mahan, *Retrospect and Prospect* (London: Sampson, Low, Marston & Co. Ltd., 1902), p. 144.

8 Ibid, pp. 177–178.

9 Alfred Thayer Mahan, *The Problem of Asia and its Effect Upon International Policies* (London: Sampson, Low, Marston & Co. Ltd., 1900), p. 99.

10 Gang Deng, *Chinese Maritime Activities and Socioeconomic Development c.2100 BC–1900 AD* (Westport, CT: Greenwood Press, 1997), pp. 155–158.

11 P.E. and E.F. Matheson (eds), *Francis Bacon* (Oxford: Clarendon Press, 1964), pp. 137–160.

12 Commonwealth of Australia, *Australia's Oceans Policy*, Vol. 2 (Canberra: Environment Australia, 1998), p. 7.

13 A good introduction to this point is in Sam J. Tangredi, (ed.) *Globalization and Maritime Power* (Washington, DC: National Defense University Press, 2002).
14 See Government of Canada, *G8 Muskoka Declaration Recovery and New Beginnings*, Muskoka, Canada, 25–26 June 2010, Annex II Part II, http://g8.gc.ca/g8-summit/summit-documents/g8-muskoka-declaration-recovery-and-new-beginnings/.
15 It ought to be said, though, that system defence tasks such as the control of piracy have always been a naval function and so in many ways it is unsatisfactory to apply the phrase 'non-traditional' to them. Accordingly, some (including the author of this chapter) have used the phrase modern and postmodern instead, but that terminology has its difficulties too!
16 Peter A. Lorge, *The Asian Military Revolution: From Gunpowder to the Bomb* (Cambridge: Cambridge University Press, 2008), for Japan and Korea, pp. 51–53, 59ff.; for China pp. 72–78 and 162–167; and for South-East Asia, pp. 156–160.
17 Barry Desker, 'New Security Dimensions in the Asia-Pacific', *Asia-Pacific Review*, Vol. 15, No. 1, 2008.
18 The international Joint Civilian–Military Investigation Group's report was released on 20 May 2010 and concluded that the overwhelming evidence pointed to the *Cheonan* having been sunk by a submarine-fired North Korean torpedo, and these findings were consistent with evidence on North Korean naval movements seen by the Multinational Combined Intelligence Task Force. 'Investigation Result on the Sinking of ROKS "Cheonan"', *GlobalSecurity.org*, 20 May 2010, www.globalsecurity.org/military/library/report/2010/100520_jcmig-roks-cheonan/100520_jcmig-roks-cheonan.htm.
19 Figures courtesy of AMI International. I am extremely grateful to Bob Nugent, Vice President of Advisory Services of AMI International (see http://aminter.com) for these figures and for his personal support of this project.
20 Ibid.
21 Christopher Meyer, 'A Return to 1815 is the way forward for Europe', *The Times*, 2 February 2008.
22 An interesting introduction to the problems of modern globalisation and its need for a degree of reform along the lines of greater equality is provided in Mike Moore, *Saving Capitalism: Why Globalisation and Democracy Offer the Best Hope for Progress, Peace and Development* (Singapore: John Wiley and Sons, 2009).
23 Suzy Platt (ed.), *Respectfully Quoted: A Dictionary of Quotations* (Washington, DC: Library of Congress, 1989).

3 Carriage capacity of the Straits of Malacca and Singapore

Yee Cheok Hong

Background

According to the Review of Maritime Transport 2008 published by the United Nations Conference on Trade and Development (UNCTAD), global sea-borne trade will increase by 44 per cent in 2020 and double by 2031.[1] This will consequently lead to an increase in the volume of maritime traffic through the Straits of Malacca and Singapore (SoMS).

A clear and accurate picture of the carriage capacity of the SoMS would allow the Maritime and Port Authority of Singapore (MPA) and other relevant authorities in the littoral states to understand how increases in the volume of maritime traffic could affect navigational efficiency and safety in the SoMS, and allow them to identify strategies to enhance the carriage capacity and address issues of navigational safety, if any. Towards this end, the MPA commissioned a study of the carriage capacity of the SoMS.

Overview of the SoMS

The SoMS, which are bordered by Malaysia, Indonesia and Singapore, measure about 250 nautical miles between One Fathom Bank off Port Klang in the west and Horsburgh Lighthouse in the east.

The Traffic Separation Scheme (TSS), for safer navigation in the SoMS, was brought into force on 1 May 1981. In 1998, the International Maritime Organization (IMO) adopted the Mandatory Ship Reporting System in the SoMS, known as STRAITREP, as proposed by Indonesia, Malaysia and Singapore. It aims to enhance the safety of navigation, protect the marine environment, facilitate the movement of vessels, and improve search and rescue (SAR) and oil pollution response operations. The entire TSS is divided into nine sectors with Sectors 1 to 6 lying in the Malacca Strait and Sectors 7 to 9 in the Singapore Strait. The Singapore Vessel Traffic Service (VTS) is the authority for STRAITREP in Sectors 7 to 9, while Klang VTS and Johor VTS are the authorities for Sectors 1 to 5 and Sector 6, respectively.

Along the TSS through which international shipping traverses the SoMS, the overall narrowest point lies within the Singapore Strait in Sector 8, south of

St. John's Island. This point measures about 530m westbound, 1,617m eastbound and 2,150m overall. In the Malacca Strait, the narrowest point in the westbound lane is off One Fathom Bank in Sector 1 and is 3,582m wide. The narrowest point eastbound and the narrowest point overall for the Malacca Strait, are near Tanjung Piai in Sector 6 and measure 2,959m and 8,056m, respectively. Table 3.1 summarises the narrow points in the TSS from Sectors 1 to 9.

The SoMS form the shortest sea-link between the Indian and Pacific Oceans. The importance of the SoMS as an international waterway has been well established. It represents the longest strait in the world used for international navigation and supports the bulk of maritime trade between Europe and Pacific-Asia. The SoMS are especially important for vessels transporting oil between the Middle East and the East Asian economic giants of Japan and China because they constitute the shortest and most cost-effective sea route between the two destinations. It is estimated that more than one-third of world trade and half of its oil is transported through the SoMS. The SoMS are therefore of vital importance both to European–Asian trade and to the energy needs of East Asia. It is clear that the rapid economic development of China and India will further enhance the importance of the SoMS. As a result, the number of ships and the tonnage of goods passing through the SoMS will increase.

Objectives

Given the increase in maritime traffic through the SoMS, the study commissioned by the MPA sets out to systematically examine the current situation in the SoMS and conduct a comprehensive assessment of its capacity. Outlined below are the key objectives of the study:

1 To evaluate the carriage capacity of the SoMS (Sectors 1–9 of the TSS), taking into account the historical volume and pattern of maritime traffic in the area, as well as existing navigational routes and rules employed in the area;
2 To identify the narrow or choke points and possible congestion areas in the SoMS in terms of carriage capacity;

Table 3.1 Summary of narrow points in the TSS

	Sectors 1–6 (Malacca Strait)	*Sectors 7–9 (Singapore Strait)*
Overall	8,056m (off Port of Tanjung Pelepas, Malaysia, Sector 6)	2,150m (near St John's Island, Singapore, Sector 8)
Eastbound	2,959m (off Port of Tanjung Pelepas, Malaysia, Sector 6)	1,617m (near St John's Island, Singapore, Sector 8)
Westbound	3,582m (near One Fathom Bank, Malaysia, Sector 1)	530m (near St John's Island, Singapore, Sector 8)

3 To examine possible measures that could enhance carriage capacity while at the same time maintaining navigational safety in the SoMS.

This chapter presents the preliminary results for items (1) and (2). Work on item (3) is under way and its results will be reported in due course.

Literature review

The complexity of a marine traffic system stems from the large number of vessel types, complicated operational regulations, and the autonomous control of vessel positions by shipmasters that introduces vast and irregular intersections of navigation routes, and thus makes it difficult to assess the capacity of a sea space system.[2] The capacity of sea space depends heavily on the prevailing traffic pattern, namely the mix of vessel types and sizes, and the speeds of the various vessel types, as well as their dwell times at port facilities, such as berths and anchorages. The term "capacity" is therefore only meaningful for a given set of operating conditions.

Approaches to assessing capacity typically fall within three categories: queuing theory, network analysis and computer simulation. In *queuing theory*, vessel arrivals are modelled as a Markov process, where the time taken by a vessel to pass through a facility is determined by the service level (i.e. service time required to process the vessel) and the rate of arrival of vessels entering the system. The capacity of a waterway is determined by defining the threshold for average service time. Queuing theory does not take into account the impact of the mix of different vessel or of the dynamics between vessels. The result is a rough estimate that can be used as a guideline for long-term capacity planning.

Conceptually, *network analysis* acknowledges the need to incorporate the influences introduced by different traffic patterns and considers a sea space system as a directional network consisting of links and nodes, where a node represents a specific location in the sea space, such as a pilot boarding ground, a berth or an anchorage, and a link is the fairway (or part of it) connecting any two nodes.

In such a network model, each element (node or link) has its own capacity, which is defined as the maximum number of vessels that can be served by the element within a specific time interval. The capacity of the network is then determined by that of the weakest element and the traffic demand on it. The capacity of an element can be found from the requirements on the minimum spatial separation set for different vessel types and the physical properties of the element. Although such an approach takes into account the dynamic nature of traffic patterns, the interactions, i.e. collision avoidance actions, between vessels are not modelled. Moreover, the network approach tends to assess the waterway capacity using the traffic pattern of the "peak day" with maximum number of vessel calls, which may not be representative for certain elements.

Computer simulation is the most popular way to model complex systems and has been widely used in assessing the capacities of land and air traffic systems. There is a general consensus that amongst the three approaches of assessing capacity, computer simulation is more robust and rigorous, yielding results that are more realistic. Nevertheless, applications in the maritime traffic system have relatively lagged behind, though the recent past has seen a significant increase in adopting simulation for capacity analysis and navigational risk assessment.

Existing maritime simulation programmes can be divided into two different categories: single vessel simulation and multi-vessel system. The former type of model focuses on simulating the precise path within a channel taken by a vessel given a set of external influences, such as currents, waves and wind. They are mainly used for channel design or navigation training.

The second type of simulation simulates the movements of multiple vessels along a given navigation network. Such programmes focus on the global layout of the waterway rather than the precise channel dimensions, and are mainly used to determine the capacity and safety of waterway designs. Maritime traffic simulation models move individual vessels from their source to their destination within a navigation network, abiding by the International Regulations for Avoiding Collisions at Sea or the Rules of the Road (COLREGS) to take collision avoidance manoeuvres when necessary, without considering hydrodynamic influences, as such details cannot be accurately projected for future scenarios. The main difference amongst existing models is the level of detail at which vessel movements are modelled, including parameters such as a fixed or flexible path along a channel, independent vessel behaviour, the number of collision avoidance actions and speed variations.[3]

Simulation model overview

The SoMS simulation model used for this study is built on a simulation platform called the Vessel Traffic Planning and Simulation System (VTPS^2). The VTPS^2 was built with the extensive involvement of master mariners and pilots, and has been subject to their evaluation and verification at each stage of its development. It allows users to configure waterway network and vessel details, and models detailed vessel movements, i.e. by navigating within the full width of channels at any predetermined speed and acting as a human captain to avoid collision by changing speed, changing course or both, depending on the situation.

Two separate models were built for the SoMS. The reason is twofold. First, the narrowest region in the SoMS is in the Singapore Strait and requires a more detailed investigation and, second, detailed and authoritative traffic and operations information is available only for the Singapore Strait. Given that there is less detailed traffic information available for the Malacca Strait, it is more practical to model the areas separately to acknowledge differences in reliability and detail of traffic data.

Model structure

The SoMS model is designed with maximised flexibility that allows easy configuration of parameters and scenarios in a streamlined process, while integrating input, output and simulation run windows into a single interface for effective data management. This is enabled by the modular architecture of the system, which consists of five major components:

1 A *simulation engine* and GUI (graphical user interface);
2 A *vessel arrival generator*, which generates individual vessels for each vessel type for the required duration, each vessel being assigned with related properties such as time of arrival, length overall (LOA), beam, gross tons (GT), draught and route pattern, based on historical distributions and correlations;
3 A *vessel route planning module*, which connects the source and destination of every vessel using the network of channels or fairways given as input, while taking into consideration navigation routes and guidelines for the region;
4 A *vessel navigation module*, which navigates each vessel from its source to its destination, in compliance with the COLREGS that set out the "rules of the road" upon which the safe navigation and conduct of vessels is built;
5 A *collision avoidance module*, which manoeuvres a vessel to avoid potential collisions by slowing down, overtaking, changing course or a suitable combination of these actions.

Model details

Vessel traffic

Vessels using the SoMS can be classified as either transiting vessels or vessels calling at a port for facilities, such as berths, yards and anchorages. For the Singapore Strait, detailed information on transiting vessels and calling vessels were obtained from the MPA. However, for the Malacca Strait, the numbers had to be estimated based on available information and certain assumptions made. The year 2007 was chosen as the representative base year for traffic data analysis.

Singapore Strait

For the Singapore Strait, the MPA provided data for 2007 on the number of vessels above 300 GT that called at the port of Singapore and the number of vessels that transited the Singapore Strait. This information was based on vessels that reported to the Singapore VTS, and was analysed to form representative distributions for the key attributes, such as vessel arrival times, sizes, routing and so on. Information for vessels below 300 GT was not available. It was assumed that these smaller vessels would have no impact on the waterway capacity, as they are small and swift.

The numbers of vessels transiting and calling at port for 2007 are summarised in Table 3.2 and give rise to a total of 257,000 movements in the Singapore Strait. Note that these numbers do not include intra-port movements, as they do not have any impact on the TSS, which is the focus here.

Table 3.2 Summary of vessel arrivals and transits for the Port of Singapore

	Number of vessels
Transits	41,000
Arrivals	108,000
Departures	108,000
Total	257,000

Ten types of vessels were identified as the main users of the Singapore Strait, namely (in alphabetic order) barges, bulk carriers, chemical tankers (including liquefied petroleum gas and liquefied natural gas), coasters, containerships, ferries, freighters, passenger vessels, tankers and VLCC.

The seasonality of vessel traffic was captured on a monthly basis. It was found that different types of vessels experienced different seasonal patterns. Analyses on vessel inter-arrival times were conducted for individual types, with curve fitting. The results showed exponential distributions best fit the inter-arrival times, implying a Poisson distribution of the arrival of vessels. To incorporate seasonality, a non-stationary Poisson process was used to model the vessel arrivals.

Malacca Strait

A survey was conducted on available information for vessel traffic in the Malacca Strait for the year 2007. Information from the Malaysian Marine Department showed that about 70,000 vessels reported to Klang VTS, although no further details were provided about transit and port-calling traffic, and so on. Several other unofficial sources found online cited vastly differing numbers for 2007 traffic

In the absence of complete data, an approximation was made based on known traffic for the Singapore Strait and available information for the Malacca Strait from various maritime sources and online research papers and articles and used to estimate traffic levels in the Malacca Strait, including:

1 86,000 movements at western boundary of the Singapore Strait (based on ship reports to Singapore VTS)
2 70,000 vessels reported to Klang VTS (assumed to be movements at the western end of the Malacca Strait)[4]
3 17,000 vessel calls at Port Klang[5]
4 About 77 per cent of all traffic in Sectors 1 to 6 is to Port Klang[6]
5 Items (3) and (4) above indicate that total number of arrivals in Sectors 1 to 6 is 22,000.

Based on these numbers, and assuming that eastbound and westbound transit traffic is equal, the following deductions can be made:

1. there were 28,000 eastbound and 28,000 westbound movements
2. there were 16,000 port calls from the east and 6,000 from the west
3. there were 14,000 departures to the east and 8,000 to the west.

Cross-strait ferry traffic was estimated as 26,000 per year based on information pieced together from various online sources.[7]

For intra-Malacca Strait traffic, it was assumed that:

- traffic between service points in Malaysia travels out of the TSS
- traffic between service points in Indonesia travels out of the TSS
- cross traffic (non-ferry) between service points in Malaysia and Indonesia is negligible.

Based on these assumptions, Malacca Strait traffic was approximated as shown in Table 3.3. The total number of movements, including transit and calling traffic is estimated to be 126,000.

Vessel characteristics

The physical attributes of vessels relevant to the objectives of the study include LOA, beam, GT and draught. An LOA distribution was developed for each vessel type based on Singapore Strait and Singapore Port historical data, and was used as a reference for generating the other three attributes, where each attribute was described as a function of LOA based on historical data using curve fitting.

Vessel speeds for different types of vessels in the Singapore Strait were sampled from MPA's radar records. As no speed information is available for vessels in the Malacca Strait, the same speed distributions were applied.

Similarly, for lack of a better option, it was assumed that the vessel mix and attributes of vessels in the Malacca Strait were the same as in the Singapore Strait.

Waterway layout

The waterway layout specifies the boundaries of travel for the vessels. There is a clear separation of westbound and eastbound lanes in the TSS, with the eastbound route allowing deeper draught vessels to travel. The TSS layout and

Table 3.3 Summary of vessel arrivals and transits for the Malacca Strait

	Number of vessels
Transits	56,000
Arrivals	35,000
Departures	35,000
Total	126,000

corresponding usage rules are available for the Singapore Strait and the Malacca Strait from voyage planning guides.[8] Figure 3.1 shows the TSS for Sectors 1 to 9 along the SoMS.

The figure clearly shows that the width of the TSS is not uniform along its entire stretch. As has been described in Section I.2 in the Introduction, there are some particularly narrow areas along the SoMS, especially in the Singapore Strait. These actual TSS dimensions were incorporated into the simulation model and the rules of usage were specified. Based on the width of waterways they are traversing and their own physical attributes, vessels decide whether they can travel alongside other vessels.

Navigation routes

Vessels using the SoMS are either transit vessels that do not call at any port or other facility along the SoMS or calling or departing vessels that stop at some facility along the straits. Although this study deals with traffic simulation in the straits, it is important to understand at which points along the TSS the traffic in the straits originates and terminates, so as to correctly model the movement patterns and traffic density along different sections of the TSS. For the Singapore Strait, this was obtained from the historical movement of vessels between the strait and the port waters. For the Malacca Strait, certain assumptions were made in this regard, based on the location of key ports along the TSS and their corresponding traffic as obtained from the online sources described in a previous section.

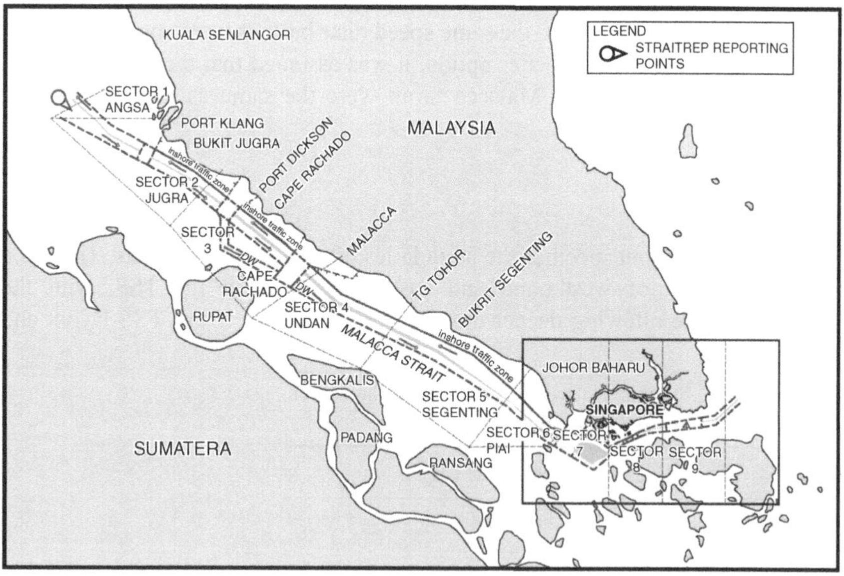

Figure 3.1 Traffic Separation Scheme in the SoMS.

Navigation guidelines and avoidance actions

All vessels in the SoMS model comply with the COLREGS, with each vessel navigating as an independent agent that reacts appropriately to the situation around it. To adequately emulate realistic vessel behaviour in the model, each vessel is given a safety domain and the undesirable overlap of safety domains would require vessels to take avoidance manoeuvres and could otherwise lead to a potential accident. The dimensions of the safety domain were approximated based on the study of radar pictures from Singapore VTS data.

As avoidance manoeuvres must be taken well before overlap of domains occurs, a monitoring range is assigned to each vessel and when another vessel enters the range, a monitoring mode is triggered to continuously monitor the safety domains of vessels within the monitoring range. If an overlap of domains is predicted (called an interaction), an avoidance action, i.e. slowing, steering and/or changing course, is taken, in adherence with the COLREGS.

Capacity definition

The capacity of a waterway network depends on its physical characteristics, navigation guidelines, the composition and characteristics (e.g. LOA, beam, speed etc.) of vessels using it and the required safety distance between successive vessels. Thus, capacity is only meaningful for a given set of operating conditions and changes if there is a change in any of the variables.

In this study, capacity is defined as the maximum efficient and safe volume of traffic (number of vessels per unit time, e.g. per year or per month) that can be sustained in the given configuration of navigational network. "Efficient" means that the travel time between any origin and destination pair should be within a predetermined range, whereas "safe" means that the risk of travelling in the waterway is below a predetermined threshold.

It is therefore critical to benchmark the average travel time of vessels using the straits and the associated navigation risk, using current levels of traffic volume. With the benchmarks in place, the carriage capacity of the straits can be assessed by comparing the increases in both travel time and risk against the increase in traffic volume.

Travel time

In this study, the travel times of transiting vessels (including eastbound transit and westbound transit) are the key capacity indicator. For each transiting vessel, its travel time in the TSS between Tanjung Piai (01° 15.54′N 103° 30.60′E) and Horsburgh Lighthouse (01° 19.81′N 104° 24.34′E) is determined by the model for the Singapore Strait, and between Batu Mandi (02° 52.2′N 100° 41.1′E) and Tanjung Piai (01° 15.54′N 103° 30.60′E) for the Malacca Strait.

Navigation risk

In quantitative risk analyses, the term "risk" is defined as the product of the risk probability and its associated consequence. By the nature of the simulation model, the scope of this assessment focuses on the probability, as it is difficult, if not impossible, to quantify the consequences of a predicted risk in maritime transport that can consist of material damage to the ship, its surroundings and the environment, as well as indirect damage such as loss of future income or even injuries and deaths. When reference is made to risk in this report, it therefore refers to the probability of a risk occurring.

Risks that are of most interest in maritime transport have been identified in Permanent International Association of Navigation Congresses (PIANC) Bulletin 95 as (1) collisions, (2) groundings, (3) strandings, (4) impacts and (5) strikings. In the SoMS model, collision risk is the main focus for two reasons. First, the water depth of most of the SoMS is deep enough to allow the majority of vessels to navigate through without risk of grounding or stranding. Second, immovable or floating objects such as buoys and vessels at anchor are not considered in the study, and there are therefore no impact or striking risks. This study on navigation risk therefore focuses on the most important factor, which is ship–ship collision.

The collision risk level is estimated by the number of interactions. The risk level in 2007 is used as a benchmark for determining the relative safety of any projected future traffic situation. To use the model in a quantitative way, an empirical relationship has to be established between the simulated number of avoidance manoeuvres and the 2007 historical collision count. However, the incident records in well-run ports are likely to contain such small samples of incidents that make such a relationship statistically insignificant. As a result, such a relationship should be used with due care.

Experiments and preliminary results

Model validation

The SoMS model inputs and logic were verified by MPA marine experts. In addition, to ensure that the simulation model is a realistic representation of vessel movements, travel time in the Singapore Strait was used as the key indicator for comparisons against the historical data. Two-sample t-tests were conducted to confirm that differences in mean travel times were not significant. Table 3.4 compares simulation and historical travel times for the different major vessel types modelled. Historical travel times were not available for the Malacca Strait and hence a similar comparison could not be conducted.

Preliminary results

Assessing the capacity of SoMS implies assessing the maximum traffic that can be sustained efficiently and safely. For this purpose, the traffic level fed into the

Table 3.4 Travel time validation

Vessel type	*Direction*	*Travel time in minutes (historical)*	*Travel time in minutes (simulation)*	*Difference (%)*
Bulk Carrier	Westward	436	453	+3.96
Bulk Carrier	Eastward	485	464	–4.20
Chemical (and LPG/LNG)	Westward	398	387	–2.69
Chemical (and LPG/LNG)	Eastward	396	394	–0.48
Container	Westward	345	330	–4.29
Container	Eastward	341	345	+1.05
Freighter	Westward	456	452	–0.95
Freighter	Eastward	494	465	–5.72
Tanker	Westward	445	453	+1.63
Tanker	Eastward	487	466	–4.35
VLCC	Westward	431	462	7.32
VLCC	Eastward	484	468	–3.43

simulation model was increased and the results of the model evaluated. Since details of traffic cannot be projected accurately into the long-term future, it was assumed that while the total volume of traffic goes up, the traffic composition, vessel mix and route patterns remain the same as today, both for the Singapore Strait and the Malacca Strait. Thus, all traffic was proportionally increased in quantum from the benchmark 2007 level and capacity indicators are also presented in terms of increase relative to the benchmark level.

Singapore Strait

The impact of increasing traffic on the efficiency indicator, or the time taken for vessels to transit the Singapore Strait, is shown in Figure 3.2. As traffic levels go up, there is a corresponding increase in travel time. When traffic volume is doubled from the base year (2007), travel time is increased by 13 per cent. This means that for a typical east to west (and vice versa) transit journey by a vessel originally taking seven hours to transit through the Singapore Strait, the travelling time would increase to nearly eight hours.

Figure 3.3 illustrates the impact of an increase in traffic on navigational safety in the Singapore Strait, quantified by the number of interactions per vessel per nautical mile travelled. At 257,000 vessel movements in the base year, each vessel is predicted to have one interaction every ten nautical miles. When traffic is doubled, the number increases to 15 interactions every ten nautical miles.

The increase in interactions is not uniform throughout the whole of the Singapore Strait. Certain areas of the TSS in the Singapore Strait recorded the highest number of interactions. The red (or shaded) zone shown in Figure 3.4 recorded up to 70 per cent of all interactions in the Singapore Strait. This is not surprising, given the high traffic density in this region because of the numerous major fairways, anchorages and pilot boarding grounds that exist here.

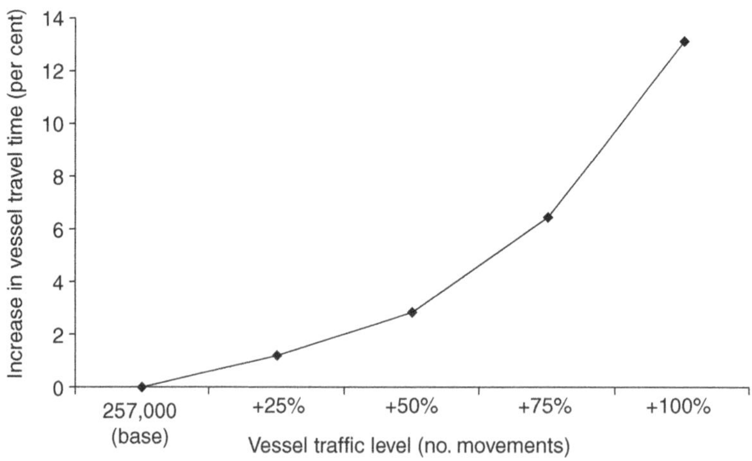

Figure 3.2 Efficiency indicator for the Singapore Strait.

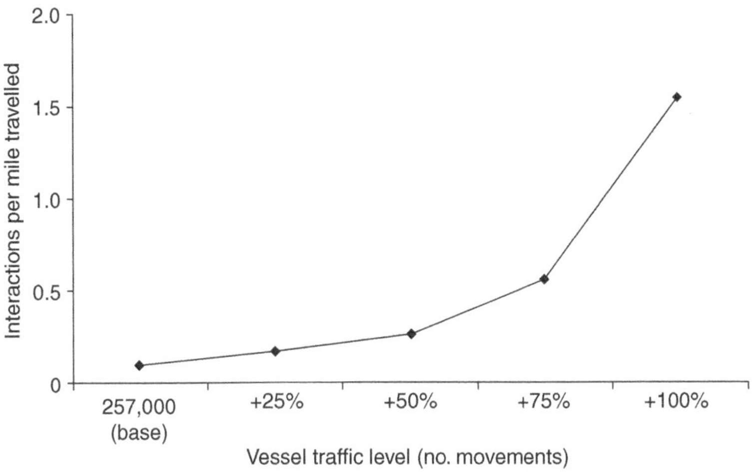

Figure 3.3 Safety indicator for the Singapore Strait.

It can be seen from both the efficiency and safety indicator charts that there is a gradual increase in vessel travel time and number of interactions per mile travelled as traffic volume is increased by up to 75 per cent over the base year level, beyond which the increase becomes more pronounced. This assumes that there are no advances in technology and no improvements to existing processes, and that these operations remain unchanged from 2007.

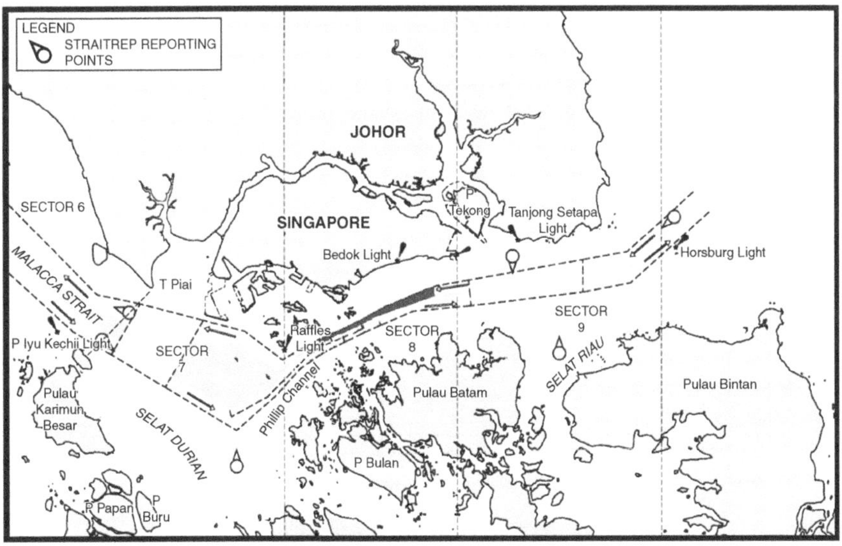

Figure 3.4 Region with high traffic density and interactions.

Malacca Strait

Based on available information and on assumptions on traffic in the Malacca Strait and using the same methodology, a preliminary assessment of capacity in the Malacca Strait was also conducted.

The impact of increasing traffic on the efficiency indicator, or the time taken by vessels to transit the Malacca Strait, is shown in Figure 3.5. As traffic levels go up, there is no significant change in the travel time, which remains stable at slightly under 20 hours, even at three times the original traffic level. In an attempt to search for a traffic level at which a more pronounced increase in travel time can be seen, a five-fold volume scenario was tested. However, travel time was unaffected even at this increased level.

Figure 3.6 illustrates the impact of an increase in vessel movements on navigational safety in the Malacca Strait, quantified by the number of interactions per vessel per nautical mile travelled. At 126,000 vessel movements in the base year, each vessel is predicted to have three interactions every 100 nautical miles. When traffic is increased three-fold, this increases to five interactions every 100 nautical miles.

As discussed, the efficiency indicator holds steady for the Malacca Strait while the safety indicator shows a slow increase as traffic levels increase up to five times the baseline level. This leads to the assessment that the Malacca Strait can sustain traffic up to five times the current level, assuming that traffic numbers and patterns used in the Malacca Strait model are reasonably realistic and that all technology, processes and operations remain unaltered.

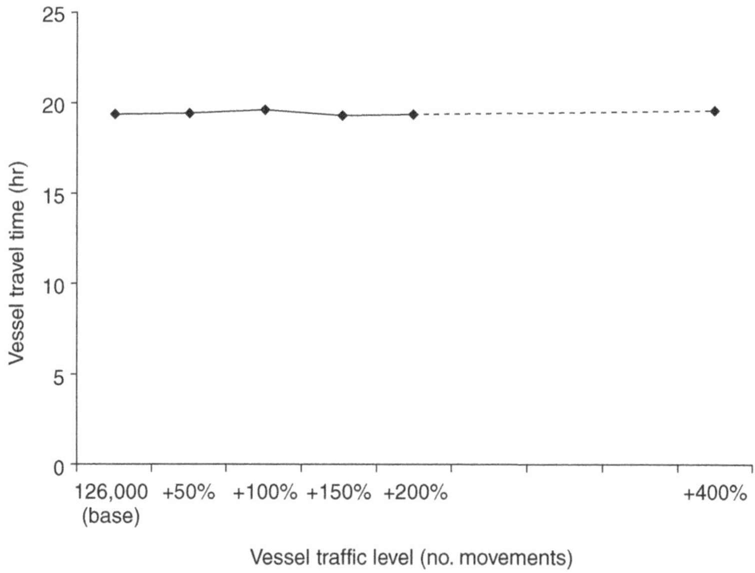

Figure 3.5 Efficiency indicator for the Malacca Strait.

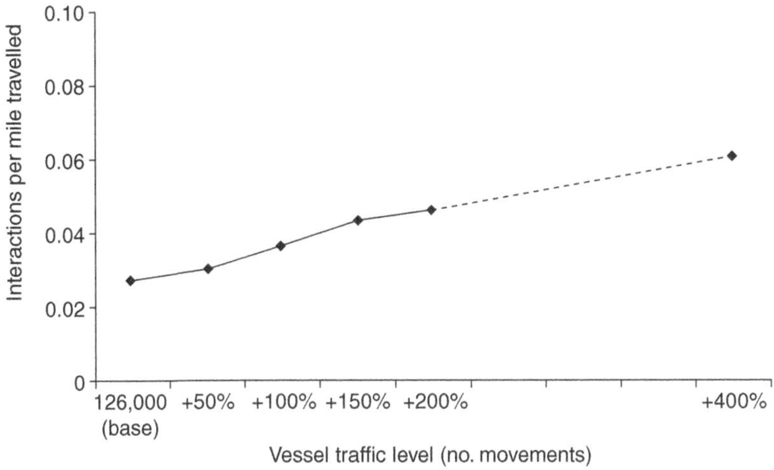

Figure 3.6 Safety indicator for the Malacca Strait.

Conclusion

The growth of vessel traffic in the SoMS will depend on many factors, including economic conditions, global trade, shipping trends and technological advances. Over time, the capacity of the SoMS can be increased even further with improved traffic management measures and technological advances. Work is underway in the second phase of this study to examine possible measures that could enhance the carriage capacity of the Singapore Strait, while maintaining navigational safety. If improved traffic volume and pattern details for the Malacca Strait become available in the future, thus providing greater confidence in the inputs, the model can be adjusted and new and more reliable results generated.

Notes

1 Review of Maritime Transport 2008, United Nations Conference on Trade and Development (UNCTAD), www.unctad.org/Templates/WebFlyer.asp?intItemID=4659&lang=1.

2 H.S.L. Fan and J.M. Cao, "Sea space capacity and operation strategy analysis system", *Transportation Planning and Technology*, Vol. 24 (2000), pp. 49–63.

3 M. Jim, *Marine Risk Assessment for Port of Melbourne*, Technical Report (2006), www.channelproject.com/global/docs/SEES_Technical_Appendix_16.pdf. See also I. Or, B. Ozbas and T. Yilmaz, "Simulation of marine traffic in Istanbul Strait", *Simulation Modelling Practice and Theory*, Vol. 11 (2003), pp. 597–608; I.W. Dand and R.D. Colwill, "Simulation of traffic flows using dynamic ship modelling", in *Proceedings of the International Conference on Marine Simulation and Ship Manoeuvrability*, Kanazawa, Japan; J.R.W. Merrick, J.R. van Dorp, J.P. Blackford, G.L. Shaw, J. Harrald and T.A. Mazzuchi, "A traffic density analysis of proposed ferry service expansion in San Francisco Bay using a maritime simulation model", *Reliability Engineering and System Safety*, Vol. 81 (2003), pp. 119–132.

4 Malaysia Marine Department website, www.marine.gov.my/service/statistik/BKP/report_all_kapal_07.pdf.
5 Port Klang official website, www.pka.gov.my/KlangSta.asp.
6 Traffic split, a *TED Case Study on MALACCA: The Impact of Transportation on Wildlife in the Malacca Straits*, www1.american.edu/ted/malacca.htm, attributed to the Marine Department Malaysia, Public Port Corporation Belawan Indonesia and Port of Singapore Authority.
7 Ferry traffic split sources: http://wikitravel.org/en/Dumai; www.m-sia.com/indomal/price.html; Maritime Traffic Pattern along Indonesian Coastal ports in southern portion of Malacca Straits, www.nmc.com.sg/2006.08.03.pdf.
8 *Singapore Port Information 2008/2009 Edition* (Singapore: Hydrographic Department of Maritime and Port Authority of Singapore, 2008); *Passage Planning Guide: Malacca & Singapore Straits*, 2nd edn (London: Witherby Seamanship International Ltd, 2008).

Part II

Maritime challenges and priorities in Southeast Asia

4 Indonesia's maritime challenges and priorities

Hasjim Djalal

Indonesian national boundaries

According to current International Law, Indonesia has several boundaries, namely land; maritime, including the seabed area; and airspace. The protection of the space within the national boundaries for the safety and security of Indonesia, and of all the resources therein, either living or nonliving, is within the sovereignty, sovereign rights, and jurisdiction of Indonesia. Equally, the security of shipping passing through (and of aviation) within the boundaries of the Archipelagic State of Indonesia, including in and through the archipelagic sea-lanes, is also within its sovereignty and jurisdiction, taking into account Indonesian national legislations, bilateral agreements, and the relevant International Laws. It is therefore essential to understand the nature of Indonesian national boundaries in order to appreciate the challenges it faces in managing its maritime resources and the security of shipping.

Airspace

According to International Law, Indonesia has sovereignty over the "airspace" above its land, archipelagic waters, and territorial sea up to the point where the airspace meets with "outer space." Until now, there has been no international agreement on the vertical limit of the airspace, although there has been general agreement that the airspace does not include outer space. The airspace of Indonesia covers an area of about 5,000,000 sq. km. However, problems may arise if the territorial sea boundaries of Indonesia are not clearly delimited with the relevant neighboring countries.

Land boundaries

The land boundaries of Indonesia are basically those agreed upon by the Government of the Netherlands (Dutch East Indies), which colonized Indonesia, the British Government, which colonized Sarawak and North Borneo (Sabah) and Papua New Guinea, and Portugal, which colonized East Timor.

Although the stipulations in those agreements maybe clear on paper, it has not been easy to determine the exact locations of these boundary lines in the field, particularly in the middle of the deep jungle, such as in Papua, or in relation to the flow of rivers, either because of marsh and swamp areas, or because rivers may have changed their course over the years. It is therefore essential to have effective cooperation between neighboring states to jointly conduct survey for border mapping on land and for constructing markers in agreed areas and locations.

Maritime boundaries

The maritime boundaries of Indonesia include the boundaries of (1) internal waters, (2) archipelagic waters, (3) territorial seas, (4) contiguous zones, (5) exclusive economic zones and (6) continental shelves. In addition, according to new legislation on autonomy and the devolution of power from central to local governments, there are also maritime zones of the districts and provinces in Indonesia.

Internal waters

According to Article 50 of the UN Convention on the Law of the Sea (UNCLOS) 1982, Indonesia may draw closing lines for the delimitation of its internal waters. However, until now Indonesia has not yet determined the boundaries of its internal waters within the archipelagic waters. It is understood that there is no right of passage of foreign ships through the internal waters of a state.

Archipelagic waters

The Indonesian "archipelagic waters" are those waters surrounded by "straight archipelagic baselines, joining the outermost points of the outermost islands and drying reefs," as stated in Article 47 (1) of UNCLOS 1982. The method for determining these lines is stipulated in UNCLOS 1982. The new coordinates for the archipelagic baselines were announced in Government Regulation No. 38/2002 and Government Regulation No. 61/1998 (for waters near the Karimata Strait and the South China Sea). The last revision to the archipelagic baselines was made under Law No. 37/2008, which was deposited with the UN Secretariat in March 2009 in accordance with Article 47 (a) of UNCLOS 1982. The revision was considered necessary as the result of the decision of the International Court of Justice on the Sipadan and Ligitan case and as the result of the separation of East Timor (Timor-Leste) from Indonesia. It should be noted, however, that foreign vessels have the right of "innocent passage" through archipelagic waters in accordance with Government Regulation No. 36/2002 and the right of "archipelagic sea-lane passage" (ASLP) through certain archipelagic sea-lanes in accordance with Government Regulation No. 37/2002. The determination of ASLP, as well as the rights and obligations of passing vessels, has been determined on the basis of UNCLOS 1982 and accepted by the International Maritime Organization (IMO). In certain parts of the archipelagic waters, certain other countries also have rights, such as the right to repair their own under-water cables or certain rights of "traditional fishing," whose implementation must be determined and regulated in separate bilateral agreements, (e.g., the Indonesian-Malaysian Treaty of February 1982, covering the traditional fishing rights of Malaysian fishermen using traditional methods in certain waters around the Anambas Islands in the South China Sea).

Archipelagic sea-lanes

Specifically regarding "archipelagic sea-lanes," Indonesia has so far determined three archipelagic sea-lanes (ALKI) in the North–South direction, namely ALKI I through the Karimata Strait, the Western Java Sea, and the Sunda Strait for navigation between the South China Sea and Indian Ocean; ALKI II through the Strait of Makassar and the Strait of Lombok for navigation between the Pacific Ocean and the Sulawesi Sea to the Indian Ocean; and ALKI III from the Pacific Ocean through the Moluccas Sea, Seram Sea, and Banda Sea, and then branching to ALKI IIIA through the Sawu Sea, ALKI IIIB to the Timor Sea, and ALKI IIIC to the Arafura Sea. The three ALKIs have been accepted by the international community through IMO and are now in force. Nevertheless, Indonesia has not yet determined the East–West ALKI through the Java Sea. The lack of determination of the East–West ALKI has the potential to create political sensitivities and conflicts in the Java Sea. It should be noted, however, that Government Regulation No. 37/2002 regulated the passage of foreign vessels through the ALKIs following many years of discussions with maritime powers, particularly with the United States and Australia.

Territorial sea

Outside the archipelagic waters, Indonesia also has sovereignty over the territorial sea up to 12 nautical miles from the archipelagic baselines that surround all Indonesian islands and seas. In cases where the waters between Indonesia and its neighbors are less than 24 miles wide, the Indonesian territorial sea boundary is determined by agreements between Indonesia and the neighboring countries concerned, or is the median line between the Indonesian archipelagic baseline and the legitimate baseline of the territorial sea of the neighboring state. So far, there are Territorial Sea Boundary Delimitation Agreements between Indonesia and Malaysia in certain parts of the Strait of Malacca, and between Indonesia and Singapore in certain parts of the Strait of Singapore. However, these two boundaries have not yet been connected.

On the eastern part of the Strait of Singapore toward the South China Sea, there is no territorial sea delimitation, either between Indonesia and Singapore or between Indonesia and Malaysia (Johor). For years, this matter depended on ownership of the Horsburgh Lighthouse and the neighboring rocks in the entrance to the South China Sea, which was disputed between Malaysia and Singapore.

Contiguous zone

Beyond the territorial sea, Indonesia may also control up to another 12 nautical miles in the contiguous zone to prevent infringement of its customs, fiscal, immigration, or sanitary laws and regulations, including jurisdiction to control the removal of objects of historical and archaeological nature found in Indonesian waters. Until now, Indonesia has not yet specifically enacted legislation on this contiguous zone. In any case, sooner or later Indonesia will also have to establish the delimitation of its contiguous zones with the opposite neighboring countries for spans of water less than 48 miles across. Indonesia is currently preparing its own legislation on this matter.

This matter is very important in view of the rampant illegal search and uplift of remnants of ancient vessels in Indonesian waters, which may sell in foreign markets for millions of dollars.

Exclusive economic zone (EEZ)

Beyond its territorial sea, Indonesia also has sovereign rights for the purpose of exploring and exploiting, conserving and managing the natural resources of its EEZ up to a distance of 200 nautical miles from its archipelagic baselines, as well as of its other jurisdictions. These entitle Indonesia to permit and regulate marine scientific research, protect and prevent pollution of the marine environment, and to construct artificial islands, installations, and other structures in the zone. Indonesia has enacted legislation on its EEZ but has not been able to agree on EEZ delimitation with its neighbors, except with Australia in the Arafura Sea, Timor Sea, South of Sumba, and between the Island of Java and Christmas Island. As I understand it, this agreement, however, has not yet been ratified by the two countries, although the agreement was concluded in 1997.

Indonesia has not been able to determine the delimitation of the EEZ boundaries with its Association of Southeast Asian Nations (ASEAN) partners, specifically Thailand and Malaysia regarding the northern part of the Strait of Malacca, Malaysia and Vietnam regarding the South China Sea, and Malaysia and the Philippines regarding the Sulawesi Sea. All Indonesian efforts to negotiate this matter with its neighbors have generally been in vain, mainly because of a lack of interest by its neighbors. These neighbors generally argue that it is not necessary, because the continental shelf boundaries that have already been agreed between Indonesia and its neighbors can be regarded as the EEZ boundaries. Indonesia disagrees with this argument because the two legal regimes, the EEZ and the continental shelf, are different: the EEZ boundary is basically for the purposes of fisheries, marine scientific research, environmental protection and is determined by distance criteria (200 miles); while the continental shelf boundaries delineate the seabed and subsoil areas for the purpose of protecting rights to oil, gas and other minerals found therein, and is therefore dependent upon geological and geomorphologic conditions in addition to “distance criteria.” In fact, the Indonesian–Australian EEZ Delimitation Agreement of 1997 is based upon this legal understanding.

The absence of accurate EEZ boundaries between Indonesia and its ASEAN neighbors has been one of the reasons for the current difficulties in managing and protecting the living marine resources of the EEZ. As it happens, there are many violations of fisheries regulations in the "gray area," in which there is no EEZ delimitation. Arrests in Southeast Asia for illegal fishing in the EEZ of neighboring countries are increasing, and these activities increasingly pose security problems, particularly for the archipelagic State of Indonesia, whose archipelagic waters, territorial seas, and EEZs are rampant with illegal fishing activities, either by its own nationals or by foreign fishermen, including those of its near neighbors. It has been estimated that Indonesia alone loses more than US$2 billion a year as the result of illegal fishing in its waters.

Continental shelf

In the seabed area beyond its territorial sea, Indonesia has sovereign rights to explore and exploit the natural resources found in its continental shelf, including sedentary organisms on the sea floor, and other minerals, oil, and gas found in the area. Under UNCLOS 1982, sovereign rights have been extended through the natural prolongation of the land territory of coastal states to the outer edge of the "continental margin," and this includes the land territories of the islands of archipelagic states. This means that in certain land territories facing the open ocean, the sovereign rights of Indonesia over natural resources on the seabed and its subsoil could extend up to 350 miles from its archipelagic straight baselines, namely to the boundary of the International Seabed Area, managed by the International Seabed Authority in Jamaica. However, this depends upon the natural and geological structure of the seabed concerned. So far, Indonesia has submitted partial delimitation of its continental margin in the Indian Ocean to the Continental Shelf Commission and is still carrying out scientific investigations on its continental margin in other parts of the country.

Indonesia has already concluded maritime boundary delimitations of the continental shelf with some of its neighbors, namely with India between the Andaman and Nicobar Islands and Aceh; with Thailand and Malaysia in the northern parts of the Strait of Malacca; with Malaysia and Vietnam in the South China Sea; with Papua New Guinea in some parts of the Pacific Ocean north of Papua; with Papua New Guinea and Australia in the Arafura Sea; and with Australia in some parts of the Timor Sea. So far, there is no agreement between Indonesia, Malaysia, and the Philippines regarding the Celebes Sea, and between Indonesia and Timor-Leste regarding the Timor Sea, Wetar Strait and Sawu Sea.

The conclusion of this continental shelf boundary agreement is also necessary for the proper exploration and exploitation of the seabed/continental shelf natural resources. The absence of a boundary agreement could disturb relations between the neighboring countries concerned and cause problems not only for the utilization and management of resources but also for maritime security in the area.

It should be noted that although the contiguous zone, EEZ, and continental shelf are areas where Indonesia has sovereign rights over natural resources and certain jurisdictions, the freedom of navigation and overflight, and other freedoms recognized in the UNCLOS 1982, continue to be respected.

District and provincial maritime zones

In addition to the various and complicated boundary problems between Indonesia and its neighboring countries, the challenges of managing Indonesian maritime resources and the security of shipping are now also being made more complicated by the problems of maritime boundaries between the provinces and the districts or autonomous cities that border the sea. Law No. 22/1999, later replaced by the Law No. 32/2004, stipulated that every province has a 12 mile maritime zone measured from the coastline, and that every district or autonomous city bordering the coast has a maritime zone of four miles measured from the coastline. This new stipulation has created sensitivities between neighboring coastal districts and cities, between individual provinces, and between provinces and the central government regarding maritime boundaries and the rights and jurisdictions to manage the natural resources in their maritime zones, especially because the provincial and districts or cities are also allowed to issue certain fishing permits in their maritime zones. As a consequence of the new legislation, conflicts have arisen between local governments with regard to the "ownership" of remote small islands, and among many Indonesian fishermen who were prevented by local fishermen from fishing in what they consider to be their own maritime zones.

With regard to shipping, more and more local governments want to have more control on ports and their facilities. It is not yet clear how these demands will affect the security of shipping.

Indonesian interest in the high seas and international seabed area

Although the territorial sovereignty and jurisdiction of Indonesia have been regulated in accordance with the provisions of UNCLOS, this does not mean that Indonesia has no interests beyond the maritime areas under its sovereignty, sovereign rights, and jurisdictions.

1 Indonesia continues to have strong interests in the airspace above its EEZ and beyond its territorial seas, mainly for navigation and ocean overflight and for defense requirements, in which it's important to anticipate and face threats that may come from neighboring airspace.
2 Indonesia also continues to have interests in the management, utilization, and freedoms of the high seas beyond its EEZ, for navigation and overflight purposes and in order to be able to protect ships navigating under its flag in the open ocean. Equally, Indonesia has interests in the management of living resources beyond its EEZ, particularly the "highly migratory species" and

the "straddling fish stocks," as the utilization and conservation of these resources are closely linked with the exploitation and conservation of its own resources in its EEZ. It is therefore important to note that Indonesia is also seeking effective cooperation with other bilateral and regional countries to deal with these problems in the Indian and Pacific Oceans.

3 Equally, Indonesia continues to be interested in the exploration and exploitation of natural resources in the International Seabed Area beyond its continental shelf. Indonesian interest in this matter has so far emphasized the need to protect its land-based mineral resources from possible commercial competition from mineral resources that may come from mining the International Seabed Area. It does not mean, however, that Indonesia is not interested in developing its own capacity for participating in mining the deep seabed international area in the future.

4 Indonesia also continues to be interested in cooperating with its neighbors in managing the "semi-enclosed seas" around Indonesia, including the South China Sea, the Celebes Sea, the Arafura Sea, the Timor Sea, and the Andaman Sea, in accordance with Article 123 of UNCLOS. This article stipulates that states bordering on enclosed or semi-enclosed seas are expected to cooperate in the management of living resources, on the protection and preservation of the marine environment, and on programs of scientific research in the sea. Indonesia has some experiences in managing potential conflicts in the South China Sea and on moving from confrontation to cooperation by developing and encouraging dialog processes, confidence building, and designing and implementing concrete cooperative programs.

Other challenges

In addition to developing Indonesian concepts of maritime jurisdiction and the ability to make use of its rights and obligations with regard to maritime zones as indicated above, there are other practical challenges that Indonesia currently faces.

Maintaining the national unity and integrity of Indonesia

Throughout its history, the continuous challenge of any Indonesian Government has been to maintain national unity and the integrity of Indonesia as a whole within the Unitary State of Indonesia. Since its early history, Indonesia has been faced with problems of provincialism, religious sectarianism, ideological bigotry, ethnic jealousy, the relationship between central and the regional governments, and many other problems. In some cases, these problems have led to armed rebellions, and even a struggle for separation, as in Aceh (which has been solved after many decades of conflicts) and from time to time in Papua.

Ideologically, Indonesia strongly believes that for an archipelagic state such as itself the sea should not "separate" peoples who live on different islands but should instead unite them. This has in fact been the essence of Indonesian struggles regarding the law of the sea and maritime issues for many decades. The challenge now is, as ever, to make this belief a reality that will strengthen the fabric of Indonesian Unitary State and of nationhood, not weaken them.

What is worse is that many Indonesians somehow still believe that there are "conspiracies" among foreign powers to undermine Indonesian national unity by encouraging and exploiting local sentiments against the central government and, in some cases, to support rebellion and separation in outlying areas.

Eliminating illegal fishing

The other Indonesian concern regards how to make those resources of the sea contribute to the welfare of the Indonesian people as a whole. Illegal fishing is one of the main concerns. As indicated previously, Indonesia has lost more than US$2 billion a year as the result of illegal fishing, although this figure may have been reduced somewhat recently.

Eliminating smuggling and other violations

Smuggling, illegal entry, intrusion of terrorist elements, the removal of border markers, and the illegal exploitation of natural resources, such as illegal logging, are rampant through Indonesian waters. It has been estimated that about US$3 billion a year of timber is illegally smuggled out of the country. The destruction of tropical forest in Indonesian provinces sometimes even takes place in "protected" or "forest conservation" areas. These smuggling activities involve not only smuggling of goods but also of laborers, including women and even children.

Recently, the smuggling and illegal trade of Indonesian endangered and protected animals have also become major problems.

All these problems require closer cooperation between neighboring countries, particularly between their law enforcement agencies, and the proper distribution of power and coordination between Central and Local Government Authorities.

Determination of clear land and maritime boundaries

It is not easy to determine national boundaries in the field, either on land or at sea, although agreements may have been made. On land, these uncertainties may create border-crossing problems between populations in the border areas. Many local populations may not know the exact locations of boundary lines, especially in remote or heavily forested areas.

At sea, there are a number of unsettled maritime boundaries between Indonesia and its neighbors, particularly in the territorial sea, EEZ, and continental shelf, as previously indicated. Unless these boundaries are settled by agreements between the countries concerned, difficulties and violations are bound to happen that may aggravate the challenges in managing maritime resources and in ensuring the security of shipping.

Shipping through the archipelagic waters

The transit of foreign vessels through Indonesian archipelagic waters, either on the principle of "innocent passage" or the principle of ASLP, is another challenge that Indonesia is sensitive to, primarily because of its shortcomings in monitoring, controlling, and supervising these vessels, and in law enforcement at sea. The challenge is to ensure that the passage of vessels, especially military vessels, vessels carrying nuclear or hazardous substances, and nuclear powered vessels, does not negatively affect Indonesian national unity, security, and stability, and its environment. It is therefore very important for Indonesia to increase its defense and law enforcement capabilities, and in such situations cooperation is needed between Indonesia and other countries, particularly regarding the users of Indonesian waters and those of neighboring states.

The problems of an archipelagic state

With such extensive land areas, maritime zones, including the seabed area, and airspace, along with the complexities of its natural resources, it is difficult to protect and maintain law and order in Indonesian maritime zones. This is complicated by Indonesia currently facing many other problems, while having limited financial and other resources to meet its challenges. In addition, Indonesia is a country with multiple distinct local cultures, which in some cases are keen to project their own identities to the nation, the region, and the international audience.

Being geographically, politically, and legally an archipelagic state, Indonesia is also confronted by other various factors, including, its geographical position at the crossroads between the Indian and Pacific oceans, as well as between the Asian and Australian continents. Indonesian maritime zones are heavily navigated by various kinds of vessels, including giant oil tankers, ships carrying nuclear and other dangerous materials, and military vessels, including submarines and other nuclear powered vessels. Indonesia is also crisscrossed by international aviation, both commercial and military. These factors have made Indonesia, together with its maritime zones and airspace, a very important strategic consideration in the minds of the regional and global powers. While this strategic geographical position is significant for other countries, it has not, however, brought significant benefits to Indonesia. In fact, it has made Indonesia becomes more sensitive to outside power maneuvers and pressures that in some cases have brought political instability to Indonesia.

While Indonesia is strategically important in the crossroads of international navigation and transportation, the geographical structure of Indonesia as an archipelagic state consisting of thousands of islands with very long coastlines and extensive sea areas between, has made Indonesian maritime zones and coastlines open and "porous," which makes it relatively easy for foreign subversion and the intrusion of smugglers, drug dealers, pirates, poachers, and terrorists, which may also upset Indonesian domestic stability.

The structure of the Indonesian population is also very uneven, with most people living in the western part of Indonesia, particularly in the island of Java. This uneven population structure has also created sensitivities between Western Indonesia and eastern regions, the people of which feel that they have been "neglected" in terms of economic and social development in favor of the development in Java. In fact, local people in some areas feel they have been economically exploited by Java and are demanding more rights to exploit nearby maritime resources.

At this moment, Indonesia is also facing many domestic problems, including issues of regional autonomy. The Regional Governments would like to increase their power through regional autonomy and devolution of powers from Central Government to the regions. These developments have also created problems in the management of maritime and other resources. While the development of regional autonomy is in itself necessary, many of its possible consequences must be carefully explored and analyzed, especially where the conditions necessary for successful autonomy do not yet exist or are lacking, either in terms of human resources or material and financial capabilities.

Indonesia has just passed the stage of political reformation from an authoritarian government to a democracy. Much progress has been achieved but a lot more is necessary, particularly in terms of human capacity building. The impact of political transformation, including the shift of political power from executive to legislative, from a bureaucracy to political parties, through regional autonomy, from government to civil society and good governance, is still to be studied and analyzed for some years ahead. This political transformation has also affected the management of Indonesian maritime resources.

The current economic and financial capacity of Indonesia to protect and maintain law and order, to defend the archipelagic state from unwanted intrusion, and to protect maritime resources and shipping interests through its maritime zones are very limited. The problems of international shipping, however, have largely taken place in western Indonesia, particularly in the straits of Malacca and Singapore. Indonesia, Malaysia, and Singapore have been cooperating for the last 40 years to promote navigation safety and protect the marine environment in the straits.

There are also the problems of law enforcement agencies. Their capacity to act is very limited in comparison with the extensive maritime areas that they have to protect. It is sad to know that the defense budget of Indonesia is generally less than 1 percent of its gross domestic product, one of the lowest percentages of defense budget in the region.

The internal conflicts in Indonesia may have also caused some problems for the border areas, which may be complicated by the cultural similarities of communities across the border. Unless specific arrangements for cross border relations is clearly defined, the border issues will be difficult to deal with and may continue to inflict damage to good bilateral neighborly relations. These issues all require close cooperation between neighboring countries, particularly for obtaining border crossing agreements, either on land or at sea, and for obtaining definitive solutions to all boundaries delimitation and demarcation issues.

Conclusion

UNCLOS 1982 has provided archipelagic states like Indonesia with varied and extensive maritime zones for either territorial purposes or jurisdictional and resources purposes. At the same time, the interests of shipping communities, particularly foreign shipping communities, have also been protected commensurately. Yet, archipelagic states like Indonesia are facing many challenges in utilizing the opportunities provided by UNCLOS 1982, primarily due to domestic shortcomings and financial and economic constraints. Archipelagic states like Indonesia need cooperation and understanding from their neighbors, regional and international communities in order to implement UNCLOS 1982 appropriately. What is needed, therefore, are cooperation and not confrontation, mutual understanding and not recrimination from neighbors. It should be understood that proper implementation of UNCLOS 1982 and the protection, proper utilization, and sustainable development of marine resources, as well as the security of shipping passing through Indonesian maritime zones, are in the interests of all concerned.

5 The search for sustainability and security

Malaysia's maritime challenges and opportunities

Mohd Nizam Basiron

Introduction

Malaysia's maritime realm encompasses a total area of 614,159 square kilometers[1] comprising areas of the Strait of Malacca, the South China Sea, the Sulu Sea and the Sulawesi (Celebes) Sea, as well as parts of the Straits of Singapore and the Gulf of Thailand.[2] The extent of Malaysia's maritime realm is shown on the two sheets of the *Peta Baru* (New Map) *1979*.[3] Malaysia's sea area, which is almost twice the size of its land-mass, poses a spectrum of issues and challenges for maritime policy makers and managers in Malaysia. Each of the sea areas mentioned above presents different issues and challenges including traditional and non-traditional maritime security issues, as well as environmental and social issues. This chapter discusses and analyses Malaysia's maritime challenges and opportunities by examining each of the seas and the issues that they pose to the country's policy makers and managers, as well as the crosscutting issues that affect the governance of Malaysia's maritime realm.

The Straits of Malacca and Singapore

The challenges posed by the Strait of Malacca (SOM) to Malaysia's policy makers and managers stems partly from its multiple uses as a strait used for international navigation, a fertile fishing ground, which provided Malaysia with more than half of its fish landings in 2009, and an important location for social and economic activities such as tourism. The interaction between these three uses, however, is limited and multiple use conflicts lie more in the realm of the "potential" rather than the "actual," especially in situations where maritime casualties result in oil spills that could adversely affect the fisheries and tourism sector. Sectoral issues, on the other hand, appear to be more critical, especially with regard to fisheries, safety of navigation and crime at sea.

In 2009, landings from the west coast of Peninsular Malaysia which borders the SOM amounted to 729,558 metric tonnes (tonnes) compared to the national total of 1,393,226 tonnes.[4] This is an increase of almost 36,000 tonnes from 2008. The increase in fisheries landings, however, belie what has been described by environmentalists as a crisis in fisheries resource management, which has manifested itself in the many symptoms of overfishing, such as a decrease in catch-per-unit-effort, a reduced fish biomass and an increase in landings of trash fish within the demersal fisheries subsector in the Straits of Malacca and Singapore (SOMS).[5] Because of the significance of the SOMS to Malaysia's fisheries sector, any dramatic decline in the resource could affect the industry as a whole and the supply of protein to Malaysians, whose per capita consumption of fish in 2004 was 45.4 kilograms (kg)[6] and was expected to increase to 56 kg in 2010.[7] Overfishing is not the only threat to the fishing industry. Over the years, the SOM has seen a steady decline in the ecosystems that support the burgeoning fisheries, namely the mangroves. From 1973 to 2005, states bordering the SOM have lost between 20 to 90 percent of their mangrove coverage.[8] On the other hand, a research cruise conducted by the University of Malaya to the islands of Perak and Jarak in the straits in 2004 discovered hitherto unknown and biologically diverse terrestrial and marine ecosystems, including corals and seaweed habitats.[9]

More than 74,000 vessel movements were recorded in the SOM in 2010.[10] In the past, the increase in vessel movements in the SOM has raised concerns regarding safety of navigation in the area. However, studies have shown that with the traffic separation scheme, aids to navigation and a vessel management system in place the SOM may be able to assimilate up to 120,000 vessels.[11] Safety of navigation in the SOM is closely related to environmental protection. While the tools for ensuring safe navigation are in place and functioning, the possibility of maritime incidents and the subsequent ill effects on the environment are ever present. Maritime security is an essential element of safe navigation. From 1999 to 2006, the SOM experienced an increase in the recorded number of piracy attacks, which peaked in 2000 with over one hundred cases. The number declined after 2006 following the establishment of the Malacca Straits Patrols initiative by the littoral states.[12]

The South China Sea

The South China Sea is important to Malaysia for geopolitical, ecological and economic reasons. Almost all of Malaysia's off-shore hydrocarbon resources are located in this area and the South China Sea is the second most important fisheries area for Malaysia.[13] It is also an area of ecological and environmental significance to Malaysia, hosting major ecosystems such as coral reefs and sea-grass beds, which are crucial breeding and nursing grounds for fish.[14] Historically, the South China Sea was an important trading route for merchants dating back to the eighth and ninth centuries and probably earlier, as evidenced by the discovery of Chinese ceramics from wrecks in Malaysia's South China Sea area.[15]

Unlike the SOM, Malaysia's challenges in the South China Sea are more geopolitical and environmental in nature. Malaysia's maritime territory in the South China Sea encompasses 12 features (islands, rocks, reefs, shoals and atolls in the Spratly Islands, as well as many other features further south).[16] From 1978 onwards, Malaysia has maintained a physical presence on five of the features it claimed in the Spratly Islands: Pulau Layang-Layang (Swallow Reef), Terumbu Mantanani (Mariveles Reef), Terumbu Ubi (Ardasier Reef), Terumbu Siput (Erica Reef) and Terumbu Peninjau (Investigator Reef). Two other features, Pulau Amboyna Kecil (Amboyna Cay) and Terumbu Laksamana (Commodore Reef), are occupied by Vietnam and the Philippines, respectively.[17] The level of Malaysia's presence on these features varies from the highly developed Layang-Layang, which has an airstrip, a resort, a naval station and more recently a marine research station,[18] to the more basic accommodation and meteorological modules on the other features. A chronology of Malaysia's activities in the Spratly Islands is given in Table 5.1.

Notwithstanding the unresolved claims in the South China Sea, Malaysia in 1992 signed an agreement with Vietnam to jointly develop hydrocarbon resources in an area claimed by both countries.[26] Malaysia has also sought to alleviate tension in the South China Sea by becoming a signatory to the non-legally binding ASEAN–China Declaration on the Conduct of Parties in the South China Sea, 2002 (DOC).

The whole of the South China Sea has experienced environmental stresses related to human activities, such as ecosystems modification, pollution and over-fishing.[27] Malaysia's South China Sea area is not spared these problems and has also had to contend with additional problems, such as coral bleaching associated with increased sea-level temperatures.[28] Other environmental issues in the South

Table 5.1 Chronology of Malaysia's activities in the Spratly Islands

Year (month)	*Features*	*Activity*
1978 (–)	Amboyna Kecil	Malaysian Navy Special Forces landed on the features and placed markers. The marker on Amboyna Kecil was subsequently destroyed by Vietnam, who now occupies the feature.[19]
1983 (May)	Pulau Layang-Layang	Malaysian Navy Special Forces landed on Layang-Layang.[20]
1986 (April)	Pulau Layang-Layang	Naval station "Lima" constructed on Layang-Layang.[21]
1986 (April)	Terumbu Ubi	Naval station "Uniform" constructed on Ubi.[22]
1986 (November)	Terumbu Mantanani	Naval station "Mike" constructed on Mantanani.[23]
1991 (–)	Pulau Layang-Layang	Resort constructed on Pulau Layang-Layang.[24]
1992 (May)	Pulau Layang-Layang	The then Yang Di-Pertuan Agong of Malaysia Sultan Azlan Shah visited Layang-Layang.[25]
1999 (April)	Terumbu Siput	Naval station "Sierra" constructed on Siput.
1999 (April)	Terumbu Peninjau	Naval station "Papa" constructed on Peninjau.
2004 (July)	Pulau Layang-Layang	Marine Research Station, Pulau Layang-Layang (MARSAL) opened.

China Sea include encroachment by foreign fishing vessels, which also target endangered species such as turtles.[29] To better understand the environment in the South China Sea, Malaysia is also actively enhancing its scientific knowledge of the area through research voyages such as the Matahari Expeditions (1985–1989), the Research on the Seas and Islands expedition (2004)[30] and the Prime Scientific Sailing Expedition 2009.[31] Malaysia also participated in a United Nations Environment Programme (UNEP) sponsored project on "Reversing Environmental Degradation Trends in the South China Sea and Gulf of Thailand," which ran from 2002 to 2009.

The Gulf of Thailand

The Gulf of Thailand is probably the least problematic of Malaysia's sea areas and illustrates the possibility of cooperation even in areas where maritime boundary delimitation has not been completed. Malaysia has two joint development areas in the Gulf of Thailand with Thailand and Vietnam respectively. The Malaysia–Thailand Joint Development Area (JDA) covers a continental shelf area of about 7,250 square kilometers and was established in 1979,[32] while the Malaysia–Vietnam Agreed Common Area (ACA) was established in 1992.[33]

The Sulu Sea

There is less written about Malaysia's Sulu Sea compared to the South China Sea and the SOM. This is presumably because, unlike these other areas, Malaysia's territory in the Sulu Sea is less well researched, is not often highlighted in the media and is geographically confined to the maritime boundary between Malaysia and the Philippines around Sabah. However, this is an area which has gained notoriety following the kidnapping of tourists from the resort islands of Sipadan and Pandanan in April and September 2000, respectively.[34] This prompted the Government of Malaysia to initiate an integrated security operation known as Ops Pasir in September of that year, intended to secure the area by placing Malaysian troops on all Malaysian islands in the Sulu Sea and enhancing naval patrols in the area. Non-traditional maritime security issues in the Sulu Sea and in the waters off Sabah in general also include the smuggling of various contrabands such as cigarettes, alcohol, narcotics, counterfeit currency and explosives, as well as human trafficking.[35] Human trafficking is fast becoming a major issue in this area and results from the "push-and-pull" factors related to security, political stability, the better economic opportunities in Sabah, and family ties between the populations of Sabah and the southern Philippines.

The biologically diverse reefs in the Sulu Sea sometimes are subject to pressure resulting from the increasing demand for life reef food fish. In order to meet the demand for 13,000 tonnes of reef fish valued at over US$810 million in 2003, illegal destructive fishing methods such as cyanide fishing are sometimes used. Another common destructive fishing method used in this area is dynamite fishing or fish bombing: 67 arrests were made from 2005 to April 2007 for fish bombing offences, with 327 detonators and more than 7,000 kg of fish being confiscated.[36] The situation vis-à-vis fisheries in parts of the Sulu Sea is approaching what has been described as "Malthusian overfishing," where over-exploitation of local fisheries resource occurs as a result of poverty, population growth and a lack of alternative income[37] Enforcement is made difficult by the proximity of the numerous islands in the area, cross-border movements of transient indigenous communities and the difficulty of policing a porous maritime border.[38]

The Sulawesi Sea

The non-traditional security situation in the Sulawesi (Celebes Sea) mirrors that of the Sulu Sea. However, the Sulawesi Sea is for Malaysia an area where traditional maritime security concerns predominate. The decision by the International Court of Justice (ICJ) in favor of Malaysia on sovereignty over the Sipadan and Ligitan islands and the ongoing exercise with Indonesia to delimit the waters off the islands has not precluded the navies of both countries from coming into close contact. This situation, which started prior to the ICJ judgment of 2002, continued well after the decision has been delivered and almost came to the boil in 2008 when an Indonesian navy vessel reportedly almost fired on the Royal Malaysian Navy (RMN),[39] with a further incident being reported in 2009. This situation notwithstanding, the RMN and the Tentara Nasional Indonesia – Angkatan Laut (TNI–AL) did sign a prevention of incidents at sea (INCSEA) agreement in January 2001. Why the agreement was not adhered to is a question that should be asked if such agreements are to be promoted further in areas where maritime boundary disputes occur, such as in the South China Sea.

Crosscutting issues

Maritime boundary delimitation

Malaysia has maritime boundaries with Indonesia, Singapore, Thailand, Vietnam, Brunei and the Philippines and has signed various agreements to delimit these boundaries (Table 5.2). However, Malaysia's undelimited maritime boundaries pose a challenge for maintaining sovereignty and control over parts of its maritime realm and the development of its resources. The most contentious of these thus far is the maritime boundary in the waters off Sipadan and Ligitan, which is contested by Indonesia. More recently, however, Indonesia has also exerted its claims over the northern part of the SOM and the eastern part of the Straits of Singapore, resulting in the apprehension of Malaysian fishermen and Indonesian fisheries officials, respectively, in these areas. Unresolved maritime boundaries could also have repercussions on maritime security, including the prevention of transboundary maritime crime such as smuggling and human trafficking and the rendering of humanitarian assistance during disasters.[40]

Table 5.2 Malaysia's maritime boundary agreements[43]

Signatories	*Type of boundary*	*Date signed*	*Entry into force*	*Sea area*
Indonesia and Malaysia	Continental shelf	27 October 1969	7 November 1979	Strait of Malacca and South China Sea
Indonesia and Malaysia	Territorial sea	17 March 1970	8 October 1971	Strait of Malacca
Malaysia and Thailand	Continental shelf Territorial sea	24 October 1979	15 July 1982	Gulf of Thailand
Indonesia, Malaysia and Thailand	Continental shelf	21 December 1971	16 July 1973	Strait of Malacca
Malaysia and Vietnam	Common area	5 June 1992	5 June 1992	South China Sea
Malaysia and Singapore	Territorial sea	7 August 1995	7 August 1995	Johor Straits

Malaysia has adopted different approaches for delimiting its maritime boundaries:

- It went to the ICJ to resolve the question of sovereignty over Sipadan, Ligitan, Pedra Branca, Middle Rocks and South Ledge. The implementation of the ICJ judgment, however, is being carried out through bilateral negotiations.
- In the case of overlapping claims in the Gulf of Thailand, Malaysia and the other claimants, Thailand and Vietnam, agreed to develop the hydrocarbon resources in the areas while placing boundary disputes on the back burner.
- Malaysia's long-running maritime delimitation issue with Brunei was resolved through bilateral negotiations leading to the signing of a Letter of Exchange on 17 March 2009 and the establishment of a Commercial Agreement Area for the joint exploitation of hydrocarbon reserves in the overlapping area.[41] Commercially, the agreement unlocked potentially vast petroleum resources in the deep-water area where exploration was halted in 2003. From a security and sovereignty standpoint, however, it has the effect of dividing Malaysia's exclusive economic zone (EEZ) in the waters of Sarawak and Sabah into two distinct areas straddling Brunei's EEZ. The implication of this division on Malaysian law enforcement and defence has yet to be clarified by the government and was the subject of a lengthy debate in Malaysia's parliament.[42]

Institutional structure for ocean governance

Malaysia's ocean management is divided among 14 ministries, nine departments and the Prime Minister's Department,[44] while the legislative framework comprises seven major laws and many other subsidiary laws (Table 5.3). This fragmentation and its implications have long been recognized by the government and scholars alike. Problems include a failure to use a conflict resolution mechanism among Government agencies, non-holistic decision-making and the inefficient use of financial resources.[45] Efforts to address these problems at the national policy level have unfortunately been a "stop–start" affair and there is still no public body with a large enough mandate to coordinate the work towards an integrated ocean policy.[46] Part of the problem in relation to maritime enforcement was resolved with the establishment of the Malaysian Maritime Enforcement Agency (MMEA) in 2005, which is intended to be the single maritime enforcement agency in Malaysia. Given the current security and sustainability challenges that Malaysia faces, it is pertinent that the government should act on the need for an overarching ocean policy to address the myriad of issues involved.

Despite the presence of these laws, there are still gaps in the national maritime legal framework of Malaysia, particularly in fully implementing the provisions of the 1982 United Nations Convention on the Law of the Sea on the

Table 5.3 Summary of principal maritime laws in Malaysia

Law	*Purpose*
Continental Shelf Act, 1966	• Defines the extent of Malaysia's continental shelf • Regulates exploration and exploitation of resources on Malaysia's continental shelf
Emergency Essential Ordinance, 1969. Nos 7 and 11	• Defines the extent of Malaysia's internal waters and territorial sea
Exclusive Economic Zone Act, 1984	• Defines the extent of Malaysia's EEZ • Regulates use of the EEZ • Protects the EEZ from pollution
Fisheries Act, 1985	• Regulates fisheries industry through issuing of licences, specifying allowable fishing gears and defining fishing zones • Protects endangered marine species • Establishes marine protected area
Environmental Quality Act, 1974	• Protects the marine environment from land-based and vessel-based pollution, and development impact
Merchant Shipping Ordinance, 1952	• Regulates shipping practices, including those related to pollution • Implements MARPOL 73/78
Malaysian Maritime Enforcement Agency Act, 2004	• Enabling act granting the MMEA powers to enforce all maritime laws in Malaysia

delimitation and pronouncement of various maritime zones,[47] as well as on emerging maritime security issues such as crimes at sea, maritime terrorism and the transportation of weapons of mass destruction.

Conclusions

Malaysia faces the dual challenge of sustainability and security in the governance of its maritime realm. These broad challenges affect all of the seas under Malaysia's national jurisdiction but vary in terms of their specific nature, the level of threat and the efforts undertaken by Malaysia to address them. Table 5.4 summarizes the nature of these challenges.

In addition to site-specific challenges, there are challenges that have crosscutting implications for Malaysia, particularly maritime boundary delimitation and the present institutional structure for maritime management in Malaysia. The former is an ongoing issue that Malaysia is currently addressing and has addressed using different means but is still problematic in the Sulawesi Sea and is emerging in the straits of Malacca and Singapore, despite regular bilateral meetings. The latter also have wide-reaching implications, but these can be addressed through the institution of an overarching ocean policy to address

Table 5.4 Summary of Malaysia's maritime challenges

Sea area	*Challenges*	*Mitigating efforts*
Strait of Malacca	• Ensuring safety of navigation • Overexploitation of fisheries resource • Piracy	• Ongoing application of various safety of navigation tools • Malacca Straits Patrol
South China Sea	• Overlapping claims and maritime boundary delimitation • Environmental degradation • Encroachment of foreign vessels	• Signing of DOC and bilateral negotiations • Regional cooperation and national actions • Stricter enforcement activities
Gulf of Thailand	• Overlapping claims	• Joint development of hydrocarbon resources
Sulu Sea	• Smuggling and human trafficking • Movement of transient population • Kidnapping by separatist or terrorist groups • Use of destructive fishing methods	• Implementation of integrated security measures under Ops Pasir • Continued enforcement
Sulawesi Sea	• Maritime boundary delimitation with Indonesia • Naval tension	• Bilateral negotiations • INCSEA

long-recognized deficiencies in the current institutional and legal framework. In the final analysis, Malaysia needs to urgently address a myriad of maritime challenges that could affect the sustainability of its maritime resources and its security as a maritime nation.

Notes

1 Department of Survey and Mapping Malaysia, 1999.

2 See V.L. Forbes and M.N. Basiron, *Malaysia's maritime realm atlas* (Kuala Lumpur: Maritime Institute of Malaysia, 2008).

3 The *Peta Baru 1979* was published in 1979 and its full title is "Map Showing Territorial Waters and Continental Shelf Boundaries of Malaysia." See R. Haller-Trost, *The contested maritime and territorial boundaries of Malaysia* (London: Kluwer Law International, 1998), for an analysis of the origin and a critique of the map.

4 Department of Fisheries, Malaysia, *Fisheries Statistics 2009* (Putrajaya: Department of Fisheries, Malaysia, 2010).

5 A. Abu Talib, "Demersal Fisheries: Have we surpassed the Straits' sustainable capacity?" in F.M. Yusoff, M. Shariff, H.M. Ibrahim, S.G. Tan and S.Y. Tai (eds), *Tropical Marine Environment: Charting Strategies for the Millennium* (Serdang: MASDEC, 2002).

6 M.M. Dey and Y.T. Garcia, Demand for fish in Asia: A cross-country analysis, in B. Johnson (ed.), "Economics and market analysis of the live reef-fish trade in the Asia-Pacific region," *ACIAR Working Paper No. 63*, 2007, pp. 13–31.

7 Ministry of Agriculture, Malaysia, *Third National Agricultural Policy* (Kuala Lumpur: Ministry of Agriculture, Malaysia, 1999).
8 K.H. Tan, *Protection and Management of Mangroves in Malaysia: Challenges and Strategies*, paper presented at the National Conference on Coastal and Marine Biodiversity, 17–18 April 2007, Kuala Lumpur, Malaysia.
9 P. Siew Moi, *Gems in the Straits of Malacca: the natural history of Pulau Jarak and Pulau Perak* (Kuala Lumpur: University of Malaya, 2007).
10 M. Shahryari and Mohd Arshad Atta Mohamad, "Tipping Points in the Strait of Malacca," *MIMA Bulletin* 18(1), 2011, pp. 4–11.
11 Ibid.
12 International Maritime Bureau's International Piracy Report, various years.
13 *Annual fisheries statistics 2007* (Putrajaya: Department of Fisheries, Malaysia, 2008).
14 M.N. Basiron, K.H. Tan and Z.M.Z. Zakariah, "Wither our ecosystems," *MIMA Bulletin*, 14(1), 2007, pp. 4–9.
15 R. Brown and S. Sjostrand, *Maritime archaeology and shipwreck ceramics in Malaysia* (Kuala Lumpur: Department of Museums and Antiquities, 2001).
16 Ibid.
17 For a list of the features in the Spratly Islands, see M.J. Valencia, *Malaysia and the law of the sea: the foreign policy issues, the options and their implication* (Kuala Lumpur: ISIS Malaysia, 1999) and D.J. Dzurek, "The Spratly Islands dispute: Who's on first?" *Maritime Briefing* 2(1), International Boundaries Research Unit, Durham, 1996.
18 The Marine Research Station, Pulau Layang-Layang (MARSAL) was officially opened on 19 July 2004. See Southeast Asian Fisheries Development Centre, Marine Fisheries Resource Development and Management Department, *The fourth department: a pictorial journey to distinction* (Kuala Terengganu: SEAFDEC-MFRDMD, 2007).
19 D.J. Dzurek, "The Spratly Islands dispute: Who's on first?"
20 Ibid.
21 Ibid; and personal communication with officers from the Policy Division, Ministry of Defence, Malaysia.
22 Personal communication with the Policy Division, Ministry of Defence, Malaysia.
23 Dzurek and Malaysia's Ministry of Defence differ on the actual date of the construction of the naval station "Mike."
24 J.R.V. Prescott, "The Spratly Islands: past and present," *MIMA Bulletin*, 17(1), 2010, pp. 14–18.
25 "King and Queen visited Layang-Layang," *The New Straits Times*, 23 May 1992.
26 V.L. Forbes and M.N. Basiron, "Unresolved maritime boundaries and implications for maritime security in Southeast Asia," *MIMA Bulletin* 17(1), 2010, pp. 3–13.
27 L. Talaue-McManus, "Transboundary Diagnostic Analysis for the South China Sea," *EAS-RCU Technical Report* No. 14, 2000.
28 "More dive sites hit by coral bleaching, may close," www.themalaysianinsider.com/malaysia/article/more-dive-sites.
29 "Mass turtle poaching: A case study from Southeast Asia," http://seaturtlestatus.org/pdf/r3_impact.pdf.
30 S. Md. Salleh, *The Royal Scientific Expedition to the South China Sea: investigation and planning*, final report of short-term grant (Pulau Pinang: School of Biological Sciences, Universiti Sains Malaysia, 2005).
31 Statement by YAB Dato' Sri Mohd Najib Tun Abdul Razak, Prime Minister of Malaysia at the Coral Triangle Initiative, 15 May 2009, Menado, Sulawesi, Indonesia, www.pmo.gov.my/?menu=speech&page=1676&news_id=124&speech_cat=2.
32 See www.mtja.org/whatisjda.php.
33 Nguyen Hong Thao, "Joint Development in the Gulf of Thailand," *IBRU Boundary and Security Bulletin*, 7(3), 1999, www.dur.ac.uk/ibru/publications/view/?id=153.

34 "20 kidnapped from Malaysian resort island," *NY Times*, 25 April 2000, www.nytimes.com/2000/04/25/news/25iht-malay.2.t_3.html.
35 Presentation by Assistant Commissioner of Police Abdul Manaf bin Othman at MIMA Seminar on Security in Sabah Waters, 2 September 2009.
36 Presentation by Deputy Superintendent of Police Robert Salisip at the MIMA Conference on Marine and Coastal Biodiversity, 17–18 April 2007.
37 L. Teh and R. Sumaila, "Malthusian Overfishing in Pulau Banggi?" *Marine Policy* 31(4). 2007, pp. 451–457.
38 Iskandar Sazlan Mohd Salleh, "Sempadan Maritim yang Bolos," *Majalah Massa*, April 1997.
39 M.J. Valencia and N. Khalid, "The Sulawesi Sea Situation: Stage for tension or storm in a teacup?" *Nautilus Institute Policy Forum 2009–2010*, www.nautilus.org/publications/essays/napsnet/forum/2009–2010/09060ValeniaKhalid.pdf/view.
40 V.L. Forbes and M.N. Basiron, "Unresolved Maritime Boundaries and Implications for Maritime Security in Southeast Asia," *MIMA Bulletin* 17(1), 2010, pp. 3–13.
41 J.J. Smith, "Malaysia and Brunei Resolve Outstanding Maritime Boundary Issues," *LOS Reports* Vol. 1, 2010.
42 Details of the debate can be read from the parliamentary Hansard of Monday, 7 June 2010.
43 V.L. Forbes and M.N. Basiron, "Unresolved Maritime Boundaries and Implications for Maritime Security in Southeast Asia," p. 9.
44 H.W. Wong, *Maritime Institutions and Agencies in Malaysia: An Overview* (Kuala Lumpur: MIMA, 1995).
45 E.L. Miles, *Consultant's Report on an Integrated National Ocean Policy* (Kuala Lumpur: MIMA, 1996), p. 51.
46 F.M. Yusoff, M. Shariff, H.M. Ibrahim, S.G. Tan and S.Y. Tai (eds), *Tropical Marine Environment: Charting Strategies for the Millennium*. (Serdang: MASDEC, 2002).
47 J. Ramli, *Status of Maritime Related National Laws and Maritime Conventions in Malaysia* (Kuala Lumpur: Maritime Institute of Malaysia, 1998).

6 Myanmar's maritime challenges and priorities

Maung Aung Myoe

This chapter examines the Myanmar government's perspective on the country's maritime challenges and priorities. It argues that the Myanmar government's maritime strategy largely remains traditional in outlook, that it pays little attention to other forms of maritime challenges, and that its most obvious priority is the defense of the sovereignty and territorial integrity of the state.

Myanmar is situated in Southeast Asia and is bordered on the north and northeast by China, on the east and southeast by Laos and Thailand, on the south by the Andaman Sea and the Bay of Bengal, and on the west by Bangladesh and India. It is located between latitudes 09° 32′N and 28° 31′N and longitudes 92° 10′E and 101° 11′E. The total length of contiguous frontiers is 6,159 kilometers (3,828 miles) and the coastline from the mouth of Naaf River to Kawthaung is 2,228 kilometers (1,385 miles). The coastline can be subdivided into three sections: the Rakhine coastline of 713 kilometers (443 miles), the Ayeyarwaddy Delta coastline of 437 kilometers (272 miles), and the Tanintharyi coastline of 1,078 kilometers (670 miles). Myanmar has 29,043 square nautical miles of internal waters and 9,895 square nautical miles of territorial waters (Table 6.1). There are 852 big and small islands in Myanmar waters.

Although the Myanmar government publicizes its multi-dimensional approach to security from time to time,[1] little is known or reported about its perceptions of maritime security or maritime strategy. This does not mean that Myanmar does not have any problems concerning maritime security. In reality, there are many

Table 6.1 Myanmar's claimed waters

Myanmar waters	*Area (nm^2)*
Internal waters (shore to baselines)	2,9043.6
Territorial sea waters (baseline to TS limit)	9,895.2
Contiguous zone (TS limit to CZ limit)	9,879.7
Exclusive economic zone (CZ limit to EEZ limit)	92,392.1
TOTAL MYANMAR WATERS	141,210.6

Source: Myanmar Ministry of Defense.

issues that the Myanmar government needs to address in the context of maritime security, and some are serious. In terms of challenges and priorities, in the view of the present military regime the issue of maritime boundary disputes appears be at the top of the list.

Maritime boundary disputes

Myanmar shares maritime boundaries with Thailand, India and Bangladesh. While some maritime boundaries with Thailand and India have been delimited, problems remain in the delimitation of the maritime boundary between Myanmar and Bangladesh. Maritime boundaries and disputes are complex, as the 1982 Law of the Sea Convention allows a country to claim a considerably large area of territorial waters and an exclusive economic zone (EEZ) on the basis of possession of even one small island or reef. There are currently three maritime boundary issues or disputes involving Myanmar. These include the unresolved maritime boundary disputes with Bangladesh and Thailand, and protests by some countries over Myanmar's use of straight baselines.

For Myanmar, the maritime boundary dispute with Bangladesh is the most serious maritime security issue. It has the potential to escalate into a major armed conflict, since the disputed area appears to hold a huge reserve of oil and gas. The Myanmar–Bangladesh boundary measures approximately 168.5 miles, including the Naaf River boundary of about 39.8 miles. The land and river boundary had previously been properly demarcated in accordance with the international law of state succession. At the time of Myanmar's independence in 1948 and that of Pakistan in 1947, both countries inherited and accepted the de jure Burma–Bengal boundary line drawn by the British during the colonial period. This being the case, Myanmar lost its historically owned Shinmaphyu (Shahpuri) Island and Ohnkyun (St. Martin) Island to (East) Pakistan.[2]

The most problematic aspect of the Myanmar–Bangladesh boundary is the maritime boundary, which covers the territorial sea, the EEZ and the continental shelf. As Prescott and Schofield explain:

> Its [Bangladesh] boundaries with Burma [Myanmar] and India meet at a trijunction near 19°5′N and 90°05′E, only about 167 nm from the most seaward point of Bangladesh. The boundary with Burma starts at the entrance of the Naf Estuary in which the land boundary between the two countries is located. The line of equidistance extends for 160 nm almost perpendicular to the mainland coast. Its course is governed for most of its length by Saint Martin Islands [known in Myanmar as Ohn-Kyun], belonging to Bangladesh and Oyster Island [known in Myanmar as Mayu-Kyun], that is part of Burma. The islands lie about 25 nm apart. Only for the last 25 nm of the equidistant line does a second Bangladeshi basepoint take effect. It is a low-tide elevation, located near 21°23′N and 90°34′E, south of Dakhin Shahbazpur island. It seems that this line of equidistance is equitable in terms of the water column.[3]

However, the equidistance principle applied by both Myanmar and India is contested and rejected by Bangladesh. Thus, the maritime boundary between Myanmar and Bangladesh has not been delimited, as both sides have failed to reach common ground. Several rounds of talks have been held in the past without any major breakthroughs. Myanmar has adhered to the principle of equidistance or the true median line, while Bangladesh has stood on the principle of equality during the talks, with several changes in methods of delimitation. Between 1974 and 1986, there were eight rounds of talks – two at ministerial level (the fourth and sixth rounds) and the rest at a technical level.

During the second round of negotiations, both sides reached a conditional agreement to apply the equidistance or median line principle. This agreement was clearly stated in the "Agreed Minute" signed by both parties in Dhaka on 23 November 1974. The minute established that the territorial sea between the Myanmar coastline and the St. Martin Islands of Bangladesh was to be delimited on the basis of the median line principle and that a treaty guaranteeing free passage of vessels from Myanmar in the waterways that extended into the Bangladeshi side of the territorial boundary was to be concluded. The minute included seven reference points for delimitation of the territorial sea boundary (shown in Figure 6.2).

Based on these reference points, a territorial sea boundary line was drawn on the Myanmar Naval Hydrographic Chart No. 114, and the chart was attached to the "Agreed Minute" signed on 23 November 1974. Therefore, it is safe to state that the territorial sea boundary between Myanmar and Bangladesh has been delimited.

However, the delimitation of the EEZ and the continental shelf is altogether a different story. Bangladesh has a concave-shaped coastline that lies between India and Myanmar (see Figure 6.1) and is the only country with a baseline that does not touch the low-water line of an island or mainland at any point; thus, the 222 nautical mile baseline is constructed on eight points at 60 feet (ten fathoms) of water. In the case of a concave coast, the effect of the equidistance method is to pull the line of the boundary inwards in the direction of the concavity; therefore, where two equidistance lines are drawn from two adjacent coastal states, they would inevitably meet at a relatively short distance from the coast, resulting in a much smaller EEZ and continental shelf, or may cut off the coastal state from the continental shelf altogether. It is in this context that Bangladesh sticks to the principle of equality, while, like India, Myanmar stands firmly on the principle of equidistance.

The equidistance line or true median line between Myanmar and Bangladesh starts from the midpoint between St. Martin Islands (Bangladesh) and Oyster Island (Myanmar) that runs along 243 degrees for about 160 nautical miles and then turns to 210 degrees for another 40 nautical miles before meeting with another median line that delimits the India–Bangladesh maritime boundary. In this situation, Bangladesh will end up with a closed EEZ about 167 nm from the baseline.

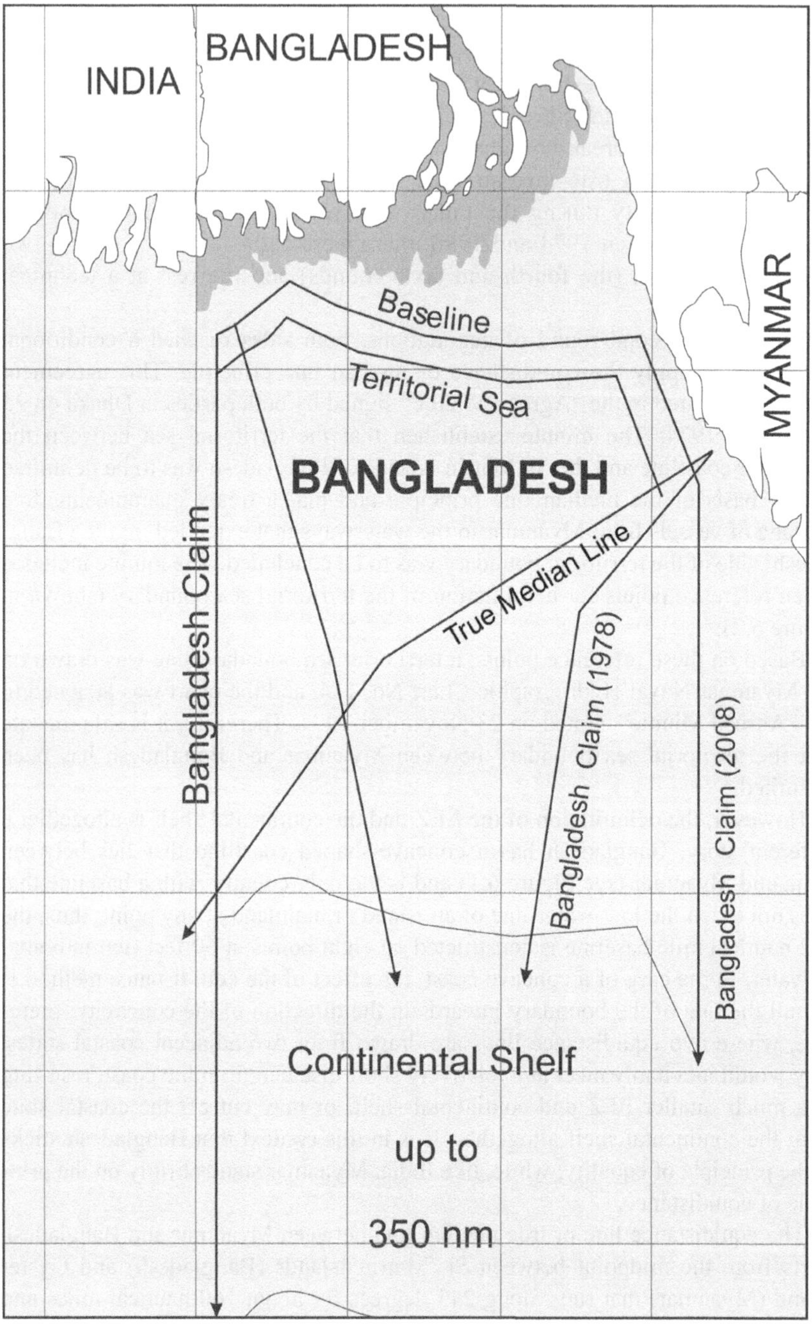

Figure 6.1 Map showing Bangladesh's maritime boundary claims (source: *Daily Star*, 5 December 2008; map redrawn by I. Made Andi Arsana, Gadjah Mada University, Yogyakarta, Indonesia, on the basis of additional information supplied by the author).

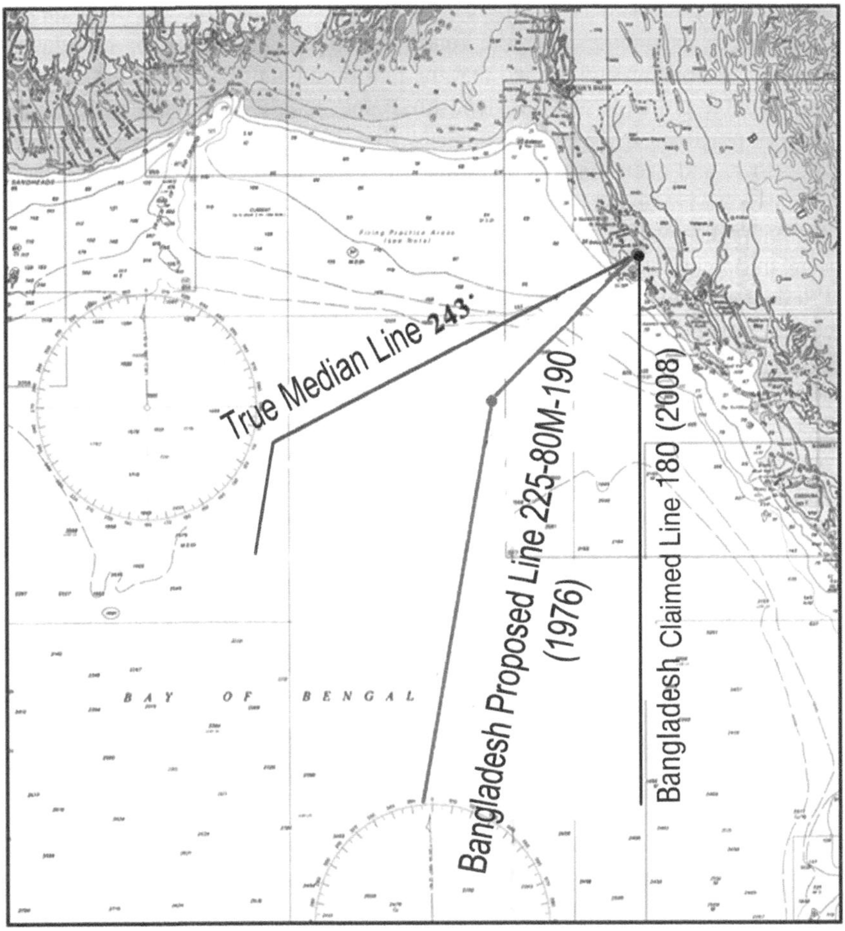

Figure 6.2 Bangladesh's maritime boundary claims with Myanmar (source: map drawn by I. Made Andi Arsana, Gadjah Mada University, Yogyakarta, Indonesia, on the basis of information supplied to the author by the Myanmar Ministry of Defense).

In the first three rounds of talks, each side rejected the other's proposals and, thus, there was no progress on the subject. During these talks, the Bangladeshi delegations, while resting their arguments on the principle of equality, referred to the *North Sea Continental Shelf Case*[4] as a prime example to be considered and applied in the Myanmar–Bangladesh maritime boundary delimitation. This could mean that Bangladesh was asking for a corridor towards the EEZ, as in the case of North Sea Continental Shelf, where the equidistance or median line was modified to give Germany access to the continental shelf. Myanmar was also prepared to offer a modified equidistance line in delimiting the EEZ and the continental shelf, with a view to enabling Bangladesh to claim up to 200nm of EEZ. Myanmar's position was in accordance with the existing Law of the Sea and state practices of the time.

However, beginning with the fourth round of talks in 1976, Bangladesh changed its position and argued that the maritime boundary should be based on the equitable principle and on friendship, rather than on international legal procedures practiced by Western countries. It rejected the equidistance principle altogether, and even the modified one. Bangladesh then proposed a friendship line, which Myanmar could not accept, as it was not based on any principles of international law. The proposed friendship line (see Figure 6.2) starts from the same midpoint but runs along 225 degrees for 80 nautical miles and then turns to 190 degrees, which would allow Bangladesh to enjoy up to 350 nautical miles of continental shelf. This would have taken away nearly 10,000sq. km from Myanmar's EEZ. Myanmar could not accept this proposed friendship line and has never recognized it. In fact, Myanmar documents only mention the 225–80nm–190 line as "the 1976 Bangladesh proposed line" and never referred to it as "the friendship line." At the sixth round of talks in 1985, the Bangladesh delegation cited the applicability of the 1982 UNCLOS (United Nations Convention on the Law of the Sea) and stressed the principle of equality in delimitating the maritime boundary while completely rejecting a modified equidistance line. Both sides therefore could not find common ground and talks were suspended in 1986.[5]

After nearly 21 years in abeyance, bilateral talks on maritime delimitation were finally resumed on 31 March 2008.[6] The two-day technical meeting ended inconclusively, as the two sides failed to narrow their differences. The second round of talks took place in Bagan, Myanmar, on 4–5 November 2008, after a naval standoff between the two countries in early November. This was closely followed by a third meeting on 17 November, during Myanmar Deputy Foreign Minister Maung Myint's visit to Dhaka. Although both sides agreed to hold another round of technical meetings in January 2009, the fourth meeting actually took place only on 30 June 2009 in Naypyitaw. During the 2008 meetings, Bangladesh came up with a far more aggressive maritime claim. It now draws a line running 180 degrees from the most eastward point of the baseline, taking more than 18,000sq. km from Myanmar. Dhaka no longer talked about the friendship line. It now argued for equality and proportionality. Myanmar argued that the 180-degree line did not conform to existing state practices and that it simply could not accept it. Myanmar remained inflexible about the application of the equidistance method and also maintained that the line must start, on the basis of the equidistance method, from the midpoint of St. Martins Island and Oyster Island. Meanwhile, Myanmar offered Bangladesh a corridor towards the EEZ, similar to the North Sea Continental Shelf case. The government of Bangladesh did not accept the Myanmar offer and, on 17 October 2009, took the case to the International Tribunal for the Law of the Sea (ITLOS) for final arbitration.

In accordance with Article 287, paragraph 1 of the 1982 UNCLOS, on 4 November 2009 the Myanmar government issued a declaration stating that it "accepts the jurisdiction of the ITLOS for the settlement of dispute between the

Union of Myanmar and the People's Republic of Bangladesh relating to the delimitation of maritime boundary between the two countries in the Bay of Bengal." This was closely followed by a declaration of the same content by the Bangladeshi government on 12 December 2009. The ITLOS has already placed the case of the Myanmar–Bangladesh maritime boundary dispute on the list of cases as Case No. 16 on 14 December 2009. However, on 14 January 2010, the Myanmar government notified the secretary general of the UN that it had decided to withdraw the declaration issued on 4 November 2009. The ITLOS held consultation meetings with "agents" from Myanmar and Bangladesh on 25–26 January 2010 and issued Order 2010/1 on 28 January. The president of the ITLOS has fixed the time limit for the filing of the Memorial (1 July 2010) for Bangladesh and the Counter-Memorial (1 December 2010) for Myanmar. The order also stated that "should the Tribunal find it necessary to authorize the presentation of reply and rejoinder," the time limits for the filing of these pleadings should be 15 March 2011 for the filing of the Reply by Bangladesh and 1 July 2011 for the filing of the Rejoinder by Myanmar. In this context, with Order 2010/2 dated 17 March 2010, the ITLOS "authorizes the submission of a Reply by Bangladesh and a Rejoinder by Myanmar" according to the time limits (see Table 6.2).

Meanwhile, the fifth round of talks was held in Chittagong on 8–9 January 2010; both sides agreed in principle to resolve their arguments on the maritime boundary through bilateral negotiations by "accommodating the principle of equity and principle of equal distance." The sixth round was held in Naypyitaw on 17–18 March 2010. As yet, no details of the method for delimitation have been reported.

Myanmar shares a 1,309 mile (or 2,107 km) border with Thailand.[7] Myanmar and Thailand also share a maritime boundary in the Andaman Sea (see Figure 6.3). An agreement to delineate the maritime boundary was signed on 25 July 1980 and was ratified on 14 February 1982, but sovereignty over three islands at the mouth of the Pakchan River remained unsettled. The maritime delimitation was based on British Admiralty Chart No. 830. The maritime boundary is 142.2 nautical miles long and there are nine reference points; the boundary is an equidistance line formed by a series of straight lines connecting the nine points (Table 6.3).

Table 6.2 Reference points for the Bangladesh–Myanmar maritime boundary

Point No.	*North Latitude*	*East Longitude*
1	20° 42′ 12.3″	92° 22′ 18″
2	20° 39′ 57″	92° 21′ 16″
3	20° 38′ 50″	92° 22′ 50″
4	20° 37′ 20″	92° 24′ 08″
5	20° 35′ 50″	92° 25′ 15″
6	20° 33′ 37″	92° 26′ 00″
7	20° 22′ 53″	92° 24′ 35″

Source: Myanmar Ministry of Defense.

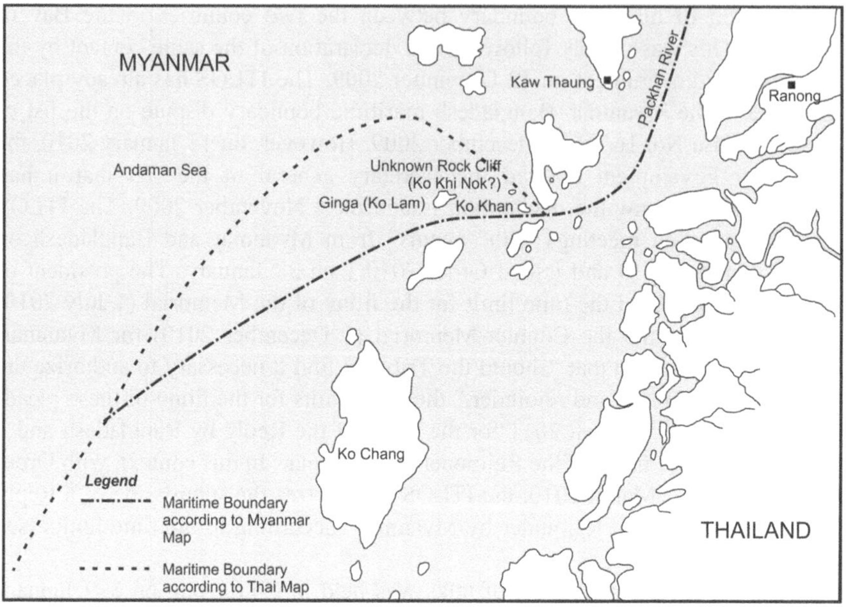

Figure 6.3 Map showing maritime territorial dispute between Myanmar and Thailand (source: map drawn by I. Made Andi Arsana, Gadjah Mada University, Yogyakarta, Indonesia, on the basis of information supplied to the author by the Myanmar Ministry of Defence).

Segments of the maritime boundary between point No. 1 and point No. 5 constitute the boundary between the territorial seas of Myanmar and Thailand, and the others are between the continental shelves of the two countries. However, during negotiations between Myanmar and Thailand on delimitation of the territorial sea boundary and the continental shelf cum EEZ from 1977 to 1980, the two sides had agreed that the precise delineation of Myanmar–Thai internal waters should be carried out after the issue of ownership of the three islands at the mouth of Pakchan River had been settled on the basis of historical evidence. The three islands in question are Ginga Island (Ko Lam in Thailand), Ko Khan Island and an unnamed rock cliff (Ko Ki Nu in Thailand).

According to a treaty signed between the British government in Myanmar and the Thai government in 1868, the three islands belong to Myanmar. Subsequent British maps, Indian hydrographic charts and Myanmar national charts indicate that the three islands are indeed Myanmar's. However, in 1975, based on information provided by Thailand (Thai Naval Chart No. 331) and the Thai–American Joint Mapping Operation, the British Naval Headquarters published Naval Chart No. 216 in which the three islands were identified as part of Thailand, even though the Thai national chart published in 1973 had identified the three islands as belonging to Myanmar.

Table 6.3 Turning points for Myanmar–Thailand maritime delimitation

Point no.	*North latitude*	*East longitude*
1	90° 32′ 15″	97° 56′ 20″
2	90° 34′ 29″	97° 52′ 10″
3	90° 34′ 54″	97° 51′ 12″
4	90° 35′ 39″	97° 45′ 29″
5	90° 36′ 02″	97° 43′ 39″
6	90° 37′ 24″	97° 37′ 36″
7	90° 40′ 35″	97° 26′ 36″
8	90° 45′ 30″	96° 29′ 35″
9	90° 38′ 00″	95° 35′ 25″

Source: Ministry of Defense.

In its search for historical evidence, the Myanmar government managed to uncover pertinent records of marine surveys, old charts, tracings and correspondence since 1880. With these documents in hand, the Myanmar government positively identified that the three islands had historically belonged to Myanmar. In 1985, a Thai delegation came to Yangon and discussed matters relating to the ownership of the islands, but no agreement was reached. The issue was raised again in April 1989 and in May 1990, again without any progress. The first meeting of the Myanmar–Thailand Joint Boundary Committee was held in Yangon on 18–21 February 1993. In the agreed minutes, it was stated that the two sides agreed that the issue had been pending for quite some time and that it would be taken up at an appropriate forum in due course. The second meeting of the Myanmar–Thailand Joint Boundary Committee was held in Bangkok on 29–30 March 1995. In this meeting, officials on both sides were urged to convene a technical meeting to discuss and exchange views on the subject.

In March 1995, the Thai side furnished documents relating to the status of the three islands and handed over their findings to the Myanmar authorities. In order to make an assessment of the documents, a meeting was held at the Myanmar Ministry of Foreign Affairs on 8 June 1995. Officials from the Naval Hydrographic Department and the Ministry of Foreign Affairs attended the meeting. After much scrutiny, the meeting came to the unanimous opinion that the documents had no relevance whatsoever to the islands in question. The meeting further decided to make an exhaustive appraisal of past developments with regard to the three islands. This decision was intended to encourage the Thai side to resume technical level talks on the question of the three islands and the alignment of the inner sector boundary between Myanmar and Thailand.

Meanwhile, the Central Hydrographic Unit (CHU) of the Myanmar Navy (MN) undertook the task of producing a naval chart based on British and Indian naval charts. Chart No. 12 (Myeik Archipelago – Myanmar Sakhanthit to Taungsune Island), drawn by the CHU and accompanied by relevant documents, was sent to the United Kingdom Hydrographic Office (UKHO) on 2 October 1996. The UKHO subsequently corrected its naval chart. Therefore, the British Admiralty

Chart No. 216, published in 1997, placed the three islands on the Myanmar side of the maritime boundary. However, Thailand protested and sent notes to the UKHO urging it to remove the approximate boundary line shown on the chart. Myanmar also sent a note in support of its claim. As a result, the UKHO informed both countries that any future Admiralty Chart No. 216 would not show the approximate boundary line unless both parties reach an agreement. Although there were no specific meetings and negotiations on the issue of the three islands, it was brought up from time to time at various meetings. The two countries finally declared the three islands a "no man's land" and the issue has remained a source of tension, leading to a series of naval confrontations and clashes in late 1998 and again in 2003. So far, the problem of the three islands remains unsettled.[8]

Baselines in Myanmar territorial waters

On 15 November 1968, in a Ministry of Foreign Affairs statement, Myanmar claimed a system of straight baselines and declared that its territorial sea would henceforth extend 12 nautical miles seaward from these baselines. However, Myanmar was not a party to the 1958 Convention on the Territorial Sea and the Contiguous Zone. The Myanmar government justified its move on the grounds that the prevailing geographical conditions along its coastline and the need to safeguard "the vital economic interest of the inhabitants of the coastal regions" required it to claim straight baselines. The Myanmar government restated its claims on 9 April 1977 through the 1977 Territorial Sea and Maritime Zones Law (Pyithu Hluttaw Law No. 3). Myanmar's 21 straight baselines segments extend for a total of 826.4 nautical miles, starting from the southern point of Oyster Island (known as Mayu Island) on the Rakhine coast and terminating at the western point of Murray Island on the Thanintharyi coast. The baselines on the Rakhine coast measure 304.8 nautical miles, on the Gulf of Martaban 222.3 nautical miles and along the Thanintharyi coast 299.3 nautical miles. The straight baselines run the entirety of Myanmar's coastline with the exception of an approximately 30 nautical mile stretch of normal baselines extending southwards from the terminus of the country's land boundary with Bangladesh at the mouth of the Naaf River. None of the base points is situated on the mainland: all are on islands along the coast. The baselines appear to depart from the general direction of the coastline, and islands that are not in the immediate vicinity of the coast are used as turning points. In addition, a single baseline segment across the Gulf of Martaban, between Alguada Reef (Pathein Light) and the western point of Long Island, extends 222.3 nautical miles, setting the record as the longest single straight baseline segment in the world. The consequence of this extraordinary claim is that, at one point along the Gulf of Martaban, the distance from the landmass to the baseline is 132 nautical miles (see Figure 6.4).[9] This has apparently raised the issue of whether the baselines depart from "any appreciable extent from the general direction of the coast" or whether the waters so enclosed are "sufficiently linked to the land domain to be subject to the regime of internal waters," as required under Article 7(3) of the UNCLOS.

There are numerous cases of international protests against straight baselines claims and the United States leads the field in this regard, protesting against any practices that it deems to be excessive or contrary to the provisions of the UNCLOS. The United States asserts that no baseline segment should exceed 48 nautical miles in length.[10] However, the US position is by no means universally accepted. There are 23 countries that have more than 50 nautical miles in some

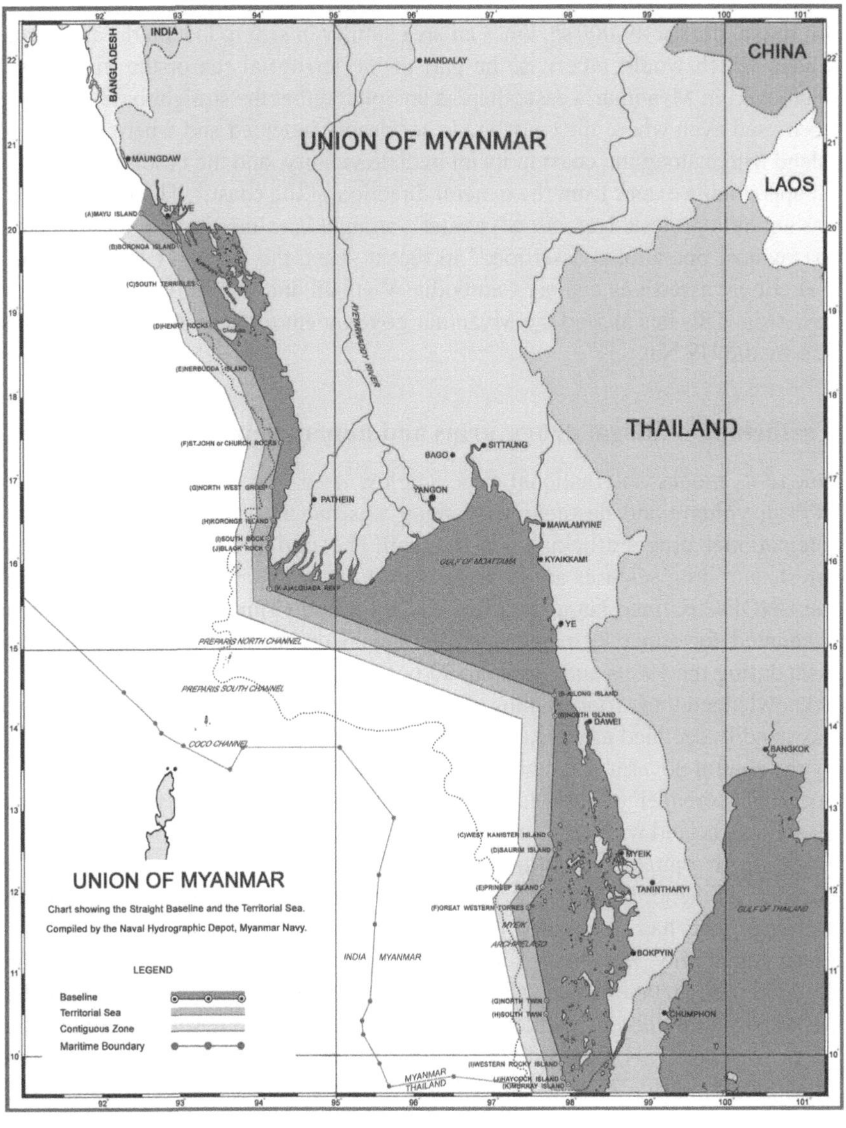

Figure 6.4 Map showing Myanmar's claimed territorial waters (source: Myanmar Ministry of Defense).

segments of their straight baselines. Of these, 16 have been the subject of objections by the United States.[11]

The straight baselines claimed by the Myanmar government drew protests from several countries, most notably from the United States in 1982, as they were considered not to be in compliance with the 1958 Convention or the 1982 Law of the Seas. As mentioned previously, Myanmar set the record by drawing a single straight baseline of 222.3 nautical miles across the Gulf of Martaban; in the view of the United States, it thereby claims an additional approximately 14,300 sq. nm (or 49,000 sq. km – an area similar in size to Denmark) as internal waters which would otherwise be part of the territorial sea or the high seas.[12] Moreover, in Myanmar's case, there is an opinion that the straight baselines have been used even where the coastline is not deeply indented and where there is no island fringe along the coast in its immediate vicinity, and the baselines depart to an appreciable extent from the general direction of the coast.[13] The United States has not only protested against Myanmar's straight baselines but has also declared the right of operational assertion.[14] In recent years, the US Navy has conducted operational assertions against Cambodia, Vietnam and the Philippines in Southeast Asia. This has alerted the Myanmar government to the possibility of similar acts by the US Navy.[15]

Trafficking of illegal drugs, arms and human beings via sea

Due to its modest international trade and low level of container traffic, in terms of both volume and destination, Yangon was not an attractive transit port for international drug trafficking via sea until the mid-2000s. Most drug-related arrests and drug seizures are in areas close to production centers. Nevertheless, the UNODC (United Nations Office on Drugs and Crime) noted that Myanmar accounted for about 80 percent of the annual opium production of Southeast Asia during the 1980s and for about 90 percent during the 1990s.[16] The UNODC acknowledged that, after peaking in 1996, opium poppy cultivation in Myanmar has steadily declined as a result of increased eradication and control efforts, both by the central government and by local authorities. Another important factor has been the surrender of the Mao Thai Army (MTA), an ethnic insurgent group closely connected with drug production and trafficking.

Although opium cultivation in Myanmar has declined, the production of cheaper synthetic drugs in the country's porous border areas has dramatically increased, and has constituted a challenge for both Myanmar and the international community. Myanmar is identified as a major source of methamphetamine and other amphetamine-type substances (ATS). Yet, it is important to note that Myanmar has a limited chemical industry and does not domestically produce the precursor chemicals required for the production of ATS. These chemicals are imported, primarily from Thailand, China and India. Drug trafficking takes place mostly along the land border: illegal drug trafficking via sea has thus not been a major security problem for Myanmar. Nevertheless, from time to time, Myanmar authorities have arrested people involved in drug trafficking via sea. Observers say that drug traffickers are increasingly using maritime routes to smuggle drugs out of Myanmar due to a tougher suppression campaign by neighboring countries such as Thailand and China, and Yangon is emerging as an attractive transit port. This will be a challenge for Myanmar law enforcement authorities in the future.[17]

Myanmar does not have a problem with arms trafficking via sea. However, the border area between Myanmar and Bangladesh is a sanctuary for arms smugglers, due mainly to the absence of an adequate security establishment. Smugglers ship various types of small arms from Thailand and transit through the area before selling them to insurgents in Myanmar and India.[18] For example, on 8 February 1998 on Andaman's Landfall Island, during Operation *Leech*, the Indian Navy seized a boat and captured at least 34 Arakan and Karen insurgents shipping arms to Myanmar from Thailand. Those captured were members of the Karen National Union (KNU) and the National Unity Party of Arakan (NUPA). Six NUPA leaders were killed in the incident.[19] However, it must be stressed that Myanmar is neither a source nor a transit country for arms trafficking.

In the case of human trafficking, while Myanmar has a serious problem as a source as well as a transit region, trafficking usually takes place along the Myanmar–Thai and Myanmar–China borders, not by sea. Although human trafficking via sea is not a major security problem for the Myanmar government, there is one issue of concern that has political and security implications. This is the issue of the so-called Rohingya boat people. At least since 1962, as far as the Myanmar government is concerned, the Rohingyas do not constitute an indigenous nationality. Hence, they are not entitled to Myanmar citizenship. According to some reports, there are about 800,000 so-called Rohingya people living along the Myanmar–Bangladesh border, of which about 250,000 are reportedly living as refugees in Bangladesh. However, the problem is that these so-called Rohingya people are caught up in international human trafficking networks. While there are stories of their alleged abuse and repression by the Myanmar government, most observers agree that Rohingya boat people are actually economic refugees in search of better living conditions. Most Rohingya boat people started their sea journey in Bangladesh, not in Myanmar. Their destination is usually either southern Thailand or Malaysia. The Rohingya boat people issue surfaces from time to time, drawing international attention and prompting criticism against the Myanmar government.[20]

Illegal, unreported and unregulated fishing and exploitation of marine resources

Illegal fishing is an important maritime security issue for Myanmar. Thai fishing trawlers have been illegally operating in Myanmar waters at least since the early 1980s, ever since marine resources in Thai waters began to be depleted due to an extended period of over-exploitation. In the 1980s, the MN was very weak and there was no way to check the extent of illegal fishing activities along the Thanintharyi coastline.

In December 1988, the military government in Myanmar granted fishing rights for Thai trawlers. Hence, 241 Thai fishing trawlers were legally fishing in Myanmar waters by mid-1989. Despite this, there have been problems with illegal fishing and arrests of Thai fishermen operating illegally in Myanmar waters are not uncommon. Between September 1988 and 1992, the Myanmar government seized 231 illegal Thai fishing trawlers with a total of 2,346 crewmen. IUU fishing in Myanmar waters has persisted due to a lack of monitoring and surveillance and corruption among law enforcement authorities. There have been several reports about Myanmar naval officers taking bribes from Thai trawlers in exchange for turning a blind eye to illegal fishing. Myanmar protested to the Thai government against Thai trawlers fishing in restricted zones, as well as the duplication and production of forged permits by Thai fishermen. Illegal fishing has become a major source of tension between the two countries since the MN has become more effective in patrolling Myanmar waters and pursuing illegal trawlers. While illegal fishing is mainly around the Thanintharyi coastal area, the Rakhine coastal area has the same problem, although illegal fishing by foreign vessels has rarely reported in this area: it appears that most illegal fishing activities are carried out by local fishermen. In these cases the issue is either overlooked or resolved through bribes.[21] Some argue that the figures for the Thanintharyi coastal area do not reflect the scale of illegal fishing: corruption is rampant and protection money is not uncommon. The situation is considered to be worse than official figures reveal. IUU fishing has been happening on a fairly large scale in Myanmar waters and the Myanmar government appears to be unable to resolve it.[22]

Another issue related to illegal fishing is the unregulated exploitation of marine resources. Myanmar's marine fisheries comprise both inshore and offshore fisheries. Inshore fishery is carried out within five nautical miles from the shore on the Rakhine coast and within ten nautical miles on the Ayeyarwaddy and Thanintharyi coasts. This fishing is usually carried out using passive fishing gear such as gill nets, drift nets, long lines and traps. Offshore fishery is carried out in an area extending from the outer limit of the inshore fishing zone. This fishing involves the use of bottom trawls, purse seines, surrounding nets, drift nets and long nets. Until the late 1980s, marine products were mostly taken for domestic consumption. However, since the early 1990s, the Myanmar government has promoted the production and export of marine products.

Between 1988 and 2008, marine fish production tripled, the volume of marine product exports increased 70 fold, and export earnings grew from US$10 million in 1988 to US$561 million in 2008. Yet, it is important to note that by 2003, marine fish production had already passed Myanmar's Maximum Sustainable Yield (MSY) of 1.05 metric tonnes per year. In 2008, the marine fish production (of 1.679 metric tonnes) was far beyond the MSY. The situation is far more alarming than it appears since the official figures are much lower than the actual catch by legal and illegal fishermen. If the government fails to address this issue, Myanmar's fishery resources will be depleted in the near future.

Another aspect of marine resource conservation to be considered is the marine ecosystem. The Rakhine coastline is shallow and deltaic in the north and rocky in the south; it has a narrow continental shelf. The coastline is heavily influenced by the monsoon. The Ayeyarwaddy coastline is also deltaic and three major rivers in Myanmar, the Ayeyarwaddy, the Sittaung and the Thanlwin, end their journey here. This coastline receives an annual sediment of 250 million tons from the Ayeyarwaddy alone. It has a wide continental shelf and the delta is expanding seawards at the rate of 5 km per 100 years. The Thanintharyi coastline, the longest of the three coastlines, includes the Myeik Archipelago, comprising more than 800 islands of various sizes.

Mangrove forest can be found on all three coastlines, but are heavily concentrated in the Ayeyarwaddy Delta region. In 1924, the total area of mangrove forest in Myanmar was recorded at 242,811 hectares. Thirty years later, in 1954, it was about 234,515 hectares, suffering an annual loss of 277 hectares. Another 30 years later, in 1984, the area of mangrove forest had shrunk to 178,642 hectares, representing an annual loss of 1862 hectares. According to a 1990 assessment, the mangrove forest had suffered an alarming annual loss of 7,775 hectares. By the early 1990s, the total area of mangrove forest was 85,533 hectares and by 1998 it was only 48,562 hectares. Therefore, between 1924 and 1998, Myanmar lost about 80 percent of its mangrove forests. The Post-Nargis Joint Assessment (PONJA) reported that, in May 2008, Cyclone Nargis had destroyed 16,800 hectares of mangrove forest (about 30 percent of the total mangrove forest area) and another 21,000 hectares of mangrove plantations in Yangon and the Ayeyarwaddy Delta.[23] The main causes of mangrove deforestation are the extension of paddy fields and the over-exploitation and illegal felling of mangroves for firewood and charcoal, especially in the 1950s and the 1960s. Much of the losses in the 1970s and 1980s were due to a boom in the charcoal industry, when demand for cheap cooking fuel was high in cities. In the 1990s, agricultural encroachment in the form of land reclamation and the introduction of shrimp farms further cut into the mangrove forests.

The Forest Department in Myanmar began to promote the conservation of mangrove forests in 1975, but their achievements have been modest and they have failed to prevent further losses. The 1990 assessment revealed the serious problem of mangrove deforestation. The Myanmar government therefore began to take measures to address the issue. A firewood-substitution fuel program was popularized, the production and sale of firewood or charcoal from the mangrove forests of the Ayeyarwaddy delta were strictly prohibited, and reforestation was also carried out. Some international organizations, local and international non-government organizations, and individuals are involved in the reforestation. Although the total area of mangrove forest has increased gradually, the results have been far from satisfactory. The tragic loss of life and property caused by Cyclone Nargis in Myanmar in May 2008 could have been avoided had there been a sizable area of mangrove forests along the coastline. In terms of coral reefs, the Myeik Archipelago is famous for its abundant and diverse coral communities, yet little is known about the current state of the reefs. However, many people hold the view that the reefs are not yet spoiled and that Myanmar is still basically clean and unpolluted. The same is true in the case of the sea grass ecosystem, which can be found everywhere except in the Ayeyarwaddy Delta. Unfortunately, the Myanmar government does not appear to take the marine environmental protection issue seriously. The apparent lack of sufficient and effective marine environmental protection has triggered a chain reaction in human security issues.

Maritime piracy, armed robbery against ships and the threat of maritime terrorism

While most Southeast Asian littoral states have confronted the issues of maritime piracy, armed robbery against ships and the threat of maritime terrorism, Myanmar has been relatively untroubled by the problems. According to International Maritime Bureau annual reports, between 1991 and 2008 there were only 14 actual or attempted attacks in Myanmar waters. The problem of maritime piracy in Southeast Asia was at its worst in the decade between 1996 and 2005. Nearly 50 percent of world piracy took place in Southeast Asia waters, with the highest concentration in Indonesian waters and the Malacca Strait area.

Concern for naval force modernization in the region

As far as naval force modernization in the region is concerned, Myanmar appears to observe the navies of Bangladesh and Thailand closely and carefully. Because of the dispute over the maritime boundary, the MN is particularly concerned about the naval build-up in Bangladesh. At present, the MN has about 15,000 service personnel, with five naval regional commands, three flotillas, one naval dockyard and one naval training command, among other facilities. Until the early 1990s, the primary role of the MN was restricted to patrolling rivers and inshore waters and to supporting the army in counter-insurgency operations. Due primarily to the nature of these missions and to financial limitations, the MN maintained a very modest fleet of mostly small and lightly armed boats. Yet, it never lost sight of coastal surveillance and territorial waters protection issues, reflected in the procurement of a small number of corvettes and costal patrol crafts. Yet, for all practical purposes, the MN was primarily a coastal navy and its effective patrols never extended beyond the country's brown waters. In 1988, the MN's order of battle included four aging corvettes, two offshore patrol vessels (OPVs), seven coastal patrol boats (CPs), 12 river patrol boats (PRBs) and a few landing craft. There were neither torpedo boats nor minesweepers in the MN. The MN envied the navies of neighboring countries for their frigates, corvettes and missile crafts.

In 1990, the MN, along with the Myanmar Army and Air Force, began a major naval procurement program. In that year, it commissioned three ex-Yugoslav PB-90-class coastal patrol boats. A year later, it placed an order for ten Hainan-class FAC-SCs (fast attack craft – submarine chasers) from the People's Republic of China (PRC).[24] In March 1994, the MN signed another procurement contract with the PRC for a delivery of six Houxin-class FAC-Ms (fast attack craft – missile).[25] With the technical assistance and weaponry from the PRC, the MN also built locally six 50-meter long FAC-Gs (fast attack craft – gun) between 1995 and 2006.[26] There have also been unconfirmed reports that the navy constructed four FAC-Ms in its naval dockyard. The naval dockyard also built four river patrol craft in the 1990s. In the same period, the Myanmar shipyard built two Burma PGM-type coastal patrol craft. The MN also constructed three 77-meter long corvettes and one frigate, with the assistance of the PRC, in its own dockyards in recent years. There have been some reports that the MN is building several more frigates in its dockyards.

The MN is apparently interested in building up its blue water capabilities, although it has a long way to go in this area. Yet, the MN argues that it needs to protect the country's EEZ and that it is under pressure from naval force modernization programs in neighboring countries. Illegal fishing in Myanmar waters, prominently by Thai trawlers, is a concern for the MN. Moreover, the overlapping claims of maritime boundaries, with Bangladesh in particular and to a lesser extent with Thailand, is cited as a reason for the projected build-up. The MN is aware that while naval modernization in Thailand is primarily aimed at countering any possible power projection by the Vietnamese Navy into the Gulf of Thailand, the Bangladeshi naval build-up is more directly concerned with denial, if not control, of the sea in the case of a naval confrontation with Myanmar over the disputed maritime boundary. Myanmar appears to understand that Thailand has a coastline of 2,637 kilometers – 1,700 km on the side of the Gulf of Thailand and 937 km on the Andaman Sea – and so needs a powerful navy to protect its territorial waters and maritime resources. However, Myanmar has been curious for a long time about the naval build-up in Bangladesh, which has a coastline of 580 km, just one-quarter that of Myanmar. Therefore, the MN is cautiously watching the naval modernization program in Bangladesh.

At present, according to its official homepage, the Bangladesh Navy (BN) has a total of 79 warships of various types and sizes and nearly 15,000 service personnel, of which 2,800 are civilians. Their order of battle includes five frigates, five OPVs, seven FAC-SCs, ten FAC-Gs, nine FAC-Ms, eight FAC-Ts (fast attack craft – torpedo), five minesweepers, three survey ships, nine landing craft and 18 auxiliary ships.[27] These vessels are deployed in two naval area commands and a flotilla: Commodore Commanding Khulna (COMKHUL), Commodore Commanding Chittagong (COCHIT) and Commodore Commanding BN Flotilla (COMBAN). The Chittagong Naval Area has the highest concentration of warships under five naval squadrons, and also is the location of the Commodore Superintendent Dockyard (SCD) and the Bangladesh Naval Academy (BNA).[28]

In term of naval build-up, in the early years of independence, the BN concentrated its efforts mostly on brown water capabilities, namely in riverine and coastal patrols. By 1975, it had begun to build up its offshore patrol capability. Between 1975 and 1983, the BN procured three frigates, three FAC-SCs, eight

FAC-Gs, four FAC-Ms and four FAC-Ts. Except for three ex-British frigates, these were mostly obtained from Chinese People's Liberation Army-Navy (PLAN). Since 1988, after a five-year break, the BN has actively engaged in the process of naval force modernization, in terms of acquisition of new warships and weaponry upgrade. Between 1988 and 2004, the BN procured two new frigates, five OPVs (ex-British), two FAC-SCs, four FAC-Gs, six FAC-Ms, six FAC-Ts and five minesweepers. Although there have been no more acquisitions of warships since 2005, the BN has upgraded its naval weaponry. It replaced its SY-1 anti-ship missiles with more advanced C-802As and bought FM-90N SAMs for its two frigates. A new combat data link system and more advanced sonar were installed on the BNS *Osman*, an ex-PLAN frigate commissioned into the BN in November 1989. With the help of PLAN, the BN also upgraded its naval weaponry. On 12 May 2008, the BN test-fired a C-802A missile and hit a target at 140 nm.[29]

On 23 February 2009, the newly elected Bangladesh government, led by Sheikh Hasina of the Awami League, told parliament that it had decided to buy US$2 million worth of anti-ship missiles for the BN before the end of June 2010. Then, on 22 June 2009, the Ministry of Defense submitted a report to parliament, which detailed a ten-year force modernization plan for the BN. According to this plan, the BN would procure three frigates (possibly to replace three aging frigates in the existing order of battle), three OPVs, 12 patrol craft (some presumably corvettes), two landing craft, one survey ship, four FAC-Ms and one replenishment ship between 2010 and 2020. The plan also includes buying three maritime patrol aircraft, four helicopters and one submarine. The price tag for the plan is estimated at Taka 6,200 crores (nearly US$920 million).[30]

More alarming for the Myanmar government has been the Bangladeshi military's closer contact with the United States in recent years. At the invitation of the BN, US Pacific Fleet Commander Admiral Robert F. Willard visited the country in January 2008 and held talks with Bangladeshi senior commanders. Then, after Cyclone Nargis struck in May 2008, the BN allowed the US Navy to use port facilities on St. Martin Island for any future relief operations in the area. In addition, in early November 2008 the BN conducted a joint naval exercise with a US warship just a few days before a naval standoff between Bangladesh and Myanmar. Then, in February 2009, during his visit to Bangladesh, the US Assistant Secretary of State for South Asia expressed "the US willingness to assist Bangladesh in maritime patrol and secure its unprotected territorial sea lanes."[31] The Myanmar military is also aware that the Bangladesh military has been upgrading Cox's Bazar Airfield into an advanced air force base, possibly with the help of the United States. In fact, in September 2009, the Bangladeshi prime minister decided to build an advanced air force base in Cox's Bazar. The Myanmar military is cautiously watching these latest developments in Bangladesh.

Myanmar also observes the Royal Thai Navy (RTN) very closely. The RTN has about 140 warships of various types and sizes and 70,600 service personnel: 44,750 are regular and the rest are on national service. It has three Fleet Headquarters in Sattahip, Songkhla and Phuket. Moreover, the RTN maintains six naval bases and three naval garrison detachments. On the Andaman side of the Thai coast, the RTN has a naval base in Phang Nga. The current order of battle includes one aircraft carrier, 12 frigates, five corvettes, six FAC-Ms, three FAC-Gs, 14 OPVs, seven minesweepers, 31 PCs (coastal patrol craft), 18 PBRs (Riverine Patrol Craft), 20 landing craft and 19 auxiliary ships.

Since 1991, the RTN has been actively engaged in naval force modernization. Between 1991 and 1997, the RTN procured one aircraft carrier, six frigates, three corvettes, two harbor tugs and one replenishment oiler. The RTN temporarily halted its naval procurement program for about three years due to Asian financial crisis, but had already resumed by mid-1999. Between mid-1999 and late 2008, the RTN acquired two frigates (ex-US Navy), eight OPVs, two minesweepers, three landing craft and one oceanographic research ship. Moreover, the RTN built four high-speed craft for the Royal Thai Navy SEALs. The RTN also has naval aviation units: about 95 aircraft, with fixed or rotary wings, are placed under two air wings based in Utapao and Songkhla. At present, according to the Thai press, the RTN is building four new OPVs to be commissioned in the near future. In addition, on 22 September 2009, the Thai government announced that it would spend 989 million baht (US$250 million) to upgrade anti-submarine capabilities on RTN warships. Moreover, it also announced a plan to buy three diesel submarines with a price tag of US$500 million. Interestingly, this decision came after Vietnam's announcement on 27 April 2009 that it would buy six Kilo-class submarines from Russia, worth US$1.8 billion in total. This could arguably fit into the action–reaction pattern of force modernization that many observe in the Southeast Asian region.

Conclusion

The most serious maritime challenges and the foremost priorities for the Myanmar government appear to be the maritime disputes over territorial waters, the EEZ and the continental shelf. In the view of the Myanmar government, the issue of these maritime disputes is closely linked to naval force modernization in neighboring coastal states. This is particularly true in the case of Myanmar's maritime dispute with Bangladesh. The overlapping maritime boundaries claimed by Bangladesh in the resource-rich Bay of Bengal, which entails a potential loss of 18,000 square kilometer of Myanmar's EEZ, seems to be a top priority in the Myanmar government's maritime security issues. While the Myanmar government remains steadfast in its adherence to the principle of equidistance, it has been willing to modify the median line so that Bangladesh can claim up to 200 nautical miles of its own EEZ. The Bangladeshi government has rejected this offer, stands firmly on the principle of equality, has proposed different methods of delimitation and has finally taken the case to the United Nations. As far as the maritime delimitation with Bangladesh is concerned, the Myanmar government appears to watch India's position on the Indo-Bangladesh maritime delimitation issue very carefully, since the two cases are similar. Myanmar cannot be expected to compromise where India would not, and there is a possibility that Myanmar and India may cooperate and coordinate their approaches in their disputes with Bangladesh on maritime boundary delimitation.

Another maritime security challenge for the Myanmar government is the possibility of an infringement of Myanmar's waters by foreign navies. Perhaps the most cited case of this nature by the Myanmar government was the sighting of five US warships, including the aircraft carrier *Coral Sea*, within Myanmar territorial waters on 12 September 1988. In addition, the MN sighted HMS *London* near Preparis Island on 9 January 1993 and two Indian frigates near Pathein lighthouse and Thamihla Island on 15 and 16 April 1998. The Myanmar government was fully aware of the US policy of operational assertion in Myanmar waters as a protest over the country's unusually long straight baselines. In the early days of the post-Cyclone Nargis relief operations in May 2008, when a US fleet led by the aircraft carrier *Essex* and three amphibious ships, carrying 22 heavy-lifting helicopters and a small fleet of landing craft, appeared near Myanmar waters for relief operations (against the background of going into a disaster area without permission from the host government in the name of humanitarian intervention), the MN was on the high alert for any possible incursion into Myanmar territorial waters by the US fleet.

For the Myanmar government, serious maritime security challenges are mostly in the form of traditional security threats. However, it appears that some non-traditional maritime security issues are also of growing importance for Myanmar. While trafficking of human being, drugs and arms via sea, and maritime piracy or maritime terrorism are not yet major problems, illegal and unregulated exploitation of marine resources are serious enough and require immediate attention from the government. Living and non-living marine resources have been depleted at an alarming rate with serious consequences. While inadequate resources, ineffective laws and legislation, poor coordination among various government departments, and corruption among law enforcement agencies are partly to blame for the depletion of marine resources, one cannot avoid questioning the political will of the government to address these issues.

Myanmar's maritime strategy remains largely traditional in outlook and the most important objective appears to be the defense of the sovereignty and territorial integrity of the state. The principal task of the navy is to protect territorial waters and maritime interests in the EEZ. Myanmar's maritime cooperation with other regional countries is still weak and its accession to international conventions or protocols is minimal. In the age of globalization, the growing importance of maritime trade, and the excessive exploitation of living and non-living marine or natural resources in the sea or under the seabed, should impel Myanmar's maritime strategy planners to aim at meeting challenges from both state and non-state entities, as well as from traditional and non-traditional issues.

Notes

1 For example, in the mid-1990s, the Defense Services Historical Museum held an elaborate exhibition on the multi-dimensional security threats to Myanmar.

2 With regard to the Myanmar–Bangladesh land boundary, the "Agreement on the Demarcation of the Land Section of the Boundary North of the Naaf River" was signed in Dhaka on 23 May 1979, between the foreign ministers of the two countries. Following this agreement, a joint survey was conducted and boundary markers were erected by 1984. Boundary maps were prepared and signed by the two countries in Yangon on 12 August 1985. In 1997, a joint boundary inspection was carried out for the maintenance of boundary markers. Finally, the "Treaty on the Demarcation of the Land Section of the Boundary North of Naaf River (Nat River)" was signed by the foreign ministers of both countries on 12 November 1998 in Yangon. Due to the porous nature of the boundary, issues of illegal migration into Myanmar arose. As a result, in 1979 and again in 1992, the Myanmar government conducted immigration checks, leading to tensions along the border and the flight of illegal immigrants back into Bangladesh. These came to be known in the international media as "Rohingya" refugees. In fact, there is no such ethnic group as the "Rohingyas" in Myanmar and the so-called "Rohingya people," which was essentially a political identity created in the early 1950s by some Myanmar politicians, have constituted a major security problem for Myanmar, since they frequently clash with the local Rakhine people. Hence, the Myanmar government decided to erect barbed wire fences unilaterally on its side of land border with Bangladesh in early 2009. Another aspect of the Myanmar–Bangladesh boundary is the internal waters in the Naaf River (Nat River). The internal waters boundary line was fixed in the mid-1960s. After a brief military confrontation between Pakistani and Myanmar forces and several rounds of talks over the ownership of some islets in the Naaf River in 1952, both governments signed the "Memorandum of Agreement for the Demarcation of a Fixed Boundary in the Naaf River" on 21 January 1964. As a result, a joint hydrographic survey was carried out between 1964 and 1966 and a chart was finally produced. On 9 May 1966, in Rawalpindi, General Ne Win and General Ayub Khan signed the "Agreement on the Demarcation of a Fixed Boundary between Myanmar and Pakistan in the Naaf River." In accordance with the agreement and the accompanying chart, the middle line of the main navigable channel was designated as a fixed boundary and beacons and reference markers were subsequently erected to denote the boundary line. In addition, procedures for the maintenance of boundary markers were also prescribed in the agreement. The first joint inspection of boundary markers and beacons was carried out in 1978, seven years after East Pakistan became independent as Bangladesh. Subsequently, the "Supplementary Protocol on Joint Inspection" was signed by the two countries on 17 December 1980. River boundaries are inevitably subjected to the impact of natural phenomenon such as floods, sedimentation and erosion, as well as human encroachment. In this context, there was an exchange of fire between troops from Myanmar and Bangladesh on 8 January 2001 over an attempt by Myanmar to dam the Naaf River – the thalweg of which constitutes a part of the boundary. The Bangladeshi government viewed the embankment as a violation of the boundary agreement and protested against the construction of a dam on the Myanmar side at the mouth of Ale-Chaung (Dubfari Creek) of the Naaf River. The Myanmar government explained that the construction was done by local people to prevent erosion of banks along Kyee-Kyun Island caused by the development of new prawn cultivation farms on the opposite (Bangladeshi) bank. The matter was peacefully resolved through joint inspection in February 2001 and the Myanmar side agreed to halt construction. A year later, on 14 January 2002, Myanmar protested against the construction of a dam on Bilasaudi Creek and said that this was contrary to the agreement. The Bangladeshi side then stopped the construction. Although these kinds of disputes arose from time to time, they did not affect the boundary line in the Naaf River.

3 Victor Prescott and Clive Schofield, *The Maritime Political Boundaries of the World*, 2nd edn (Leiden: Martinus Nijhoff Publishers, 2005), pp. 463–464.

4 *North Sea Continental Shelf (Federal Republic of Germany* v. *Denmark; Federal Republic of Germany* v. *The Netherlands)*, (1969) ICJ Rep 3.

5 In the meantime, both countries signed the UNCLOS, which required them to publish maps of their maritime boundary and EEZ within ten years of the date of signing. Therefore, Myanmar had to delimit the border and file its claim to the UN on 21 May 2006, while Bangladesh has to do it before 27 July 2011.

6 A Myanmar delegation led by Commodore Maung Oo Lwin met a Bangladeshi delegation led by M.A.K. Mahood in Dhaka.

7 This extends from the confluence of the Mekhong River and the Nam Ruak River (the tri-junction of Myanmar, Laos and Thailand) to Bayint Naung Point (formerly known as Victoria Point). For the most part, the boundary coincides with mountain crests and major water divides, or the thalwegs, or deep-water channels, of various rivers.

8 On 12 February 1998 a Thai warship attacked the *Yan Naing 510* and fired 25 rounds of artillery in the disputed waters. On 25 March 2003, around Kawthaung waters, Myanmar's naval vessel *Yan Naing 517* was chased by about 30 fishing boats. When it received a distress call, the MN sent two warships to the scene. Meanwhile, the Thai navy also sent a warship and fired at the *Yan Naing 517*, but left when it saw the two Myanmar warships approaching.

9 Prescott and Schofield, *The Maritime Political Boundaries of the World*, p. 654.

10 US Department of State, "Developing Standard Guidelines for Evaluating Straight Baselines," *Limits in the Seas No. 106* (1987), p. 14.

11 Prescott and Schofield, *The Maritime Political Boundaries of the World*, pp. 654–655.

12 US Department of State, "United States responses to Excessive National Maritime Claims," *Limits in the Seas No. 112* (1992), p. 24.

13 J. Ashley Roach and Robert W. Smith, "Excessive Maritime Claims," *International Law Studies*, Vol. 66 (Newport RI: Naval War College, 1994), p. 69.

14 The United States has conducted multiple assertions of rights against Myanmar's claimed baselines, especially in the Gulf of Martaban sector, between Pathein Lighthouse of Alguada Reef and the western point of Long Island, which extends for 222.3 nautical miles.

15 The MN established three naval regions in Heingyi (at the mouth of Ayeyarwaddy River), Yangon and Heinze (Long island), and located two naval flotillas to maintain security in the territorial waters enclosed by the Gulf of Martaban. During the Cyclone Nargis crisis in May 2008, Myanmar appeared to be acutely worried about the prospect of operational assertion by the US. Myanmar is unlikely to step back from its straight baselines system and to redraw the baseline in the Gulf of Martaban. Therefore, this area could be a potential flash point in the future.

16 UNODC, *Myanmar Country Profile*, December 2005, p. 19, www.unodc.org/pdf/myanmar/myanmar_country_ profile_2005.pdf.

17 For example, 9 January 2003, a state-owned newspaper reported in connection with an arrest, that in December 2000 a resident of Mandalay had loaded 240 kilograms of heroin and 6.5 million stimulant pills onto a boat in Yangon and handed it over to a Thai fishing boat on the Andaman Sea. The same person was charged with trafficking of 1,427 kilograms of heroin, 138.7 million stimulants, 28,197.2 kilograms of ephedrine, 12,100 kilograms of caffeine and 12 viss (18.2 kilograms) of opium since 1992. A recent arrest over drug trafficking in Yangon port took place on 25 January 2009. The anti-narcotic force in Yangon found 29 kilograms of drugs in a container on board the Singaporean-flagged ship, *Kota Tegap*. The container was bound for Singapore and was reportedly owned by the Myanmar Timber Enterprise, but no further details are known. A few days earlier, another person was arrested and charged in Myanmar for smuggling 32 kilograms of heroin out of the country aboard a container ship. About the same time, on 29 January 2009, the Central Narcotics Bureau of Singapore revealed that it seized 17.2 kilograms of heroin in 2007 and 44.2 kilograms in 2008. See "Heroine Arrests Spike Again," *The Straits Times*, 29 January 2009, www.straitstimes.com/Breaking%2BNews/Singapore/Story/STIStory_331784.html.

18 Ramtanu Maitra, "India bids to rule the waves," *Asia Times Online*, 19 October 2005, www.atimes.com/atimes/South_Asia/GJ19Df03.html.

19 For details, see Nandita Haksar, *Rogue Agent: How India's Military Intelligence Betrayed the Burmese Resistance* (New Delhi: Penguin Books, 2009).

20 For example, in January 2009 Indonesian authorities found 114 Rohingya boat people who had drifted ashore. About the same time, Thailand also detained 146 Rohingyas in Southern Thailand. In February 2009, the House Committee on Security in the Thai Parliament concluded that they were economic refugees and found evidence showing that transnational human traffickers were behind the influx of Rohingya boat people. The objective of these traffickers was to take the Rohingyas to a third country. See "MPs blame traffickers for Rohingya," *Bangkok Post*, 2 February 2009, www.bangkokpost.com/breakingnews/136144/human-traffickers-behind-the-influx-of-rohingya.

21 Nevertheless, between 1993 and 2000, out of 582 Thai citizens arrested for various charges, more than 450 were for illegal fishing. Between 1988 and 2003, the MN seized 3,157 illegal fishing boats of various sizes, including 923 foreign boats, and commodities on board worth nearly 9,900 million kyat. The arrest of people involved in illegal fishing was particularly high in the period between 1988 and 1993.

22 In early January 2009, the Independent Mon News Agency reported that Myanmar authorities seized at least one illegal fishing boat per day in Myanmar waters and that about 100 more are operating without official permits, but obtain "unofficial tickets" through bribery. Boat owners pay between 50,000 and 60,000 baht per month for unofficial fishing rights, depending on the size of the boat. Boats that fail to get unofficial fishing tickets are seized but they are released once they pay the bribe. The report quoted an interview with a man who negotiated with a local MN officer for the release of a fishing boat and its crew by paying three motorbikes and various commodities worth 150,000 baht. The same report stated that despite the Myanmar government's ban on shellfish harvesting, along with a sentence of 20 years imprisonment, illegal activities have continued and that a boat could catch, on average, enough shellfish to make a profit of 60,000 baht, and sometimes up to 150,000 baht. See "Thai fishing boats seized daily by authorities in southern Burma," *Burma News International*, 7 January 2009, www.bnionline.net/news/imna/5647-thai-fishing-boats-seized-daily-by-authorities-in-southern-burma.html.

23 PONJA, p. 127, www.aseansec.org/21765.pdf.

24 These coastal patrol crafts (submarine chasers) were numbered and named: 441-*Yan Sit Aung*, 442-*Yan Myat Aung*, 443-*Yan Nyein Aung*, 444-*Yan Khwin Aung*, 445-*Yan Min Aung*, 446-*Yan Ye Aung*, 447-*Yan Paing Aung*, 448-*Yan Win Aung*, 449-*Yan Aye Aung* and 450-*Yan Zwe Aung*.

25 These fast attack craft are named after astrological stars (*Seik-hta*, *Mar-ga*, *Han-tha*, *Ze-Hta*, *Ban-Na* and *Du-wa*) and their pennant numbers are from UMS 471 to UMS 476.

26 Their pennant numbers are from UMS 551 to UMS 556. UMS 551 was commissioned on 2 January 1996.

27 Moreover, there are about 15 warships (both riverine and coastal patrol craft) under the command of the Bangladesh Coast Guard.

28 See the BN website, www.bangladeshnavy.org.

29 Wendell Minnick, "Bangladesh Navy Tests Chinese Anti-Ship Missile," *Defense News*, 14 May 2008, www.defensenews.com/story.php?i=3528643.

30 "Navy eyes sub, new frigates: Prepares Tk 6,000 cr plan to turn it into '3-dimesional' force," *Daily Star*, 24 June 2009, www.thedailystar.net/newDesign/news-details.php?nid=93936. See also "Navy plans to add submarine, aviation unit to its fleet in 10 years," *New Age*, 24 June 2009, www.newagebd.com/2009/jun/24/front.html.

31 "No plans for military base in Bangladesh waters," *Thaindian News*, www.thaindian.com/newsportal/world-news/no-plans-for-military-base-in-bangladesh-waters-us_100152741.html.

7 Maintaining good order at sea

Maritime challenges and priorities in the Philippines

Mary Ann Palma

Good order at sea and maritime security concept in the Philippines

The concept of "good order at sea"[1] has similar elements to the maritime security policy of the Philippines. Maritime security is defined under the Philippine National Marine Policy of 1994 as a "state in which the country's marine assets, maritime practices, territorial integrity, and coastal peace and order are protected, conserved, preserved and enhanced".[2] This definition, although embedded in a broader marine policy that has not been amended for more than a decade, captures the thrust of the security envisioned by the Philippines in its waters. This concept of maritime security is also widely adopted and elaborated, particularly by Philippine law enforcement agencies in their policies and programmes.

There are five components to the maritime security policy of the Philippines. The first component is the promotion and enhancement of maritime security as an element of national security. The second is the provision of a stable and peaceful socio-political and administrative environment in the country that fosters sustained profitability and growth for maritime industries. The third aspect is the protection and defence of the integrity of Philippine marine resources, while the fourth is ensuring preparedness for and an effective response to natural calamities and man-made disasters. The fifth and last component of maritime security in the Philippines is the provision of leadership and guidance in the proper and effective collection, processing and distribution of strategic information supportive of the National Marine Policy. Threats to good order at sea, such as piracy and armed robbery at sea, illicit trafficking of drugs, people and arms, maritime terrorism, illegal fishing, illegal dumping of wastes, and maritime accidents, run counter to these objectives and are deemed as challenges to the attainment of maritime security in the Philippines.

This chapter examines the challenges confronting the Philippines in maintaining good order at sea. It also highlights the priorities of the government in terms of the development of the maritime sector, current issues with respect to the delineation of its territorial and maritime jurisdiction, protection of offshore oil and gas resources and facilities, and some of the recent maritime safety and security concerns of the Philippines, such as threats to the safety of seafarers off the coast of Somalia and occurrence of maritime accidents. Lastly, this chapter discusses some of the existing regional and subregional initiatives involving the Philippines to address threats to good order at sea.

Maritime threats in the Philippines

The geographic characteristics of the Philippines primarily define the scope and breadth of the maritime interests of, and the threats confronting, the country. The Philippine archipelago, comprising more than 7,100 islands connected by water, is home not only to a unique socio-cultural diversity but also to abundant marine resources. The waters around and between the islands are used for both domestic and international commerce and are greatly relied upon by Filipinos for their livelihood. Hence, the security of its people, islands, waters and resources in their entirety is a principal concern for the Philippines.

The security of the Philippine archipelago and its people is continuously threatened by a number of maritime security challenges, such as the trade of illicit drugs, the smuggling of goods including arms, trafficking in people, illegal fishing, illegal dumping of waste, piracy and armed robbery, and maritime terrorism. Although it is difficult to obtain accurate information on the nature and extent of these threats to good order at sea, a number of official sources, academic literature and anecdotal evidence point to the existence of these illegal activities as a result of inadequate monitoring of the long coastline and extensive maritime jurisdiction of the Philippines. The discussions that follow provide an indication of the nature of these maritime security challenges and the factors contributing to the proliferation of illegal activities in the Philippines.

Illegal trafficking of drugs

The Philippines is geographically at the crossroads of drug trafficking in the Asia-Pacific region. It is in a strategic location for the transit and market of drugs. The Philippines is known as a producer, exporter and consumer of cannabis plant-based drugs and an importer and consumer of synthetic drugs.[3] In a global review on drug consumption and production, the Philippines has been cited to have reported an increasing trend in cannabis consumption and methamphetamine production, and is identified as source of synthetic drug precursors to various destinations in the world.[4] The Philippines is also a transit point for the international trade of heroin and cocaine, a recreation place and an investment and money laundering haven for international drug syndicates.[5]

Since 2004 the Philippines has the highest estimated methamphetamine prevalence rate globally, and since then the number has been stable or slightly declining.[6] It is estimated by the National Drug Law Enforcement and Prevention Coordinating Centre that about 14 per cent of the total number of local municipalities is drug infested.[7] About 5 per cent of the total population are dependent on illicit drugs, including 7 per cent of the total youth population.[8] The local illegal drug trade in the Philippines is a multi-billion dollar industry involving foreign nationals and local drug groups who concentrate their activities in Metro Manila.

A number of factors have been attributed to the increase in drug trafficking in the Philippines. Economic difficulties and poverty may be identified as the main reasons for people resorting to drug trade as an alternative source of income. There has also been an influx of members of transnational criminal organisations masquerading as legitimate investors and tourists in the country. Liberalisation and deregulation have also been cited as reasons for the movement of illegal goods, including illicit drugs.[9] For these reasons, law enforcement agencies regard drug trafficking as a national security threat.

Apart from contributing to the increasing level of crime in the Philippines, it is surmised that drugs can finance activities of insurgent and secessionist groups. Some areas of the Philippines with a high incidence of insurgency activities are major sites of marijuana production. It is unclear how much illegal drugs are transported by sea; however, some areas have been identified as coastal trafficking points around the archipelago.[10] Seizures of illegal drugs can enable them to be traced from their origin in certain parts of Asia to their point of entry into the country through small ports along the extensive coastline. In May 2008, for example, the Philippine Drug Enforcement Agency identified the Subic Bay Freeport in Zambales as a transhipment point for illicit drugs from several countries in Asia.[11]

Illegal trafficking of arms

There are about 630,000 licensed firearms in the Philippines, with an average increase of 65,802 registered firearms each year.[12] Most of these firearms are made locally or imported legitimately from the United States, China, Israel and Europe.[13] It is estimated that that there are now more than 300,000 loose firearms in the Philippines in the possession of gun enthusiasts, hobbyists, political warlords or criminal groups.[14]

Smuggling of firearms is conducted through air and seaports in the Philippines, through the delivery of packages, big equipment, appliances and international aid. However, the most common mode of smuggling some of these loose firearms is through ports. Gunrunners have been known to use the Manila North Harbour, the various ports of Cebu, Leyte and Negros provinces, and other areas in Luzon and the southern Philippines as landing sites and storage points for arms sold to ideological political groups and local bandits.[15] Local guns, usually of less firearm power, are manufactured in the Philippines and shipped to both local and foreign markets on board passenger vessels and fishing boats. More sophisticated and high-powered firearms are smuggled into the country.[16]

A number of factors have contributed to the proliferation of illegal trafficking of arms in the Philippines. The high marketability of firearms and the involvement of unscrupulous officials in arms smuggling for use in private armies are the two main reasons that this problem remains unabated in the Philippines. The lack of control of gun dealership and manufacturing in the Philippines, as well as the pilferage of arms from the military and police, also lead to arms smuggling.[17]

Trafficking in people

Smuggling and trafficking of people, mostly women and children, is a component of the illegal migration of Filipinos overseas.[18] The Philippines is a major source of people trafficked to other countries, particularly to the United States, Singapore, Canada, Japan, Italy, the United Kingdom, Jordan, Malaysia, South Korea and Saudi Arabia.[19] Philippine authorities report that the number of victims of trafficking in people increased from 220 in 2004 to 359 in 2007.[20]

The major schemes of trafficking Filipinos to these countries are illegal immigration by fraudulent documentation, mail-order bride schemes, cultural exchange and adoption.[21] As the Philippines witnesses an increasing number of Filipino women migrating to other countries, the trafficking of these women in the hands of illegal recruiters, slavers and prostitution rings has also increased.[22] Some of these Filipinos become subject to domestic violence, as well as to labour and human rights abuses.

The extent of trafficking of Filipinos by sea, particularly to neighbouring states, is unknown. However, incidents have been cited by the Philippine government of women trafficked in cargo vessels, and in freezer vans and drums, and some of these women do not survive the journey.[23] A more common problem associated with the illegal transport of people by sea is the illegal migration of refugees to the Philippines. The migration of asylum seekers and refugees under the human rights programmes of the government is not in itself illegal.[24] However, there are vessels transporting people to the Philippines through the western and southern seas undetected by border patrols, and these migrants are therefore undocumented and illegal.

Economic instability is no doubt the major driving force for the migration of Filipinos to other countries. However, the labour export policies and programmes of the Philippines, together with the international demand for cheap labour, may also be identified as facilitating the massive migration of Filipinos overseas. Such policies and programmes, which may promote unfavourable conditions for workers, are used by illegal recruiters and criminal syndicates to exploit Filipinos who want to obtain jobs outside the Philippines.

Smuggling of goods

Smuggling of goods, as a way to avoid payment of taxes and duties, is rampant in the Philippines.[25] The goods illegally transported into the country are wide-ranging, and include garments, ceramic tiles, luxury cars, agricultural products, electronic equipment, appliances and jewellery.[26] These goods are brought into and taken out of the country illegally by different modes of smuggling, such as actual smuggling, technical smuggling, through the use of falsified documents or smuggling in the open sea.

Ports and open waters are major conduits for smuggled goods, with plastic and oil as the most common illegally traded products. Smuggling of oil at sea occurs when tankers plying Philippine waters conduct shipside unloading to small vessels.[27] Pilferage of oil is most common in Manila and is conducted at sea and along the Pasig River where oil firms are located.[28] Oil barges on their way to depots are also illegally boarded by robbers.[29] In 2003, 232 million litres of fuel were reported to have been smuggled in Subic Bay Freeport.[30] Other landing sites of smuggled fuel include ports in southern Philippines.

Despite a number of anti-smuggling campaigns conducted by the Bureau of Customs, smuggling of oil at sea continues. Corruption in the government, particularly within the systems of trading, monitoring, taxation and auditing, may be identified as key factors in uncontrolled smuggling in the Philippines. Inadequate penalties for smuggling-related offences are also responsible for the proliferation of such illegal activity.

Piracy and armed robbery at sea

There are relatively few recorded piracy incidents in the Philippines. There have only been 63 incidents of piracy in Philippine waters from 2001 to 2008, compared to a total of 1,318 incidents in the Southeast Asian region.[31] While strengthened regional cooperation and reporting of incidents may be considered as contributing to the decline of piracy incidents in the Philippines, this problem nevertheless remains a threat to the good order at sea in the country.

In certain parts of the country, particularly in the southern Philippines, armed robbery at sea or raiding is an endemic problem and is sometimes regarded as piracy.[32] Sulu pirates used to attack coastal communities and vessels[33] and armed robbers are known to have camps throughout the Sulu Archipelago coastline, which serve as resupply points, safe havens and bases for raiding expeditions.[34] The insurgency problem in the Philippines has further presented piracy as a means of raising funds for their operations. Secessionist groups, such as the Moro Islamic Liberation Front (MILF) and the Abu Sayyaf Group (ASG), have ethnic affinities with seafaring families and contribute to the prevalence of piracy in the southern Philippines.[35]

Maritime terrorism

In addition to insurgency, the southern Philippines has been associated with a number of terrorist activities.[36] Three major home-grown non-conformist groups in the southern Philippines are the MILF, the ASG, and the Moro National Liberation Front (MNLF).[37] However, only the ASG has so far been considered to have a significant intent to conduct maritime terrorism.[38] Current terrorist threats posed by the ASG have existed since the 1990s. Various incidents have been associated with this group including the bombing of the inter-island ferry MV *Our Lady of Mediatrix* in Iligan in 2000, the abduction of foreign tourists in a diving resort in Sipadan and the bombing of the MV *SuperFerry 14* in Manila

Bay in 2004.[39] While these cases are indications of the capability of ASG to carry out piracy and maritime terrorism, further studies still need to be conducted to substantiate claims for the potential use of piracy as a tool for terrorism.[40]

Illegal fishing

The full extent of illegal fishing in the Philippines is not known, but it is reported to occur mostly in rich fishing grounds within areas of the country with ineffective fisheries enforcement. Some of the illegal fishing activities conducted by both domestic and foreign fishing vessels include fishing without a licence and the use of destructive fishing methods, such as blast fishing, cyanide poisoning and illegal gears. It is estimated that the Philippines loses PhP50 billion or almost US$1 billion dollars annually to illegal fishing activities.[41] This estimate only accounts for the value of the seized fish and does not reflect the actual loss that may result from the impact of such activities on fish habitat and the social dislocation of artisanal fishers. Most of the illegal fishing practices have irreversible impacts on fisheries resources and their habitats.

Another problem in Philippine fisheries affects the live reef fish trade. The live reef fish trade is a lucrative industry in the Asia-Pacific valued at approximately US$30 million for the Philippines alone.[42] The main problems associated with live reef fish trade is not only undocumented trade and the use of destructive fishing methods affecting coral reefs and habitats, but also the involvement of organised criminal groups. The high prices and demand for fish have made it difficult for the Philippines to address this problem for several decades.

Illegal dumping of waste

There is scant information on illegal dumping of waste at sea in the Philippines. Such illegal activity is generally regarded as part of marine pollution. Marine pollution in the Philippines is caused by land- and sea-based sources, including sewage, agricultural runoffs, chemical discharges, hazardous and toxic substances, and operational and accidental oil discharge. An account of marine pollution in the Philippines suggests that the country experiences an average of 23 oil spills a year.[43]

Some of the major incidents of oil and chemical spills have affected multiple municipalities to the detriment of coastal resources and livelihood. An example of a massive oil spill incident in the Philippines involved a power barge running aground on the coast of Antique Province in 2005. It dumped 364,000 litres of oil and polluted about 40 kilometres of coastline.[44] The clean-up and rehabilitation costs to the Philippines for this oil spill incident was US$2 million.[45] A similar incident occurred when an oil tanker sank off the southern island of Mindanao in 2006. M/V *Solar I* leaked 200,000 litres of oil, which reached a number of coastal areas and contaminated 1,000 hectares of mangrove areas, including several marine sanctuaries and coral reefs.[46]

Without adequate monitoring, it is difficult to distinguish between illegal dumping of waste at sea and accidental marine pollution.

Maritime security threats as transnational crimes

Similar to global trends, the Philippines has associated some of the maritime security threats with a wider context of transnational crime. Illegal trafficking in drugs, goods and persons, piracy, and terrorism all have land and sea components and are linked to transnational criminal groups. These activities are deemed criminal in nature, and their proceeds are linked with money laundering under Philippine law.[47] However, illegal fishing and illegal dumping of waste, which are considered in the realm of environmental crime, are not included in the list of unlawful activities that may be associated with money laundering. There have been legislative initiatives to extend the scope of the predicate offences for the crime of money laundering to address corrupt practices and terrorism, as well as violations of environmental and fisheries legislation.[48] However, these bills are yet to be approved by the Philippine Congress. Providing a stronger legal link between threats to good order at sea and other illicit activities, such as corruption and money laundering, may be seen as an effective means to strengthen mechanisms to address maritime security challenges.

The Philippines estimates that the profit from drug trafficking is almost half the country's national budget, while terrorist groups have used laundered money to support their activities and expand their facilities.[49] Some activities of terrorist groups also include kidnapping or hostage for profit, such as the kidnapping by ASG of 21 people at the Sipadan Beach Resort, Malaysia in 2000 and 20 people at Dos Palmas Beach, Palawan, in 2001, the victims of whom were brought to Southern Mindanao.[50] There are other examples of kidnapping incidents inspired by terror and profit-making, such as the kidnapping of Indonesian sailors at the Sulu Sea in 2002 and of five workers from the Borneo Paradise Beach Resort in Sabah, Malaysia, in 2003.[51] Although the economic benefits from conducting these illegal activities at sea have yet to be accurately determined, a holistic approach in addressing these concerns not just from a maritime security perspective but also from a national security perspective is warranted.

Maritime priorities of the Philippines

Apart from identifying domestic laws and regulations that address maritime threats in the Philippines,[52] it would be difficult to identify the current priorities of the country when it comes to maintaining good order at sea because of the lack of a clear national maritime agenda. One has to look at a number of sources in order to determine the maritime priorities of the country, such as the various plans, programmes and activities of each relevant government department, the work programme of the government under the Medium Term Development Plan, bills and resolutions filed before the Philippine Congress, and other government actions that address current maritime challenges confronting the Philippines.

Sectoral programmes and activities

There are more than 40 individual and inter-agency institutions governing the marine and maritime sectors in the Philippines, which involve some functions related to maintaining good order at sea. Each of these government institutions has a number of priorities set out in their mandates, annual plans and programmes. For example, the Bureau of Fisheries and Aquatic Resources of the Department of Agriculture, as part of its many priorities, is focussing on the implementation of the country's obligations under regional fisheries management organisations and on its compliance with the European Union regulation to combat illegal, unreported and unregulated (IUU) fishing. The Maritime Industry Authority has adopted a ten-point programme that institutionalises an advocacy campaign for the safety of travel and protection of the environment. The Department of Energy, in pursuit of energy independence under the Philippine Energy Plan, aims to attain a sustainable 60 per cent energy self-sufficiency beyond 2010. Such an objective is to be achieved through accelerating the exploration, development and utilisation of indigenous energy resources; intensifying renewable energy resource development; increasing the use of alternative fuels; and enhancing energy efficiency and conservation.

Law enforcement agencies have mandates to protect the territorial integrity of the Philippines, promote maritime safety and security, protect the marine environment and provide services such as search and rescue, and vessel traffic management. Enforcement agencies cooperate in order to carry out more effective mechanisms against illegal activities at sea, such as the joint manning of vessel traffic monitoring centres by the Philippine Ports Authority and the Philippine Coast Guard, and port state control by these agencies along with the Bureau of Customs, the Bureau of Immigration and Deportation, the Bureau of Quarantine and Inspection Services and the Philippine National Police.

A number of other initiatives have been established by the Philippines, such as the deployment of sea marshals or counter-terrorist teams on board vessels in the aftermath of the *SuperFerry 14* incident. Each sea marshal team is composed of officers from the Philippine Coast Guard, the Armed Forces of the Philippines, the Philippine National Police and private ship security agencies. In support of the sea marshal operations, coast guard K-9 units are also used to search for bombs, firearms and illegal drugs in cargo containers as a pre-departure port security measure. Several task forces have also been created such as the Coast Guard Anti-Terrorist Unit (CGATU).[53]

The issues addressed through inter-agency cooperation also demonstrate the maritime priorities of the Philippines. Some of the existing collaborative mechanisms established by various government institutions include the Anti-Terrorism Council (ATC), the Inter-Agency Counter-Narcotics Operations Network – Philippine Drug Enforcement Agency (ICON–PDEA), the Inter-Agency Philippine Border Management Network (IPBMN), the National Committee on Illegal Entrants (NCIE), the National Intelligence Coordinating Agency (NICA), the National Law Enforcement Coordinating Committee (NALECC) and the Presidential Anti-Smuggling Group (PASG).[54] Law enforcement agencies, particularly the Philippine Coast Guard, are also cooperating with the Land Transportation Office to inspect documents of vehicles being transported by ferry and to monitor the illegal transport of smuggled and stolen vehicles. Similarly, a Joint Coastal Coordination Desk was formed by the Philippine Coast Guard and the Bureau of Customs to identify coastal ports where no customs official or employee is regularly stationed. The Joint Coastal Coordination Desk is also tasked to receive confidential information related to smuggling operations; take testimony, receive evidence, administer oaths, summon witnesses and require the submission of documents by subpoena; and assist in the prosecution of smuggling cases.[55]

In recognition of and response to the various maritime security threats in the southern Philippines, the government is in the process of establishing Coastwatch South, an inter-agency coordinating body to ensure maritime security in the Philippines.[56] Coastwatch South aims to provide a strategic and comprehensive maritime surveillance and response mechanism in the southern Philippines.[57] Members of the coordinating body would include the National Security Council, the Department of National Defense, the Department of Justice, the Department of Interior and Local Government, the Department of Agriculture, the Department of Energy, the Department of Environment and Natural Resources, the Department of Health, the Department of Transportation and Communications, and attached agencies such as the Office of Transportation Security, the Philippine Navy, the Philippine Coast Guard, the Philippine National Police, the Philippine Drugs and Enforcement Agency, the Bureau of Immigration, the Bureau of Customs, the Bureau of Fisheries and Aquatic Resources, the NICA and the Philippine Center on Transnational Crime.

Economic development plans for the marine sector

The Medium Term Development Plan of the Philippines 2004–2010 (MTPDP),[58] which sets out the programme of work of the government, is similarly sectoral in approach and does not provide a strict maritime agenda for the country. However there are goals under the MTPDP that directly affect the maritime industry and economy of the Philippines, such as in shipbuilding and the promotion of marine products for export. The MTPDP provides that

> [i]nvestments in the establishment of additional shipbuilding/ship repair capacities in the country for the production of ocean-going vessels, bulk-carriers, inter-island ships/ferries and catamarans for export and domestic shipping shall be encouraged and supported. The customer base shall be expanded through leveraged selling missions and business matching facilities. The Philippine Navy shall continue its collaboration programme with the shipbuilding industry.[59]

The MTPDP also highlights a number of goals with respect to the export of marine products, such as advocating compliance with standards for fresh and marine products; embarking on an intensive marketing promotions of value-added marine products through informational campaign and participation in trade shows; promoting product development for seaweed and carrageenan; promoting branding of Philippine marine products as quality products through country of origin logo; pursuing bilateral fisheries agreements to gain market access to fishing grounds for tuna and to reduce tariff and nontariff barriers to marine products; and promoting new investments in cold storage facilities to assure a continuous supply of fresh and frozen marine products.[60]

The Philippine Medium Term Development Plan has broader and more ambitious goals with respect to protecting the marine environment, biodiversity and coastal and marine ecosystems. Some of these goals include the expansion of coverage and the strengthening of coastal and marine ecosystems protection; the delineation of 6.3 million hectares of coastal and marine area for the protection of biodiversity; the establishment of a management system and facilities for toxic and hazardous wastes; and the total phase-out of the consumption of ozone-depleting substances nationwide. Specific objectives to achieve these goals include the creation of 14 coastal law enforcement alliances with non-government sectors and communities; the provision of technical assistance to 570 local government units in coastal protection and management; the management of 39 priority wetlands; the zoning of 77 protected areas to delineate areas suitable for development; and the conversion of production systems to ozone-friendly technologies.[61]

Congressional bills and resolutions

A number of bills and resolutions addressing marine and maritime issues have been submitted to the Fourteenth Congress of the Philippines and this provides an indication of the maritime priorities as perceived by the legislative assembly. There are bills relating to institutional development, such as the establishment of a National Maritime Authority, the Philippine Coast Guard as an independent organisation and the creation of a Permanent Secretariat for the Inter-Agency Council Against Trafficking.[62] Other bills refer to the development of a maritime agenda;[63] the development of coastal resources, the fisheries sector and shipping;[64] and the protection of the coastal and marine environment, particularly the management of hazardous and radioactive waste.[65] There are also legislative drafts on the establishment of a national oceanic and coastal observation system and disaster mitigation;[66] marine resource and environmental education and awareness;[67] maritime safety;[68] and climate change.[69] House and Senate Bills were also submitted to address illegal activities and other security concerns.[70] These legislative proposals however, are yet to be successfully adopted into law.

Other current issues

There are other concerns related to the maintenance of good order at sea currently being addressed by the Philippines. Some examples are the delineation of territorial and maritime jurisdiction of the Philippines, the protection of offshore oil and gas resources and facilities, the safety of Filipino seafarers from piracy attacks in the Gulf of Aden, and the occurrence of maritime accidents.

Territorial and maritime jurisdiction of the Philippines

The delineation of territorial and maritime jurisdiction is a longstanding issue in the Philippines and may be considered as a fundamental element in upholding good order at sea. Neither the legal and geographic limits of Philippine waters nor the existing maritime boundary disputes with neighbouring countries will be discussed in this chapter.[71] However, the four most current issues being addressed by the Philippines are highlighted. The first is the question of constitutionality of Republic Act 9522 on the Archipelagic Baselines of the Philippines, which was enacted in March 2009.[72] The new baselines law adopts a straight archipelagic baselines system consistent with Article 47 of the United Nations Convention on the Law of the Sea (UNCLOS). The Archipelagic Baselines Law also provides that baselines in the Kalayaan Island Group (KIG) and Scarborough Shoal will be determined based on the "regime of islands" provided under Article 121 of the UNCLOS.[73] A petition for certiorari and prohibition to nullify the Archipelagic Baselines Law for being unconstitutional was filed before the Supreme Court of the Philippines[74] and has yet to be addressed by the court. The legislation has also been the subject of protests by neighbouring countries of the Philippines.

The second issue relates to the submission for a continental shelf beyond 200 nautical miles by the Philippines. In April 2009, the Philippines presented a partial submission to the Commission on the Limits of the Continental Shelf (CLCS) on the outer limits of its continental shelf extending beyond 200 nautical miles from the baselines in the Benham Rise region, in the eastern part of the Philippines.[75] This area is not subject to maritime boundary disputes or claims. However, the Philippines also maintains that it has continental shelves in the western region that encompass areas in the South China Sea subject to territorial disputes. There is therefore a question on how the Philippines can proceed with its submission for a continental shelf beyond 200 nautical miles in these disputed areas.

The third and fourth relevant issues for the Philippines are the joint submission of Malaysia and Vietnam for the limits of their extended continental shelves,[76] as well as Palau's submission for the limits of its continental shelf.[77] The Philippines has officially requested the United Nations to refrain from considering both submissions.[78] An area subject to the joint submission of Malaysia and Vietnam partially overlaps with some of the Philippine-occupied islands in the KIG. On the other hand, the submission of Palau seems to have taken into account the Philippine exclusive economic zone; therefore, the legal and political reasons for such protest from the Philippines remain unclear to the author.

Protection of offshore oil and gas resources and facilities

For decades, offshore oil and gas resources in the Philippines have remained largely untapped due to huge costs and logistical challenges. However, since 2007 oil production has increased in the country because of the development of new offshore deep-water oil deposits.[79] It is estimated that about 3.9 billion barrels of oil equivalent exist within an extensive 709,000 square kilometres of rich resource regions in the Philippines.[80] About 80 per cent of these regions comprise offshore areas.

Compared to the offshore oil resources, gas production in the Philippines has become more significant because of the Malampaya gas field in the western seas. Inaugurated in 2001, the Malampaya Deepwater Gas-to-Power Project is the largest natural gas development project in the history of the Philippines and one of the largest foreign investments in the country. All of the gas production in this area is consumed domestically.

In addition to current gas production, the Philippine Department of Energy estimates significant undiscovered oil and gas resources in the South China Sea areas adjacent to the Philippines.[81] Compared to the eastern Philippines, almost all of the oil and gas resources in the western Philippines are situated in offshore areas. The potential for these oil and gas resources and their geographic location has three major impacts on good order at sea in the Philippines. First, the co-existence of navigation and non-living resource exploration activities in the area signifies the need to address safety and security concerns of vessels and oil and gas platforms. Second, the development of oil and gas resources, as well as access to fishing grounds, in the South China Sea increase the possibility of conflict among littoral states, as has been evident in the past. Third, the existence of these resources, coupled with unresolved territorial disputes, raises some national patrimony and sovereignty issues for the Philippines. The most relevant example in this case is the Joint Marine Seismic Undertaking in the South China Sea, signed by the Philippines with Vietnam and China in 2005, which was challenged, among other things, as violating the Philippine Constitution and domestic laws that reserve the exploitation of such resources to Filipinos.[82]

In addition to the offshore oil and gas resources in disputed areas, the Philippines is investigating the potential of ocean energy to augment current power supplies. According to some studies, the prospective capacity of this renewable source of energy is estimated at 170,000 megawatts.[83] Some of the initial ocean energy sites identified include the Hinautan Passage, the Camarines, North-Eastern Samar, Surigao, Batan Island, Catanduanes, Tacloban, the San Bernardino Strait, Babuyan Island, Ilocos Norte, Siargao Island and Davao Oriental.[84] Although this may seem to be an issue for the distant future, the Philippines needs to be conscious that any development of this nature would require the establishment of a framework to address not only the sustainability and protection of ocean resources, but also the safety and security of energy platforms and facilities. A similar framework would also need to be developed for any exploration of resources in continental shelf areas beyond 200 nautical miles.

Piracy in the Gulf of Aden and Filipino seafarers

As a major supplier of seafarers in the world, the Philippines is at the forefront of addressing issues with respect to the security and welfare of its seafarers on board commercial vessels. Filipino seafarers have been held as hostages by Somali pirates in light of increasing piratical attacks in the Gulf of Aden. There have been 470 Filipino seafarers kidnapped and held hostage by Somali pirates since 2006.[85] As of December 2009, 56 Filipino seafarers were being held by Somali pirates.[86] Although some commercial vessels and Filipino seafarers have been released by Somali pirates, kidnapping of vessel crews persists in the Gulf of Aden. As of February 2011, some reports have noted that 118 Filipino seafarers were still held captive by Somali pirates.[87] These incidents merited a congressional enquiry into the existing legislation and policies of the Philippines on the safety and welfare of seafarers, and how such legal and policy instruments can be improved.[88] Although threats to the safety of Filipino seafarers on board vessels do not occur within Philippine waters, it is nevertheless considered a national maritime security concern. The government has been trying to address the problem by issuing safety and security directives to manning agencies of ships plying the Gulf of Aden and requiring seafarers to undergo anti-piracy training. The Philippines has also established an Ad Hoc Committee on Piracy and Armed Robbery against Ships under the Office of the President. Furthermore, the Department of Foreign Affairs and the Department of Labour and Employment are coordinating their efforts with manning agencies for the release and repatriation of seafarers. Needless to say, the assistance of foreign governments has been instrumental in the release of Filipino seafarers held hostage by Somali pirates. Political visits and more active communication between the Philippines and Somalia have also been necessary to facilitate the release of captive Filipino seafarers and to discuss potential areas of cooperation to address the problem.[89]

Threats to maritime safety

Another challenge to maintaining good order at sea is the threat to safety of life and property at sea. Compiled incident reports by the Philippine Coast Guard in the past 20 years include 170 recorded marine accidents, most involving Philippine-flagged vessels in the country's waters.[90] Some of these incidents involve grounding of vessels, oil pollution, collision, capsizing of vessels, fire on board vessels and engine explosions. While some of these incidents have been caused by typhoons and natural disasters, some cases have been due to human error or malicious attacks and have resulted not only in the loss of ships but, more importantly, in the loss of lives of crew and passengers. Among the most disastrous cases in terms of loss of lives were the collision of the MV *Super Ferry 12* and the MV *San Nicholas* in 2003, the fires on board the MV *Maria Carmela* in 2002 and the MV *Super Ferry 14* in 2004, and the capsize of the MV *Princess of the Stars*, the MBca *Don Dexter*, and the MBca *Mae Juan* in 2008.[91]

Other incidents may not have involved the loss of lives but have caused injury to numerous passengers and crew and damage to property.

A number of marine disasters are still under investigation by the Board of Marine Inquiry as at 2010, such as the collision between the M/V *Catalyn B* and the F/V *Anatalia D.R.* in the vicinity of Limbones Island, Cavite; and the sinking of the MV *Baleno 9* in the vicinity of San Agapito, Verde Island and Batangas. The House Committee on Transportation is also conducting its own enquiry into these accidents at sea.[92]

Regional cooperation

Perhaps the only feature of good order at sea that has not been directly discussed in the National Marine Policy is the contribution and participation of the Philippines in regional and subregional arrangements to promote maritime security. Nevertheless, it does not mean that the Philippines does not give priority to its relations and cooperation with neighbouring states in Southeast Asia and the wider Asia-Pacific regions. On the contrary, the Philippines has entered into venerable bilateral, subregional and regional arrangements with its neighbours.

The Philippines conducts naval exercises and has established bilateral arrangements with neighbouring states on defence cooperation, border control, intelligence sharing, joint exercises and military education. Two examples are the Philippines–Indonesia Border Crossing Agreement and the Philippines–Malaysia Memorandum of Agreement on Anti-Smuggling Cooperation.[93] Anti-terrorism has also been the subject of strengthened ties and cooperation between the Philippines and the United States after September 11.[94] Aside from the United States, the Philippines also maintains bilateral ties with Australia. Agreements concluded between the Philippines and Australia include a memorandum of understanding to combat international terrorism and transnational crime, as well as border control and migration management.[95] One of the components of a counter-terrorism package funded by the Australian Government is the implementation of the Philippine Australia Port Security Capacity Building project.[96] This project includes continuous training on the International Ship and Port Facility Security (ISPS) Code. In May 2007, the two countries also signed a Status of Forces Agreement.[97] Furthermore, the Philippines cooperates with other states in strengthening law enforcement against drug trafficking and trafficking in persons.[98] Such cooperation is also extended to private companies, non-governmental institutions and civic organisations to promote measures to address these illegal activities.

Among the many examples of subregional and regional cooperation involving the Philippines, the country has been active in promoting the security of key subregional areas in the region, such as in addressing IUU fishing in the Sulu–Sulawesi Sea and in protecting sea trade routes in the Brunei–Indonesia–Malaysia–Philippines East Asian Growth Area (BIMP–EAGA).[99] At the regional level, the Philippines serves as a forum for various types of functional cooperation under the Association of Southeast Asian Nations (ASEAN), such as on biodiversity conservation, environmental protection, promotion of regional security and prevention of transnational crime. It participates actively in the work of the Regional Cooperation against Armed Robbery and Piracy at Sea (ReCAAP), particularly through the organisation's Information Sharing Centre. In fisheries, the Philippines is a member of various regional fisheries management organisations, such as the Western and Central Pacific Fisheries Commission, and is a participating country to the Regional Plan of Action to Promote Responsible Fishing Practices, including Combating IUU Fishing.

Conclusion

The Philippine maritime security policy has its similarities to the concept of good order at sea in terms of the elements and recognised threats. Most of the challenges to maintaining good order at sea faced by other states are also present in the Philippines, such as illegal trafficking of arms, people, drugs and other goods, piracy and armed robbery at sea, and maritime terrorism, although they may vary in terms of magnitude. The transnational nature of these illegal activities at sea require the Philippines to seek cooperation with its neighbouring states, and where mechanisms for cooperation already exists, to enhance them in order to achieve good order at sea in the region. Other relevant maritime threats, such as illegal fishing, illegal dumping of waste and marine disasters, may have a more national focus but nevertheless requires inter-agency and regional cooperation, particularly with respect to membership and engagement in regional organisations and arrangements, and the ratification and implementation of relevant international conventions.

In maintaining good order at sea, there is not only a need for the Philippines to strengthen policies and legislation, but more importantly to consider investing more heavily in supporting law enforcement activities in terms of providing sufficient resources and training of personnel. The Philippines may also want to examine a number of other issues, some of which are not discussed in great detail in this chapter, such as addressing emerging issues related to trafficking in human organs,[100] securing continental shelf areas beyond 200 nautical miles, protecting the marine environment from invasive alien species, monitoring the live reef fish trade and protecting the rights of fish workers. In order to assist the international community in promoting maritime security, the Philippines also needs to ensure the implementation of relevant agreements on the suppression of unlawful acts against maritime navigation, long-range identification and tracking of vessels, and seafarers identify documentation.

Notes

1 Geoffrey Till, *Seapower: A Guide for the Twenty-first Century*, 2nd edn (Oxon: Routledge, 2009), pp. 286–321; Sam Bateman, Joshua H. Ho and Jane Chan, *Good Order at Sea in Southeast Asia*, RSIS Policy Paper (Singapore: RSIS, May 2009); and Sam Bateman, "Navies and the Maintenance of Good Order in Peacetime", in

Andrew T.H. Tan, *The Politics of Maritime Power: A Survey* (London: Routledge, 2007), pp. 95–114.

2 Philippines, Cabinet Committee on Marine Affairs, *National Marine Policy*, 8 November 1994.

3 Philippine Centre on Transnational Crime (PCTC), *Role of the Philippines in International and Regional Cooperation Effort on Drug Trafficking*, paper presented to the United Nations International Narcotics Control Board, 5–8 September 2000, p. 5, www.pctc.gov.ph; see also United Nations Office on Drugs and Crime (UNODC), *World Drug Report 2009* (Vienna: UNODC, 2009), pp. 75, 111.

4 See UNODC, *Amphetamines and Ecstasy: 2008 Global ATS Assessment* (Vienna: UNODC, 2008); UNODC, *World Drug Report 2009*, see note 3, pp. 127, 139.

5 PCTC, *Role of the Philippines in International and Regional Cooperation Effort on Drug Trafficking*, see note 3, p. 5.

6 UNODC, *Amphetamines and Ecstasy: 2008 Global ATS Assessment*, see note 4, p. 43.

7 PCTC, *The Worldwide Drug Situation*, 2000, p. 9, www.pctc.gov.ph.

8 Ibid.

9 Ibid.

10 UNODC, *Amphetamines and Ecstasy: 2008 Global ATS Assessment*, see note 4, p. 42.

11 Ibid., p. 43.

12 PCTC, paper on *Illicit Trafficking and Manufacturing of Firearms: Philippine Context*, p. 2, www.pctc.gov.ph.

13 Ibid.

14 Ibid., p. 3.

15 Ibid.

16 Ibid.

17 Ibid.

18 UNODC, *Global Report on Trafficking in Persons* (Vienna: UNODC, 2009), p. 55.

19 PCINSP CEO Abrenica, *Situation Report on Trafficking in Persons in the Philippines*, p. 2, www.pctc.gov.ph.

20 UNODC, *Global Report on Trafficking in Persons*, see note 18, p. 181.

21 Abrenica, see note 19.

22 Ibid., p. 5.

23 Ibid.

24 See Florentino B. Feliciano and Marissa P. de la Cerna, "Refugees in Southeast Asia: A Note on Philippine Practice and Recent Developments", *World Bulletin* VI:6, 1990, p. 2.

25 See Bienvenido P. Aleno, Jr, "Import Smuggling in the Philippines: An Economic Analysis", *Journal of Philippine Development*, 21, 1984.

26 UPI Asia.com, *Rampant Smuggling in the Philippines*, 18 March 2008, www.upiasia.com.

27 Col. Ramon Roque M. Jueves (CE) GSC PA, *An Assessment of Government Initiatives in Curbing Illicit Trade of Oil*, thesis, Masters in National Security Administration, National Defense College of the Philippines, August 2006, p. 4.

28 Ibid., p. 2.

29 Ibid.

30 Ibid.

31 ReCAAP Information Centre, *Annual Report 2008*, p. 14, www.recaap.org.

32 Stefan Eklöf Amirell, "Political Piracy and Maritime Terrorism: A Comparison Between the Straits of Malacca and the Southern Philippines", in Graham Gerard Ong-Webb (ed.), *Piracy, Maritime Terrorism and Securing the Malacca Straits* (Singapore: ISEAS, 2006), p. 59.

33 Stefan Eklöf Amirell, *Pirates in Paradise: A Modern History of Southeast Asia's Maritime Marauders* (Copenhagen: NIAS Press, 2006), p. 9.

34 Adam J. Young, *Contemporary Maritime Piracy in Southeast Asia: History, Causes and Remedies* (Singapore: ISEAS, 2007), p. 39.

35 Eduardo Ma. R. Santos, "Piracy and Armed Robbery Against Ships in the Philippines", in Graham Gerard Ong-Webb (ed.), *Piracy, Maritime Terrorism and Securing the Malacca Straits* (Singapore: ISEAS, 2006), p. 39.

36 For more discussions, see Rommel C. Banlaoi, *Philippine Security in the Age of Terror: National, Regional and Global Challenges in the Post-9/11 World* (Boca Raton: CRC Press, 2009); Graham Gerard Ong, "Ships Can Be Dangerous, Too: Coupling Piracy and Terrorism in Southeast Asia's Maritime Security Framework", in Derek Johnson and Mark Valencia (eds), *Piracy in Southeast Asia: Status, Issues, and Responses* (Singapore: ISEAS, 2005), pp. 49–50; Angel Rabasa, "Case Study: The Sulawesi-Mindanao Arc", in A. Rabasa, S. Boraz, P. Chalk, K. Cragin, T.W. Karasik, J.D.P. Moroney, K.A. O'Brein and J.E. Peters, *Ungoverned Territories: Understanding and Reducing Terrorism Risks* (Santa Monica: RAND Corporation, 2007), pp. 111–145.

37 Ronnie Gil Gavan, *Border Security Dilemma: Operational Responses to Maritime Security Threats in the Southern Philippines*, thesis, Masters in Maritime Studies Research, University of Wollongong, 2008, p. 50.

38 Ibid.

39 Eklöf, *Political Piracy and Maritime Terrorism*, see note 33, pp. 61–63.

40 Rommel C. Banloai, *Al-Harakatulal Islamiyyah: Essays on the Abu Sayyaf Group* (Quezon City: Philippine Institute for Political Violence and Terrorism Research, 2008), p. 62.

41 Mary Ann Palma, *Analysis of the Adequacy of the Philippine Legal, Policy, and Institutional Framework to Combat Illegal, Unreported and Unregulated Fishing*, Doctor of Philosophy thesis, University of Wollongong, Australia, 2006; Mary Ann Palma and Martin Tsamenyi, *Case Study on the Impacts of Illegal, Unreported and Unregulated Fishing in the Sulawesi Sea*, APEC Fisheries Working Group, FWG 02/2007 (Wollongong: University of Wollongong), 2008.

42 Robert S. Pomeroy, Michael D. Pido, John Francisco A. Pointillas, Benjamin S. Francisco, Alan T. White and Geronimo T. Silvestre, *Evaluation of Policy Options for the Live Reef Food Fish Trade: Focus on Calamianes Islands and Palawan Province, Philippines, with Implications for National Policy* (Palawan: FISH Project, 2005), p. 2.

43 Philippine Coast Guard, *Emergency Preparedness Plan*, p. 2, www.coastguard.gov.ph.

44 "Large Oil Spill in the Philippines Threatens Marine Ecosystem", WWF website, 17 August 2006, www.panda.org.

45 Ibid.

46 Ibid.

47 Republic Act 9160, An Act Defining the Crime of Money Laundering, Providing Penalties Therefor and for Other Purposes, or otherwise known as the Anti-Money Laundering Act of 2001, sect. 3(l).

48 See, for example, the Fourteenth Congress of the Philippines, Second Regular Session, Senate Bill No. 3005, introduced by Senator Lacson, An Act to Further Strengthen the Anti-Money Laundering Law, Amending for the Purpose Republic Act No. 9160, otherwise known as the Anti-Money Laundering Act of 2001, as amended and for other purposes.

49 PCTC, *Money Laundering*, p. 16, www.pctc.gov.ph.

50 PCTC, *Kidnapping in the Philippines*, 2004, p. 2, www.pctc.gov.ph.

51 Ibid.

52 Examples of these national laws are the Revised Penal Code, the Republic Act (RA) 6425 or the Dangerous Drugs Act 1972, Presidential Decree (PD) 532 or Anti-Piracy and Anti-Highway Robbery Law 1974, RA 9160 or the Anti-Money Laundering Act

2001, RA 9372 or the Human Security Act 2007 (more commonly known as the Philippine Anti-Terror Law), firearms laws and regulations, the National Internal Security Plan and draft national plans of action to combat piracy and armed robbery against ships, trafficking of illegal drugs, trafficking in persons, smuggling of firearms and terrorism. See also RA 6955 or An Act to Declare Unlawful the Practice of Matching Filipino Women for Marriage to Foreign Nationals; RA 7658 or An Act Prohibiting the Employment of Children Below 15 Years of Age; RA 7659 or An Act to Impose the Death Penalty on Certain Heinous Crimes; RA 8042 or An Act to Institute the Policies of Overseas Employment; RA 8043 or An Act Establishing the Rules to Govern Inter-Country Adoption of Filipino Children; and RA 9105 or An Act Defining the Crime of Art Forgery.

53 Philippine Coast Guard website, Maritime Security Measures, www.coastguard.gov.ph.

54 Examples of executive issuances establishing these inter-agency cooperation are Executive Order (EO) 220 Creating an Executive Council to Suppress Trafficking in Persons, Particularly Women and Children; EO 8 Creating a Presidential Anti-Organized Crime Commission and a Presidential Anti-Organized Crime Task Force to Investigate and Prosecute Criminal Elements in the Country, as amended by EO 295; EO 61 Creating the National Drug Law Enforcement and Prevention Coordinating Center to Orchestrate Effort of National Government Units, and Non-Government Organization for a more Effective Anti-Drug Campaign; EO 62 Creating the Philippine Center on Transnational Crime to Formulate and Implement a Concerted Program of Action of all Law Enforcement, Intelligence and Control of Transnational Crime; and EO 101 Providing the Immediate Organization and Operationalization of the Interim Internal Affairs Service (IAS) of the Philippine National Police.

55 Philippine Coast Guard website, see note 35.

56 Economy Report on Maritime Security Philippines, www.apec-tptwg.org.cn/new/Archives/tpt-wg30/Maritime/Mar-sec/Philippinr%20Economy%20Report%20MEG%20SEC.doc.

57 See Gavan, see note 37, p. 57.

58 National Economic Development Authority, *Medium-Term Philippine Development Plan 2004–2010* (Manila: NEDA, 2004).

59 Ibid., p. 16.

60 Ibid., p. 18.

61 Ibid., ch. 3.

62 Please note that some of these bills have counterpart bills at the House of Representatives. SBN-3545, Philippine Marine Act of 2009; SBN-3389, Philippine Coast Guard Law of 2009; SBN-3228, Anti-Trafficking in Persons Act.

63 SBN-3545, Philippine Marine Act of 2009.

64 SBN-3413, Agricultural and Fisheries Mechanization (AFMECH) Law; SBN-3245, Philippine Shipping Industry Reform Act of 2009; SBN-3208, Marine and Coastal Resources Protection Act of 2009.

65 SBN-3508, Clean Coastal Environment and Public Health Act of 2009; SBN-3422, Philippine Hazardous and Radioactive Wastes Management Act of 2009; SBN-3194, Toxic Waste Information Clearinghouse.

66 SBN-3490, National Oceanic and Coastal Observation System Act; SBN-3541, Predisaster Hazard Mitigation Enhancement Program Act of 2009; SBN-3216, Disaster Preparedness Plans; SBN-3126, Ocean Acidification Research and Monitoring Act of 2009; SBN-3086, Philippine Disaster Risk Management Act of 2009.

67 SBN-3338, Environmental Education; SBN-3276, Marine Resources Awareness and Education Act.

68 SBN-3394, Vessel Security and Accountability Act of 2009; SBN-3029, Maritime Safety Act of 2009.

69 SBN-3274, Climate Change Act of 2009; SRN-1525, Safety Measures for Filipino Sailors.

70 SBN-3270, Anti-Trafficking in Persons; SB-3268, Weapons of Mass Destruction Non-Proliferation and Strategic Items/Goods Regulation Act of 2009; SBN-3041, Stop Smuggling Act of 2009; SBN-3007, Comprehensive Dangerous Drugs Act; SBN-3005, Anti-Money Laundering Act; SBN-3180, Migrant Workers and Overseas Filipino Act.

71 In brief, the Philippines exercises sovereignty over some areas contested by neighbouring states: Bajo de Masinloc (Scarborough Shoals), the KIG, and Sabah. Bajo de Masinloc and the KIG, both found within the South China Sea areas, are known for their rich fishing grounds and potential for oil and gas and mineral resources. The Philippine exercise of sovereignty over these areas has been the subject of disputes with other claimant countries. For relevant literature, see Mary Ann Palma, "The Philippines as an Archipelagic and Maritime Nation: Interests, Challenges and Perspectives", *RSIS Working Paper No. 182*, S. Rajaratnam School of International Studies, Singapore, July 2009; Merlin M. Magallona, "Problems in Establishing Archipelagic Baselines for the Philippines: The UNCLOS and the National Territory", in the Institute of International Legal Studies, *Roundtable Discussion on Baselines of Philippine Maritime Territory and Jurisdiction* (Quezon City: University of the Philippines Law Center, 1995), pp. 1–21; Jay L. Batongbacal, "The Maritime Territories and Jurisdictions of the Philippines and the United Nations Convention on the Law of the Sea", *Philippine Law Journal* 76(2), 2001, pp. 122–168; Lowell B. Bautista, "The Historical Context and Legal Basis of the Philippine Treaty Limits", *Asia-Pacific Law and Policy Journal* 10(1), 2008, pp. 1–31.

72 Republic Act 9522, An Act to Amend Certain Provisions of Republic Act No 3046, as Amended by Republic Act No 5046, to Define the Archipelagic Baselines of the Philippines, and for Other Purposes, 10 March 2009.

73 RA 9522, sect. 2.

74 Petition for Certiorari and Prohibition with Prayer for the Issuance of a Write of Preliminary Prohibitory Injunction and/or a Temporary Restraining Order, S.C. G.R. No 187167, April 2009.

75 Republic of the Philippines, A Partial Submission of Data and Information on the Outer Limits of the Continental Shelf of the Republic of the Philippines Pursuant to Article 76(8) of the United Nations Convention on the Law of the Sea, 8 April 2009, www.un.org/Depts/los/clcs_new/submissions_files/submission_phl_22_2009.htm.

76 Malaysia and the Socialist Republic of Vietnam, Joint Submission to the Commission on the Limits of the Continental Shelf, pursuant to Article 76, para. 8 of the United Nations Convention on the Law of the Sea 1982 in respect of the southern part of the South China Sea, May 2009.

77 The Republic of Palau, Executive Summary, Submission to the Commission on the Limits of the Continental Shelf, Pursuant to Article 76 of the United Nations Convention on the Law of the Sea, 8 May 2009.

78 Philippine Mission to the United Nations, Communication Nos. 818, 819, and 820, New York, 4 August 2009.

79 Energy Information Administration, "Country Analysis Briefs: Philippines", www.eia.doe.gov.

80 See Department of Energy, Petroleum Resources Development Division, *Map of Oil and Gas Potential in the Philippines*.

81 Ibid.

82 For relevant information, see, for example, Abigail Ho, "PNOC: JMSU Area All in RP", *Inquirer.net*, 19 March 2008, www.inquirer.net. "Philippine Navy says JMSU beneficial to country", *GMANews*, 11 March 2003, www.gmanews.tv.

83 Department of Energy, "Renewable Energy: Biomass, Solar, Wind and Ocean", www.doe.gov.ph.

84 Ibid.
85 "Philippines orders sailors to take anti-piracy classes", *BBC News*, 4 January 2010, http://news.bbc.co.uk/2/hi/asia-pacific/8439198.stm.
86 "56 Filipino Seafarers still in Somali Pirates' Custody", *Manila Times*, 20 December 2009, www.manilatimes.net.
87 "Somali Pirates Free Ship, 20 Pinoys", *ABS-CBN News.com*, 28 February 2011, www.abs-cbnnews.com.
88 Senate of the Philippines, SRN-1525, Directing the Proper Senate Committee to Conduct an Inquiry, in aid of Legislation, on the Alleged Lack of Protection and Safety Measures for Filipino Sailors, introduced by Senator Miriam Defensor-Santiago, 15 December 2009.
89 "Somali officials discuss measures vs piracy with RP coast guard", *GMA News*, 25 December 2009, www.gmanews.tv.
90 Department of Transportation and Communications, Philippine Coast Guard, *Summary of Marine Accident 1986–2008*, May 2009.
91 Ibid.
92 House of Representatives, Press Release: House to Probe Recent Maritime Accidents, 6 January 2010, www.congress.gov.ph.
93 Republic of the Philippines and Republic of Indonesia, Joint Implementation of the Border Patrol Agreement and Border Crossing Agreement between the Government of the Republic of the Philippines and Government of the Republic of Indonesia signed in Jakarta, Indonesia on 11 March 1975, Manila, 1 July 1975; Philippines and Malaysia: Memorandum of Understanding on Defence Cooperation between the Government of the Philippines and the Government of Malaysia, done in Quezon City, Philippines on 26 September 1994; Memorandum of Understanding on the Establishment of a Joint Commission for Bilateral Cooperation between the Government of the Philippines and the Government of Malaysia, done in Kuala Lumpur, Malaysia on 22 July 1993; Second Protocol (1994) to the 1976 Agreement on Anti-smuggling Cooperation between the Government of the Philippines and the Government of Malaysia, done in Kuala Lumpur, Malaysia on 29 March 1995.
94 Larry Niksch, "Abu Sayyaf: Target of Philippine–U.S. Anti-Terrorism Cooperation", *CRS Report for Congress*, 25 January 2002, www.fas.org/irp/crs/RL31265.pdf.
95 Australian, Department of Foreign Affairs and Trade, "Republic of the Philippines Country Brief", www.dfat.gov.au/geo/philippines/philippines_brief.html.
96 Economy Report on Maritime Security Philippines, see note 56.
97 Philippines–Australia the Status of Visiting Forces Agreement (SOVFA), signed in Canberra, Australia, May 2007. This agreement is yet to be ratified by the Philippines.
98 UNODC, thirty-second Meeting of Heads of National Drug Law Enforcement Agencies, Asia and the Pacific, Bangkok, Thailand, 10–13 February 2009, item 4 of the Provisional Agenda, Implementation of the Recommendations Adopted by the Thirtieth Meeting of Heads of National Drug Law Enforcement Agencies, Asia and the Pacific, *UNODC/HONLAP/2009/32/3*, 26 January 2009, paras. 12, 24.
99 Capt. Jaime S. Bernardino PN (GSC), *Maritime Security Concerns of the BIMP-EAGA Maritime Trade: An Assessment*, unpublished thesis, Masters in National Security Administration, National Defense College of the Philippines, August 2008, p. 83.
100 See Fourteenth Congress of the Philippines, SRN-1519, Resolution Urging the Committees on Health and Demography and Public Order and Illegal Drugs to Review, in Aid of Legislation, the Existing Statutes and Policies Addressing Organ Donation and Trafficking in Order to Halt this Criminal Activity as well as to Educate the Filipinos on the Health Implications of Organ Transplantation, introduced by Senator Manny Villar, 9 December 2008.

8 Singapore's maritime interests

Joshua H. Ho

Introduction – the emergence of Singapore as an entrepot port in the modern era

Stamford Raffles was a clerk of the English East India Company with a keen interest in Malay studies and natural history. He engineered the succession to the Johor Sultanate and established himself in Singapore in order to establish a trading base in Singapore conceived on geopolitical and commercial principles. He managed to conclude an agreement with the sultan on the 6 February 1819, which entitled the East India Company to use a defined area as a port and settlement.

Singapore possessed an advantageous location whose potential was vastly enhanced by the application of free trade principles and advances in technology. Raffles thought of free trade for Singapore as a way to beat the competition from ports under indigenous rulers, such as Riau, or under the Dutch rule, notably Batavia (Jakarta), where traders were encumbered by all sorts of taxes and restrictions. Free trade as Raffles decreed it was "virtually unknown" in the region, and he scored handsomely by being the first mover.[1] Yet his move was also dictated by necessity as, apart from its geographical position, Singapore had few natural resources and no products to tempt the trader. Singapore's trade, as the British merchants coming long after Raffles realized, "was an artificial creation."[2]

This artificial creation was entrepot trade, meaning that the goods transacted were not produced in the island but were brought in from outside. The British merchants believed that free trade was essential to keep the Singapore entrepot going. These merchant pioneers were not only opposed to the imposition of duties on imports and exports, they were also against the fees normally charged at any port, namely tonnage and port dues, pilotage, wharfage and anchorage duties, and port clearance fees.[3] Revenue was raised through excise duties, licenses and property taxes.

Singapore's strategic location

The geographical location of Singapore became more important with the opening of the Suez Canal in 1869. Steamships began to call more often and used it as a coal-bunkering center. Then, in 1871, telegraphic communications linked

Europe, Australia and Hong Kong. Tin from Malaya and the Sumatran islands of Banka and Billiton made Singapore a world market for this mineral. Trade in rubber also produced more links, in particular with the Chinese and between the traders in Singapore and the growers in remote rivers and jungles in Netherlands India.[4] Singapore also hosted the oil industry, and oil companies chose Singapore because it was well connected by shipping routes to the world and the region, and it was where they could store, blend, distribute and ship the oil, all at one convenient center.[5] Singapore gained from the sheer volume of oil handled, the repair of oil tankers and the bunkering of oil-fired ships. In addition to being a staple port, Singapore was also a center for the import and distribution of manufactures, in particular textiles, where the British and European agency houses were supreme but where the Japanese also competed successfully based on price.

In 1960, Singapore began to refine oil sent from the Middle East, but Indonesia and Malaysia also sent their crude to be processed. Eventually Indonesia started to refine its own oil in 1985[6] and Malaysia followed suit with a refinery in Malacca.[7] These developments did not affect Singapore too much, as Middle East and Chinese crude were also the basis of Singapore's oil refinery business. What mattered was that Singapore had the best refineries in the region, as the multinational oil companies located in Singapore had seen to this, making it the Houston of Asia. Hence, in summary, three things, namely location, free trade and a primary producing hinterland covering British Malaya (the Malay states) and, "even more, Netherlands India" had come together to make Singapore so important.[8] This importance continues today.

Singapore as a maritime hub

Today, the port of Singapore is a central node that sits astride the Straits of Malacca and Singapore, which link the Indian Ocean and the South China Sea, and which provide the main artery through which a huge proportion of global trade and energy flow. Tankers and bulk carriers move vast quantities of oil, coal, iron ore and minerals to the manufacturing centers of Southeast and Northeast Asia, whilst millions of containers flow in the opposite direction to feed consumer markets all over the world. Singapore has today become the world's top container port and is a major transshipment port, with 80 percent of its container cargo transshipped; the world's top bunkering port; the world's third largest oil refining center; a thriving international center for shipbuilding, ship repairs and conversions; and a regional cruise center.[9] Because of the importance of the sea to Singapore's material well-being, it has adopted a comprehensive approach to maritime security and developed an integrated response to promote Singapore's maritime interests in the Malacca and Singapore Straits.

Adopting a comprehensive approach to maritime security

A comprehensive approach to maritime security addresses not only traditional inter-state conflict and tackles the challenge of maritime terrorism but also includes the prevention of illicit smuggling of weapons of mass destruction and items needed to develop nuclear weapons by sea. In the past, it was normal in the shipping sector to make a distinction between safety and security, but now there is also recognition of the close relationship between maritime safety and maritime security. Even the International Maritime Organization (IMO) has changed its motto from "safer ships, cleaner oceans" to "safe, secure and efficient shipping on clean oceans" to reflect the close relationship between safety and security.[10] Maritime safety is part of a comprehensive concept of security that includes maritime safety services, marine aids to navigation and services, and hydrographic surveying. However, the links do not stop at safety and security, as the new IMO motto also emphasizes protection of the marine environment as an important goal. Hence, a comprehensive approach to maritime security has emerged that includes issues relating to maritime safety, security and environmental protection, addressed from the perspective of both the users of the seas, comprising the ships, their owners and operators, and service providers, comprising port and terminal operators, maritime authorities, navies and coast guards.

Singapore's maritime interest

Singapore's maritime interest can be defined as minimizing disruption to shipping and port activities and ensuring open, safe and secure access to sea-lanes through active policy prescription in the areas of maritime safety, security, environmental protection and international law. As disruptions can come in the form of armed conflict, piracy and armed robbery, maritime terrorism, restrictions to transit passage, accidents and marine pollution, Singapore has adopted various measures to enhance the safety, security and environmental protection of the Straits of Malacca and Singapore.

Measures to enhance maritime safety

Providing adequate aids to navigation

Ensuring the navigational safety of the 70,000 ships annually that ply the Singapore Straits is an important task.[11] With the approval of the IMO and the cooperation of Malaysia and Indonesia, a routing system and traffic separation scheme (TSS) was implemented in the Malacca and Singapore Straits to enhance the safety of navigation. A mandatory ship reporting system has been implemented in the straits with effect from 1 December 1998. This system, known as STRAITREP, requires ships proceeding through the Singapore Straits to report to the Vessel Traffic Services (VTS), in this case the Maritime and Port Authority (MPA), on designated communications channels so that the authority can track its movements for safety purposes. A Vessel Traffic Information System (VTIS), comprising a chain of radar stations along the Singapore coast, has also been developed to monitor shipping traffic, and its operators, located at the Port Operations Control Center (POCC), can directly contact vessels to advise if there is an impending close-quarter situation developing that might result in collision. However, collision avoidance directions are only advisory in nature and the ship's captain retains final responsibility for his actions.

Other measures to improve safe navigation in the Singapore Straits include the launching of Electronic Navigation Charts (ENC) and the implementation of the Differential Global Positioning System (DGPS), which improve the accuracy of position information to the meter range. With the increased usage of the Electronic Chart Display and Information System (ECDIS), shipmasters can know their ship's positions accurately at a glance and be warned of any potential close-quarter situation. Singapore has also implemented IMO-mandated Automatic Identification System (AIS) for ships above 300 gross tonnes, which has improved safety of navigation tremendously as ships' identities, positions, courses and speed information are now displayed on the radar of the VTS stations and nearby ships. With all these measures in place, the MPA's safety record continues to stand at a very low 0.03 incidents per 1,000 vessel movements.[12]

Providing search and rescue services

Besides preventive measures to ensure the safety of navigation, Singapore has also implemented search and rescue arrangements to facilitate the recovery of personnel should an accident happen in its Search and Rescue Region (SRR).[13] Singapore has promulgated the Singapore Plan for Search and Rescue (SAR) Services, and the Maritime Rescue Coordination Center (MRCC) in Singapore coordinates the search and rescue effort by utilizing the assets of the Singapore Armed Forces (SAF) and the Police Coast Guard (PCG). The assets include helicopters from the Republic of Singapore Air Force (RSAF), maritime patrol aircraft and patrol vessels (PV) from the Republic of Singapore Navy (RSN), as well as patrol craft from the PCG. Singapore has also implemented a bilateral search and rescue arrangement with Indonesia and has conducted Search and Rescue Exercise (SAREX) Indopura with Indonesia on a regular basis. Singapore has also ratified the 1979 Convention on Maritime Search and Rescue (SAR Convention), which encourages cooperation between Parties and search and rescue organizations with regard to search and rescue operations at sea.

Measures to enhance maritime security

Protection of critical maritime infrastructure

Being the world's top container port, Singapore is a major node that sits astride the Malacca Straits and is a top bunkering port and a major oil-refining center. To ensure that Singapore's connection to the global maritime system continues uninterrupted and free of disruption, there is a need to physically defend the extensive maritime infrastructure that has been developed.[14] Protection is provided by the PCG and the RSN, with the army in support, against both state and non-state threats. The PCG and the RSN conduct continuous and extensive daily patrols as deterrents. The army also conducts land patrols at Singapore's key petrochemical complex on Jurong Island. As maritime terrorism has become a threat since 9/11, actions have been taken to mitigate vulnerabilities to three scenarios: (1) the turning of hijacked container ships into Trojan horses for dirty bombs, (2) the turning of hijacked ammonium nitrate carriers, LPG (liquefied petroleum gas) and LNG (liquefied natural gas) carriers by turning them into floating bombs, and (3) the use of bomb-laden small boats to attack shipping.

For example, the Accompanying Sea Security Teams (ASSeT) board selected merchant ships that are deemed more vulnerable to hijacks when they enter and leave the port of Singapore. Selected merchant ships are also escorted by PVs along the Straits of Singapore. To reduce the threat posed by small boats, dedicated ferry routes have been mandated that avoid anchorages and sensitive installations, like naval bases, and the VTIS radars continuously monitor the movements of these vessels within the port limits. The identities of small craft are also facilitated through the mandatory installation of the Harbor Craft Transponder System (HARTS), AIS, for the 3,000 small harbor and pleasure craft that are licensed to operate in Singapore. The requirement to fit the HARTS is over and above the requirements of the Safety of Life at Sea (SOLAS) Code, which only mandates that ships above 300 gross tonnes should fit an AIS transponder for identification purposes. In addition, the port of Singapore has installed scanning machines to detect illicit material transported in containers, implemented the International Ship and Port Facility Security Code (ISPS), and participated in the Container Security Initiative (CSI) and Radiation Detection Initiative. Singapore has also ratified major counter-terrorism conventions, such as the 1988 Convention for the Suppression of Unlawful Acts against the Safety of Maritime Navigation (SUA Convention).

Defending access to sea lanes

Besides the protection of critical maritime infrastructure, there is also a need to defend the sea-lanes that lead to the port.[15] As a result, extensive seabed surveillance has been conducted in the waters around Singapore to ensure that any anomalous mine-like objects can be detected quickly. Bilateral mine clearance exercises and coordinated patrols have also been conducted with both the Royal Malaysian Navy (RMN) and the Indonesian Navy (TNI-AL). In addition, the RSN, with the RSAF, has the capability to protect and ensure access to its sea-lanes up to a considerable range from Singapore. This is achieved through extensive surveillance provided by maritime patrol and airborne early warning aircraft, coupled with a lethal ship strike capability provided by stealth frigates and submarines, and supported by advanced strike aircraft with air-to-air refueling capability.

Singapore also jealously guards its continued access to the sea-lanes and stoutly defends the transit passage regime in straits used for international navigation enshrined in the United Nations Convention on the Law of the Sea (UNCLOS). Singapore opposes any action taken by coastal states to impose regimes over straits used for international navigation that has the effect of hampering the right of transit passage. It views such actions as excessive coastal state interference in an area where the coastal state does not have jurisdiction under UNCLOS and is the reason why it has opposed Australia's pilotage system in the Torres Strait.[16]

Delimiting maritime boundaries

However, ensuring physical security through law enforcement action by the national security agencies is only one aspect of maritime security. The other aspect is to ensure that law enforcement can be exercised within areas where the legal jurisdiction is clear. As a result, Singapore has sought to delimit its maritime boundaries with its neighbors, as it realizes that without a clear delineation of jurisdictional responsibilities, malevolent individuals and organizations can exploit the legal gray zones to perpetrate their criminal activities. Singapore opts to delimit its maritime boundaries with its neighbors through bilateral and, if necessary, trilateral negotiations and has had success in delimiting most of the maritime boundaries with both Malaysia and Indonesia. What remains to be delimited in the Singapore Straits are areas where the maritime boundaries of the three countries of Singapore, Indonesia and Malaysia meet, which require trilateral negotiations and currently forms the next stage of the negotiation process. Where an issue cannot be negotiated bilaterally, Singapore has opted to commit such territorial differences to third party dispute settlement, an example of which was the referral of the dispute between Singapore and Malaysia over the ownership of Pedra Branca, Middle Rocks and South Ledge to the International Court of Justice (ICJ) for binding dispute settlement after almost 30 years of bilateral exchange of letters, documents and negotiations.[17]

Measures to enhance marine environmental protection

Besides the threat of physical attacks, the port of Singapore and its surrounding waters are extremely vulnerable to oil pollution due to the high number of shipping activities within its port limits. Singapore has adopted a comprehensive approach to deal with marine pollution that begins with prevention, implementation of strict regulations, and putting in place emergency plans for quick and effective clean-up operations when cases of pollution occur. There is also a mechanism to ensure that adequate compensation for pollution clean-up costs is recoverable from the perpetrators. The measures can be classified into legislative and contingency plans to deal with a pollution situation.

Implementation of legislative measures

Singapore has put in place appropriate legislation to take polluters to task, as well as to prepare and respond to oil pollution incidents and obtain compensation.[18] The Prevention of Pollution of Sea Act was enacted in 1971 and updated in 1990 when Singapore acceded to the MARPOL 73/78 Convention, which deals with the prevention of pollution of the sea by oil, chemicals, garbage, and sewage from ships. One significant feature of the act is that it provides for a penalty of up to S$1 million and/or a maximum prison term of two years for a person found guilty of polluting Singapore's waters. The act was amended again in 1999 when Singapore acceded to the 1990 International Convention on Oil Pollution Preparedness, Response and Cooperation (OPRC). Singapore has also acceded to Annexes I, II, III, V, and VI of the MARPOL 73/78, to the OPRC-HNS 2000, and to international conventions established for oil pollution claims, such as the 1992 Protocol to the International Convention on Civil Liability for Oil Pollution Damage (CLC 92), the 1992 Protocol to the 1971 International Convention on the Establishment of an International Fund for the Compensation for Oil Pollution Damage (Fund 92), and the International Convention on Limitation of Liability for Maritime Claims, 1976 (LLMC), all of which ensure that Singapore would have access to sufficient compensation for the cost of the pollution clean-up operations and possible damages and losses from marine incidents.

Developing contingency plans

Despite the best preventive and legislative measures in place, pollution incidents can still occur and robust contingency arrangements are required. The private sector in Singapore has taken several measures that facilitate oil spill response. The first measure is the establishment of the East Asia Response Private Limited (EARL). The shareholders of EARL include BP Singapore, Caltex, Esso, Eastern, Mobil, Shell and BHP Billiton. EARL has its regional center in the western part of Singapore (Jurong), where it stores and maintains a wide range of oil spill response equipment. EARL has also entered into a global alliance with Oil Spill Response Limited (OSRL) of Southampton, United Kingdom. The alliance enables both companies to pool their resources and expertise and make the combined resources available to all of their customers when required.[19]

The second measure is an oil spill response program undertaken by the Petroleum Association of Japan (PAJ) since 1993. PAJ's program consists of stockpiling and lending oil spill response equipment free of charge to government agencies or parties upon their request. This stockpile is kept by the Singapore Oil Spill Response Center (SOSRC).[20]

The third measure is the setting up of the SOSRC by SembCorp Logistics Limited in 1994.[21] The SOSRC, together with its parent company, is able to deal with almost any type of marine accident or emergency, and many companies have signed contracts with SOSRC to ensure a rapid response. Not only does SOSRC maintain its own stockpile of oil pollution response equipment, it is also involved in the maintenance of equipment belonging to the PAJ. Singapore is well prepared to tackle oil pollution in and around its waters through careful planning and regular exercises directed by the MPA and involving other government agencies, local oil companies and pollution response companies.

The MPA is also capable of coordinating various national agencies, foreign agencies and companies in response to a clean-up effort. For example, the MPA-led clean-up effort arising from the collision of the *Orapin Global* and the *Evoikos* in October 1997 involved a total of 16 ministries/agencies, oil terminals, salvage companies, oil spill response companies and one foreign agency, with the involvement of some 80 craft and 650 personnel. Fortunately for Singapore, the impact of the spill was well contained, traffic in the Singapore Straits was not disrupted and the straits remained open. Singapore's container terminals, oil and petrochemical complexes and power stations were also able to continue their operations without disruption. Damage to sensitive areas and the mainland was prevented and adverse ecological effects were limited to a few small, uninhabited offshore islands that were immediately hit in the initial aftermath of the spill due to their close proximity to the location of the incident.[22]

Regional cooperative regimes

The comprehensive definition of maritime security adopted by Singapore puts a premium on inter-agency coordination at both the national and the regional levels. A lack of coordination will be a barrier to effective maritime security in the region. Already we are witnessing trends in the region where the need for an integrated approach has resulted in the setting up of new organizations or the implementation of new coordinating mechanisms. For example, in Singapore this comprehensive approach and integrated response is termed the "whole of government" approach and Singapore has a high-level committee that coordinates the activities of the three agencies in Singapore with responsibilities for maritime security, namely the Maritime and Port Authority (MPA), the PCG and the Maritime Security Task Force (MSTF) of the RSN.[23] The committee looks at ways to enhance maritime security and to promote Singapore's broader maritime interests even as the individual agencies continue to exercise responsibility within each of their functional areas. Similarly, Malaysia has established the Malaysian Maritime Enforcement Agency (MMEA) and Indonesia the BAKORKAMLA, or the Indonesian Maritime Security Coordinating Board (IMSCB), which will form the basis of an Indonesian Sea and Coast Guard, in response to similar concerns.[24]

In terms of inter-agency coordination at the regional level, three cooperative regimes stand out: the Cooperative Mechanism (CM), the Malacca Straits Patrols (MSP) and the Regional Cooperation Agreement to Combat Piracy and Armed Robbery against Ships in Asia (ReCAAP) Information Sharing Center.

The Cooperative Mechanism (CM)

In recognition that addressing the disruption to shipping in the Malacca and Singapore Straits is an important issue, the IMO convened a series of three meetings under its Protection of Vital Shipping Lanes Initiative in the capitals of the littoral states from 2005 to 2007. The outcome of the three meetings was the development of a framework for cooperation between the users of the straits and the littoral states. The framework for cooperation, known as the CM, was a historic breakthrough, as Article 43 of the 1982 UNCLOS was implemented for the first time in any part of the world. Even Ambassador Tommy Koh, the president of the Third United Nations Conference on the Law of the Sea, has said that it was a historic achievement.[25]

The Cooperative Mechanism for the Enhancement of Safety, Security and Environmental Protection of the Straits of Malacca and Singapore consists of three components. The first is the Forum for Cooperation, comprising senior officials and technical experts from the maritime authorities of Indonesia, Malaysia and Singapore. This forum forms the main avenue for interested user states and other parties to meet and cooperate with the littoral states.[26]

The second component is the Project Coordination Committee. This committee was primarily formed to oversee a package of projects proposed by the littoral states. To ensure the progress of these projects, funding and participation from the user states and interested parties have been sought. Projects include the removal of wrecks, and cooperation and capacity building on Hazardous and Noxious Substance (HNS) preparedness and response. One of the demonstration projects for equipping small vessels with AIS transponders is also being considered. Other projects include the replacement and maintenance of aids to navigation, the setting up of tide, current and wind measurement systems, and the replacement of navigational aids damaged by the 2004 tsunami. The third component is the Aids to Navigation Fund, in which interested stakeholders can volunteer to finance the maintenance of the critical aids to navigation.[27]

Since its inception, many countries and industry-related organizations have participated and contributed to the CM and this bears testimony to the successful implementation of UNCLOS Article 43. Countries that have participated include Australia, China, Germany, Greece, India, Japan, Saudi Arabia, South Korea, the United Arab Emirates and the United States. Industry-led organizations that have participated include the IMO, the Nippon Foundation, the International Chamber of Shipping (ICS), INTERTANKO and the International Tanker Owners Pollution Federation Limited (ITOPF).[28]

The CM is managed by the Tripartite Technical Experts Group (TTEG), comprising maritime officials of the three littoral countries of Indonesia, Malaysia and Singapore. Since 1975, these three littoral countries have worked together at the technical level to put in place measures to enhance the safety of navigation in the Malacca and Singapore Straits. Some of these measures include the implementation of a TSS and a mandatory ship reporting system called STRAITREP, which have both greatly contributed to enhancing the safety of navigation through the straits. Both these measures were implemented with the approval of the IMO.

However, the CM is only one aspect of the cooperative efforts undertaken to keep the straits open, safe and secure. Whilst the CM has mainly addressed the safety and environmental protection aspects and has involved both users and the littoral states, the security aspect has largely been undertaken only by the navies of the littoral states and in a low-key manner.

The Malacca Straits Patrols (MSP)

Prior to 2004, efforts to secure the straits had largely been undertaken at national and bilateral levels. However, the situation changed in 2004. As a result of the perceived threat of piracy and maritime terrorism to shipping in the straits, there was increasing pressure placed by extra-regional countries, particularly the United States, for something to be done. The Lloyd's Joint War Committee also added the Malacca Strait to its list of war-risk areas in mid-2005. In response, Operation *MALSINDO* was launched in July 2004 to demonstrate the resolve of the littorals to secure the straits on their own, with navies patrolling within their respective territorial waters and exclusive economic zones round the clock. Operation *MALSINDO* has since been renamed the Malacca Straits Patrols (MSP). The MSP also encompasses air patrols, as well as security arrangements between the three littoral states, including the Intelligence Exchange Group, the Joint Coordination Committee and the Standard Operating Procedures, as well as the MSP Information System. In September 2008, Thailand also became a member of the MSP and commenced its sea patrols in October 2008 and air patrols in January 2009.[29]

Joint Coordinating Committee (JCC)

The JCC, co-chaired by the respective Head of Naval Operations, is the decision-making body in the MSP. It provides a channel of communications between top officials from the four participating countries in intelligence exchange and coordination for all operational security measures relating to the Straits of Malacca and Singapore.[30] Under the JCC is the Intelligence Exchange Group (IEG), formed in 2006, which comprises the naval intelligence agencies of the participating countries. The IEG meets regularly to exchange information and each incident in the MSP area of operation is studied carefully by the various intelligence agencies. Observations are later shared and discussed during the meetings for further recommendation related to the conduct of future sea and air patrols.[31]

Malacca Straits Patrol Information System (MSP-IS)

The four littoral countries have also developed the Malacca Straits Patrol Information System (or MSP-IS) to aid them in the conduct of patrols.[32] The MSP-IS is a data sharing system that allows users to share information about shipping and vessels of interest, in order to boost security in the Straits of Malacca and Singapore. The system includes a reference database on more than 150,000 vessels and is able to flag up anomalies, such as ships with fake identities. It also allows information of an incident to be disseminated quickly to agencies in the four littoral states so that a coordinated response can be mounted.[33]

In March 2008, the RSN conducted the inaugural information-sharing exercise using the MSP-IS at the Information Fusion Center (IFC), then located at the Tuas Naval Base (TNB). The exercise saw participation from the SAF, the Malaysian Armed Forces (MAF), the Armed Forces of Indonesia (TNI) and the Royal Thai Armed Forces (RTARF). During the exercise, participants were given a short training workshop on the enhanced MSP-IS system before a live information-sharing exercise was conducted. Following feedback from the four countries, the MSP-IS has since been enhanced to include the Open and Analyzed Shipping Information System (OASIS), the Sense-Making, Analysis and Research Tool (SMART) and chat functions to facilitate better information sharing.[34]

ReCAAP Information Sharing Center (ISC)

The third cooperative regime in the Malacca and Singapore Straits is the Regional Cooperation Agreement on Combating Piracy and Armed Robbery against Ships in Asia (or ReCAAP). In November 1999, former Japanese Prime Minister Keizo Obuchi first mooted the concept of a regional cooperation agreement to combat piracy and armed robbery at the Association of Southeast Asian Nations (ASEAN)+1 Summit Meeting held in Manila.[35] The concept was proposed at a time when there was concern over the numerous incidents of piracy and armed robbery against ships in Southeast Asia and the Malacca Straits in particular. After three years of negotiations, 16 member countries – the ten ASEAN countries, the South Asian trio of Bangladesh, India and Sri Lanka, and the Northeast Asia trio of China, Japan and South Korea – finalized the scope and content of the ReCAAP agreement on 11 November 2004.[36] The agreement called for the setting up of an ISC in Singapore and required ten ratifications from the member countries before it could come into force. On the 4 September 2006, the agreement came into force, with 14 ratifications from member countries or contracting parties having been obtained. To date, there are three additional contracting parties to the agreement: Norway, the Netherlands and Denmark.[37] Subsequent to the agreement coming into force, the ISC was launched on 29 November 2006 in Singapore.

The ReCAAP ISC is the first multilateral government-to-government anti-piracy and armed robbery effort in the region and has the status of an international organization (IO), with locally recruited staff and overseas secondees from the member countries. At the moment, the ISC has secondees from China, India, Japan, South Korea and the Philippines. The ReCAAP ISC operates under the three pillars of the agreement, namely information sharing, capacity building and cooperative arrangements. Its first and key function is to be a platform for information exchange. Its second function is to collate and analyze statistics on piracy and armed robbery incidents with a view to producing reports that provide an appreciation of the piracy situation in the region. Its third function is to facilitate capacity building and cooperative arrangement efforts among the contracting parties. The operating principles adhered to by the ISC are the respect for sovereignty, effectiveness in terms of adding value to current anti-piracy efforts, and the transparency of ISC operations to all contracting parties.

Besides setting up the ISC and the secretariat in Singapore, there are also other key features of the agreement. For example, the agreement enabled the formation of a governing council (GC) with one representative per contracting party to oversee the operations of the ISC, and the decisions made by the GC are by consensus. The agreement also called for the identification and designation of a focal point per contracting party, which would act as the point of contact for the ISC. ReCAAP ISC is the platform for information exchange, with the focal points being linked via the Information Network System (IFN), a web-based and secure network. Funding for the ISC comes from voluntary contributions from the contracting parties.

Conclusion – creating a stable maritime regime

In conclusion, the Asia-Pacific century is poised to begin, with China, India and Japan leading the way. Fueling the Asia-Pacific engine will be the continued economic growth of China, as well as of India, Japan and the United States. As a by-product of regional economic growth, trade and energy flows into and within the Asia-Pacific will continue to grow, leading to an increasing reliance on the sea as a mode of transport, since the sea continues to be the most economical transport mode. Already, the increasing trend of shipping traffic is apparent from the traffic data reported via STRAITREP, where traffic has increased by 74 percent over the ten-year period from 1999 to 2008.[38] A study completed by the Ministry of Land, Infrastructure and Transport of Japan has also projected that the volume of ships through the Malacca Straits will increase from 94,000 in 2004 to 117,000 in 2010, with a further increase to 141,000 in 2020.[39] This surge in the use of the sea means that it is ever more crucial to safeguard the sea-lanes and critical port infrastructure that lies along them by enhancing their safety, security and environmental protection.

Because countries in the region share significant maritime interests, the creation of a stable maritime regime through bilateral and multilateral cooperation needs to remain high on the regional political agenda. However, in pursuing cooperative initiatives, it is important to keep in mind the three broad principles espoused by Singapore's Deputy Prime Minister and Defense Minister Teo Chee Hean at the March 2005 ARF Confidence Building Measure Conference on Regional Cooperation in Maritime Security and the 2005 Shangri-La Dialogue.[40] The three principles are that littoral states have the primary role in addressing maritime security issues, other stakeholders have important roles to play, and consultation should be pursued and the rule of international law be observed in the implementation of any new initiatives.

Notes

1 Wong Lin Ken, "Commercial Growth before the Second World War," in Ernest C.T. Chew and Edwin Lee (eds), *A History of Singapore* (Singapore: Oxford University Press, 1991), p. 47.
2 C.M. Turnbull, *The Straits Settlements 1826–67: Indian Presidency to Crown Colony* (London: Athlone Press, 1972), p. 190.
3 Ibid., pp. 190–191.
4 W.G. Huff, *The Economic Growth of Singapore: Trade and Development in the Twentieth Century* (Cambridge: Cambridge University Press, 1994), p. 204.
5 Ibid., pp. 236–243.
6 Fereidun Fesharaki, "Singapore as an Oil Centre," in Kernial Singh Sandhu and Paul Wheatley (eds), *Management of Success: The Moulding of Modern Singapore* (Singapore: Institute of Southeast Asian Studies, 1989), pp. 307, 309.
7 Ibid., pp. 307, 311.
8 Huff, *The Economic Growth of Singapore*, p. 273.
9 "The World's Busiest Port," *MPA Corporate Information Kit*, 2009, www.mpa.gov.sg/sites/pdf/infokit2.pdf.
10 Sam Bateman, Catherine Zara Raymond and Joshua H. Ho, "Safety and Security in the Malacca and Singapore Straits: An Agenda for Action," *IDSS Policy Paper*, May 2006, pp. 15–16.
11 "A Safe, Secure and Clean Port," *MPA Corporate Information Kit*, 2009, pp. 2–6, www.mpa.gov.sg/sites/pdf/infokit3.pdf.
12 Ibid, p. 2.
13 Sam Bateman, Joshua H. Ho and Jane Chan, "Good Order at Sea in Southeast Asia," *RSIS Policy Paper*, May 2009, p. 25.
14 National Security Coordination Secretariat, *1826 Days: A Diary of Resolve, Securing Singapore Since 9/11* (Singapore: SNP International Publishing, 2006), pp. 23–28.
15 RSN, *Onwards and Upwards: Celebrating 40 Years of the Navy*, (Singapore: SNP International Publishing Pte. Ltd, 2007), pp. 39–75.
16 Robert Beckman, "Australia's Pilotage System in the Torres Strait: A Threat to Transit Passage?" *IDSS Commentaries 125/2006*, 7 December 2006, www.rsis.edu.sg/publications/Perspective/IDSS1252006.pdf.
17 The ICJ ruled that the sovereignty over Pedra Branca belongs to the Republic of Singapore, whilst sovereignty over Middle Rocks belongs to Malaysia and sovereignty over South Ledge belongs to the state in the territorial waters of which it is located. See S. Jayakumar and Tommy Koh, *Pedra Branca: The Road to the World Court*, (Singapore: NUS Press, 2009).
18 "A Safe, Secure and Clean Port," pp. 9–11.
19 Global Response Network Leaflet, April 2009, www.oilspillresponse.com/pdf/grn/grn_leaflet.pdf.
20 "A Summary of Oil Spill Response Arrangements & Resources Worldwide, Country Profiles: Singapore," *International Tanker Owners Pollution Federation Limited (ITOPF)*, December 2007, www.itopf.com/_assets/country/singapore.pdf.
21 Ibid.
22 "A Safe, Secure and Clean Port," p. 9.
23 National Security Coordination Center, *The Fight Against Terror: Singapore's National Security Strategy* (Singapore: Atlas Associates Pte. Ltd, 2004), p. 50.
24 Joshua H. Ho, "Piracy in the Gulf of Aden: Lessons from the Malacca Strait," *RSIS Commentaries 9/2009*, 22 January 2009, www.rsis.edu.sg/publications/Perspective/RSIS0092009.pdf.
25 Tommy Koh, "A New High in Straits Cooperation," *Singapore Nautilus, 1Q 2008*, www.mpa.gov.sg/sites/pdf/singapore_nautilus_issue2.pdf.

26 See "The Co-Operative Mechanism Between The Littoral States And User States On Safety Of Navigation And Environmental Protection In The Straits Of Malacca And Singapore," IMO, Singapore Meeting On The Straits Of Malacca And Singapore: Enhancing Safety, Security And Environmental Protection, 4–6 September 2007, www.mpa.gov.sg/sites/pdf/spore-mtg-co-op-mechan-070904.pdf.

27 Ibid.

28 Joshua H. Ho, "Enhancing Safety, Security, and Environmental Protection of the Straits of Malacca and Singapore: The Cooperative Mechanism," *Ocean Development and International Law*, 40, 2009.

29 See "Thailand Joins Malacca Straits Patrols" *MINDEF News*, 18 September 2008, www.mindef.gov.sg/imindef/news_and_events/nr/2008/sep/18sep08_nr.html.

30 Donald Urquhart, "Malacca Strait Air and Sea Patrols Brought under One Umbrella," *Business Times* (Singapore), 22 April 2006.

31 See "Factsheet: Milestones of Malacca Straits Patrols," *MINDEF News*, 28 March 2008, www. mindef.gov.sg/imindef/news_and_events/nr/2008/mar/28mar08_nr/28mar08_fs.html.

32 See "Inaugural Malacca Strait Patrols Information Sharing Exercise," in *MINDEF News*, 28 March 2008, www.mindef.gov.sg/imindef/news_and_events/nr/2008/mar/28mar08_nr.html.

33 See "Factsheet: Malacca Straits Patrols Information System" *MINDEF News*, 28 March 2008, www.mindef.gov.sg/imindef/news_and_events/nr/2008/mar/28mar08_nr/28mar08_fs2.html.

34 "Inaugural Malacca Strait Patrols exercise held at Tuas Naval Base," *Channel News Asia*, 28 March 2008, www.dsta.gov.sg/index.php?option=com_content&task=blogcategory&id=0&Itemid=809&limit=9&limitstart=333.

35 Press Release of the Chairman on the ASEAN+1 Summit Meetings between the Heads of State/Government of ASEAN and China, Japan and the Republic of Korea, Manila, 28 November 1999, www.mofa.go.jp/region/asia-paci/asean/pmv9911/release_c.html.

36 IMO MSC 83/19/2, Piracy and armed robbery against ships: Regional Co-operation Agreement on Combating Piracy and Armed Robbery against Ships in Asia, 27 July 2007.

37 "ReCAAP Information Sharing Centre Annual Report: 2010 January to December" (Singapore: ReCAAP, 2011), p. 54.

38 Data obtained from STRAITREP, a mandatory ship reporting system proposed by the littoral states of Indonesia, Malaysia and Singapore, and adopted by the IMO on 1 December 1998. Ships of 300 gross tonnes and above and not less than 50 meters in length, vessels carrying hazardous cargo, passenger vessels and others entering a defined operational area are required to report to the VTS authorities through VHF radio channels.

39 Takashi Ichioka, "Traffic Patterns, Safety, and Security in the Straits of Malacca", in Hongyi Lai (ed.), *Asian Energy Security: The Maritime Dimension*, (New York: Palgrave Macmillan, 2009), p. 164.

40 *1826 Days: A Diary of Resolve*, p. 23.

9 Thailand's maritime challenges and priorities

Wilfried A. Herrmann

At the beginning of the second decade of the twenty-first century, the Kingdom of Thailand faces an array of maritime challenges, and needs to set priorities for coping with these. However, from its historical developments and structures, the kingdom is used to following a more continental than maritime focus, despite the geographical setting of two long-separate coastlines; this aspect will be highlighted in the first two parts of this chapter. Following this is an intensive look at the strategic developments of the naval or maritime sector in Thailand after World War II, before an overview of the actual challenges and international cooperation leads to a discussion of Thailand's maritime capabilities and plans.

Geography

The Kingdom of Thailand is located in a strategic position in Southeast Asia. With two long coastlines on the Gulf of Thailand and the Andaman Sea with a combined length of about 3,219 km, the kingdom has access to two major oceans: the Pacific via the South China Sea and the Indian Ocean via the Andaman Sea. Thailand's territorial sea area is about 2,230 sq. km, about 5 percent of its total landmass,[1] while the exclusive economic zone (EEZ) covers about 324,812 sq. km.[2] Furthermore, strategic value is added by its position at the northern mouth of the Malacca Straits, one of the most important sea lines of communication (SLOCs) in the world, with more than 50,000 ships passing through annually. However, as the east and west coasts of the country are separated by Malaysia and Singapore, strategic planners have to take into consideration either the military build-up of two separate fleets or, if the country cannot meet/afford this requirement, a close cooperation of political, diplomatic and military means in order to avoid turning this advantage into a disadvantage.

Thailand shares land borders with four neighbors: Myanmar (approximately 1,800 km), Laos (approximately 1,750 km), Cambodia (approximately 800 km) and Malaysia (approximately 500 km), many of which are not clearly defined and therefore require border negotiations, which are currently either ongoing or partly completed. Thailand also shares direct sea borders with Myanmar, Cambodia and Malaysia, while the introduction of the EEZ regime has increased its sea areas more than threefold. Some maritime experts state in this context that

> Thailand now becomes an EEZ-locked nation surrounded by two layers of other countries. The inner layer comprises Cambodia, Vietnam, Malaysia, Indonesia, India's Nicobar Island and Myanmar. The outer layer is made up of China, Philippines, India, Sri Lanka and Bangladesh.[3]

However, Joint Development Areas were established with some of these countries (e.g. with Malaysia[4]) in order to avoid tensions and to try to obtain useful gains for the countries involved while other negotiations are still ongoing or creeping along (e.g. with Indonesia on the demarcation of the EEZ).

The fact that the major harbors and the capital of Thailand are located in the Gulf of Thailand about 400 nm away from any major shipping lanes is unfavorable for trade and defense. Consequently, about 70 percent of all sea-borne imported goods to Thailand have to pass through Singapore. However, as its distant neighbors do have extremely good and close relationships with Thailand, this factor does not create any concern for the Thai maritime planners. Nevertheless, one problem is that some of the sea borders – especially with Cambodia and Myanmar – are not completely defined yet, a fact further complicated by the international continental shelf agreement under the 1982 UNCLOS[5] as the sea areas being claimed have expanded and negotiations have been stalled, rescheduled or their discussion topics have been changed. Nevertheless, with Vietnam and Indonesia concords have already been concluded (including the much-needed continental shelf agreements), while –following domestic political problems – the sea border with Cambodia, for example, remains a major issue for the government agencies involved.[6]

From the economic point of view, the sea is considered by some Thai decision-makers as a major contributor to the well-being of the country. Unfortunately, this approach is not shared by the majority of the predominantly continental-thinking Thai population, and most of the elites, officials, business community and interest groups also lack a distinct maritime sense. For the "maritime" thinkers, the economic gains are generated by the tourism industry, sea-borne trade and offshore oil and gas reserves, which are exploited in close cooperation with multinational companies.[7] Against this backdrop, the overall attitude of the Thai people towards the maritime environment is based on a limited knowledge of sea/maritime-related issues and is therefore rather nebulous. Thai people seldom think in a maritime context and consequently the national strategy of the Kingdom of Thailand is not an inherently maritime strategy, but is instead continental in its essence. Even the introduction of the United Nation Convention Law of the Sea (UNCLOS) in 1982, the increased dependence on sea-borne trade, the rapid depletion of resources on land due to population growth and industrialization, and the discovery of natural gas at sea, and the increased incomes from fishing and tourism industries could not motivate the majority of Thai to take maritime affairs more seriously.

However, after almost two decades of intense lobbying by the Royal Thai Navy (RTN), related government agencies and the maritime industrial sector public awareness of the increasing importance of the sea in the twenty-first century is slowly rising. This is an important step forward, as public opinion – especially in times of challenging domestic political situations – determines the new governments (by elections) and thus the outcomes of the national budgeting process, essential for improvements and modernizations of the security sector, in this case the RTN and all maritime-associated government organizations, as well as the maritime private sector. However, since the first formally integrated maritime policy was obtained in 1993, followed by its revision and its full endorsement in 1999, implementation stages always lagged behind the projected needs and plans, as there was a lack of appropriate public, political and – consequently – fiscal support.

Historical background

The Kingdom of Thailand –previously the Kingdom of Siam – despite being continent-orientated, has a long history of sea-borne trading routes to Vietnam, Philippines, China and Japan in the east, while Thai goods have been taken to Malaysia and Indonesia in the south, as well as to India, Sri Lanka and Persia/Iran in the west. The first trading contacts with major European colonial powers started with Portugal in 1516, while Dutch shipbuilders shared their knowledge in building European-designed ships from the beginning of the seventeenth century onwards. At that time, the Siamese Kingdom also employed capable and thus influential foreigners at the royal court who advised its rulers to widen the scope of sea-borne trade and increase the wealth of the kingdom via this international trading tool. However, this "golden age" of sea-borne trade did not last long, as treaties with the Dutch (1664) and the British (1687), as well as domestic rifts within the kingdom, caused setbacks to sea-borne trading, especially after the reign of King Narai the Great (1656–1688). Later, during the eighteenth and nineteenth centuries, Siamese sea-borne trade was conducted largely with China, as many of the European countries were at war. The 81 Siamese ships at that time were locally built wooden sailing ships of 300–1,000 tons capacity. However, as soon as steamship technology arrived, the kingdom failed to obtain the capability to this build new type of ship, with severe consequences for the nation's security and economic interests as dependency on outside countries grew rapidly. The main reason for this development was the lack of political will to support new maritime technical developments and implement them for the benefit of trading and naval fleets.

In contrast to the use of the sea for commercial benefits, which had been well developed in early Siamese history, the use of the sea for military purposes was largely restricted to troop transportation and logistic support for land operations combined with a limited role for "swimming artillery" depending on the range of the canons installed on board ships. These circumstances were mirrored by a substantial lack of maritime thinking and naval strategy combined with a lack of capability of military naval personnel at that time. From the end of the eighteenth century until the close of the nineteenth century, imperial or colonial threats of a maritime nature loomed large and the kingdom adopted a defensive maritime strategy of sea denial. The main aim of this naval strategy was to prevent foreign naval forces from entering the Chao Phraya River and threatening the capital, Bangkok. However, even with this in mind, the main efforts focused on ground-based troops and installations, such as forts built on the riverbanks, while torpedoes, mines, nets and warships were deployed at the mouth of the river. Nevertheless, these strategic maneuvers failed to prevent French warships from fighting their way through in 1893 and subsequently forcing Bangkok to make enormous concessions.

After this devastating experience, the kingdom put more emphasis on maritime modernization programs by acquiring more capable ships. Additionally, the lack of trained personnel was addressed by sending more military naval personnel for education and training to Europe. Nonetheless, the overall limited resources kept the Siamese Navy on a defensive maritime strategy, focusing mainly on the Gulf of Thailand in order to protect the capital. But, in a small step forward, the new naval capabilities allowed some expansion of the overall area covered for sea denial from the mouth of the Chao Phraya River to Sichang Island, and later to Kut Island.[8]

These long-term historical developments are still alive today as

> during the long Thai history the Royal Thai Navy (RTN) has paid attention only to surveillance of the Andaman Sea, concerned mostly with protection of the Thai fishing fleet and dissuading the arrival of refugees from Burma and nearby Bangladesh. In the past two years, thousands of Rohingya refugees have successfully sneaked into Thailand's eastern coastal provinces through extensive human trafficking operators. Since 2005, the conflict in southern Thailand has for the first time raised the possibility of maritime support for insurgent groups.[9]

These quotes from *The Nation* newspaper in 2008 highlight the fact that historical experiences and points of view remain strong in some RTN planning circles. However, more recent strategic developments are increasingly taken into consideration for naval analysis and planning, indicating that the RTN leadership is capable of adapting, adopting new ideas and improving the naval situation and strategic planning.

Strategic developments

During the Second World War, only short maritime skirmishes occurred, which failed to cause major changes to the kingdom's maritime strategy. As soon as World War II ended, the Kingdom of Thailand turned towards and joined forces with the West, to contain the communist expansion in Asia, with the headquarters of the South East Asian Treaty Organization (SEATO) being located in Bangkok. During this time, the major supporter of hardware and training was the United States, which also supported Thai economic development after the war. With improved assets, better-trained personnel and a new strategic environment, the maritime strategy of the RTN shifted from its long-term sea denial strategy against foreign (colonial) navies towards coastal interdictions of communist infiltrations, as a close maritime battlefield support for the land-based armed forces. Substantial training support and funding were provided from the United States, as Thailand was considered a "front line state" facing communism.

However, after the American retreat from Vietnam, the RTN was left alone to cope with the communist infiltrations and expansions, which led the naval military planners to consider the development and transformation of the navy from a purely "close" coastal force into a modern navy equipped with missile boats for fighting a conventional war in wider coastal waters. During this time – from the aftermath of World War II until the height of the Cold War – the RTN was described by some experts as a "gunboat navy"[10] because its main aim was fighting sea-borne (communist) infiltrations, as well as piracy and armed robbery against ships along the sea borders to Cambodia and inside the Gulf of Thailand. Consequently, modern requirements for (coastal) navies, such as anti-submarine warfare, sea-based anti-aircraft warfare and ship-to-ship missiles, were not the main focus of RTN planners and procurers.

Additionally, Thailand maintained good and close relationships with all neighboring countries and the naval capabilities of most neighboring countries (e.g. Cambodia, Myanmar and Vietnam) did not threaten any major national interests of the kingdom, while the increased capability of the Royal Malaysian Navy did not cause a major concern as naval cooperation between the two countries was growing. Additionally, the effects of the 1997 financial crisis led to major cuts in defense budgets for several years. Thus, the pace of modernization was slow during the Cold War and post-Cold War times, even though the United States needed a strong pillar inside ASEAN to rely on and tried via diplomatic channels to increase the rate of maritime modernization of the Kingdom of Thailand.

However, a major change for Thai national strategic thinkers and planners occurred after the events of 2001. When Thai Prime Minister Thaksin Shinawatra took office in January 2001, the strategic environment for the RTN was comparatively calm, despite some disputes with neighboring countries concerning fishery rights and anti-piracy activities on the high seas in the Gulf of Thailand and the Andaman Sea. In addition, the almost annual need for disaster relief operations – mostly in southern Thailand – could be fulfilled with existing equipment. However, the overall budget, which was still struggling with the consequences of the financial crisis of 1997, was considered insufficient by the RTN as it blocked the way for necessary modernization and upgrade of many ships bought or built on the basis of "fitted for but not with."

But in 2001 the strategic environment changed drastically because the overarching influence from the events of September 11 (2001) required the adjustment of Thai politics to the United States-declared and United States-led "War on Terrorism," which reached Thailand in 2002 after the United States pronounced Southeast Asia a "second front in the war on terrorism."[11] While at the beginning, major issues were mostly concerned with intelligence collection and sharing with the United States, but were also within the ASEAN framework, later, especially inside the ASEAN regional grouping, a change of mind concerning security issues took place. This was highlighted by the signing of the final Bali document of the meeting of the head of states and prime ministers of ASEAN in October 2003. In this document security and the cooperation against terrorism was inked out and thus manifested the will of closer security ties in the ASEAN region. In this context, the ASEAN Navies Interaction (ANI) group, consisting of the chiefs of navies of the ASEAN nations, increased their respective activities in order to improve cooperation in the intelligence and operational sectors. As a result, in a meeting in July 2003 in Malaysia all ASEAN navy chiefs underlined maritime security as essential for the safety and the economic development of their countries, as terrorist attacks on vulnerable maritime targets like (tanker) ships and offshore oil and gas drilling rigs could have also enormous effects on the (maritime) environment and resources, e.g. fish stocks.

In this context, the international SLOCs running through Southeast Asian waters are considered by some experts as the "soft belly" of the adjacent states in their war against terrorism, as land-based potential targets are easier to protect. Consequently, this leaves the high seas an attractive opportunity for terrorists, as shown by the attacks on the USS *Cole* in Yemen (2000) and the French flagged oil tanker *Limburg* in the Arabian Sea (2002). Some experts even have even foreseen a crucial development in the terrorist strategies: the hijacking of a ship –possibly a chemical or oil tanker – in order to carry out a suicide attack on vital harbor facilities.[12] Despite the fact that this scenario has not occurred –some experts are even urging to reduce the risk calculation on this possible event in 2010 to a real level[13] – at least it forced closer cooperation between the ASEAN navies, occasionally including some of the larger neighboring countries, such as the People's Republic of China and India. As a result, the number of bilateral maneuvers and multilateral approaches steadily increased inside ASEAN. Therefore, the RTN and the other regional navies had to rethink their structure and operational readiness concerning compatibility with the other partners. The main steps in this direction were improvements to the intelligence gathering technology and the general communication equipment. In addition, the RTN envisaged and implemented an upgrade of surface ships and reconnaissance planes in order to meet the requirements for the new situation that evolved from the war on terrorism.

On the other hand, there is an increased demand on Thailand for contributing troops to UN-sanctioned or United States-led missions. However, only during the Korean War was a Royal Thai Navy contingent requested and submitted, while later contributions to UN-missions, including East Timor (1999–2002), Darfur (starting in 2010) and Iraq (2003–2004, leading to the status increase for Thailand by the United States as a "Major Non-NATO Ally"; MNNA) consisted only of land forces. Although all of these actions were and are considered vital for the security interests of the Kingdom of Thailand, they also posed a challenge to the planning process for long distance deployments and the necessary logistical support and operational implementation. Key questions included, for example, the need for long-range capability in transportation and evacuation. As a result, these missions added to the existing scale of use – which already includes regional disaster relief– of the only aircraft carrier operated by an ASEAN nation, the HTMS *Chakri Naruebet* of the RTN based in Sattahip in the Gulf of Thailand. However, with the 2003 MNNA status, more American training and funding could be channeled to Thailand, which also benefited the RTN. In fact, today almost 50 ships of the RTN originate from the United States, while the number of United States-trained Thai naval personnel has also significantly increased.

With the end of the Cold War, major land threats diminished or disappeared, so the national focus of Thailand shifted towards the fast-changing maritime environment, with the SLOCs becoming vital focal points for both national security as well as national economic interests. Political, military and, increasingly, economic strategists are pointing at the heavy dependency of the economic well-being of the kingdom on a flourishing export trade, mostly via sea. Consequently, Thailand must consider itself a safeguard for the trade routes and SLOCs within its national reach and in the adjoining high seas, the latter in close cooperation with neighboring countries. This was the main motivation in September 2005 for Thailand to join Indonesia, Malaysia and Singapore in the "Eye in the Sky" (EiS) program with two planes from the Royal Thai Air Force.[14] Three years later, on 18 September 2008, the then Thai Supreme Commander General Boonsrang Niumpradit signed two agreements, the Terms of Reference (TOR) and the Standard Operation Procedures (SOP), for the RTN to join the Malacca Straits patrol agreement to conduct joint sea and air patrols alongside Indonesia, Malaysia and Singapore.[15] The sea operations commenced in October 2008 and the air patrol started in January 2009.[16]

Other vital national aims for Thailand include securing sufficient energy supplies at a reasonable price, protecting fishery rights and products as well as tourism inside the area of the EEZ, implementing strict maritime conservation measures and chasing maritime polluters, in addition to improving the maritime surveillance system and law enforcement in order to combat crimes at sea more effectively. These economic vital points have a growing influence not only on the operational planning of the RTN but also on the procurement process, where priorities for the safety of the SLOCs and coastal areas have been defined anew. For example, the use of maritime patrol aircraft (MPA) to conduct long-range surveillance and to monitor oil spills aims to protect natural resources as well as the tourism industry as vital economic assets of the kingdom. Further, the focus shift of naval planners from coastal defense to offshore operations with a limited "blue-water capability"[17] is indicated by the purchase of larger ships and longer-range aircraft to handle these new responsibilities.

Actual challenges

Based on the previously outlined strategic developments and the resulting political requirements, the actual strategic concepts for the Royal Thai Armed Forces to protect the country from external threats are outlined in a "Total Defense Strategy" document[18], and in the White Paper on "Defense of Thailand 2008," published in late 2008 by the Ministry of Defence[19] in order to clarify operational, tactical and technical needs to the parliament and the public, as well as to regional neighbors. In the latter document, the actual strategy related to outside threats consists of three pillars: cooperative security building, collective national defense and proactive defense. Additionally – as there is some unrest in southern Thailand – tasks related to maintaining the internal security within the legal framework of the Internal Security Act B.E. 2551 (2008) and the protection of the monarchy are laid down in the respective documents.

In this particular context, the RTN and the Royal Thai Marine Corps are tasked with several missions, focusing on defense military operations, law enforcement and civil action, as well as international affairs assistance.[20] This set of assignments includes traditional missions, including defending the territorial integrity of the Kingdom of Thailand, but also so-called Military Operations Other Than War (MOOTW), consisting of disaster relief operations, supporting the development of the Kingdom of Thailand, protecting sea-based resources (e.g. offshore oil and gas), protection against illegal fishing and fighting against illicit drug/arms smuggling, as well as coping with refugees and human trafficking via sea. However, sometimes conducting these tasks is made difficult by the complex situation regarding sea borders with neighboring states, as there are still several hundred miles of territorial/EEZ/continental shelf undefined, especially between Thailand and Myanmar and between Thailand and Cambodia.

In this strategic context, Thailand and the RTN are facing substantial challenges, as Admiral Khamthorn Pumhiran, Commander-in-Chief, Royal Thai Navy pointed out in March 2009:

> The maritime security threat has changed from dealing primarily with international conflicts to the more complex circumstantial environments, which are politically, economically, and socially interrelated. These threats – maritime terrorism, transnational crimes, piracy, drug-trafficking, illegal immigration, human trafficking, illegal labor, and natural and environmental disasters – adversely affect national security. This gradually undermines and eventually destroys the favorable environment for greater prosperity and well-being of a nation and its people.[21]

As Thailand has not face any direct hostility from its neighbors by sea for a long time, the current mission of the RTN to combat piracy and armed robbery against ships in its territorial waters is almost traditional. Until now, this mission has been quite successful given the fact that there is no immediate threat of pirates in the waters of Thailand.[22]

A new perspective, however, opens up with the anticipated threat of maritime/sea-bound terrorism. As a result, Thailand, as part of the global United States-led anti-terrorism campaign, joined the Container Security Initiative (CSI) in 2003.[23] The implementation framework required was later put in place and operates smoothly. However, despite the fact that the Kingdom of Thailand has endorsed in general the principles of the Proliferation Security Initiative (PSI) announced by President George Bush in May 2003 to counter or stop Weapons of Mass Destruction (WMD) proliferation, and the fact that Thailand participated in several workshops, seminars and training, the signing of this document has been delayed. The reasons for this relate to the situation in the three – predominantly Muslim – southern border provinces and the lack of ASEAN support, as only Brunei Darussalam, Cambodia, the Philippines and Singapore are members of this agreement.[24] Another negative point is the perception from some Thai experts that the PSI chooses to bypass UN processes.

Nonetheless, Thailand is an active member of the "Megaports Initiative," in which responsible personnel participate in port and border security programs. The main tool for this initiative is the Export Control and Related Border Security Assistance (EXBS)[25] program, which enables the kingdom to strengthen its control on the export of ammunition, dual-use goods and related technologies. Additionally, Thai military and police personnel participated in United States-supported training programs in Bangkok sponsored through the Antiterrorism Assistance (ATA) program, the Force Protection Detachment (FPD) and the International Law Enforcement Academy (ILEA). Consequently, United States and Thai military personnel cooperated in a training program designed to build counter-terrorism capacity to respond to terrorist acts on land and sea. The culmination of these activities was the Cobra Gold 2008 Joint-Combined Military Training Exercises, in which peacekeeping, humanitarian assistance and disaster relief objectives were for the first time combined for responding to the changing nature of the security environment in Southeast Asia.[26]

Besides anti-terror efforts, Thailand also supports the main endeavors of the International Maritime Organization (IMO), including adaptations of the International Convention for the Safety of Life at Sea (SOLAS) and the Long Range Identification and Tracking (LRIT) System. After a regional workshop in March 2008, Thailand proposed including LRIT matter in a regular agenda to be discussed at the ASEAN Maritime Transport Working Group Meetings, where ASEAN member countries are encouraged to exchange their experiences and practices in preparation for the implementation of LRIT in their respective countries. Today, most Thai vessels are capable of transmitting LRIT information to the National Data Center and are therefore form an integrated part of the LRIT system. Additionally, the expansion of Thailand's international sea-borne trade has resulted in the need for an efficient and effective traffic control system to monitor the increasing vessel traffic at Thailand's major ports. Therefore, in order to cope effectively with this situation and also to better comply with IMO requirements, Thailand has established the Vessel Traffic Control and Maritime Security Centre (VTCMSC) under the Marine Department at Laem Chabang Port. From the technical side, the installation of the Vessel Traffic Management and Information System (VTMIS) project, consisting of surveillance systems and communication systems, has led to a remarkable enhancement of the capabilities of the VTCMSC. The complete system is planned to be fully operational in 2010.[27] With this high level of engagement and its role as model system for increased cooperation between different maritime related agencies, Thailand could secure re-election as a member of the IMO Council for the third times in a row and is currently serving the 2010–2011 term.

Another major domestic step has been the resulting enhancements in inter-agency coordination. As Admiral Khamthorn Pumhiran described,

> the Thailand Maritime Enforcement Coordination Center, with the Royal Thai Navy as the core unit, was established to coordinate the efforts of other maritime governmental units and agencies. This provides consistency and avoids effort redundancy through sharing and exchanging information and persistent intelligence. We are confident that such combined efforts of internal and external cooperation will enhance our capability to address these problems effectively.[28]

With all these steps being taken to improve the necessary legal and operational framework for strengthening the overall maritime strategy, it has become clear that Thailand now regards seriously maritime transnational threats going far beyond piracy or refugees and including non-traditional security, such as maritime terrorism or protecting energy sources and routes, as well as keeping an eye on maritime conservation.

In 2005, related to the field of marine environmental protection, the Global Environment Facility/United Nations Development Program/International Maritime Organization Regional Program on Partnerships in Environment Management for the Seas of East Asia (PEMSEA) introduced the Port Safety, Health and Environment Management System (PSHEMS) to the Port Authority of Thailand (PAT). The PSHEMS initiative aim to promote the regional implementation of international conventions related to port safety, health and the environment through the sustainable development of coastal and marine areas and activities, specifically the safe operations of ports and harbors. As an integrated approach, PSHEMS provides a well-defined structure of policies, procedures, documentation, records and continual assessment for the measurement of performance over time. After the successful implementation, Bangkok Port was awarded a PSHEMS certificate of recognition by PEMSEA in December 2006. Additionally, Thailand supports the implementation of the MARPOL 73/78 Convention; a study on Port Waste Management conducted in three Thai ports (Bangkok Port, Laem Chabang Port and Map Ta Put Port) with technical assistance sponsored by the government of Denmark. The results of this study were transformed into an operational plan for the management of ship-generated waste and should serve as a model of ship waste management for other ports in Thailand and the ASEAN region.[29]

Many of these activities have improved inter-agency communication among the Thai domestic agencies but, as one expert points out, "streamlining of overlapping boundaries and centralization of the enforcement authorities are far from adequate. Creation of a comprehensive coast guard is unlikely to happen soon in

Thailand, given the intensive turf battles among the domestic agencies."[30] A similar point of view is taken by some Thai experts, whose discussions are summarized as, "In the future, Thailand would need to consider a centralized body such as a coast guard agency to undertake a more comprehensive maritime security."[31] External pressure is also present, including from Japan, pointing out that overlapping jurisdiction over maritime security issues increase the vulnerability of maritime security enforcement agents to corruption. Experts argue that the scattering of authority of arrest, seizure, investigation and prosecution across multiple agencies is further complicated by geographical (territorial water, EEZ, the high seas) and functional boundaries (i.e., immigration, customs, fisheries and so on). Therefore, Japanese experts elaborate, criminals often find it easy to pay off one in the chain of such agencies in order to remain free.[32] However, even though the Institute for Advanced Naval Studies in Bangkok is providing more details of this issue, no move towards forming a coast guard is expected in the near future, because the creation of a new governmental body with new budget lines, equipment, personnel and logistics is considered un suitable by many naval/maritime planners and strategists.

International cooperation

The Chief of the RTN, Admiral Khamthorn Pumhiran, continues to emphasize – knowing that these are huge tasks for the existing forces of the RTN and the Royal Thai Marine Corps – that

> Thailand cannot deal with these issues alone, nor can any one country. The crucial factor in solving these problems lies in cooperation among every country in the region.... Given a due regard to the importance of cooperation, the Royal Thai Navy has continually developed and expanded its interaction with many allied countries, both bi- and multilateral. Thailand, for example, has cooperated in the joint maritime patrol and aerial reconnaissance in the Malacca Strait with Indonesia, Malaysia, and Singapore. In addition, our nation has conducted joint maritime patrol with Malaysia, India, and Vietnam.[33]

The latter development is of overarching importance, as Thailand never previously considered itself as part of the littoral states along the straits, even though the country shares maritime territorial waters, EEZ and long coastlines with Malaysia, Indonesia, Burma and India that encompasses the Bay of Bengal. Therefore, at a deeper level, the maritime security cooperation in the Malacca Straits underlines the new security mindset in Thailand's defense strategic thinking towards taking on more international (i.e., regional) responsibility.

Consequently, as one expert openly put it,

> after decades of ambivalence and recalcitrance, Thailand has now embarked on a whole new security scheme – maritime security cooperation – that

would allow the country to provide full surveillance and protection of its territorial waters as well as ensuring the safety of nearby international sea lanes for communications.[34]

In this context, as many events show, Thailand is well aware of the ASEAN framework and the need for cooperation at the regional level. As a result, in the field of piracy and armed robbery against ships, Thailand is an active member of the Regional Cooperation Agreement on Combating Piracy and Armed Robbery against Ships in Asia (ReCAAP) and currently Mr Pornchai Danvivathana, a senior diplomat from the Thai Ministry of Foreign affairs, holds the chairmanship of the governing council 2009–2010 of the Information Sharing Center (ReCAAP-ISC). Furthermore, in the area of disaster relief the Royal Thai Armed Forces contribute substantially with medical and logistic support on a regional and super-regional level, including assets from the RTN in recent years. In this context, Thailand is also using and supporting the ASEAN Regional Forum's (ARF) scheme to assist navies in member countries to work together and build up mutual confidence. As a result of this endeavor, ARF started to motivate joint military exercises for disaster relief and rescue operations in order to improve disaster relief performance, for which some major coordination problems were especially obvious following the 2004 tsunami. In 2009, parallel to these developments, Thailand initiated an ASEAN-wide dialog between Military and Civil Society Organizations (CSO) on disaster relief in order to include a wider spectrum of actors in this field into the disaster preparation, policy recommendation and drafting phases.[35] In order to broaden its maritime and security engagement, Thailand is also a member of the Western Pacific Naval Symposium (WPNS) and the Council for Security Cooperation in the Asia Pacific (CSCAP), to name a few.

Additionally, on the international stage, several countries are trying to establish closer maritime relationships with Thailand and/or ASEAN. While the United States are a long-term maritime ally with a huge impact via "hardware" (ships, material, etc.) and "software" (training and exchange programs), the upcoming sea powers with regional and super-regional "blue-water" ambitions – India and the People's Republic of China – are striving to catch up and establish themselves as reliable, "geographically closer" partners with Thailand and in some cases also with ASEAN. While – up to some years ago – "hardware" formed the main focus of these attempts, recent developments include the People's Republic of China offering scholarships for military personnel and India pressuring for more Thai attendees in their military training programs. At the same time, the naval presence of these two up-and-coming naval (regional) powers in the waters adjacent to Thailand is more visible than ever. Port calls, political initiatives for Malacca Strait protection, arms sales and training course offers are part of the variable strategic maritime approaches by these countries.[36] Thailand benefits from the increased "shop window," although it never forgets that its main partner is the United States and despite smaller differences stands steadfast to the dominant global sea power. This is documented in the annual maneuver COBRA GOLD, although now other countries are invited to participate in and observe this originally bilateral maneuver. Another main exercise "Cooperation Afloat Readiness and Training" (CARAT), funded by the United States Navy, is adding to the strong maritime relationship between the countries involved, including Thailand. Other United States allies like Australia and the United Kingdom are also profiting from the broadened view of Thailand either by being recognized as part of a special relationship documented by intensive training exchange programs or by vessel purchases. In addition, the kingdom takes opportunities from other distant states (e.g., Spain, delivery of aircraft carrier and relevant training; Germany, delivery of MPA as well as training; Brazil, delivery of ERJ 135 MEDEVAC aircraft, and possibly in future Russia, submarines), but also turns to immediate (ASEAN) neighbors for modernizing the RTN (e.g., Singapore, delivery of "Endurance" class landing ship tanks; LSTs). In this framework, the international maritime cooperation of Thailand is dominated by two factors: equidistance to the major powers; and a reasonable price tag combined with the options for barter trade or a compensation policy, so that the investment of Thailand can – at least partly – flow back to the country.

On the global level, Thai vessels are among those affected by the acts of piracy and armed robbery off the coast of Somalia and the Gulf of Aden. For this reason, Thailand supported UNSC Resolutions 1803 (2008), 1816 (2008) and 1838 (2008), which call upon the member states to take an active part in the fight against piracy on the high seas off the coast of Somalia. However, at the beginning Thailand did not deploy any naval vessels or military aircraft in the region as this was not considered to be cost-effective. This led to criticism from several private ship owners. With growing pressure from domestic and international actors, the government led by Prime Minister Abhisit Vejjajiva decided to send two ships on an anti-pirate mission in September 2010. The task group consisting of the 1,500-tonne offshore patrol vessel (OPV) HTMS *Pattani*, the fleet replenishment tanker HTMS *Similan* and two helicopters, and two Special Forces units from the RTN Special Warfare Group were scheduled for an initial 98-day assignment. The vessels sent for this duty were built by the Hudong Shipyard in Shanghai and were equipped with flight decks and hangars to support maritime helicopter operations suitable for anti-piracy missions. However, before the return date of 12 December 2010, Navy Commander Admiral Khamthorn Pumhiran asked for the first extension of this tasks, with the return of a new task force to the Somalia seas in January 2011.[37] In the case of further need and calls by other nations it is expected that the mission will be further prolonged. In addition, considering the international mixture of ships along the coastline of Somalia, Thailand's authorities have developed guidelines for ship owners and operators whose vessels sail through this geographical area, providing suggestions on how to avoid pirate attacks and how to protect affected crews.[38]

All in all, the political and strategic framework has improved maritime issues remarkably; however, there is still room for improvement, including signing international agreements and considering the introduction of comprehensive security approach measures, but the general direction of the maritime strategists and planners is positive. The next section includes a short analysis of the main operational actor in this context, the RTN.

RTN – capacities and plans

Nowadays, being one of the main strategic and the operational maritime actors of Thailand, the RTN has a fleet of over 130 mostly modern vessels, which makes it one of Southeast Asia's larger, and better-equipped, maritime forces. At present, the RTN has about 69,849 personnel, including 1,200 Naval Aviation men and 23,000 Marines.[39] The operational structure consists of the 1st Naval Area Command Royal Thai Fleet in the North Thai Gulf, the 2nd Naval Area Command Royal Thai Fleet in the South Thai Gulf and the 3rd Naval Area Command Royal Thai Fleet in the Andaman Sea, as well as the Royal Thai Marine Corps.[40] Additionally, there is a Naval Air Division and the Mekong River Operating Unit, the latter close to the border with Laos. Besides the aircraft–helicopter carrier HTMS *Chakri Naruebet* – equipped with AV-8A Harriers and Seahawk Helicopters – the RTN operates 12 frigates, nine corvettes, approximately 90 patrol and coastal combatants, 19 mine counter-measure vessels, eight amphibious units and 15 logistics and support vessels.[41]

The HTMS *Chakri Naruebet* – after being fitted with a medium-range radar and flight-deck landing aids – will remain as the core of the RTN and the only Southeast Asian operated carrier for the foreseeable future. It will serve as an offshore base for Thai forces involved in peacekeeping missions or disaster relief in the region (Southeast Asia) or even outside the region (South and East Asia). Additionally, the major warships are potent symbols of national sovereignty, and regularly provide a high-profile Thai presence in regional exercises with foreign navies and thus can add to the diplomatic efforts of Thailand in the regional maritime framework.

However, as regional concerns are mounting over maritime territorial sovereignty, offshore resource protection, resurgent piracy, terrorism, search and rescue and, in the wake of the 2004 tsunami, disaster relief, the RTN switched its acquisition priorities from "blue-water" warships with surface, underwater and air warfare capabilities, to OPVs, suitable for cost-effective patrol, enforcement, response and surveillance duties. Meanwhile, three locally built "Hua Hin" class OPVs commissioned in 2000 and two Chinese designed "Pattani" class 96-meter-long OPVs commissioned in 2005–2006 will be followed in the coming years by a set of British-designed 90-meter-long, helicopter-capable OPVs. A main improvement concerning long distance deployment, evacuation and logistical support was the acquisition of the "Endurance" class LST built by Singapore Technologies Marine (STM) in 2008, which should increase the regional reach of the RTN during traditional missions as well as for MOOTW.

In the naval aviation arm, the situation also improved remarkably by the purchase of two MH 60S Knighthawk multi-role naval helicopters and the ERJ 135 MEDEVAC, as well as communication improvements. However, the operational level of the AV-8S Matador/Harrier gives still cause for concern, but there is no immediate solution visible.[42] On the other hand, major progress will be made by the introduction of nine to 12 unmanned aerial vehicles (UAVs) into the aviation arsenal of the navy. These new assets will significantly enhance the capabilities of reconnaissance and sea surveillance.

Against the regional backdrop of massive spending on subsurface vessels in Asia and the wording in the White Paper on "Defense of Thailand 2008"[43] speculation is high that conventional submarines are still high on the requirement list. But, as many high-level Royal Thai Navy officers point out, this kind of acquisition should be more or less restricted to second-hand boats.[44] Russia, with a "Kilo" class submarine offer, seems to be at the forefront, while German, French, British and even Korean shipbuilders are waiting for the next developments, mainly regarding the domestic political situation of Thailand and the subsequent new budget for the fiscal year 2010–2011, as well as the new ten-year procurement plan of the armed forces for 2011–2020. But even if the budget remains unchanged or is slightly increased, Thai naval procurement officials are flirting more with the idea of leasing submarines as a first step, as this may be the only way by which RTN can bring submarines into service during the foreseeable future. However, the introduction of submarines alone is not the final point, given that new logistic lines, new training and education facilities are needed, as well as underwater medicine improvements, and so on. Time will show the progress of this ambitious program of the RTN and if or when it will materialize. From the operational point of view, given the analysis of the immediate threats, submarine warfare should not, however, be the first priority in the opinion of several naval experts.

With its modernization completed as described, the RTN will have closed the gap with some of the more sophisticated navies in the region and beyond, if the budget situation will allow complete modernization and operational training for crews.

Conclusion and outlook

The analysis of the factors elaborated in this chapter lead to the conclusion that the recent developments initiated by the United States, the IMO and the ASEAN, as well as by Thai maritime strategists, based on existing shared norms and standards of maritime practices, have definitely encouraged Thailand to increase its engagement in multilateral maritime cooperation. As there was also a change of perception of part of the wider Thai public, these developments fit well into the overall maritime interests of Thailand, covering the main topics significant for security and the economy. In addition, Thailand wants to be accepted as a good member of the world community by abiding by the rules of law and international norms in the process of achieving and protecting its national maritime interests and goals. This can be underlined by active participation at regional or super-regional levels.

In Southeast Asia, all countries are members of ASEAN and therefore pose no immediate (maritime) threat. However, some potential maritime conflicts can be contained and resolved by peaceful means, such as the reduction of disputed maritime areas by clearly demarcating sea borders and increased joint development and/or joint patrols. These activities will be mutually beneficial for all parties involved.

In the foreseeable future, the Kingdom of Thailand will be able to protect its trade routes and other interests further out at sea either alone or (most likely) in collaboration with friendly countries, if the budgetary and domestic political situation supports this approach. Hand in hand with these developments will be the further improvement of the maritime political level, the strategic and operational level and public support, including the increased participation of the CSO in suitable operational areas, including disaster relief, maritime environment protection and so on. This is necessary because unless the public and interest groups understand and accept these maritime strategies, one cannot expect them to give sufficient support to any plan for the acquisition of new capabilities needed to meet the upcoming challenges. The then Supreme Commander General Boonsrang Niumpradit pointed out in Defense White Paper 2008 that "[t]he rapid change of the strategic environment, domestically and internationally, has created both challenges and opportunities for the armed forces in developing appropriate roles in national defense."[45] Thailand is taking on these challenges and opportunities, especially in the maritime sector, more seriously than ever.

Notes

1 CIA World Fact Book, www.cia.gov/library/publications/the-world-factbook/geos/th.html.

2 H.J. Buchholz, *Law of the Sea Zones in the Pacific Ocean* (Singapore: Institute of Southeast Asian Studies, 1987), Table 6.

3 See Admiral Chart Navavichit, "Thailand's Maritime Strategy in the Twenty First Century," in Juergen Schwarz, Wilfried A. Herrmann and Hanns-Frank Seller (eds), *Maritime Strategies in Asia* (Bangkok: White Lotus Books, 2002), p. 411.

4 Report of the Ninth Meeting of the Maritime Cooperation Working Group (MCWG) of the Council for Security Cooperation in the Asia-Pacific, Manila, Philippines, 19–22 November 2000. At this conference, Captain Boonruang Homkachorn (CSCAP Thailand) gave a paper entitled "The Influence of Exclusive Economic Zone on Thailand," which considered Thailand's various maritime boundaries and the problems of enforcement within the EEZ, www.victoria.ac.nz/css/docs/CSCAP_Reports_Contributions/2000/9MCWG.pdf.

5 UNCLOS, the 1982 United Nations Convention on the Law of the Sea, signed by Thailand but not ratified. World Trade Organization Appellate Body, AB 1998–4, WT/DS58/AB/R, United States – Import Prohibition of Certain Shrimp and Shrimp Products, p. 10, FN 110.

6 A comprehensive overview with related maps can be found at: "Thailand and Cambodia Maritime Disputes," Captain Somjade Kongrawd, Royal Thai Navy, www.navy.mi.th/judge/Files/Thailand%20Cambodia.pdf.

7 Oil production, 310,000 bbl/day (2007); oil consumption, 929,000 bbl/day (2005), proven oil reserves, 291,000,000 bbl (2006), source www.globalfirepower.com/country-military-strength-detail.asp?country_id=Thailand.

8 To get an overview about the history of RTN, see Rear Admiral (Ret.) Chaen Pachusanon, RTN, *History of the Royal Thai Navy* (Bangkok 1965).

9 Kavi Chongkittavorn, "Thailand embarks on maritime security cooperation," *The Nation*, 6 October 2008, www.nationmultimedia.com/2008/10/06/opinion/Thailand-embarks-on-maritime-security-cooperation-30085175.html.

10 Keith Jacobs, "The Royal Thai Navy," *Naval Forces*, Issue V, 2009, p. 18.

11 Bill Tarrant, "Balancing powers in the Malacca Strait," *Reuters*, 7 March 2010, http://blogs.reuters.com/global/2010/03/07/balancing-powers-in-the-malacca-strait.

12 Graham Gerald Ong, "Next wave of terror targets: Will they be at sea?" *The Straits Times (Singapore)*, 15 September 2003, p. 15.

13 Sam Bateman, "Terror in the Malacca Strait: The Risks of Overreaction," *RSIS Commentary 31/2010*, 10 March 2010.

14 Nancy-Amelia Collins, "Southeast Asian Nations to Begin Air Patrols Over Malacca Strait," *GlobalSecurity.org*, Jakarta, 8 September 2005, www.globalsecurity.org/military/library/news/2005/09/mil-050908-voa01.htm.

15 Kavi Chongkittavorn, "Thailand embarks on maritime security cooperation," *The Nation*, 6 October 2008, www.nationmultimedia.com/2008/10/06/opinion/opinion_30085175.php.

16 "Joint patrol in the Straits of Malacca and Singapore," *Thailand as a Member of IMO Council*, www.md.go.th/IMO/HTML/safety.htm.

17 Wilfried A. Herrmann, "Die regionale Rolle Thailands – von der national resilience, zu einer treiben Kraft in Suedostasien," *Muenster* 1996, p. 84.

18 Keith Jacobs, "Naval Forces," p. 17.

19 National Defense Studies Institute (NDSI), *Defense of Thailand 2008* (English) (Bangkok: NDSI, 2008).

20 Ibid, p. 57.

21 This citation comes from a transcript of the answer of the Commander-in-Chief of the RTN, "Commanders Response," *US Naval Institute Proceedings Magazine* – March 2009, Vol. 135/3/1,273.

22 Results of several meetings and discussions with RTN "leader board" in Feb. –Mar. 2010, as well as participants of the Phuket Maritime Forum, organized by the Human Development Forum Foundation from 7–10 January 2010, www.hdff.org.

23 "Kingdom of Thailand Joins Container Security Initiative to Target and Pre-Screen Cargo Destined for U.S." *Press Release by the United States Department for Homeland Security*, 10 June 2003, www.cbp.gov/xp/cgov/newsroom/news_releases/archives/cbp_press_releases/062003/06102003.xml.

24 "Proliferation Security Initiative Participants," www.state.gov/t/isn/c27732.htm.

25 "A Resource on Nonproliferation export controls," www.exportcontrol.org.

26 UNHCR, Country report on terrorism Thailand 2008, www.unhcr.org/refworld/country,,USDOS,,THA,4562d8cf2,49fac688c,0.html.

27 See www.md.go.th/IMO/HTML/safety.htm.

28 Commander-in-Chief, RTN, "Commanders Response."

29 "Joint patrol in the Straits of Malacca and Singapore," www.md.go.th/IMO/HTML/safety.htm.

30 Yoichiro Sato, "Southeast Asian Receptiveness to Japanese Maritime Security Cooperation," *Asia-Pacific Center for Security Studies Commentary,* September 2007, www.apcss.org/Publications/Maritime security cooperation Japan-SE Asia Sato.pdf.

31 Chongkittavorn, "Thailand embarks on maritime security cooperation."

32 Sato, "Southeast Asian Receptiveness."

33 Commander-in-Chief, RTN, "Commanders Response."

34 Chongkittavorn, "Thailand embarks on maritime security cooperation."

35 Human Development Forum Foundation (HDFF/www.hdff.org) and the author are main discussion partners in the ASEAN Defense Establishments and CSOs Cooperation on Non-Traditional Security (Disaster Management), which commenced for the first time in June 2009 and is taking place again in June 2010.

36 A good overview on the increasing Thai–Chinese military relations can be found in Ian Storey, "China and Thailand: Enhancing Military-Security Ties in the 21st Century," *China Brief*, 8(14), 2008.
37 "Move to extend piracy measures," *Bangkok Post*, 1 December 2010, p. 5.
38 See www.md.go.th/IMO/HTML/safety.htm.
39 International Institute for Strategic Studies, *The Military Balance 2010* (London: Routledge, February 2010), pp. 430–431.
40 NDSI, *Defense of Thailand 2008* (English) (Bangkok: NDSI, 2008), p. 50.
41 International Institute for Strategic Studies, *The Military Balance 2010* (London: Routledge, February 2010), pp. 430–431; the Defense White Paper Thailand 2008 does not give detailed numbers, just general numbers for personnel (73,000), capital ships (56) support ships (15) aircraft (29) and helicopters (25). See also NDSI, *Defense of Thailand 2008* (English) (Bangkok: NDSI, 2008), p. 58.
42 Detailed procurements of the last years can be found under Keith Jacobs, "The Royal Thai Navy."
43 NDSI, *Defense of Thailand 2008*, p. 57.
44 Wassana Nanuam, "Navy could sink B1bn on submarine," *Bangkok Post*, 1 January 2010, www.bangkokpost.com/news/local/30323/navy-couldsink-b1bn-on-submarine.
45 NDSI, *Defense of Thailand 2008*, p. V.

10 Good order at sea

The challenges and priorities of Vietnam

Nguyen Hong Thao

Entering the second decade of the twenty-first century, the world is now facing several challenges, including a global financial crisis; climate change; the proliferation of weapons of mass destruction and ballistic missiles; a rapid military power build-up; territorial and sovereign disputes; human rights; and terrorism. Thus, sustainable development and ensuring security have become top priorities. All members of the world community depend on each other more and more. Because of the global integration process and peaceful movements of people between countries, national security cannot be separated from common development and security issues. In other words, common development and security help boost national development and security, and vice versa. This is also true for the South China Sea region and Vietnam.

Encompassing a portion of the Pacific Ocean stretching roughly from Singapore and the Strait of Malacca in the south-west to the Strait of Taiwan (between Taiwan and China) in the north-east, the South China Sea is surrounded by ten coastal states, including some of the world's most rapidly industrializing and fastest-growing countries in the world.[1] As a consequence of its distinctive geographical features, the South China Sea serves as a resource and a medium of transportation and exchange. It is a unique ecosystem and a repository for valuable natural resources such as oil and gas. The economic growth of coastal countries depends on the exploitation of fish and oil resources and, in turn, the exploitation of maritime resources increases the over-exploitation of resources and illegal, unregulated and unreported (IUU) fishing problems, degradation of the marine environment, and competition for control over natural resources in the area. The vital sea routes linking the Pacific and the Indian oceans provide passage for over half of the world's merchant fleet (by tonnage) sailing through the South China Sea every year, most of the fuel transportation by sea from the Middle East and Africa to Japan, China and South Korea,[2] and the huge volume of import–export goods between Association of Southeast Asian Nations (ASEAN) countries and the rest of the world. For other major distant shipping states, such as the United States, the role of China, India and Australia in maintaining freedom of navigation for merchant shipping and naval vessels in the South China Sea is of considerable interest.[3] The interest in maritime transportation has brought new challenges from the marine pollution, maritime accidents and marine search and rescue (SAR), as well as piracy and armed robbery and illegal drug trafficking in the region. The development of the modern international law of the sea focusses more attention on the South China Sea as a medium of dominion, with approximately 60 maritime boundaries still required to be settled in the region.[4] The United Nations Convention on the Law of the Sea (UNCLOS) of 1982 has now been in force for 15 years. This is sufficient time to create an initial legal framework but not long enough to provide a basis to settle all of the problems raised. The South China Sea constitutes a distinctive maritime region for competing security interests.[5] Transboundary issues, such as marine pollution, the management of straddling and highly migratory fish stocks, anti-terrorism and combating piracy and armed robbery, or even maritime delimitation, need to be solved by cooperation among coastal states. Each coastal state has its own interests and priorities. However, good order in the South China Sea is necessary for all, from each separate coastal state to regional and extra-regional countries. Over the years, it has become increasingly clear that the South China Sea issues need to be treated in a comprehensive manner by the littoral states. The maritime challenges and priorities of each country are the focus of the whole region. Good order at sea and maritime security covers not only national but also bilateral, regional and international interests; not only military maritime security but also environmental, economic, societal and political security. *In the undividable liquid volume*, good order at sea and maritime security have been ensured by both national and regional efforts.

Bordering the South China Sea, Vietnam is in a good position to exploit the sea. With its long coastline of 3,260 kilometres and more than 3,000 scattered islands, Vietnam has the opportunity to extend its maritime zones under the International Law of the Seas. The coastal and marine zones of Vietnam are rich in flora and fauna, including over 2,000 marine fish species, 300 species of coral, and an unknown number of plant species, and are characterized by 13 major ecosystems. The fisheries industry is extremely important to Vietnam. Most sealanes across the South China Sea pass maritime zones under the jurisdiction of Vietnam. The country is therefore in a strong position to develop maritime ports, and navigation and SAR services. Vietnamese waters have become some of the most active sites for oil and gas exploration and exploitation, with an estimated oil reservoir of 700 million tonnes.

The sea plays a very important role in the country's present and future development. At the same time, the South China Sea causes huge challenges for Vietnam. If marine delimitation of territorial seas, the economic exclusive zone (EEZ) or the continental shelf is considered separately, Vietnam has more 20 maritime disputes remaining to be settled with neighbouring states, i.e. one-third of the total number of maritime disputes in the region.[6] Maritime disputes may concern not only two parties but also three (Vietnam, China and Taiwan on the Paracel Islands) or even six parties (Vietnam, the Philippine, Malaysia, Brunei, China and Taiwan on the Spratlys Islands). The competition and cooperation on the management of marine resources remain a priority among Vietnam and neighbouring countries. International routes bring new concerns about marine pollution, SAR operations, piracy and armed robbery. Coastal development, industrial pollution, environmental deterioration, reduction of biodiversity, over-fishing, destruction of mangroves, swamps, wetlands and coral systems are the most serious problems facing development at present. The Strategy on Marine Economic Development approved in 2007 affirmed new orientations for developing the marine economies; for further expanding international cooperation relating to the sea; for closely combining rapid economic growth with strengthened security, national sovereignty and national jurisdiction; and for protecting social order and safety, as well as the nation's interests at sea. Marine challenges and priorities in Vietnam have focused on some choke points, such as maritime delimitation and settlement, fishing rights and enforcement, marine transportation, SAR operations, anti-piracy and anti-terrorism, marine environmental protection and other issues.

Maritime delimitation and the settlement of maritime disputes

The big challenge for Vietnam is to settle the delimitation of maritime zones with opposite and adjacent states in the South China Sea. Unsettled EEZ and continental shelf issues can cause difficulty for the resource development and enforcement against illegal fishing.[7] Since 1977, Vietnamese maritime zones have been defined and negotiations on maritime delimitation with neighbouring countries have been carried out continually. Vietnam holds the position that all disputes should be settled through peaceful means. Concerning this issue, clause 7 of the 12 May 1977 Declaration of the Socialist Republic of Vietnam on the Territorial Sea, the Contiguous Zone, the EEZ and the Continental Shelf of Vietnam clearly states:

> The Government of the Socialist Republic of Vietnam shall, together with the concerned countries through negotiations on the basis of mutual respect of independence and sovereignty, in compliance with international law and practices, resolve the issues relating to the maritime zones and the continental shelf of each side.[8]

Since 1991, the settlement of maritime disputes has been a top priority in Vietnam's maritime policy. As a result of maritime settlements during the last two decades Vietnam is now the leading South-East Asian country with respect to the settlement of maritime delimitation issues in accordance with the UNCLOS 1982. Several agreements on maritime delimitation have already been concluded, such as the Agreement on Maritime Delimitation with Thailand on 9 August 1997, the Agreement on the Delimitation of Bac Bo (Tonkin) Gulf and the Agreement on Fishery Cooperation in Bac Bo Gulf with China on 25 December 2000, and the Agreement on the Delineation of the Continental Shelf with Indonesia on 26 June 2003. Vietnam has, however, had a flexible approach to negotiations to reach a final delineation solution: if deemed necessary and on the basis of agreement, Vietnam and its counterpart countries may select the application of provisional arrangements in the spirit of Articles 74 and 83 of the UNCLOS 1982. Vietnam has had historical waters under joint management with Kampuchea since 1982, reached an agreement with Malaysia on joint petroleum exploitation in the overlapping area in 1992; and has accelerated negotiations on the cooperation on joint petroleum exploitation in the overlapping areas of Vietnam, Thailand and Malaysia (negotiations started in 1998). This form of joint exploitation has been also applied to delineated sea areas, such as the Common Fishery Zone and the Transitory Fishery Zone with China in the Bac Bo Gulf (effective from 30 June 2004). In addition, the Tripartite Agreement for Joint Marine Seismic Undertaking in the Agreement Area in the South China Sea was signed on 14 March 2005 between the National Oil Companies of the Philippines (Philippines National Oil Company, PNOC), the People's Republic of China (Chinese National Offshore Oil Company, CNOOC) and Vietnam (PETROVIETNAM).[9] Development through cooperation constitutes an intermediate measure toward achieving the final delimitation at the appropriate time (see Table 10.1).

Among unsettled disputes, the one regarding the Paracels and Spratlys has seriously affected good order at sea for the whole region. These disputes have lasted over a century and have drawn most papers and ink for their discussion. However, events of 2009 have made all concerned countries understand that they must cooperate to find a solution acceptable to all if they don't want to risk good order at sea.

First, the incident of 8 March 2009 between Chinese patrol ships and the US ocean surveillance vessel USNS *Impeccable*[10], and the collision of Chinese submarine with the sonar cable of the USS *John McCain* in June 2009 marked the decisive return of Americans to the South China Sea after the Vietnam War, as well as the Chinese intention to be dominant in this area. The root cause of these recent incidents are the different interpretations of the rights and duties within an EEZ. China argues that these American activities violated the rights of the Chinese EEZ, while US strongly maintains that these activities are part of the freedoms of navigation and overflight that are available to other states in an EEZ. The second development relates to the submission of a claim over the extended continental shelf to the United Nations Commission on the Limits of the Continental Shelf (CLCS) before the deadline of 13 May 2009. Vietnam, Malaysia, Indonesia and the Philippines made their submissions of the outer limit of the continental shelf to extend beyond the 200 nautical miles distance measured from their baselines to the CLCS. The Philippine's submission in the Benham Rise region[11] and the Indonesian one in the north-west of Sumatra[12] have not met with any objections, but the Vietnamese and Malaysian joint submission in the southern part of the South China Sea[13] and Vietnam's own submission in the North Area (VNM-N)[14] have been criticized by China and the Philippines. Vietnam is of the view that the area of continental shelf that is the subject of Vietnamese report and joint Vietnam–Malaysia submission are not the subject of any overlap and dispute[15] and that the submissions are without preju-

Table 10.1 Vietnam's maritime delimitation and settlements

Country	*Geographic zone*	*TS*	*EEZ*	*CS*	*Remarks*
Vietnam–China	Gulf of Tonkin	Yes	Yes	Yes	Agreement on the Delimitation of Bac Bo (Tonkin) Gulf and the Agreement on Fishery Cooperation in Bac Bo Gulf, 25 December 2000
Vietnam–Indonesia	South China Sea	NR	No	Yes	Agreement on the Delineation of the Continental Shelves, 26 June 2003
Vietnam–Malaysia	Gulf of Thailand	NR	No	No	Agreement on the Joint Petroleum Exploitation, 5 June 1992
Vietnam–Thailand	Gulf of Thailand	NR	Yes	Yes	Agreement on Maritime Delimitation, 9 August 1997
Vietnam–Malaysia–Thailand	Gulf of Thailand	NR	No	No	Negotiation on Joint Development
Vietnam–Kampuchea	Gulf of Thailand	No	No	No	Agreement on Historic Waters, 7 July 1982
Vietnam–China–Taiwan	Paracel Islands	No	No	No	Declaration on the Conduct of Parties in the South China Sea, 14 December 2002
Vietnam–China–Taiwan–Malaysia–Philippines–Brunei	Spratlys Islands	No	No	No	Declaration on the Conducts of Parties in the South China Sea, 14 December 2002

Notes
NR = Boundaries are not required; TS = Territorial Sea; EEZ = Exclusive Economic Zone; CS = Continental Shelf

dice to the maritime delimitation between Vietnam and other relevant coastal states. In note HA 24/09 of the Malaysian Permanent Mission to the United Nations, Malaysia shares the view with Vietnam in affirming that the joint submission of Malaysia and Vietnam to the CLCS to establish the limits of the continental shelf appurtenant to Malaysia and Vietnam beyond 200 nautical miles from their baselines, from which the breath of their respective territorial seas is measured, in respect of the southern part of the South China Sea constitutes legitimate undertakings in implementing the obligations of states party to the UNCLOS 1982 and conforms to the pertinent provisions of UNCLOS 1982, as well as the Rules of Procedure of the CLCS. This joint submission was made without prejudice to the question of delimitation of the continental shelf between states with opposite or adjacent coasts, as well as to the positions of states that are parties to a land or maritime dispute.[16] In its rejection on 7 May 2009 to the Secretary-General of the United Nations, China considered those submissions to infringe its sovereignty, sovereign rights and jurisdiction over the waters and islands bounded by the nine-dotted line (the map of line attached with the note).[17] This was the first time China that presented the dotted line to a UN body in the context of Chinese claim to maritime delimitation in the South China Sea. Many law of the sea experts have commented that the Chinese dotted line is not based on any of the UNCLOS 1982 scientific criteria for delimiting the outer limits of the continental shelf."[18] Despite the Chinese position, the protest made by the Philippine authority on 4 August 2009[19] reserves the possibility to have discussion. The note submitted by the Philippines stated that the submission for an extended continental shelf made by Vietnam and the joint submission made by Malaysia and Vietnam lay claims on disputed areas that overlap with those of the Philippines.[20] The Philippines requested the commission to refrain from considering these submissions unless and until the parties have discussed and resolved their disputes. Brunei had no objection, but the country made preliminary information indicative of a future submission that the edge of the continental margin should be beyond 200 nautical miles from Brunei's baselines, which lie at the transition between the Dangerous Grounds (Spratlys Islands) and the deep ocean floor of the South China Sea.[21] Indeed, the confrontation of interested parties is linked to territorial disputes over islands in the South China Sea.[22] Claimant countries are all members of the UNCLOS 1982 and have all shown an intention to implement Article 76 to fix the outer limit of the extended continental shelf beyond 200 nautical miles on different levels: submission or preliminary information or objection. While Vietnam and Malaysia intend to separate the submission of outer limit of extended continental shelf beyond 200 nautical miles from sovereignty disputes over islands, China and the Philippines want to link the two problems. From the text of its preliminary information, Brunei would also like to fix the outer limit of its extended continental shelf beyond 200 nautical miles measured from the baseline of land territory, without consideration of islands under dispute. The concerned countries have different views because of uncertainties in the UNCLOS 1982 over the status of islands. Article 121 (3) states that "rocks which cannot sustain human habitation or economic life of their own shall not have an exclusive economic zone or continental shelf". This uncertain provision has caused an active dilemma among researchers. Some consider that the geological features of the Spratlys Archipelago cannot generate an EEZ or a continental shelf. Others suggest that some of the features in the archipelago – which are above water at high tide – can generate more than just territorial waters.[23]

The third development relates to "the hot situation" caused by the recent activities of China and other claimants in the South China Sea. Since March 2009, Chinese activities in the South China Sea have been multiplying in intensity and capacity in line with a strategic vision. US and other foreign oil companies operating in the South China Sea have been asked to withdraw from it.[24] Chinese fisheries patrol vessels have been sent to protect China's fisheries resources in its claimed island EEZs.[25] On 15 May 2009, China renewed the fishing ban in the South China Sea and intensified the detention of Vietnamese fisherman near the Paracel Islands[26] Vietnam launched diplomatic protests. The Vietnamese news media reported that the Vietnamese fishing boats were stopped, boarded and sunk and that the catches of the fishing boats were seized by Chinese vessels.[27] On the 8 November 2009, following a decision by the authorities in Hainan Province, China set up hamlet administration in Yongxing and Zhaoshu islands, also known as Phu Lam Island (Woody Island) and Dao Cay island (Tree Island) of the Paracels Archipelago, respectively, and the subject of a dispute between Vietnam and China.[28] In November 2009, China sent two Yuzheng vessels to the Paracels Archipelago and a medical ship to the Spratlys Islands.[29] Chinese media continually repeats its intention to deploy air-carrier ships in the South China Sea. By the end of 2009, on 26 December, the Chinese Law on defending the islands was approved.[30] A programme to launch tourist tours on Hainan, including the Paracels, will be launched in 2010.[31] These events warn that Chinese activities will be greatly increased in the coming years and that the situation may deteriorate further.

Malaysia and the Philippines have also taken steps to reinforce their presence. On 5 March 2009, there were reports that Malaysian Prime Minister Badawi visited Swallow Reef.[32] The Philippines approved the Archipelagic Baseline Law (Filipino Republic Act 9522) on 10 March 2009, which classifies the Kalayaan Island Group and Scarborough Shoal as "regimes of islands".[33] The recent activities and measures taken by concerned parties, especially by China, may hinder not only the economic development of Vietnam but also security and free communication in the region.

The fourth issue is the inactive implementation of the Declaration on Conducts of Parties in the South China Sea (DOC). Approved by the ASEAN and China in 2002, the DOC was aimed at helping to manage conflict in the South China Sea in the period 2002–2007.[34] The DOC aimed at avoiding military actions and promoting mutual understanding between ASEAN and China, and the adoption of confidence-building measures in less sensitive areas. The parties were encouraged to explore or undertake cooperative activities in the fields of marine environmental protection; marine scientific research; safety of navigation and communication at sea; SAR operations; and combating transnational crime, including but not limited to trafficking in illicit drugs, piracy and armed robbery at sea, and illegal traffic in arms. However, the declaration is a more political than a legal document, depending only on the "bonne fois" of all claimants. The ASEAN–China technical expert meetings have not reached any agreement on guidelines or projects because of the different views of parties. While ASEAN countries consider that document is a "common pact" between the two sides (i.e. ASEAN and China), Beijing has continued to have talks on a bilateral basis with each claimant and not with the association as a whole. China doesn't agree with the regionalization or internationalization of disputes in the South China Sea, despite of the fact that such disputes concern more than the two parties.[35]

Before the intensified actions of China and America's recent interest in the South China Sea, good order and security at sea had become a higher priority for the whole region, for all concerned parties, inside or outside of the region, and especially for Vietnam. Talks on maritime settlement and cooperation between claimant countries must be promoted in close future. Before the start of 2010, Deputy Prime Minister and Minister of Foreign Affairs of the Socialist Republic of Vietnam, H.E. Pham Gia Khiem expressed the view that Vietnam and China should focus their talks on maritime issues.[36] The experience of the negotiations to complete the land boundary demarcation and delimitation of the Tonkin Gulf is useful for reaching a common understanding. An agreement on the principles for settling maritime issues will be the first step. In its capacity of president of ASEAN in 2010, Vietnam must unite the efforts of the association and China to renew the talks on the DOC and move it to a higher level. The concerned parties must develop guidelines for its implementation and to promote projects in less sensitive areas, such as the Joint ASEAN–China Table-Top Maritime Search and Rescue Exercise; a workshop on marine ecosystems and biodiversity; a workshop on marine environment protection, regional oceanographic and climate exchanges; disaster prevention and reduction; establishing disaster monitoring and warning systems; or a training programme on ecosystem monitoring and monitoring technology.[37] The concerned parties should move forward to confidence-building measures, such as a code of conduct or a conflict management agreement for overlapping areas. They should gradually narrow their differences. The current situation calls for new efforts to establish a legal arrangement for cooperation between concerned parties in the South China Sea. In this, a framework for cooperation and the status of islands will be a hot topic for discussion.

Fishing competition and cooperation

The fisheries industry provides approximately 60 per cent of the total animal protein consumed by Vietnamese citizens. Marine capture is primarily nearshore-based, and is undertaken by a fleet of over 60,000 motor-, wind- and human-powered fishing boats. Aquaculture activities in the coastal zone produce include fishing, crustaceans (shrimps and crabs), molluscs and seaweed. The total

Vietnamese fisheries stock is estimated at 4–4.2 million tonnes including 1.7 million tonnes of pelagic fish. The sustainable yield is approximately 1.6–1.7 million tonnes. In 2010, the capture of marine fisheries product is predicted to be 1.5–1.8 million tonnes.[38] If the illegal capture of foreign fishing boats in the Vietnamese maritime zone is taken into account, the total marine fisheries product reaches the upper limit of the sustainable yield. Overfishing is the major problem for Vietnam in both coastal and offshore areas and the cause of pollution problems and the destruction of coral reefs and natural habitats. The reasons for these problems include:

- The concentration of fishing activity in the shallow waters of the nearshore zone;
- The use of destructive fishing techniques, including the use of dynamite and undersized mesh nets;
- The increasing size of the national fishing fleet;
- The lack of management and enforcement capabilities;
- The intrusion of foreign fishing fleets.

During the last decade, Vietnam has taken active measures to manage the protection and development of aquatic resources through its policies, overall planning and plans, and by integrating educational, technical, economic and legal measures to this end. The Law on Aquatic Resources 2003 provides that the protection and development of aquatic resources must be closely associated with the protection of their habitat to ensure the reproduction rate of aquatic species is maintained to support the immediate and long-term livelihood of fishermen as well as the economic efficiency of the entire society. All acts that endanger aquatic resources and their habitat, or obstruct the protection and development of aquatic resources are strictly forbidden. For the purpose of sustainable development, Vietnam has taken some effective measures. Organizations and individuals assigned to water areas for farming and exploiting aquatic resources are responsible for drawing up plans or economic technical feasibility studies that should incorporate measures for fighting pollution of the aquatic environment and for protecting and developing aquatic products with a view to increasing business and upgrading production, as well as maintaining the reproduction of aquatic products. Several legal documents are approved that ban the use of noxious substances, explosives, ammunition and electric currents for catching aquatic resources; forbid the destruction of submerged forests, upstream forests, rock ridges and coral reefs, underwater floral grounds and other special natural structures; and forbid the building, dismantling or repairing of structures and installations relating to water areas and the habitat of aquatic resources that may cause substantial harmful effects to aquatic resources. Regarding fish stocks, regulations relate to areas where fishing is forbidden or permitted only for specific periods; the different types of harvesting means and methods permitted, including a ban on the use of undersized nets with undersized meshes; on the species that may be caught, including a ban on the exploitation of species less than a prescribed size; on the allowable catches for waters less than or more than 30 metres deep. The permitted quota of fish and other species smaller than the prescribed size cannot be more than 15 per cent per catch or total harvested aquatic products per ship. Harvesting and trading of species banned from exploitation are also strictly forbidden. A network of 20 marine protected areas has been created in the framework of the programme on research on Vietnamese marine protected areas sponsored by the government, the GEF and the WB.[39]

However, the highest priority for fishing for Vietnam is related to the combat of illegal fishing in Vietnamese marine areas and protection against armed robbery of fishermen in the disputed areas. In recent years, foreign ships, especially Chinese, often trespass Vietnamese internal waters, territorial sea and EEZ to catch aquatic resources. After unilaterally issuing the fishing ban in the South China Sea during 15 May to 31 August 2009,[40] the Chinese fishing patrol force has increased the number of seizures of Vietnamese fish boats operating near the Paracels and Spratly islands. Diplomatic notes between the two countries have been exchanged at high rates, in which Vietnamese authorities have demanded their Chinese counterparts to release immediately Vietnamese fishermen and fishing boats.[41] In some cases, Vietnamese fishermen complained that their boats had been fired upon and hit by the foreign patrol force.[42] Media reported that an attack by an unidentified ship sank Vietnamese fishing boats,[43] while the Chinese authorities reported that Vietnamese fishermen had committed acts of robbery.[44]

On 20 June 2009, Indonesia stated that 75 Chinese fishermen were caught fishing within Indonesia's EEZ in the South China Sea, while Chinese media reported that they were captured by an Indonesian patrol boat in their traditional fishing grounds.[45] To combat against so-called illegal fishing by foreigners in Indonesian waters,[46] severe punishments are permitted under the new Indonesian Law on Fishery approved on 15 September 2009. Under this law, any party found guilty of illegal activity in the sea – including illegal fishing, or fishing that is not in line with existing regulations, such as the use of explosive materials – could be sentenced to up to ten years in prison or given a two billion rupiah (US$217,000) fine. Furthermore, patrol forces are allowed to open fire against the illegal fishing boats; however, this point does not conform to international laws on fishery and human rights. China, Vietnam, Malaysia and Thailand have all shown their concern about the new Indonesian Law on Fishery.[47] Indonesian authorities confirmed that they will pay strong attention to giving humane treatment and safe repatriation to foreign fishermen who are found engaging in illegal fishing. To avoid illegal fishing activities, it is also expected that the fishing companies of concerned countries will be encouraged and helped to establish joint fishing businesses.[48] Fishing competition, IUU fishing and bad treatment for fishermen will continue as long as disputes over sovereignty and jurisdiction are not resolved. Pending maritime delimitation, confidence-building measures and cooperative arrangements should be set up immediately. The legal basis of cooperation for preserving living resources and protecting the marine environment is set by the Article 123, Part V, Part IX of the 1982 UNCLOS, the 1995 Agreement for the Implementation of the Provisions of the United Nations

Convention on the Law of the Sea of 10 December 1982 Relating to the Conservation and Management of Straddling Fish Stocks and Highly Migratory Fish Stocks (UNFSA), FAO Code of Conduct for Responsible Fisheries, and the Regional Plan of Action of 2007 to promote responsible fishing practices and combat illegal fishing in South-East Asia.

Problems with fisheries competition arise due to the lack of EEZ boundaries and underdeveloped fishing cooperative management in South-East Asia. To avoid the bad treatment of fishermen and to preserve the living resources and the marine environment, concerned countries must have talks to reach a regional agreement on fishing activities in the disputed areas. A more cost-effective, integrated regional mechanism, such as a Regional Fishing Management Cooperation Organization in the South China Sea, must be set up. The 2001 UN Agreement on the Conservation and Management of Straddling Fish Stocks and Highly Migratory Fish Stocks must be ratified. The initiatives taken by Vietnam and other countries must be studied and implemented. In the Gulf of Tonkin, the Agreement on Fishery Cooperation of 25 December 2000 created the Common Fishery Zone (CFZ), the zone of transitional arrangement for fishing activities (Transitory Fishery Zone) and the Buffer Zone for small fishing boats. These have provided a new experience in the practice of settlement of maritime disputes.[49] The Joint Sino-Vietnam Committee for Fishery Management in the Gulf promulgated the Regulations for Management of the Fishery Resources in the Common Fishery Zone in 2004. All people fishing in the CFZ, the Zone of Transitional Arrangements and other related waters are bound by these legal documents. The competent authorities of the contracting parties are responsible for monitoring and controlling the nationals and fishing vessels of both parties in their own water areas of the CFZ. If necessary, they may coordinate to conduct joint monitoring, control and surveying (MCS) operations, and to handle any breach of the regulations laid down by the Sino-Vietnamese Joint Committee. From 2004 to 2008, three joint MSC operations by the two countries were organized, which helped to reduce the annual figure for illegal fishing operations in the gulf.[50] In relation to Thailand, in March 1994, Thai–Vietnamese Joint Committee on Fisheries and Order at Sea was established. The Agreement on Maritime Delimitation in the Gulf of Thailand of 9 July 1997 stopped the chaotic situation of fishing activities between the two countries.[51] Some measures to establish order at sea were implemented effectively by the competent authorities of both countries. These include:

- Establishing joint patrols;
- Establishing a contact channel for early warning of any potential violation of laws and regulations of either country;
- A joint programme of information dissemination to fishermen. The two sides reiterated the need for both sides to educate their fishermen in respect of fisheries laws and regulations of the other party;
- Cooperation in the prevention of violation of fisheries laws and regulations;

- Promotion of business cooperation in fisheries and related downstream industries between the two countries. This is considered a confidence-building measure, which is eventually hoped to lead to the establishment of a desired order at sea;
- Conducting a joint assessment and management of marine resources in the Gulf of Thailand.

During 1997–2009, the navies of Vietnam and Thailand conducted 18 joint patrols, and established a hotline informing each other of violations of the joint agreement for helping to re-establish order at the sea in the Gulf of Thailand.

To solve the fishing competition and IUU problems, Vietnam has opted to cooperate with and sign fisheries agreements with neighbouring countries in the future, first with Indonesia, Philippines and China. Vietnam is trying to alleviate this problem by accurately defining the conditions and procedures for permitting foreign nationals to exploit marine living resources in its waters, by intensifying supervisory and monitoring work, by reinforcing the Maritime Police, by setting up communication channels with those countries whose nationals are fishing in Vietnam's maritime zones and in whose waters Vietnamese fishermen have activities, by enforcing sanctions and penalties against infringements, and by further promoting the legal education activities.

Exploitation of non-living resources

The South China Sea is a major hotspot of energy conflict in the world, and countries in the region have increasing concerns about the exploration and exploitation of offshore oil and gas reserves for their energy security and jurisdiction claims at sea. Like other countries, Vietnam has exercised its sovereign and jurisdiction rights in conformity with the UNCLOS 1982. It has implemented policies to attract investment, offering numerous preferences to foreign petroleum firms, especially for offshore areas with difficult exploration and exploitation conditions. Vietnam's petroleum exploration and exploitation activities have been carried out on the basis of mutual benefit, respect for sovereignty and sovereign rights over the natural resources in Vietnam's continental shelf.

The growing energy demands and the nine-dotted claim line of China are major causes of incidents in the South China Sea. China needs energy to support its rapidly growing economy. With an oil consumption level of 6,534,000 barrels per day (the second in the world after the USA), China's imports of oil rose by nearly 13 per cent in the first five months of 2008.[52] Chinese studies estimate the potential oil resources of the Spratly and Paracel Islands to range from 105 to 213 billion barrels of oil, and the potential production levels of the Spratly Islands could be 1.4–1.9 million barrels per day.[53] Seizing the right of control over maritime areas is a policy for oil assurance. China has reiterated its claims to most of the South China Sea within the so-called nine-dotted lines.[54] This claim overlaps with Indonesia's claims to the north-east of Indonesia's Natuna island group, which is said to have considerable natural gas deposits. It also partly overlaps with the Philippines' Malampaya and Camago natural gas and condensate fields, with Malaysia's natural gas fields offshore Sarawak, and with Vietnam's Tu Chinh and Dai Hung fields. In 2007–2009, China put pressure on British Petroleum (BP), Conoco Phillips, Exxon Mobil and the Indian Oil and National Gas Company (ONGC) to stop their joint activities with Vietnam under licences provided by the Vietnamese Government.[55] It is also notable that in November 2008, CNOOC launched a plan to invest 200 billion Yuan (US$29 billion) to develop the exploration and exploitation of oil deposits in the South China Sea together with its partners.[56]

The effect of exploiting oil and gas reserves in offshore areas will depend on the cooperation of concerned countries in implementing the DOC and starting negotiations on the status of rocks and islands in the South China Sea.

Marine transportation and related issues

Vietnam's geographic position in the South China Sea provides favourable conditions for developing a marine transport system along its coast. According to the strategies for the development of Vietnam's maritime sector until 2010 and 2020 and the master plan on Vietnam's seaport system (issued together with the Prime Minister's Decision No. 202/1999/QD-TTg of 12 October 1999), by 2020 Vietnam will have 114 seaports, compared to 90 at present. Vietnam's fleet will have more big ships with technical specifications that comply with the provisions of the UNCLOS 1982 and the International Maritime Organisation (IMO) marine conventions. Development of the Vietnamese marine transportation sector and petroleum activities, as well as international maritime transportation in the routes along the coast, have brought several problems including marine pollution, marine accidents, piracy, terrorism and illegal trafficking.[57] Solutions to those problems demand the country's effort and participation with the regional community.

In the transport field, Vietnam has quickly built a legal structure and applied effective measures for exercising the rights and fulfilling the obligations of a coastal state, a port state and a flag state, in accordance with the provisions of the 1982 UNCLOS and relevant international commitments. The new revised Maritime Code of 2005, the Civil Code, the Civil Procedure Code and the Order on the Ship Arrest Procedure form a solid legal basis to attain this goal.

With the duties of a flag state, Vietnam has promulgated numerous regulations concerning ships flying its flag, such as regulation on registration of seagoing ships and crew, issued together with the government Decree No. 91/CP of 23 August 1997, circular No. 259/1998/TT-BGTVT of 18 August 1998 from the Transport Ministry guiding the implementation of Decree No. 91/CP, the government Decree No. 23/2001/ND-CP revising a number of articles of Decree No. 91/CP; regulations on systems for the prevention of marine pollution by ships (TCVN 6276:1997) and regulations on the safety of seagoing ships (TCVN 6278:1997), issued together with decision No. 902/QD-TDC of 7 November 1997 from the Science, Technology and Environment Ministry (now the Science and Technology Ministry). A technical safety certificate for ships, a crewman's certificate and a pollution prevention and control certificate have been proscribed and granted in accordance with Vietnam's laws and international maritime conventions. Vietnam's fleets have fully satisfied not only the conditions for operation in Vietnam's sea but also for entry, exit and operation in seaports and sea areas of other countries, as well as in the high seas.

The system of lighthouses and navigational signals, navigational notices and navigational piloting services for ships operating in, entering and leaving seaports and seas areas or passing through Vietnam's sea have been strengthened, with 72 lighthouses situated from the north to the south and in the East Sea to Truong Sa, 29 navigational channels and 29 systems of navigational signals along the channels. Vietnam has participated in the International Convention of the International Maritime Satellite Organization (INMARSAT) and the Global Maritime Distress and Safety System (GMDSS). It has established a system of 14 coastal communication stations serving communication between ships, and between ships and the coast. This system has been connected to the international maritime communication system, assisting vessels operating on the sea in receiving and sending information, especially on salvage. The International Convention for the Safety of Life at Sea (SOLAS 74) has been implemented with the setting up of the Vietnam Maritime Rescue Coordination Centre (VMRCC). Ship control has been conducted at seaports according to the regional Memoranda of Understanding on Port State Control (MOU on PSC). Heavier penalties have been meted out for violations of maritime safety and marine pollution prevention.

Vietnam has participated in nine IMO conventions (not to mention the Convention on IMO), including:

- The 1973 International Convention for the Prevention of Pollution from Ships and the 1978 Supplementary Protocol (MARPOL 73/78);
- The International Convention on Tonnage of Ships (Tonnage 69);
- The Convention on International Regulations for Preventing Collisions at Sea (COLREG 72);
- SOLAS 74;
- The International Convention on Load Lines (Load Line 66);
- The International Convention on Standards of Training, Certification and Watchkeeping for Seafarers (STCW 78/95);
- The International Convention on the International Maritime Satellite Organization and the Operating Agreement on the International Maritime Satellite Organization (INMARSAT and OA);
- The International Convention for the Suppression of Unlawful Acts against the Safety of Maritime Navigation (SUA 88) and the Protocol for the Suppression of Unlawful Acts against the Safety of Fixed Platforms Located in the Continental Shelf;
- The International Convention on the Limitation of Civil Liability of Ship Owners for Oil Pollution Damage (CLC 1992).

Vietnam has signed many joint agreements among the ASEAN member countries concerning ocean shipping and maritime services, such as the 1975 Agreement on the Facilitation of Search of Ships in Distress and Rescue of Survivors of Ship Accidents, the 1998 ASEAN Framework Agreement on the Facilitation of Goods in Transit, the ASEAN Framework Agreement in the Facilitation of Inter-State Transport, and the 2004 Regional Cooperation Agreement on Combating Piracy and Armed Robbery against Ships in Asia (ReCAAP). Vietnam is actively supporting the initiative to establish the ASEAN Maritime Forum.

The reinforcement of Marine Police and paramilitary forces in 2009 has contributed to the effective action against maritime piracy and robbery, and maritime terrorism in Vietnamese waters. In 2008–2009, the cases of maritime piracy and terrorism registered in Vietnamese waters went down significantly by 5–7 cases per year. These figures are relatively small in the region, compared to the current situation in the Indonesian, Singaporean and Malaysian coasts.[58]

Marine SAR is important for Vietnam as it has huge vessels and large numbers or personnel operating in the South China Sea. For directing and organizing the search and salvage of people and means (aircraft, vessels and petroleum facilities) in distress in the air, on the sea and in adjacent areas between Vietnam and other countries, Vietnam's National Committee for Search and Rescue has developed three command and control centres along the coast. The bilateral SAR arrangement will be extended between Vietnamese, Chinese and Philippines authorities in the near future. In November 2006, a three-day joint regional SAR exercise (SAREX) was carried out by the SAR forces of seven ASEAN countries, including Vietnam.[59] Those efforts must be developed at the regional scale to ensure that all regional SAR agencies are able to coordinate assistance during major emergencies. The rescue of 17 Chinese seafarers during the November 2009 typhoon in Vietnamese waters demonstrated the necessity of cooperation between the SAR agencies of neighbouring countries. However, Vietnam, China, Singapore and IMO must concentrate on talks to clearly define the Search and Rescue Responsible boundaries in the South China Sea and cooperative arrangements in the disputed areas. The difference between SRR boundaries and national maritime boundaries has caused difficulties for effective cooperation in the SAR field.

Good order at sea in South-East Asia also requires a high level of information sharing. Vietnam has supported having a regional centre of data and information to ensure that maritime accident, pollution, piracy and armed robbery, terrorism and illegal trafficking at sea are promptly reported to the relevant authorities. The implementation of hotlines and joint exercises and patrols are effective tools for managing conflicts in the disputes areas pending maritime delimitation.

Vietnam has not yet enacted any law or regulation on ocean dumping. Vietnam has also not yet signed the 1972 London Convention on Dumping and its 1996 Protocol. However, being party to the UNCLOS 1982, Vietnam is obliged to establish the necessary legal and institutional framework to implement the provisions of the convention. Article 210 of the UNCLOS 1982 requires states to adopt laws and regulations to prevent, reduce and control pollution of the marine environment by dumping. National laws, regulations and measures shall be no less effective in preventing, reducing and controlling such pollution than the generally accepted international rules and standards. According the 1995 Report of the UN Secretary-General on the Law of the Sea, the London Convention is considered as a generally accepted international rule in the field of preventing, reducing and controlling pollution by ocean dumping.[60] So, in reality, states party to the UNCLOS 1982, but not party to the London Convention and the 1996 Protocol shall be bound by its provisions.[61]

Vietnam is also seriously considering its participation in the system of the 1992 Civil Liability Convention, the 1992 Fund Convention and the Oil Pollution Preparedness, Response and Cooperation Convention.

Conclusion

Good order at sea constitutes an urgent challenge in the South China Sea and for Vietnam. The development of marine resources, ensuring the safety and security of shipping, and the extension of coastal jurisdiction in accordance with agreed principles of international law are closely related with disputed areas in the South China Sea. The lack of maritime delimitation and a regional arrangement pending the maritime delimitation have seriously affected the assurance of good order at sea. Maritime accidents and pollution, fishing competition, IUU fishing and marine natural hazards, piracy and armed robbery against ships, maritime terrorism, illicit trafficking in drugs, arms and people smuggling are transboundary threats requiring large and effective regional cooperation. Conformity to the UNCLOS 1982 is necessary for overcoming these challenges to national and community interests at sea and sustainable development. Vietnam supports all initiatives and efforts for wide participation in regional arrangements and in cooperation in less sensitive fields. The maritime priority of Vietnam in the future will concentrate on the implementation of confidence-building measures; on talks to find a rational solution for disputes in the South China Sea; on concluding agreements on fishery activities, usually in the disputed areas; and on the coordination of relevant authorities in realising transboundary issues.

Notes

1 During the global financial crisis of 2009, China and Vietnam were two of the few countries to have a positive rate of development.

2 About 70 per cent of the fuel imports of Japan, China and South Korea are transported through the South China Sea. Hasjim Djalal and Ian Townsend-Gault, "Preventive Diplomacy: Managing Potential Conflicts in the South China Sea", in Crocker, Hampson and Aall (eds), *Herding Cats: Multiparty Mediation in a Complex World* (New York: United States Institute of Peace Press, 1999), pp. 107–133, http://faculty.law.ubc.ca/scs/cats.htm.

3 David Rosenberg and Christopher Chung, "Maritime security in the South China Sea: Coordinating Coastal and User State Priorities", *Ocean Development and International Law*, Vol. 39, Issue 1, 2008, pp. 51–52.

4 Sam Bateman, Joshua H. Ho and Jane Chan, *Good Order at Sea in Southeast Asia*, (Singapore: RSIS Policy Paper, April 2009), p. 16.
5 Ibid., p. 5.
6 Ibid., p. 16.
7 Ibid.
8 Kriangsak Kittichaisaree, *The Law of the Sea and Maritime Boundary Delimitation in Southeast Asia* (Singapore: Oxford University Press, 1987), Annex IV.
9 Nguyen Hong Thao and Ramses Amer, "Managing Vietnam's Maritime Boundary Disputes", *Ocean Development & International Law*, 38, 2007, pp. 305–324.
10 Sam Bateman, "Clashes at Sea: When Chinese vessels harass US Ships", *RSIS Commentaries 27/2009*, Singapore, 13 March 2009.
11 Submissions to the Commission on the Limits of the Continental Shelf (CLCS): Submission by the Republic of the Philippines, Executive Summary, www.un.org/Depts/los/clcs_new/submissions_files/submission_phl_22_2009.htm.
12 Submissions to the Commission on the Limits of the Continental Shelf (CLCS): Submission by the Republic of Indonesia, Executive Summary, www.un.org/Depts/los/clcs_new/submissions_files/submission_idn.htm.
13 "Vietnam's Submission on its Outer Limits of the Continental Shelf", Ministry of Foreign Affairs' Spokesman Mr Le Dzung answers question, 8 May 2009, www.mofa.gov.vn/en/tt_baochi/pbnfn/ns090508180346.
14 Vietnam Foreign Press Centre, "Vietnam submits report on continental shelf", 10 May 2009, http://vfpc.com.vn/Vietnam denounces China's objection regarding continental shelf report.htm.
15 Socialist Republic of Vietnam, Executive Summary, Submission to the Commission on the limits of the continental shelf, Pursuant Article 76, para. 8 of the United Nation Convention on the Law of the Sea 1982, Partial Submission in respect of Vietnam's extended continental shelf North Area (VNM-N), May 2009, www.un.org/Depts/los/clcs_new/submissions_files/submission_vnm_37_2009.htm/vnm2009n_executivesummary.pdf. See also Malaysia and Socialist Republic of Vietnam, Executive Summary, Joint Submission to the Commission on the limits of the continental shelf, Pursuant Article 76, para. 8 of the United Nation Convention on the Law of the Sea 1982 in respect of the southern part of the South China Sea, May 2009, www.un.org/Depts/los/clcs_new/submissions_files/submission_vnm_37_2009.htm/vnm2009n_executivesummary.pdf.
16 HA 24/09 Malaysian Permanent Mission Note to the United Nations, www.un.org/Depts/los/clcs_new/submissions_files/submission_vnm_37_2009.htm/mys_re_chn_2009re_mys_vnm_e.pdf.
17 CML/18/2009, New York, Note of the Permanent Mission of the People's Republic of China to the Secretary-General of the United Nation on 7 May 2009.
18 Tran Du, "Maritime Boundaries and the Spratlys: China causes concern", *OpinionAsia*, 29 June 2009, http://opinionasia.com/Chinamaritimeboundaries.
19 Note 000818, the Permanent Mission of the Republic of the Philippines to the Unites Nations, 4 August 2009, www.un.org/Depts/los/clcs_new/submissions_files/submission_vnm_37_2009.htm/clcs_37_2009_los_phl.pdf.
20 Tessa Jamandre, "RP hits Kalayaan claims", *Business Mirror*, VERA Files, 11 August 2009, http://businessmirror.com.ph/home/top-news/14424-rp-hits-kalayaan-claims.html 01:33.
21 Brunei Darussalam's Preliminary Submission concerning the Outer Limits of its Continental Shelf.
22 For a more detailed overview of the claims, see Nguyen Hong Thao and Ramses Amer, "The Management of Vietnam's Maritime Boundary Disputes", *Ocean Development and International Law*, Vol. 38, Issue 3, July 2007, pp. 306–309 (hereafter Nguyen and Amer, *The Management*).
23 Van Dyke and Bennett proposed a 12 mile territorial sea for rocks in the Spratlys Islands in J.M. Van Dyke and D.L. Bennett, "Islands and the Delimitation of Ocean

Space in the South China Sea", in E.M. Borgese, N. Ginsburg and J.R. Morgan (eds), *Ocean Yearbook*, Vol. 10 (Chicago: The University of Chicago Press, 1993), p. 54. See also John M. Van Dyke and Robert A. Brooks, "Uninhabited Islands: Their Impact on the Ownership of the Ocean's Resources", *Ocean Development and International Law*, Vol. 12, Issues 3–4, 1983, p. 265.

24 Yee Kai Pin, "China Pressures Exxon, Vietnam on South China Sea Project", *Dow Jones Newswires*, 24 July 2008, www.rigzone.com/NEWS/article.asp?a_id=64661.

25 "Vietnam criticizes Chinese fishing bans in South China Sea", *Asia-Pacific News*, 18 May 2009, www.monstersandcritics.com/news/asiapacific/news/article_1477907.php/Vietnam_criticizes_Chinese_fishing_bans_in_South_China_Sea_#ixzz0NfqC9K8q; "Beijing sends patrol ship to South China Sea", *AFP Asian Edition*, 14 March 2009, www.blnz.com/news/2009/03/16/Beijing_sends_patrol_ship_South_6459.html; "Patrol ship off to South China Sea", *Shenzhen Daily*, 16 March 2009, http://paper.sznews.com/szdaily/20090222/ca2910518.htm; "China charts course toward secure South China Sea", *People Daily Online*, 1 July 2009, http://english.peopledaily.com.cn/90001/90776/90786/6690696.html.

26 Nga Pham, "Hanoi protests China fishing ban", *BBC News*, http://news.bbc.co.uk/2/hi/asia-pacific/8089654.stm.

27 "Patrol ships trawl for disorder in Beibu Gulf", *China Daily.com*, 28 May 2009; "One more ship to patrol South China Sea", *China Daily.com*, 15 May 2009; "Reinforced patrol sails from Hainan", *China Daily.com*, 19 May 2009; "Controversial Chinese ban affects more Vietnamese fishing vessels", *Thanh Nien News*, 5 June 2009; "Fishermen intimidated and harassed by Chinese patrol boats", *Thanh Nien News*, 8 June 2009; "MOFA Spokesman answers reporters' question", *Nhan Dan*, 27 June 2009; "Calling for signs of goodwill from China", *Thanh Nien News*, 28 June 2009; "VN official asks for Chinese counterparts help in detained fishermen case", *VietNamNet Bridge*, 23 July 2009; "China arrests Vietnamese fishermen, demands astronomical fines", *Vietnam.net*, 30 June 2009; "China again demands money for Vietnamese fishermen", *Vietnam.net*, 7 July 2009; "Fishermen team up for protection, Vietnam asks China to lift ban", *Thanh Nien News*, 8 June 2009; "China detains Vietnamese fishermen fleeing storms", *DPA*, 4 August 2009; "Vietnam asks China to release fishermen", *DPA*, 5 August 2009; Beth Thomas, "China Releases Vietnamese Fishermen Seized Near Paracels Islands", *Bloomberg*, 12 August 2009; "Chinese Recurring Seizures of Vietnamese Fishermen and Boats Cause Concern" and "December 7–8 incident in which Chinese authorities busted three fishing boats from Quang Ngai province which were operating normally in Vietnam's Hoang Sa Archipelago, seizing two boats with equipment and possession of the fishermen before releasing 43 fishermen in one boat", Ministry of Foreign Affairs' Spokesperson, Ms Nguyen Phuong Nga, on 15 December 2009, www.mofa.gov.vn.

28 "Viet Nam Protests the Establishment of Hamlet Administration in Yongxing and Zhaoshu Islands", Ministry of Foreign Affairs' Spokesperson, Ms Nguyen Phuong Nga, on 16 November 2009, www.mofa.gov.vn.

29 "Vietnam reaffirms its indisputable sovereignty over Hoang Sa and Truong Sa archipelagos", Ministry of Foreign Affairs' Spokesperson, Ms Nguyen Phuong Nga, on 27 November 2009, www.mofa.gov.vn.

30 "Vietnam mentioned about the Chinese Law on defending islands", Ministry of Foreign Affairs' Spokesperson, Ms Nguyen Phuong Nga, on 29 December 2009, www.mofa.gov.vn.

31 "*Vietnam yeu cau Trung Quos cham dut tour du lich o Hoang Sa*", Ministry of Foreign Affairs' Spokesperson, Ms Nguyen Phuong Nag, on 4 January 2009, mofa.gov.vn.

32 "Vietnam's position on reports on March 5 saying that Malaysian Prime Minister Bandai visited the Swallow Reef", Ministry of Foreign Affairs' Spokesperson, Mr Le Dung, on 9 March 2009, www.mofa.gov.vn.

33 Tessa Jam André, "Baseline law signed; China protests", *Vera Files*, 11 March 2009, www.verafiles/185-baseline-law-signed-china-protests.htm.

34 The text of the 2002 ASEAN–PRC Declaration on the Conduct of Parties is reproduced as an Annex to Nguyen Hong Thao, "The 2002 Declaration on the Conduct of Parties in the South China Sea: A Note", *Ocean Development and International Law*, Vol. 34, Issues 1–2, 2003, pp. 282–285, www.aseansec.org/13165.htm. See also Nguyen Hong Thao, "The Declaration on the Conduct of Parties in the South China Sea: a Vietnamese perspective, 2002–2007", in Sam Bateman and Ralf Emmers (eds), *Security and International Politics in the South China Sea. Towards a co-operative management regime* (London and New York: Routledge, 2009), pp. 207–222.

35 Some Chinese scholars share the view of ASEAN countries that the DOC is significant in the sense that the South China Sea issue having originally been bilateral has now become a regional issue and should be solved under the framework of China–ASEAN cooperation. Zou Keyuan, "Suppressing piracy in the South China Sea: Toward a new cooperative establishment", paper presented at the international workshop on The South China Sea: Cooperation for Regional Security and Development, Ha Noi, 26–27 November 2009.

36 "*2010, Vietnam se lo thao luan bien gioi bien*", *Megaplus*, www.vnn.vn.

37 Nguyen Hong Thao and Ramses Amer, "A New Legal Arrangement for the South China Sea?", *Ocean Development & International Law*, Vol. 40, 4, 2009, pp. 333–349.

38 Nguyen Hong Thao, "*Cong uoc luat bien nam 1982 va chien luoc bien cua Vietnam, NXB Chinh tri quoc gia*" ("United Nations Convention on the Law of the Sea in 1982 and the Vietnamese Maritime Policy, Edt. Chinh tri quoc gia, 2008"), *Ha Noi*, 2008, pp. 254–256.

39 Nguyen Hong Thao, "*Cong uoc luat bien nam 1982 va chien luoc bien cua Vietnam, NXB Chinh tri quoc gia*" ("United Nation Convention on the Law of the Sea in 1982 and the Vietnamese Maritime Policy, Edt. Chinh tri quoc gia"), *Ha Noi*, 2008, pp. 259–287.

40 The fishing ban in the South China Sea has been imposed since 1998 for the period from 1 June to 31 August. In 2009, the ban was extended from 15 May to 31 August.

41 "Vietnam requests that Chinese side refrain from hampering normal fishing by Vietnamese fishermen", Ministry of Foreign Affairs' Spokesperson, 7 June 2009, www.mofa.gov.vn. On June 4, MOFA Deputy Foreign Minister Ho Xuan Son held an exchange with the PRC Ambassador to Vietnam, Sun Guoxiang, drawing the latter's attention to the fact that recently the Chinese ordered a fishing ban in some sea areas in the Eastern Sea, including those under Vietnam's sovereignty and increased patrol ships, made more arrests and imposed fines in these areas. The Deputy Minister was of the view that these acts had affected normal fishing activities by Vietnamese fishermen in Vietnam's traditional fishing grounds. They caused discontent among the public and do not serve the interest of bilateral relations between the two countries. He requested that the Chinese side refrain from any activities preventing normal work by Vietnamese fishermen in sea areas under Vietnamese sovereignty. The Chinese Ambassador promised to report the Vietnamese request to his capital. "Concerning Chinese patrol forces' arrest of a number of Vietnamese fishing boats and fishermen", Ministry of Foreign Affairs' Spokesperson, 25 June 2009, www.mofa.gov.vn. On 21 June 2009, Chinese patrol forces arrested three fishing boats manned by 37 fishermen from the Quang Ngai province of Vietnam while they were conducting normal fishing activities in the waters of the Hoang Sa Archipelago of Vietnam. The Vietnamese Government pays special attention to the safety of Vietnamese fishermen at sea. On 25 June 2009, two fishing boats and 25 fishermen returned safely to Vietnam. The Vietnamese authorities are now requesting the Chinese to release the remaining boat and fishermen and not to conduct any further acts to prevent the normal activities of Vietnamese fishermen in the waters under Vietnam's sovereignty. "Requesting the

Chinese side to immediately release 13 fishermen and their boat *QNg 95031TS*", Ministry of Foreign Affairs' Spokesperson on 3 August 2009, www.mofa.gov.vn. Vietnam's reaction to the news that on 1 August 2009, China seized fishing boat *QNg 95031TS* and 13 Vietnamese fishermen while moving to avoid a tropical depression in the area of Vietnam's Hoang Sa (Paracels) Archipelago. "Chinese Recurring Seizures of Vietnamese Fishermen and Boats Cause Concern", Ministry of Foreign Affairs' Spokesperson on 16 December 2009, www.mofa.gov.vn. Concerning the question from the media about the 7–8 December incident in which Chinese authorities arrested three fishing boats from Quang Ngai province that were operating normally in Vietnam's Hoang Sa Archipelago, seizing two boats with equipment and possession of the fishermen before releasing 43 fishermen in one boat, Vietnamese Ministry of Foreign Affairs' Spokesperson, Ms Nguyen Phuong Nga, responded that "Vietnam is concerned about the Chinese repeated seizures of Vietnamese fishing boats and fishermen while they operate normally in the waters of Vietnamese sovereignty. Such wrongful acts are a serious violation of Vietnam's sovereignty and sovereign rights, not in line with the friendship relations between the two countries and puts to harm life and property of Vietnamese fishermen. On 15 December 2009, the Ministry of Foreign Affairs of Vietnam handed a diplomatic note to the Embassy of China in Vietnam, demanding the Chinese side to return boats, equipment and property of the Vietnamese fishermen and take measures to prevent similar recurrence".

42 On 21 October 2009, in response to a question from the media about Vietnam's reaction to the late September incident in which Chinese armed officers opened fire against the entry of 16 boats of Quang Ngai province fishermen to Hoang Sa Archipelagos for shelter in the wake of Typhoon No. 9, and later beat them and took away their possessions and equipment, Vietnamese Ministry of Foreign Affairs' Spokesperson, Ms Nguyen Phuong Nga, responded that "The Ministry of Foreign Affairs of Vietnam in the October 21st afternoon handed a diplomatic note to the Ambassador of China to Vietnam in protest of the inhumane acts by the Chinese armed officers toward Vietnamese fishermen upon their refuge in Phu Lam Island (Tru Cau by Vietnamese fishermen) in Vietnam's Hoang Sa Archipelago, occupied by China. The Ministry demands in the note the Chinese side promptly look into the incident, strictly discipline the officers who acted cruelly against Vietnamese fishermen, return possessions to and compensate losses for the fishermen, and take measures to prevent recurrence of similar acts", Ministry of Foreign Affairs' Spokesperson on 21 October 2009, www.mofa.gov.vn.

43 On 15 July 2009, while operating in Vietnamese waters at 13°45' N 110°32' E, fishing vessel *QNg 2203* was hit and sunk by an unidentified ship, injuring nine fishermen on board. On 22 July 2009, answering correspondents' question about what Vietnam has been doing about the case, Vietnamese Foreign Ministry's Spokesman Le Dzung said, "The Vietnamese Government pays special attention to the safety of Vietnamese fishermen at sea. Right after the incident occurred, Vietnamese competent authorities have promptly launched an investigation, particularly the identification of the ship. On 16 July 2009, Vietnamese Foreign Ministry sent notes to other countries in the region, informing them of the case and asking for their cooperation to conduct investigation in order to ensure safe fishing activities for fishermen and maritime security", Ministry of Foreign Affairs' Spokesperson on 18 July, 2009, www.mofa.gov.vn.

44 Baiying Kang, "Hainan's Role in the Management of the South China Sea Issues – A Case Study of the Gulf of Tonkin", paper presented for the international workshop on Dispute Settlement and Conflict Management in Pacific Asia, organized by the Department of Oriental Languages, Stockholm University, Stockholm, 21–22 August 2009. According to the paper, while more illegal fishing cases are carried out by Hainan fishers, all seven armed robbery cases are of Vietnamese vessels robbing Hainan fishermen.

45 "China Asks Indonesia to Free Fishermen", *Jakarta Globe*, 26 June 2009.

46 "Neighboring countries poach Indonesia's fish", *PNA/Antara*, 25August 2009.
47 "Indonesia adopts new law on fishery", *Xinhua*, 15 September 2009, www.people.com.cn.
48 An Dien, "Indonesia pledges safe, humane treatment of Vietnamese fishermen", *Thanh Nien Weekly*, 13 November 2009.
49 "Viet Nam, China Sign Cooperation Agreements", statement by Vietnam's Foreign Affairs Ministry, 25 December 2000, www.mofa.gov.vn/; "Two China-Vietnam Beibu Gulf agreements take effect", *People.com*, 1 July 2004, http://english.people.com.cn/200407/01/eng20040701_148157.html; Zou Keyuan, "The Sino-Vietnamese Agreement on Maritime Boundary Delimitation in the Gulf of Tonkin", *Ocean Development and International Law*, Vol. 34, No. 1, January 2003, pp. 13–24; Nguyen Hong Thao, "Maritime Delimitation and Fishery Cooperation in the Tonkin Gulf", *Ocean Development and International Law*, Vol. 34, No. 1, January 2003, pp. 25–44; Zou Keyuan, "Sino-Vietnamese Fishery Agreement for the Gulf of Tonkin", *The International Journal of Marine and Coastal Law*, Vol. 17, No. 1, January, pp. 127–148.
50 S. Huang, "Joint MCS in the Beibu Gulf to Maintain Security in the Fishing Ground", *Zhongguang Net*, 1 July 2009, http://211.89.225.4:82/gate/big5/www.cnr.cn/gundong/200907/t20090701_505385400.html.
51 Nguyen Hong Thao, "Thailand-Vietnamese boundary agreement", *Boundary and security bulletin*, V. 5, N. 3, Autumn 1997, pp. 74–78.
52 According to MarketWatch, China's imports of crude oil in the January to May period totalled 75.97 million metric tonnes (659.8 million barrels). See also Douglas McIntyre, "China oil consumption jumps", *Market Watch*, 11 Jun 2008, www.bloggingstocks.com/2008/06/11/china-oil-consumption-jumps/.
53 "Oil Gas Resources and Shipping Terminals in South China Sea", 9 May 2006, www.oilgasarticles.com/articles/474/1/Oil-Gas-Resources-and-Shipping-Terminals-in-South-China-Sea/Page1.html.
54 For an analysis of the "nine-dotted line" see Li Jinming and Li Dexia, "The Dotted Line in the Chinese Map of the South China Sea", *Ocean Development and International Law* Vol. 34, Issues 3–4, 2003, pp. 287–295.
55 Brian McCartan, "Rolling the waters in the Spratlys", *Asia Sentinel*, 4 February 2008, www.asiasentinel.com/index.php?option=com_content&task=view&id=1026&Itemid=31. On BP, ConocoPhillips, see "Vietnam's action on Nansha Islands infringe in China's Sovereignty, FM spokesman", *People's Daily*, 10 April 2007, http://english.peopledaily.com.cn/200704/10/eng20070410_365316.html. On BP–Conoco Phillips, see Andrew Symon, "China, Vietnam spar over gas", *Asia Times Online*, 1 May 2007, www.atimes.com/atimes/Southeast_Asia/IE01Ae01.html. On the ONGC, see Anupama Airy, "ONGC's Vietnam foray illegal says China", *The Financial Express*, 12 March 2007, www.financialexpress.com/news/ONGCs-Vietnam-foray-illegal-says-China/246000/). On Exxon, see 'China confirms telling Exxon to end Vietnam oil deal", *Reuters*, 22 July 2008, www.reuters.com/article/rbssEnergyNews/idUSPEK26391320080722.
56 Wang Yin, "CNOOC Plans $29 Billion South China Sea Exploration (Update 2)", *Bloomberg*, 24 November 2008, www.bloomberg.com/apps/news?pid=20601080&sid=aXVBShwT6cbY&refer=asia.
57 Nguyen Hong Thao, "*Cong uoc luat bien nam 1982 va chien luoc bien cua Vietnam*" ("United Nations Convention on the Law of the Sea in 1982 and the Vietnamese Maritime Policy, Edt. Chinh tri quoc gia"), *NXB Chinh tri quoc gia*, Ha Noi, 2008.
58 Eric Frécon, "Beyond the Sea: Fighting Piracy in Southeast Asia", *RSIS Commentaries 128/2009*, 21 December 2009. Sea also Sam Bateman *et al.*, *Good Order at Sea in Southeast Asia*, p. 17.
59 Sam Bateman *et al.*, *Good Order at Sea in Southeast Asia*, p. 25.
60 UN Doc. A/50/713, p. 31, para. 107.
61 Erik Jaap Molenaar, "'London Convention', Current Legal Developments", *The International Journal of Marine and Coastal Law*, Vol. 12, No. 3, 1997.

Part III

Maritime challenges and priorities in Northeast Asia

11 China's maritime security

Priorities and challenges

Wang Dong and Jiang Xin

The evolution of the Chinese maritime security discourse

Traditionally regarded as a land power, contemporary China is nevertheless highly dependent on the oceans. The five coastal provinces in East China – Shandong, Jiangsu, Zhejiang, Fujian and Guangdong – account for one-fifth of China's population and two-fifths of national gross domestic product (GDP). In coastal regions alone, there are more than 55 million people relying on jobs created by foreign trade. The dependence on foreign trade is as high as 95.95 percent in these coastal provinces. In the energy sector, up to 2008, 55 percent of China's oil had to be imported from abroad.[1] It is estimated that by the end of 2010, 57 percent of minerals, 70 percent of copper and 80 percent of aluminum will have to be imported from abroad. In addition, 70 percent of China's imported oil would have to pass the Strait of Malacca, and among all the cargoes that pass through the strait, 60 percent are bound to and from China.[2] The security of sea lines of communication (SLOCs) is therefore critical to the economic growth of China.

The idea of maritime security, however, took a long trajectory in China. China's repeated incursions by Western imperialist powers in Chinese modern history, beginning with the First Opium War of 1840, left an indelible mark on the ideational legacy of maritime security in China, which places a high premium on sovereignty and the traditional military dimension of security. It was not until the end of the Cold War that China's concept of security expanded to include non-traditional security dimensions. Consequently, the Chinese discourse of maritime security has also gradually expanded.[3] Non-traditional security issues, such as energy, people smuggling, maritime drug trafficking, maritime environmental protection, fishery disputes and so on are being incorporated into the scholarly and policy discourses of maritime security in China.

An examination of the scholarly and policy discourses on maritime security in China since 1990 reveals some interesting patterns. Table 11.1 reveals the changing scholarly and policy discourses on various aspects of maritime security in the two decades following the end of the Cold War by showing the number of journal articles published on each of the issues.

Admittedly, the data compiled here are merely suggestive rather than conclusive. Moreover, there are bound to be some overlaps among different types of

Table 11.1 Changing scholarly and policy discourses on maritime security in China, 1990–2009

No. of journal articles/issue areas	*1990–1994*	*1995–1999*	*2000–2004*	*2005–2009*
Sea power	4	22	58	133
Maritime rights and benefits (*haiyang quanyi*)	1	7	24	45
Maritime laws	13	64	38	82
South China Sea disputes/South China Sea issue	4	6	42	128
The Diaoyu Islands issue/The Diaoyu Islands disputes	2	38	61	80
Piracy (Southeast Asia)	1	1	10	13
Piracy (The Gulf of Aden/Somalia)	0	1	3	151
Maritime resources	7	32	54	129
The East China Sea (oil & gas)	0	0	12	115
The South China Sea (oil & gas)	5	2	25	68
US–China maritime relations	4	7	19	45
China–Japan maritime relations	4	12	33	109
Maritime non-traditional security	0	0	18	31
Sea lane security	2	3	13	43
Maritime people smuggling	9	19	20	15
Fishery disputes	1	5	1	3
Maritime environmental protection	1	3	14	22
Maritime drug trafficking	0	0	3	4
Small arms smuggling	0	0	6	9

Source: Data was collected from the China Academic Journal Network Publishing Database, the largest database of Chinese academic journals in the world. By November 2009, the database included over 279 million articles from 6,968 in 1915. http://acad.cnki.net/Kns55/brief/result.aspx?dbPrefix=CJFQ.

Methodological notes

The numbers of journal articles in each issue area are reported by conducting a key word/abstract search of the database, and the numbers are reported every five years to show a trajectory over time; the reported numbers could serve as a proxy measurement of the scholarly and policy discussion in each of those issue areas; the reported articles are authored by both scholars from research universities and analysts from think tanks, therefore serving as the basis for an approximate measurement of the scholarly and policy discourses in various issue areas of maritime security in China.

issues – for example, in cases where an article encompasses more than one "key word" as categorized in this table. Nevertheless, the data can at least serve as a proxy measurement of the changing patterns of scholarly and policy discourses on various aspects of maritime security in China over the past two decades. For instance, the scholarly and policy discourses on sea power (*hai quan*) more than doubled since 2005 from the previous period of 2000–2004; as did the scholarly and policy discussion on so-called maritime rights and benefits (*haiyang quanyi*). The scholarly and policy discussion on piracy rose dramatically in 2008 and 2009, with attention overwhelmingly being drawn to the piracy threats in the Gulf of Aden and off the coast of Somalia. Since 1995, the Dianyu (Senkaku) Islands have emerged as a key problem in the China–Japan relationship and have remained a prominent topic in scholarly research and policy debate of maritime security in China. The same pattern can be discerned regarding the South China Sea issue, although with relatively less research and debate going on. Maritime resources (especially concerning oil and gas), US–China maritime relations, and China–Japan maritime relations have over the past two decades consistently remained hot topics. The US–China standoff over the Taiwan Missile Crisis of 1995–1996 might have served as the overall exogenous "shock" that contributed to the systemic rise of scholarly and policy attention to maritime security since 1995.

Compared to other issues, the non-traditional dimensions of maritime security, including maritime people smuggling, maritime drug trafficking and fishery disputes, have received scant attention in scholarly and policy discussions. The only surprising exception is the issue of maritime environmental protection, which has received much more attention than most other aspects of maritime security in China.

This chapter is divided into four sections. The first section will survey the scholarly and policy debates over sea power and Chinese maritime security. The second section will examine the disputes over maritime territory and energy resources. It will be followed by an examination of the threats of piracy and maritime terrorism. The last section focuses on the challenges brought by other forms of non-traditional security challenges, such as people smuggling, drug trafficking and small arms smuggling.

Debates over sea power and China's maritime strategy

At the core of the scholarly and policy discourses on Chinese maritime security are sea power and maritime military security. It is worth providing an exposition on the meaning of sea power in the Chinese context.[4] Unlike the classic Mahanian definition, which conceptualizes sea power mainly as naval strength and the ability to dominate and control the sea, the term *quan* in *haiquan* (sea power) carries at least three different meanings.[5] The first interpretation is a legalistic one, where *quan* means *quanli* 权利 (rights); therefore *haiquan* in this context refers to *haiyang quanli* (maritime rights) and more specifically, the basic national security concept of non-infringeable maritime sovereignty.[6] The second interpretation of *quan* is more realist-oriented (defensive realism), which interprets *quan* as *quanli* 权力 (power). Thus, *haiquan* refers to maritime power, a state's capacity to realize its goals (strategic, security, military and economic) at sea.[7] Lastly, in the vein of offensive realism, *quan* could be interpreted as *baquan* 霸权 (hegemony). Hence, *haiquan* in this context would refer to dominance at sea beyond territorial waters.[8] The three different meanings of *haiquan* represent different ways of conceptualizing Chinese maritime security[9] (see Table 11.2)

A recent poll conducted by a leading Chinese newspaper, *Guoji xianqu daobao* (International Herald Leader), reveals that about 79 percent of the Chinese public polled endorse the legalistic interpretation of *haiquan*, viewing it as the maritime rights and benefits that China enjoys according to international laws, including exclusive rights of navigation, fishing, sea-farming, exploration of energy resources such as oil and gas and so on, in territorial waters and the exclusive economic zone (EEZ). In comparison, only about 16 percent of the surveyed public would take a realist interpretation of *haiquan*, viewing it as the power to control or dominate the sea.[10]

Interestingly, unlike the public's legalistic interpretation of *haiquan*, there is a considerable number of scholars who would take a hard realist view, focusing on the military security dimension of sea power. Such a school of scholarly and policy discourses take a geopolitical sound bite viewing the military presence of great sea powers, such as the United States and Japan in the Asia-Pacific region, and including American troops in Japan and the South Korea, as a potential threat to China's maritime security. Many of those scholarly and policy discourses would also tend to perceive continuous US arms sales to Taiwan as evidence of American plot of "pinning China down," and perceive Taiwan as a key component of the island chain strategy to encircle, if not contain, China.[11] With a deeply rooted victim mentality originating from the historical memories of "centuries of humiliation," many Chinese analysts and the public at large tend to perceive the outside world through the lens of conspiracy theory, thus rendering such scholarly and policy discourse appealing to both policy makers and the public.

The defensive realist-oriented scholarly and policy discourse, however, could easily morph into a more offensive realist-oriented one. Scholars and analysts of

Table 11.2 Different conceptualizations of sea power in China

	Conceptualization as	*Intellectual orientation*	*Core issues of concern*
Haiquan (sea power)	*quanli* 权利 (rights)	Legalistic-oriented	Maritime rights and benefits, as stipulated by international laws
	quanli 权力 (power)	Defensive realism-oriented	Maritime sovereignty
	*baquan*霸权 (hegemony)	Offensive-realism	Dominance at sea

the offensive realist discourse might begin with the defensive realist assumption, viewing sea power as the key to the defense of China's maritime security and, first and foremost, maritime sovereignty. However, the defensive realist logic could easily be extended to call for expansion of China's *haiquan* (sea power), especially the capability to project military forces overseas to protect China's overseas energy resources as well as trade benefits. Those hard-core realists have little faith in the liberal free trade idea, believing "there are moments when the deployment of a dozens of warships would be more valuable than holding in hands a dozens of trade agreements which could be easily scrapped." For them, military power is the most reliable asset for dealing with hegemons like the United States. Mindful of an American dominance at sea, these scholars and policy analysts argue that strengthening China's sea power holds the key to competing with the United States for a share of maritime rights and benefits.[12] Some scholars might add qualifications to the argument, calling the sea power they prescribe for China as *yougian haiquan* (limited sea power) and defensive in nature.[13] The problem in practice is, of course, that the line is difficult to draw between "limited sea power" and more ambitious goals.

The *International Herald Leader* poll reveals that a combined 53.1 percent of the surveyed public view the "biggest threat to China's maritime rights and benefits" as coming from external sources, with 32.4 percent perceiving the threat as originating from "the forces that worry about and intend to *contain* China" and 20.7 percent believing the threat comes from "the countries that have maritime boundary disputes with China." When asked about the best way to defend and protect China's maritime rights and benefits, 54.5 percent of people polled opted for "building a powerful navy and a unified and highly effective paramilitary force." Another 26.6 percent gave priority to the idea that "state should develop explicit maritime strategy," while 16.8 percent chose "to respond forcefully to acts that infringe upon China's rights and benefits."[14] It is worth noting that although quite a few of the public surveyed hold that China should play tough in response to other countries' acts that are perceived to be encroaching on China's maritime rights and benefits, less support the more aggressive idea that China should seek overseas hegemony by engaging in outward expansion.[15]

It is also against the backdrop of the increasing public awareness of sea power that debates raged over naval modernization, especially whether or not China should build aircraft carriers. A recent debate was engaged between two prominent Chinese scholars. In a February 2007 article, Ye Zicheng, a preeminent professor on strategic studies at Peking University, argued that China should postpone the building of aircraft carriers, and instead give priority to developing land power rather than sea power.[16] Ye's argument was met with fierce rebuttal from Ni Lexiong, another prominent scholar at Fudan University. Ni specifically criticizes the expansion of the conceptualization of sea power to include non-traditional maritime rights and benefits, such as exploration of maritime oil and gas fields, protection of territorial waters and EEZs, fishing rights and so on, insisting on a Mahanian, more realist-oriented conceptualization that defines sea power as a state's capability to control the sea by employing military force.

Attacking Ye's argument head-on, Ni holds that China's long-held "near sea defense" or "offshore defense" (*jinhai fangyu*) strategy might be outdated, and that aircraft carriers would play a pivotal role in deterring foreign forces from intervening in an "anti-Taiwan-independence-struggle" scenario.[17] The Ye–Ni debate aroused heated discussions in internet chat rooms and message boards in China.[18]

As the Chinese Defense Ministry announced on 23 December 2008 that China is "seriously considering" building an aircraft carrier to "protect the security of China's major sea-lanes" and "safeguard China's sovereignty of territorial waters as well as maritime rights and benefits," it seems that the debate is largely over.[19] News soon appeared from the Japanese media that China was indeed planning to build four carriers and two nuclear-powered aircraft carriers of about 60,000 tons, in addition to two conventional aircraft carriers.[20] Strategically and militarily, China's aircraft carrier battle groups would be crucial in transforming its navy from a coastal brown-water navy to a blue-water one. Arguably, China's acquisition of aircraft carriers would tip the geostrategic balance in Asia.[21] Already, worry about China's increased naval power may have triggered Association of Southeast Asian Nations (ASEAN) countries to increase security cooperation and expand joint patrols in the Strait of Malacca. So far, China has kept a low profile in its aircraft carrier program and, by and large, its sea power strategy. In terms of declared strategy and policy, China has adopted a cooperative approach, seeking to preserve maritime security through measures of confidence-building, such as navy port calls, bilateral maritime military security consultation mechanisms, joint maritime disaster relief and search and rescue exercises.[22] However, as China's sea power increases further, Beijing would have to craft a more explicit, comprehensive sea power strategy that prioritizes China's maritime security challenges and, ideally, paves the way for the peaceful rise a new great sea power.

Maritime boundary disputes

One of the potential threats to China's maritime security is the disputes over territorial waters and maritime boundaries: first and foremost, China's disputes with Japan regarding the East China Sea and China's disputes with ASEAN countries over the South China Sea.

At the core of the East China Sea issue is the China–Japan disputes over the Diaoyu Island and the oil and gas fields in the East China Sea. In both the case of the East China Sea and of the South China Sea, disputes over maritime boundary division are intertwined with the competition for maritime energy resources. Indeed, disputes over the Diaoyu Island did not emerge until late 1960s when a UN-commissioned report indicating rich oil resources located under the waters around the islands came out.[23] Since the end of the Cold War, the possibility of territorial disputes over the Diaoyu Islands escalating into armed conflict has indeed increased, as nationalist sentiments are running increasingly high in both Japan and China. In recent years, China–Japan disputes over the Diaoyu Islands caused important strategic ramifications to the region, gradually changing the dynamics of the Beijing–Washington–Tokyo strategic triangle and driving the US–Japanese alliance much closer.[24] In 1997, Japan and Washington revised the US–Japan Defense Guidelines, stipulating that US–Japan defense cooperation would govern "situation in areas surrounding Japan."[25] In the wake of the intense China–Japan standoff over the Diaoyu Islands in September 2010, top US officials, in a departure from their long-held ambivalent attitude, made it clear that the United States was under a treaty obligation to come to the aid of Japan should a military conflict over the Diaoyu Islands occur.[26] The shift in US position, partly designed to reassure its Japanese ally, nevertheless renders any possible conflict over the Diaoyu Islands potentially explosive.[27]

Differences in the guiding principles for the resolution of maritime boundaries complicate disputes over oil and gas fields in the East China Sea. While the Chinese side insists on sticking to the continental shelf principle, the Japanese side stresses that the delimitation should follows EEZs and raises a "middle line" proposal. The overlapping sovereignty claims to the Diaoyu Islands, located in the southern part of the East China Sea, add to the complexity of negotiations for resources.

Much like the case in the East China Sea, the territorial disputes in the South China Sea did not emerge until the release of the Emery Report in 1969, which made clear the enormous oil reserves in the South China Sea. The 1973 oil crisis only added to the attractiveness of the South China Sea. Beginning in the 1970s and 1980s, all claimants scrambled to occupy claimed reefs or islets scattered in the South China Sea, and did not refrain from using or threatening to use force to resolve disputes.[28]

The disputes in the East China Sea and the South China Sea have become a destabilizing factor to the regional peace and security in the Asia-Pacific. Moreover, it should be recognized that debates over purely historical evidence and different interpretations of the ocean law make any possible resolution of the Diaoyu Islands issue out of reach. Indeed, Chinese scholars and analysts generally agree that a reasonable vision of the resolution of the disputes would involve shelving sovereignty disputes by establishing Confidence Building Measures (CBMs) and trying to seek consensus gradually.[29]

For decades, China and Japan have been making competing sovereignty claims regarding the Diaoyu Islands, with the majority of Japanese commentators claiming Japanese sovereignty over the islands while the Chinese, along with a minority of Japanese scholars on the left, argue the opposite.[30] The Japanese scholar Suganuma Unryu notes that the problem of the Diaoyu Island disputes is that while both the Chinese and Japanese sides can provide historical records showing their continual control of the island, neither side is able to present definitive official documents proclaiming sovereignty over the Diaoyu Islands. Therefore, it is impossible, based on the existing international law, to rule on the sovereignty of the Diaoyu Islands. Unryu argues that the most plausible way to resolve the disputes might be to shelve them and reach agreement on joint exploration through diplomatic measures.[31]

Besides the Diaoyu Islands issue, China and Japan also have disputes over the EEZ boundary in the East China Sea, leading to controversial "incursions" of vessels into each other's claimed territorial waters. The risk of a clash increased when both sides started to drill in areas where their claims overlap. [32]

Chinese scholars and analysts generally hold the unanimous view that based on historical and geographical, as well as international law evidence, China enjoys indisputable sovereignty over the Diaoyu Islands. However, Chinese scholars do not shy away from criticism when it comes to China's strategy and policy. For instance, Liu Zhongmin, one of the major scholars on maritime security in China, is unequivocal in criticizing China's lack of "top level strategic planning," as well as its lack of "systemic studies and predictive assessment of Japan's strategies and measures." In a Ministry of Education-sponsored study of China's maritime strategy, Liu urges that China should establish a special inter-departmental agency, led by top leaders, to deal with territorial and maritime rights disputes with Japan. Such an agency should be in charge of studying and developing strategies and policies, and coordinating policies among various key institutions, including the Ministry of Foreign Affairs, the Ministry of National Defense, the Ministry of State Security and the State Oceanic Administration.[33]

Mark Valencia and Yoshihisa Amae suggest that the best way to deal with these controversial issues may be to develop an effective regime to coordinate each party's actions. First, both Japan and China should refrain from overt suspicion and hostility toward each other, i.e., China viewing Japanese naval vessel patrols as evidence of Japan's ambition to expand its naval forces, or Japan viewing "incursions" by Chinese naval vessels as evidence of the China threat. Valencia and Amae suggest that Beijing and Tokyo should, following the example of the United States and the Soviet Union in which the two reached the unprecedented Incidents at Sea Agreement in 1972, establish a military consultation and coordination regime, which could help avoid miscalculation or escalation of conflict during crisis times. The annual security dialog between China and Japan, as well as mutual port calls, has laid a foundation for the establishment of such a regime.[34]

Since the 1990s, many scholars and analysts have put forth constructive proposals for the resolution of the South China Sea disputes. Among the most comprehensive is one proposed by Mark Valencia. The essence of Valencia's proposal, which was first raised in 1990 and expanded further in the mid-1990s, is to shelve sovereignty disputes and achieve joint development of the South China Sea through the establishment of a multilateral Spratly Islands Development Authority, following the model of joint management of the South Pole by the international community. The Spratly Islands Development Authority would administer the core area and manage the exploration and exploitation of resources there. The Valencia proposal suggests that the Chinese mainland and Taiwan should be given a combined 51 percent shares in exchange for their historic "claims" to most of the South China Sea, and the remaining shares be divided among Vietnam, the Philippines and Malaysia. Valencia argues that under such a "cooperative regime," the area would be demilitarized, sovereignty claims would be frozen and the authority would be responsible for arbitrating user conflicts, facilitating exploration and the development of resources, managing fishery issues, and promoting international cooperation in scientific research and environment protection. Moreover, the legitimate transit of vessels would be allowed, keeping the strategic sea-lanes open to the international community.[35]

Valencia's proposal is echoed by the recent suggestion by Chinese analysts of a South China Sea Energy Development Organization. Believing that the problem of the South China Sea disputes lies in the exclusive claims to resource-rich maritime territories, the Chinese scholar Xue Li, affiliated with the Institute of World Economics and Politics at the Chinese Academy of Social Sciences, argues in a recent article that the best solution to the South China Sea disputes is to translate exclusive, zero-sum territorial claims to win-win joint development and economic cooperation, and transform potential armed conflict to bargaining within a regime.[36] While Xue Li's proposal focuses more on the economic dimension of the solution to the disputes, other Chinese analysts also argue that China should "actively participate in the construction of a South China Sea regional security mechanism," and "actively maintain the security of navigation in the South China Sea."[37]

The biggest challenge for scholars and policy makers of all claimant parties is how to defuse disputes over maritime oil and gas resources with sovereignty disputes remaining unresolved. China has for a long time championed the idea of "shelving disputes, and seeking joint development" (*gezhi zhengyi, gongtong kaifa*), first proposed by China's former paramount leader Deng Xiaoping in the late 1970s, as the guiding principles for resolving maritime territorial disputes.[38] There has been some limited success in that regard.

In October 2005, after three rounds of China–Japan consultations on the East China Sea issue, Japan accepted the Chinese proposal of "joint development" of the East China Sea. In June 2008, the Chinese Ministry of Foreign Affairs announced that Beijing and Tokyo had agreed to "jointly develop" a select region of 2,700 sq. km in the East China Sea. However, the joint development initiative quickly fell into abeyance due partly to domestic political oppositions on both sides.[39]

In September 1994, China and the Philippines signed an agreement to conduct joint research and development of the oil and gas resources in the South China Sea. Again, in March 2005, China, the Philippines and Vietnam signed a trilateral agreement for joint exploration of oil and gas resources in an agreed area in the South China Sea. However, the tripartite agreement, the first of its kind in history, remains largely as ink on paper as a consequence of domestic political obstacles coming from the Philippines.[40]

One of the most remarkable points of progress toward the peaceful resolution of disputes over the South China Sea was made in 2002, when China and ten ASEAN member countries signed the Declaration on the Conduct of Parties in the South China Sea (DOC). A non-legally binding document, the DOC urges the parties concerned to exercise self-restraint and not to use force or threats of force in resolving their differences.[41] The DOC marked a first step toward establishing a code of conduct in the South China Sea and indeed signified a "major leap for peace" by laying down a strong framework for future negotiations on territorial issues in the South China Sea.[42] Unfortunately, since the signing of the DOC, all parties concerned seemed to have been increasingly trapped in a "prisoner's dilemma," "defecting" from cooperation and engaging in "self-help" behavior.

The unsettling episode of 2011 concerning the alleged Chinese claim of the South China Sea as China's "core interests" and the ensuing moves by the United States and some ASEAN claimant countries to counter the perceived Chinese assertiveness has, perhaps more than anything else, highlighted the precarious and complex situation in the South China Sea.[43] The more encouraging news is that this recent controversy has already prompted Beijing to push for a stronger code of conduct in the South China Sea that aims at preventing territorial disputes from escalating into armed conflict.[44] In any event, the proposals put forth by scholars and policy makers alike are indicative of ideational evolution and the convergence of norms in the Asia-Pacific, epitomized by the so-called ASEAN Way that increasingly delegitimates the use of force in resolving differences, which might in the long run help transform self-help behavior into cooperation.[45]

Combating piracy and maritime terrorism

Among the most direct threats to China's maritime security are piracy, maritime terrorism and other forms of maritime armed hijacking.[46] It is estimated that the total annual economic losses caused by piracy worldwide are as high as US$16–25 billion.[47] Given the fact that about four-fifths of China's imported oil has to go through the Strait of Malacca, piracy constitutes a threat to the security of China's key supply line of oil and other resources.[48] In 2008 alone, there were 62 reported incidences of piracy and armed robbery in the South China Sea, accounting for 30 percent of piracy incidences worldwide. Until the surge of piracy activities along the coast of the Gulf of Aden in 2008, the South China Sea and the Strait of Malacca were the waters most susceptible to the predation of piracy and maritime violence.[49]

One worrisome trend is that piracy and maritime terrorism are becoming increasingly intertwined and indistinguishable from each another.[50] Terrorist groups such as al-Qaeda have threatened to target maritime economic lifelines.[51] If terrorists were to hijack a vessel transporting liquefied natural gas (LNG) to conduct a suicide mission in the Strait of Malacca, as an analyst warns, it would "devastate Southeast Asia's economies and environment and severely disrupt trade as the Straits could be closed to shipping and fishing."[52]

The intertwining of piracy and maritime terrorism has propelled the ASEAN to lump together piracy and maritime terrorism in its declaration for fighting against threats to maritime security. Summarizing its experiences of combating terrorist threats, the Singaporean military concluded that when you cannot distinguish pirates from terrorists, the best way is to treat them alike.[53] Analysts also point out that in terms of short-term policy measures, there are overlaps in dealing with maritime terrorism and piracy, both involving increasing maritime patrols, enhancing coordination among agencies and beefing up the self-defense capability of vessels.[54] In 2004, Malaysia, Indonesia and Singapore developed an initiative known as "Eyes in the Sky" to conduct joint air patrols of the Strait of Malacca. In September 2005, the three littoral countries conducted the first joint maritime patrol aviation. In April 2006, the Eyes in the Sky patrol was subsumed under an overarching framework called the Malacca Straits Patrols.[55] The strengthening of international coordination of counter-piracy and maritime terrorism measures among stakeholder ASEAN countries correlates with the decline of piracy attacks in the South China Sea and the Strait of Malacca regions since 2004.[56]

However, at the same time as incidences of piracy were in decline in these areas, piracy attacks in the Beibuwan Gulf (Gulf of Tonkin) and the offshore waters of China's coastal province of Guangxi were on the rise. Yang Kai, a Chinese scholar specializing in Southeast Asian studies suggests that the enhancement of regional cooperation of ASEAN countries in combating piracy might have driven pirates to "migrate" to the north. Therefore, China is now faced with an ironic situation: while the People's Liberation Army Navy (PLAN) for the first time in history dispatched fleets a thousand miles away to the Gulf of Aden for escort missions, pirates were creeping onto China's doorsteps.[57]

Singaporean Deputy Prime Minister Tony Tan once remarked, "We know very well that individual state action is not enough. The oceans are indivisible and maritime security threats do not respect boundaries."[58] However, the existing bilateral and multilateral counter-piracy frameworks such as the Indonesian–Malaysian–Singaporean mechanism are limited by the incumbent members' reluctance to open up and include more outside members. Jealously guarding their sovereignty, ASEAN countries keep a wary eye on the possibility of a great power making inroads into their backyard.[59]

The signing of the Regional Cooperation Agreement on Combating Piracy and Armed Robbery against Ships in Asia (ReCAAP) represented the first effort to institutionalize regional cooperation in combating piracy and armed robbery. With fifteen contracting countries spanning the Asia-Pacific region, including the ASEAN member countries, China, Japan, South Korea, India, Sri Lanka and Bangladesh, the ReCAAP perhaps also crystallizes the most ambitious endeavor ever to address the perennial threat of piracy and armed robbery to maritime security.[60] However, despite its declared three pillars of information sharing, capacity building, and cooperative agreements, the ReCAAP regime to date is still very much limited to the information sharing stage, with the Singapore-based ReCAAP Information Sharing Center (ISC) being the flagship institutional entity. Since the launch of the ReCAAP ISC in September 2006, China has been actively participating in institutional and capacity building, having not only sent a representative to the ReCAAP ISC but also established a Search and Rescue Center under the Ministry of Transportation that collaborates with the ReCAAP ISC and coordinates China's counter-piracy efforts.[61] However, moving from the information-sharing stage to more substantive cooperation, such as joint maritime patrols and counter-piracy/terrorism operations, will be crucial for the further institutionalization of the ReCAAP regime. Needless to say, moving to more substantive cooperation is no easy task, especially in light of the complex political relations among many of the ReCAAP member countries and the fluid geostrategic situation in Asia. For instance, as early as in 2000, China and Japan signed a memorandum to begin police cooperation in the East China Sea, partly aimed at strengthening counter-piracy measures. The initiative quickly died out as China–Japan political relations were soon strained. In addition, China's discussion with Singapore on establishing joint patrols to tackle piracy and drug deals in the South China Sea came to nothing, partly due to the wariness and uneasiness of some ASEAN member countries.[62]

One challenge for China is to find an appropriate way to take part in the institutional build-up of a counter-piracy regime in the South China Sea and the Strait of Malacca. Japan's leadership role in building the ReCAAP regime is a model that China can follow.[63] A more active and leading role in pushing forward the counter-piracy regime will help build trust between China and its neighbors in the Asia-Pacific; thus, in the long run it may help alleviate the emerging security dilemma in the South China Sea. China could substantiate its cooperation with ASEAN countries through existing international organizations such as the ReCAAP ISC, the International Maritime Bureau, the International Criminal Police Organization and the IBM Piracy Reporting Center. Moreover, the Joint Declaration of ASEAN and China on Cooperation in the Field of Non-Traditional Security Issues, released at the 6th ASEAN–China Summit in November 2002, laid out an institutional framework for the ASEAN–China cooperation in addressing non-traditional security issues, including sea piracy.[64] The challenge now is how to move from the initial stage of information exchange and personnel exchange and training to "practical cooperation" on non-traditional security issues. In this regard, China should take a leadership initiative.

Maritime governance of other non-traditional security issues

It is estimated that between 1978 and 1999, the annual number of people smuggled out of China was 20,000.[65] Most illegal emigrants used to originate in coastal provinces, such as Fujian, but are increasingly from many other regions, including inland provinces. The demographic features of the majority of illegal emigrants can be characterized as male, unemployed peasants, with a maximum education level of junior middle school or below. The main destinations for illegal emigration are mostly developed countries, such as the United States, Canada, the European Union and Japan.[66]

People smuggling, as a form of transnational crime and a maritime security threat, requires effective bilateral and multilateral cooperative mechanisms. The 2002 Joint Declaration of ASEAN And China on Cooperation in the Field of Non-Traditional Security Issues put people smuggling, including trafficking of women and children, among the priorities of China–ASEAN cooperation in addressing non-traditional security issues, and could become the institutional basis for effective cooperation and governance.[67]

In addition to people smuggling, other forms of transnational maritime crimes, such as illegal drugs trafficking and small arms smuggling also require effective bilateral and multilateral cooperation.[68] Interestingly enough, despite the scant attention that issues at the "low" end of non-traditional security, such as drug trafficking and people smuggling, have received in scholarly and policy discourses on maritime security, China has achieved a much higher level of cooperation on these issues with countries in the Asia-Pacific region. For instance, as early as in May 1991, China, Myanmar and Thailand, with assistance from the United Nations Anti-drug Agency, had already started exploring the modality of subregional, multilateral cooperation in anti-drug trafficking efforts. In October 2000, China and ASEAN signed the China–ASEAN Action Plan on Countering Drug Trafficking, formally launching the China–ASEAN cooperation on anti-drug trafficking.[69] In contrast, regional cooperation on issues at the "high" end of non-traditional security, i.e., maritime boundary disputes and piracy, has been limited. One plausible explanation is that the norms of counter-drug trafficking or human trafficking have been widely accepted in international relations, rendering the "transaction cost" of achieving cooperation on issues at the "low" end of non-traditional security much lower than that of issues on the "high" end. In contrast, regarding the issue of piracy for example, unresolved maritime boundaries in Southeast Asia have complicated the jurisdiction over piracy. For instance, many ASEAN member countries would deny cross-boundary "hot pursuit" by foreign countries against pirates due to sensitivity of their sovereignty over territorial waters.[70]

Concluding remarks

This chapter provides a preliminary assessment of the priorities and challenges of China's maritime security. Our analysis shows that traditional, military dimensions of maritime security have long dominated scholarly and policy discourses on maritime security in China. Since the end of the Cold War, with the rise of studies on non-traditional security in China, non-traditional security issues have received increasingly more attention in Chinese scholarly and policy discourses on maritime security. China's different conceptualizations of *haiquan* (sea power) not only reflect different intellectual orientations but also indicate different directions in strategic and policy planning.

Since the end of the Cold War, China's maritime security has increasingly faced a myriad of challenges, ranging from traditional threats, such as SLOCs and maritime boundary disputes, to non-traditional threats, such as piracy, fishery disputes, drug trafficking, people smuggling and so on. With China's rapid rise in the past few decades, however, China's maritime strategy seems to have lagged far behind. Meanwhile, deficiencies in institutional arrangement and capacity building have severely impeded China's ability to effectively deal with a host of threats to its maritime security. For instance, it has long been recognized that various agencies competing for jurisdiction has led to a lack of an effective administration and governance of maritime affairs in China. The uncoordinated and often times confusing efforts by those agencies to enforce maritime governance has been likened to "Five Dragons Stirring up the Sea" (*wulong naohai*).[71] It is worth noting that the disarrayed maritime governance system in China has led to repeated calls for the establishment of a comprehensive maritime administration, as well as a unified Coast Guard Force, although, as analysts have acknowledged, conflicting bureaucratic interests might hamper the creation of China's first Coast Guard Force.[72]

Facing unprecedented challenges to its maritime security, China needs to go beyond the Mahanian definition of *haiquan* and develop a comprehensive maritime strategy that will pave the way for the peaceful rise of China in the twenty-first century.

Notes

1 Shi Xiaoqin, "Huhang yu zhongguo haijun mianlin de tiaozhan" ("Naval Escort and the Challenges Facing Chinese Navy"), in Wang Jisi (ed.), *Zhongguo guoji zhanlue pinglun 2009* (*China International Strategy Review 2009*), Beijing: Shijie zhishi chubanshe, 2009, p. 315.

2 Guo Wei and Wang Ying, "Maliujia haixia: Nanhai hangxian yu dangdai zhongguo jingji fazhan" ("The Strait of Malacca: The Sea Lanes of the South China Sea and the Economic Growth of Contemporary China"), *Disiji yanjiu* (*Quaternary Research*), No. 5, 2006, p. 489.

3 For an excellent collection of studies by Chinese scholars on non-traditional security issues, see Zha Daojiong (ed.), *Zhongguo xuezhe kanshijie: feichuantong anquan juan* (*Chinese Scholars Eye the World: Volume of Non-traditional Security*), Beijing: Xinshijie chubanshe, 2007.

4 For surveys of the discussion of sea power in the Chinese literature, see Sun Lu, "Zhongguo haiquan neihan tantao" ("An Examination of the Connotation of Sea Power in China"), *Taipingyang xuebao* (*Pacific Journal*), No. 10, 2005, pp. 81–89; Shi Chunlin, "Ershi shiji jiushi niandai yilai guanyu haiquan gainian he neihan yanjiu pingshu," ("A Review of Studies on the Concept and Connotation of Sea Power since the 1990s"), *Zhongguo haiyang daxue xuebao* (*Periodical of Ocean University of China*), No. 2, 2007, pp. 7–8.

5 It has been widely recognized in the literature, though, that Chinese analysts' understanding of sea power is predominantly influenced by Captain Alfred Thayer Mahan's classic 1890 work on sea power. See James R. Holmes and Toshi Yoshihara, *Chinese Naval Strategy in the 21st Century: The Turn to Mahan*, London and New York: Routledge, 2007; Andrew S. Erickson, Lyle J. Goldstein and Carnes Lord, *China Goes to Sea: Maritime Transformation in Comparative Historical Perspective*, Annapolis, MD: Naval Institute Press, 2009. For Mahan's work on sea power, see A.T. Mahan, *The Influence of Sea Power Upon History, 1660–1783*, New York: Dover Publications, 1987.

6 Chinese works on maritime security that subscribe to this definition of sea power include Shi Jiazhu, *Haiquan yu Zhongguo* (*Sea Power and China*), Shanghai: Sanlian shudian, 2008; Liu Zhongmin, *Shijie haiyang zhengzhi yu zhongguo haiyang fazhan zhanlue* (*World Maritime Politics and China's Maritime Development Strategy*), Beijing: Shishi chubanshe, 2009; Song Yunxia, *Guojia haishang guanxiaquan: lilun*

yu shijian (*National Jurisdiction over the Sea: Theories and Practices*), Beijing: Haiyang chubanshe, 2009.

7 See Wang Chuanyou, *Haifang anquan lun* (*On Maritime Security and Defense*), Beijing: Haiyang chubanshe, 2007; Zhang Shiping, *Zhongguo haiquan* (*Chinese Sea Power*), Beijing: Remin ribao chubanshe, 2009; Ju Hailong, *Zhongguo haiquan zhanlue* (*China's Sea Power Strategy*), Beijing: Shishi chubanshe, 2010.

8 See Yu Xuebiao, *Haiquan liyi yu weixian de shuangrenjian* (*The Double-Edged Sword of Maritime Interests and Threats*), Beijing: Haichao chubanshe, 2008; Wang Shengrong, *Haiquan dui daguo xingshuai de lishi yingxiang* (*The Historical Impact of Sea Power on the Rise and Fall of Great Powers*), Beijing: Haichao chubanshe, 2009.

9 To be sure, the three conceptualizations of sea power are by no means mutually exclusive. Some Chinese scholars have developed an understanding of sea power that straddles these different conceptualizations. For instance, Zhang Wenmu, an influential Chinese scholar specializing in strategic studies, argues that a conceptualization of China's sea power should include not only "maritime rights and benefits" (*haiyang quanli*) but also "maritime capacity" (*haiyang liliang*) in order to realize and protect those rights and benefits. Apparently, Zhang's conceptualization of sea power combines a legalistic approach and a defensive realism approach. See Zhang Wenmu, *Lun Zhongguo haiquan* (*On China's Sea Power*), Beijing: Haiyang chubanshe, 2010, pp. 6–8.

10 The poll was conducted in April 2009 and the results were reported in the story, "Zhongguo gongmin haiquan yishi jueqi" ("The Emergence of the Chinese Citizens' Consciousness of Sea Power"), *Guoji xianqu daobao* (International Herald Leader), 21 April 2009.

11 Representative works include the following: Liu Zhongmin (ed.), *Guoji haiyang zhengzhi zhuanti yanjiu* (*Studies of Special Topics of International Maritime Politics*), Beijing: Zhonghao haiyang daxue chubanshe, 2007; Gao Zichuan, "Shixi 21 shijichu de zhongguo haiyang anquan" ("An Analysis of China's Maritime Security in Early 21st Century"), *Xiandai guoji guanxi* (*Contemporary International Relations*), No. 3, 2006; Jia Pei, "Riben haiyang fazhan guan yu zhongri haiquan zhengduan" ("The Japanese View of Maritime Development and the China-Japan Dispute over Sea Power"), *Riben wenti yanjiu* (*Japan Problem Studies*), No. 2, 2006.

12 Quoted in Zhang Wenmu, "Jingji quanqiuhua yu zhongguo haiquan," *Zhanlue yu guanli* (*Strategy and Management*), No. 1, 2003; Shi Chunlin, "Jin shinian guanyu zhongguo haiquan wenti yanjiu pingshun" ("A Review of the Studies of China's Sea Power Issue in the Past Decade"), *Xiandai guoji guanxi* (*Contemporary International Relations*), No. 4, 2008, pp. 54–55.

13 Li Xiaojun, "Lun haiquan dui zhongguo shiyou anquan de yingxiang" ("On the Impact of Sea Power on China's Petroleum Security"), *Guoji luntan* (*International Forum*), No. 4, 2004, p. 17; Ye Zicheng, "Dui zhongguo haiquan fazhan zhanlue de jidian sikao" ("Some Thoughts on the Development of China's Sea Power Strategy"), *Guozhi zhengzhi yanjiu* (*International Politics Quarterly*), No. 3, 2005, p. 12.

14 "Zhongguo gongmin haiquan yishi jueqi," *Guoji xianqu daobao* (*International Herald Leader*), 21 April 2009.

15 Ibid.

16 Ye Zicheng, "Sea Power is Secondary to Land Power and China Should Postpone Plan to Build Aircraft Carriers," *Guoji xianqu daobao* (*International Herald Leader*), 2 March 2007.

17 Ni Shixiong, "Aircraft Carrier and China's Sea Power Strategy," *Nanfang bushi bao* (*Nanfang Daily*), 21 March 2007.

18 Both Ye and Ni later further developed their arguments into book-length studies; see Ye Zicheng, *Luquan fazhan yu daguo xingshuai: diyuan zhengzhi huanjing yu Zhongguo de diyuan zhanlue xuanze* (*The Development of Land Power and the Rise and*

Fall of the Great Power: Geopolitical Environment and China's Geostrategic Choices), Beijing: Xinxing chubanshe, 2007; Ni Shixiong, *Wenming and zhuanxing yu Zhongguo haiquan* (*The Transformation of Civilizations and China's Sea Power*), Beijing: Xinhua chubanshe, 2010.

19 "Guofang bu: Zhongguo zhengfu jianghui renzhen kaolv jianzao hangmu de wenti" ("The Department of Defense: The Chinese Government will Seriously Considering the Issue of Building Aircraft Carriers"), 23 December 2008, http://military.people.com.cn/GB/1076/115150/8563431.html.

20 Hayoun Ryou, "Chinese Aircraft Carrier Program: Blue Water Navy on the Way," *Institute of Peace and Conflict Studies Issue Brief No. 101*, May 2009, http://ipcs.org/pdf_file/issue/IB101-Ryou-ChineseNavy.pdf.

21 Toshi Yoshihara and James R. Homes, *Red Start over the Pacific: China's Rise and the Challenge to U.S. Maritime Strategy*, Annapolis, MD: Naval Institute Press, 2010; Bernard D. Cole, *The Great Wall at Sea: China's Navy in the Twenty-First Century*, Annapolis, MD: Naval Institute Press, 2010.

22 It is worth noting that in recent years, China has been especially active in participating in maritime joint search and rescue exercises with a wide a range of countries. Notable cases include the China–India first naval joint search and rescue operation the East China Sea in 2003, followed by a second similar exercise in the Indian Ocean in December 2005; the China–South Korea–Japan joint search and rescue exercise in China's offshore waters in July 2005; the China–US first joint search and rescue exercise in the US West Coast in September 2006, followed by a second similar exercise in the South China Sea two months later; China's participation in the first ASEAN Regional Forum (ARF) maritime security shore exercise in January 2007; China's participation in the four-day sea phase of Peace 07 exercises in the Arabian Sea in March 2007, along with naval forces from Bangladesh, France, Italy, Malaysia, Pakistan, Turkey, the United Kingdom and the United States; China's participation in the Western Pacific Naval Symposium (WPNS) exercise that also involved Australia and the United States in May 2007; as well as a China–Australia–New Zealand joint search and rescue operations in October 2007. See Mingjiang Li, "China's Gulf of Aden Expedition and Maritime Cooperation in East Asia," *China Brief*, Vol. 9, Issue 1, p. 6.

23 The 1969 report, dubbed "the Emery Report," was authored by a group of oceanic geoscientists headed by American geologist K.O. Emery. It was commissioned by the Coordinating Committee for Geosciences Programs in East and Southeast Asia (CCOP) under the auspice of the United Nations Economic Commission for Asia and the Far East (UNECAFE). See K.O. Emery, "Geological Structure and Some Water Characteristics of East China Sea and Yellow Sea," *UNECAFE/CCOP Technical Bulletin*, Vol. 2, 1969, pp. 3–43.

24 Ju Hailong, *Zhongguo haiquan zhanlue*, pp. 231–232.

25 Glenn D. Hook, Julie Gilson, Christopher W. Hughes and Hugo Dobson, *Japan's International Relations: Politics, Economics and Security*, London and New York: Routledge, 2001, pp. 140–142.

26 Yoichi Kato, "China's Naval Expansion in the Western Pacific," *Global Asia*, December 2010, www.globalasia.org/V5N4_Winter_2010/Yoichi_Kato.html?PHPSESSID=85334648f6085f2a1b817371decea408.

27 For the contradictory view that the US–Japan alliance has contributed to "stability" in the Diaoyu Islands dispute, see M. Taylor Fravel, "Explaining Stability in the Senkaku (Diaoyu) Island Dispute," in Gerald Curtis, Ryosei Kokubun and Wang Jisi (eds), *Getting the Triangle Straight: Managing China-Japan-US Relations*, Washington, DC: The Brookings Institution Press, 2010, pp. 144–164. For a discussion of the historical role the United States played in the China–Japan disputes over the Diaoyu Islands, see Jean-Marc F. Blanchard, "The U.S. Role in the Sino-Japanese Dispute over the Diaoyu (Senkaku) Islands," *The China Quarterly*, No. 161, March 2000, pp. 95–123.

28 Leszek Buszynski, "ASEAN, the Declaration on Conduct, and the South China Sea," *Contemporary Southeast Asia*, December 2003, p. 346.
29 See Shi Jiazhu, *Haiquan yu Zhongguo*, pp. 107–108; Liu Zhongmin, *Shijie haiyang zhengzhi yu Zhongguo haiyang fazha zhanlue*, pp. 433–434; Jin Yongming, *Donghai wenti jiejue lujing yanjiu* (*Study on the Solutions to the Issues of the East China Sea*), Beijing: Law Press, 2008, pp. 205–206; Wu Shicun, *Nansha zhengduan de qiyuan yu fazhan*, (*The Origins and Development of the Spratly Disputes*), Beijing: Zhongguo jingji chubanshe, 2010, pp. 199–201. It is worth noting that many military scholars also argue that building up China's navy would be crucial for protecting China's maritime rights and benefits. See Shao Yongling, *Haiyang zhanguoce: Shao Yongling lun haiyang daguo de jueqi* (*Shao Yongling on the Rise of Maritime Great Powers*), Beijing: Shiyou gongya chubanshe, 2010, p. 208.
30 Shi Jiazhu, *Haiquan yu Zhongguo*, p. 85.
31 Unryu Suganuma, *Sovereign Rights and Territorial Space in Sino-Japanese Relations: Irredentism and the Diaoyu/Senkaku Islands*, Honolulu: University of Hawaii Press, 2000.
32 For instance, Chinese analysts have noted that as China launched the exploration of the Chunxiao natural gas field in the East China Sea, China–Japan tensions over maritime boundary in the East China Sea escalated. See Liu Zhongmin, *Shijie haiyang zhengzhi yu Zhongguo haiyang fazhan zhanlue*, pp. 420–421. For a study that chronologically documents the China–Japan dispute over the exploration of natural gas fields in the East China Sea, see James J. Przystup, "A Volatile Mix: Natural Gas, a Submarine, a Shrine, and a Visa," The Center for International and Strategic Studies, http://csis.org/files/media/csis/pubs/0404qjapan_china.pdf.
33 Liu Zhongmin, *Shijie haiyang zhengzhi yu Zhongguo haiyang fazhan zhanlue*, pp. 430–431.
34 Mark J. Valencia and Yoshihisa Amae, "Regime Building in the East China Sea," *Ocean Development & International Law*, April 2003, pp. 201–202.
35 Mark J. Valencia, "A Spratly Solution," *Far Eastern Economic Review*, March 1994, p. 30; the same author, *Sharing the Resources of the South China Sea*, Martinus Nijhoff Publishers, 1997.
36 Xue Li, "Nanhai nengyuan kaifa zuzhi: nanhai wenti de chulu" ("The South China Sea Energy Development Organization: A Solution to the South China Sea Issue"), *Shangwu zhoukan* (*Business Watch Magazine*), No. 12, 20 June 2009, www.business-watch.com.cn/Mag/global/2009/0717/1595.html.
37 Liu Zhongmin, *Shijie haiyang zhengzhi yu Zhongguo haiyang fazhan zhanlue*, p. 454.
38 *Deng Xiaoping Wenxuan* (*Selected Works of Deng Xiaoping*), Vol. 2, Beijing: Renmin chubanshe, 1993, p. 49. The idea of joint development can be traced back to the 1969 International Court of Justice ruling on the North Sea Continental Shelf Cases. In January 1974, Tokyo and Seoul concluded the Japan–South Korean Joint Development Agreement, the first application of the idea of the joint development of offshore oil where concerned parties failed to agree on maritime boundary delimitation. For a detailed survey of joint development cases, see Masahiro Miyoshi, "The Joint Development of Offshore Oil and Gas in Relation to Maritime Boundary Delimitation," *International Boundaries Research Unit Maritime Briefing*, Vol. 2, No. 5, pp. 1–47.
39 Shi Jiazhu, *Haiquan yu Zhongguo*, pp. 91–95; Interviews with Chinese analysts with knowledge of the agreement, May, September 2010, Beijing, China.
40 Shi Jiazhu, *Haiquan yu Zhongguo*, pp. 100, 106; Wu Shicun, *Nansha zhengduan de qiyuan yu fazhan*, p. 200; Interviews with Chinese analysts with knowledge of the agreement, May, September 2010, Beijing.
41 Wu Shicun, *Nansha zhengduan de qiyuan yu fazhan*, pp. 201–202; Nguyen Hong Thao, "The 2002 Declaration on the Conduct of Parties in the South China Sea," *Ocean Development and International Law*, Vol. 34, 2003, pp. 279–285. The text of the DOC can also be found at ASEAN's official website, www.aseansec.org/13163.htm.

42 Nguyen Hong Thao, "The 2002 Declaration on the Conduct of Parties in the South China Sea," p. 279.

43 Wang Jisi, "China's Search for a Grand Strategy: A Rising Great Power Finds Its Way," *Foreign Affairs*, Vol. 90, No. 2, March/April, 2011, p. 71.

44 "China, ASEAN Begin Discussion of Stronger Code of Conduct: Chinese Ambassador," The Xinhua News Agent, 30 September 2010, http://news.xinhuanet.com/english2010/china/2010–09/30/c_13537886.htm; Pia Lee-Brago, "China Seeks Discussion of South China Sea Issue with Phl," *The Philippines Star*, 6 April 2011, www.philstar.com/Article.aspx?articleId=673464&publicationSubCategoryId=63. Chinese analysts have argued for the need of a stronger code of conduct; see Wu Shicun, *Nansha zhengduan de qiyuan yu fazhan*, pp. 200–201.

45 For a discussion of the ASEAN Way, see Shaun Narine, "ASEAN and the ARF: the Limits of the 'ASEAN way'," *Asian Survey*, Vol. 37, No. 9, October 1997, pp. 952–971; Amitav Acharya, *Constructing a Security Community in Southeast Asia: ASEAN and the Problem of Regional Order*, London: Routledge, 2001; Gollian Goh, "The 'ASEAN Way': Non-intervention and ASEAN's Role in Conflict Management," *Stanford Journal of East Asian Affairs*, Vol. 3, No. 1, 2003, pp. 113–118; Alastair Iain Johnston, "Socialization in International Institutions: The ASEAN Way and International Relations Theory," in G. John Ikenberry and Michael Mastanduno (eds), *International Relations Theory and the Asia-Pacific*, New York: Columbia University Press, 2003, pp. 107–162.

46 Li Wenpei, *Guoji haiyang fa zhi haidao wenti yanjiu* (*Research on Piracy in International Law of the Sea*), Beijing: Law Press, 2010, p. 151.

47 John J. Brandon, *Protect Asia's Shipping*, 24 May 2002, www.csis.org/pacfor/pac0221A.htm.

48 Pang Zhonying, "Zhongguo shiyou anquan shengmingxian" ("The Life Line of China's Petroleum Security: from the Strait of Malacca to the Taiwan Strait"), *Zhongguo qingnian* (*China Youth*), 3 March 2004, http://finance.sina.com.cn/g/20040330/1001693712.shtml.

49 International Maritime Organization, "Reports On Acts Of Piracy And Armed Robbery Against Ships: Annual report 2008," annex 4, www.imo.org/includes/blastDataOnly.asp/data_id%3D25550/133.pdf.

50 For Chinese scholarly analyses of maritime terrorism, see Li Wei, "Kongbu huodong dui haishang tongdao anquan de weixie" ("The Threats to Sea-Lane Security Posed by Terrorism"), in Sea Lane Security Research Team of China Institute of Contemporary International Relations (CICIR; ed.), *Haishang tongdao anquan yu guoji hezuo* (*Sea Lane Security and International Cooperation*), Beijing: Shishi chubanshe, 2005, pp. 183–204; Shi Jiazhu, *Haiquan yu Zhongguo*, pp. 156–160; Xu Ke, *Dangdai dongnanya yanjiu* (*Contemporary Maritime Piracy in Southeast Asia*), Xiamen, Fujiang Province: Xiamen daxue chubanshe, 2009, pp. 99–133.

51 Graham Gerard Ong, " 'Ships Can Be Dangerous Too': Coupling Piracy and Maritime Terrorism in Southeast Asia's Maritime Security Framework," Working Paper of International Politics & Security Issues Series No. 1(2004), p. 6, http://web.iseas.edu.sg/ipsi12004.pdf; Rommel C. Banlaoi, "Maritime Terrorism in Southeast Asia: The Abu Sayyaf Threat," *Naval War College Review*, Winter 2005, pp. 63–80.

52 John J. Brandon, *Protect Asia's Shipping*, 24 May 2002, www.csis.org/pacfor/pac0221A.htm.

53 Graham Gerard Ong, "Haishang kongbu zhuyi he haidao weixie" ("Maritime Terrorism and the Threat of Piracy"), *Dongnanya zongheng* (*Around Southeast Asia*), No. 4, 2006, p. 15.

54 Adam Young and Mark J. Valencia, "Piracy and terrorism threats overlap," *The Washington Times*, 7 July 2003, www.washingtontimes.com/news/2003/jul/06/20030706–104801–9949r/.

55 Opening Statement by Chairman Tommy Koh at the Break-up Group 1 "Advancing Maritime Security Cooperation," at the 5th Institute for International and Strategic Studies (IISS) Asia Security Summit: The Shangri-La Dialogue, 20 June 2006, Singapore, www.spp.nus.edu.sg/ips/docs/pub/sp_tommy_Advancing%20Martime%20 Security%20cooperation_3%20June%2006.pdf.
56 ReCAAP ISC, *ReCAAP ISC Annual Report 2009*, p. 10.
57 Yang Kai, "Haidao changjue beihou de nanhai guoji boyi" ("The International Game behind the Rampant Piracy in the South China Sea"), *Shidai zhoubao* (*Time Weekly*), No. 59, 2009, www.time-weekly.com/2009/1231/2MMDAwMDAwNTE2MA.html.
58 Remarks by Deputy Prime Minister Tony Tan at the 2nd IISS Asian Security Conference Plenary Session on "Maritime Security after September 11," 1 June 2003, Singapore, www.mindef.gov.sg/imindef/news_and_events/nr/2003/jun/01jun03_nr2.html.
59 Young and Valencia, "Piracy and terrorism threats overlap"; Yang Kai, "Dongnanya haidao de quyu zhili" ("The Regional Governance of Piracy in South East Asia"), in Zha Daojiong (ed.), *Zhongguo xuezhe kanshijie: feichuantong anquan juan* (*World Politics—Views from China, Volume on Non-Traditional Security*), Beijing: New World Press, 2007, p. 240.
60 The 15 contracting countries are the People's Republic of Bangladesh, Brunei Darussalam, the Kingdom of Cambodia, the People's Republic of China, the Republic of India, Japan, the Republic of Korea, the Lao People's Democratic Republic, the Union of Myanmar, the Kingdom of Norway, the Republic of the Philippines, the Republic of Singapore, the Democratic Socialist Republic of Sri Lanka, the Kingdom of Thailand and the Socialist Republic of Viet Nam, www.recaap.org/index_home.html.
61 Interview with Lt. Colonel Xu Liang, Chinese Representative at the ReCAAP ISC, 24 November 2010, Singapore.
62 The Research Team on Sea Lane Security at the China Contemporary Institute on International Relations, *Haishang tongdao anquan yu guoji hezuo* (*Sea-Lane Security and International Cooperation*), Beijing: Shishi chubanshe, 2005, p. 233.
63 Andrin Raj, "Japan's Initiatives in Security Cooperation in the Straits of Malacca on Maritime Security and in Southeast Asia: Piracy and Maritime Terrorism," The Japan Institute for International Affairs Report, Tokyo, Japan, 2009, http://www2.jiia.or.jp/pdf/fellow_report/090331-Andrin_Raj.pdf.
64 See the text of the Joint Declaration of ASEAN and China on Cooperation in the Field of Non-Traditional Security Issues, Phnom Penh, 4 November 2002, 6th ASEAN-China Summit, www.aseansec.org/13185.htm.
65 Huang Runlong, "Zhongguo de feifa yimin wenti" ("China's Illegal People Smuggling Issue"), *Renkou yu jingji* (*Population and Economics*), No. 1, 2001, p. 12; Sun Qiongru and Hou Zhiyang, "Zhongguo feifa yimin wenti yanjiu zongshu" ("A Literature Review of the Studies of China's Illegal Human Trafficking Issue"), *Renkou yu jingji*, No. 4, 2006, p. 62.
66 Sun Qiongru and Hou Zhiyang, *Renkou yu jingji*, pp. 61–62.
67 The text of the declaration can be found at the official website of ASEAN, www.aseansec.org/13185.htm.
68 For a Chinese scholarly discussion of small arms smuggling, see Gao Yin, "Xiao wuqi kuosan yu haishang tongdao anquan" ("Proliferation of Small Arms and Sea Lane Security"), in Sea Lane Security Research Team of CICIR (ed.), *Haishang tongdao anquan yu guoji hezuo*, pp. 163–182.
69 Liu Zhi, "Zhongguo yu dongmeng jindu hezuo de xianzhuang yu qianjing" ("The Status and Prospects of China-ASEAN Anti-Drug Cooperation"), *Dangdai yatai* (*Journal of Contemporary Asia-Pacific Studies*), No. 3, 2005, pp. 34–35; "'Jinsanjiao' xinduqing gei zhongguo yu dongmeng guojia tichu xinketi" ("The New Situation in the 'Golden Triangle' Poses New Challenges for China and the ASEAN"), *Xinhua News Agency*, 23 October 2006, http://news.xinhuanet.com/world/2006–10/23/content_5237353.htm.

70 Adam Young and Mark J. Valencia, "Piracy and Terrorism Threats Overlap," *The Washington Times*, 7 July 2003, www.washingtontimes.com/news/2003/jul/06/20030706–104801–9949r/.

71 There are at least five agencies involved in maritime enforcement and governance in China, namely China Maritime Surveillance (*Zhongguo haijian*) under the State Oceanic Administration, the Maritime Police (*haijing*) under the Ministry of Public Security, China Maritime Affairs (*Zhongguo haishi*) or China Maritime Safety Administration of the Ministry of Transport, China Fishery Administration (Zhongguo yuzheng) under the Ministry of Agriculture, and China Customs (*Zhongguo haiguan*). For analyses of China's maritime enforcement and governance institutions, see Jin Yongming, *Donghai wenti jiejue lujing yanjiu*, pp. 169–176; Senior Captain Li Jie, "'Five Dragons Stirring up the Sea' has Constrained the Rise of Chinese Sea Power," *International Herald Leader*, 16 March 2009; Lyle J. Goldstein, "Five Dragons Stirring up the Sea: Challenge and Opportunity in China's Improving Maritime Enforcement Capabilities," *Naval War College China Maritime Study 5*, April 2010.

72 Interview with Lt. Colonel Xu Liang, Chinese Representative at the ReCAAP ISC, 24 November 2010, Singapore; Wang Chuanyou, *Haifang anquanlun*, pp. 258–262; Lyle J. Goldstein, "China's Coast Guard Development: Challenge and Opportunity," *China Brief*, Vol. 9, No. 23 November 2009, pp. 5–8.

12 Japan's maritime challenges and priorities

Tetsuo Kotani

Introduction

The 2008 Japan Coast Guard (JCG) annual report carried a feature article on the dramatically changing missions of the JCG.[1] Its core missions—marine environmental protection, marine surveys, rescue, law enforcement, and safety of navigation—remain intact, but, for example, heavily-armed, high-speed North Korean spy boats running wild in Japanese waters, growing tension over maritime interests, and threats from terrorism and proliferation have all made the role of the JCG more important for the protection of Japan's sovereignty and sea borders. The JCG has also come to play a greater role in countering the increased number of piracy incidents in the distant waters of Southeast Asia. In addition, it has initiated many bilateral and multilateral mechanisms to keep good order at sea.

Likewise, the Japan Maritime Self-Defense Force (JMSDF) has adapted itself to the changing maritime environment. Beyond its traditional area of operation up to 1,000 nautical miles from home, the JMSDF maintained its presence in the Indian Ocean to support the coalition maritime interdiction operations, and began counter-piracy operation in the Gulf of Aden with JCG officers aboard. It has also intensified interactions with navies of other like-minded nations, such as India and Australia. On the other hand, the 2009 Defense White Paper expressed concern over Chinese naval activities in and around Japanese waters, indicating that the role of the JMSDF will become more important for meeting Chinese naval expansion in the Western Pacific.[2]

Japan faces old and new maritime challenges in the Western Pacific and Northern Indian Oceans—from the Sea of Japan, the Philippine Sea, and the East and South China Seas, to the Straits of Malacca and Singapore, the Andaman Sea, the Bay of Bengal, the Arabian Sea, and the Persian Gulf. Japan enacted the Basic Act on Ocean Policy in 2007 and formulated the Basic Plan on Ocean Policy and other related measures to meet those challenges. This chapter first examines how Japan has met challenges within its vast sea borders. It then reviews how Japan has made efforts to secure its long and vital sea-lanes. Lastly, it analyzes the implications of the Basic Act of Ocean Policy for Japan's efforts to maintain good order at sea.

Securing sovereignty and sea borders

Japan is an island nation, sharing no land border with its neighbors, and its security and prosperity heavily depend on good order at sea. Japan is separated from the Korean Peninsula—the "dagger aimed at the heart of Japan"—by the 200 km wide Tsushima Strait. Japan's combined territorial sea and exclusive economic zone (EEZ) is about 4,470,000 sq. km (the world's sixth largest), while its territory is about 380,000 sq. km (the world's sixty-first largest). Its coastline is about 35,000 km (the world's sixth longest). Japan has 6,847 remote islands in addition to the five main islands (Honshu, Hokkaido, Kyushu, Shikoku, and Okinawa).[3] If Wakkanai, the northernmost city in Hokkaido, were Copenhagen in Denmark, then the remotest islands of Ishigaki, Okinotori, and Minamitori would be Casablanca in Morocco, Tripoli in Libya, and Alexandria in Egypt, respectively. In other words, Japanese waters cover the North Atlantic Treaty Organisation's (NATO's) Europe plus the Mediterranean.[4] On the other hand, Japan lacks strategic depth. The Japanese archipelago stretches approximately 3,000 km along the eastern coast of mainland Asia and no point in Japan is more than 120 km away from its coast.[5]

The distances between the baselines of Japan and its neighbors are less than 400 nautical miles, but the delimitation of its maritime boundaries with neighboring Russia, China, and South Korea has not been agreed. The Northern Territories and Takeshima Island are illegally occupied by Russia and South Korea, respectively, and China claims jurisdiction over the Senkaku Islands.[6] Russia claims 12 nautical miles of territorial waters around the islands of the Northern Territories. The Russian authority frequently captures Japanese fishing boats around these territories, and in 2006, for the first time since 1956, a Japanese fisherman was killed. South Korea stations security forces on Takeshima Island. So far, South Korea has captured 326 Japanese fishing boats near the island. Chinese activists began violating the territorial and contiguous seas around the Senkaku Islands in 2005 and some even landed on one of the islands in 2006.[7]

China has recently been creating a wider strategic buffer in the Western Pacific. Chinese strategy conceived of two island chains as China's maritime defense barrier.[8] The "first island chain" along the Ryukyus, Taiwan, the Philippines, and Borneo is no more than 200 nautical miles from the Chinese coast and, unless Taiwan is unified with the mainland China, the first island chain would virtually blockade China during times of crisis.[9] China has therefore enhanced its area denial or anti-access capability up to the first island chain by purchasing from Russia Su-30 ground attack aircraft, Kilo class attack submarines, and Sovremmeny class destroyers with SS-N-22 missiles—all of which the Soviet Union had developed to target US carrier strike groups—spending some one billion dollars annually.[10] China is also introducing Shang class ultra-quiet nuclear-powered attack submarines. The Chinese Navy has also expanded operational areas into the high seas toward the "second island chain" running along the Bonins and Marianas.[11]

This geographical setting requires Japan to take measures to protect its vast sea borders in the Sea of Japan, the East China Sea, and the Philippine Sea, as well as its maritime interests within the borders. The triangular sea area defined by Tokyo, Guam, and Taiwan (the TGT triangular sea area) has particular importance for Japan, since this TGT triangle is where all of Japan's lines of sea communications converge and where US reinforcement forces pass through.[12]

Securing sea borders

Recently, increasing numbers of Chinese warships have been detected in the TGT sea area. In November 2004, a Chinese nuclear submarine was detected submerged in Japanese territorial waters. JMSDF destroyers and patrol aircraft chased the submarine under a maritime security order (seaborne patrolling action) until the submarine entered the high seas. After this incident, Japan formulated guidelines to deal with violation of its territorial waters by submerged submarines so that JMSDF ships and aircraft could immediately take necessary measures under maritime security orders.[13]

The JMSDF conducts regular surveillance in the surrounding waters, especially in the TGT triangular sea area. In October 2006, a Chinese submarine surfaced in the vicinity of the USS *Kitty Hawk* off Okinawa. Further, Chinese surface warships passed though the Tsugaru Strait and the Ryukyu Islands in October and November 2008, respectively. Given the active Chinese naval activities in the TGT area, the JMSDF is considering enhancing Intelligence, Surveillance and Reconnaissance (ISR) capabilities, and building confidence with China and other neighbors as part of its "commitment strategy," while strengthening anti-submarine warfare capability to support the US Navy's operations as part of its "contingency response strategy."[14]

Remote islands are part of Japanese territory. The 2004 National Defense Program Guidelines finds that these numerous remote islands are vulnerable to foreign invasion, and calls for their defense. Such defense requires joint operations by the three services of the Japan Self-Defense Forces (JSDF), as well as regular surveillance of those islands.[15]

The JCG has detected 21 spy ships in Japanese waters since 1963. These spy boats fled in all cases but one. In the North Korean spy boat incident off Noto Peninsula of March 1999, inter-agency cooperation between the JCG and the Defense Agency did not work well. Based on the lessons from this incident, the JCG and the Defense Agency prepared a joint response manual and began joint training. The JCG has primary responsibility vis-à-vis spy boats, and the JMSDF immediately takes charge of them under maritime security order if the situation is beyond the JCG's capability.

In November 2001, the JCG law was also amended to allow the use of force against a ship for the purpose of stopping it.[16] In the December 2001 North Korean spy boat incident off Southwest Kyushu, the JCG patrol boats fired to stop the spy boat but the spy boat fired back with a rocket launcher, injuring three Japanese coastguardsmen. In the end, the spy boat blew itself up and Japan salvaged the boat and confirmed that it was a North Korean ship engaged in drug smuggling.[17] After this incident, Japan introduced 12 high-speed, high-capability patrol boats, including three 2,000-tonne helicopter patrol boats, to deal with spy boats.[18]

Counter-terrorism and counter-proliferation are new challenges to good order at sea. Japan is strengthening security at important coastal facilities, such as nuclear power plants, oil stockpile stations, ports, and US bases.[19] Japan has also intensified port state control according to the 2004 amendments to the International Convention for the Safety of Life at Sea (SOLAS).[20]

Japan is an active, core member of the Proliferation Security Initiative (PSI), and has participated in numerous PSI maritime interdiction exercises, hosting one in 2004 and another in 2007. Japan's interest in the PSI comes from concerns over North Korean nuclear and missile development. Although Japan allowed a North Korean ship inspection bill to die in the legislative session just before the August 2009 election, which resulted in a dramatic change of government, the new government pledges to take firm action against North Korea, including ship inspections under UN Security Council resolutions.[21] Japan needs to pass a law to endorse the UN Security Council Resolution 1874, which calls for the inspection of North Korean ships.

Japan combats illegal fishing by foreign ships in its EEZs based on bilateral fisheries agreements with Russia, South Korea, and China, although Japan and Taiwan have not yet reached an agreement.[22] Illegal fishing by South Koreans in Japanese EEZs is the most serious problem. Illegal foreign fishermen operate high-speed boats, GPS, and other sophisticated devices and are becoming violent. Japan regulates illegal fishing using patrol boats and aircraft in cooperation with the Fishery Agency, and by introducing more sophisticated radar and other equipment.[23]

Smuggling leads to atrocious crimes at home, while at the same time funding crime syndicates. Drug and small arms smuggling in Japanese waters is constantly uncovered, as the scale of human smuggling is decreasing. Extended inspections of foreign ships and international and inter-agency cooperation has led to an increased level of detection. Counter-terrorism measures at ports may also have positive effects on the detection of smuggling.[24]

Securing maritime interests

Growing tension over maritime interests pose serious challenges to good order at sea. China actively conducts scientific surveys in Japanese EEZs in the East China Sea and the Philippine Sea. Such activities reached a peak in 1999, when 33 Chinese survey ships were detected. Japan and China reached an agreement on prior notification regarding scientific surveys in the East China Sea in 2001, and the number of unreported Chinese surveys has decreased since. However, China still conducts unreported surveys in the East China Sea.[25] Japan deploys patrol boats and aircraft to watch scientific surveys by foreign ships in Japanese EEZs.[26]

Japan is concerned about China's oil and gas development in the East China Sea. China regards the Okinawa Trough as the boundary, based on its erroneous concept of natural extension of the continental shelf and claims the disputed waters as its EEZ, while Japan insists on a median line solution. Pending bilateral consultation, China began drilling gas fields near the median line.[27] A Chinese destroyer and other warships were witnessed in the disputed waters in September 2005.[28] Although Japan and China agreed on joint development of gas fields in the disputed waters in June 2008, China is reluctant to conclude a treaty to formalize the agreement.[29]

China conducts scientific surveys around Okinotorishima Island, located between Guam and Taiwan. It is believed that China wanted to map the sea bottom so that its submarines could intercept US aircraft carriers in a Taiwan contingency.[30] In April 2004, during bilateral talks in Beijing to discuss Chinese marine research activities within Japan's EEZs, Chinese officials argued that Okinotorishima is not an island but just a group of rocks, at the same time acknowledging Japan's territorial rights. Thus, by denying Japan's EEZ in the area, China claims that about half of its 11 cases of research activities in 2004 were legal because they were conducted around Okinotorishima.[31] Japan refused to accept the Chinese claim. Based on its possession of Okinotorishima, Japan claimed an EEZ of approximately 400,000 sq. km, larger than the area of Japanese land territory. The waters around the atoll are potentially rich in metallic minerals such as nickel, manganese, cobalt, and copper.[32] On 12 November 2008, Japan made a submission for an extended continental shelf to the Commission on the Limits of the Continental Shelf, including one extending from Okinotorishima. China and South Korea objected to Japan's request.[33]

Securing navigational safety and the marine environment

Securing navigational safety and marine environmental protection are important aspects of good order at sea. Numerous large tankers and container ships sail in Japanese waters and there have been many serious maritime accidents. There are about 2,600 maritime accidents annually in Japanese waters. Japan was the first country to introduce a MARTIS (Marine Traffic Information Service), and recently introduced a MICS (Maritime Information and Communication Service) so that those who enjoy marine leisure can obtain maritime safety information. In 2005, Japan formulated the New Traffic Vision, which called for the development of an ENSS (Electronic Navigation Support System), an IT-based comprehensive navigational safety system based on an AIS (Automatic Identification System).[34]

The accidents of the Russian tanker, *Nakhodka*, in the Sea of Japan in January 1997 and the Panama-flagged tanker, *Diamond Grace*, in Tokyo Bay in October 1997 spilled about 9,000 kiloliters of heavy oil and 1,550 kiloliters of crude oil, respectively, and led to the strengthening of Japan's oil spill countermeasures. These measures include enhanced inter-agency communication, the revision of prevention law and plans, and the introduction of new recovery and clean-up equipment. More recently, according to the Protocol on Preparedness, Response and Co-operation to Pollution Incidents by Hazardous and Noxious Substances,

2000 (OPRC-HNS), the JCG is introducing HNS prevention equipment and training a response team. In addition, given the development of the Sakhalin projects, Japan prepared an inter-agency guideline to prevent oil spills from these projects and to strengthen coordination with Russia.[35]

Building confidence

In addition to its own efforts to secure sea borders and sovereignty at sea, Japan has been promoting bilateral and multilateral partnerships to maintain good order. The JCG has bilateral agreements with its counterparts in South Korea, China, and Russia on coordinated enforcement of illegal fishing and smuggling, rescue, and regular or irregular mutual visits of ships and personnel.[36] Based on those bilateral partnerships, for example, the JCG has cooperated in a marine accident response with its South Korean counterpart. The JCG's cooperation with its Chinese counterpart also led to the detection of actual smuggling cases. Moreover, Russia has come to refrain from firing on Japanese fishing boats.[37]

Japan also initiated a multilateral forum. In December 2000, the JCG took the lead in organizing a conference among the head of coasts guards and the equivalent entities of Japan, Russia, the United States, and South Korea. China and Canada later joined this group, and it has now become an annual North Pacific Coast Guard Forum (NPCGF), comprising commandant-level and working-level meetings. The NPCGF has become a useful confidence-building mechanism, producing practical outcomes such as joint operational guidelines, combined training for counter-smuggling, and a fishery enforcement patrol.[38]

Confidence building with neighboring navies remains low-key and is affected by political circumstances. The JMSDF has conducted an annual search and rescue exercise (SAREX) with the South Korean Navy since 1994 and both navies have called each other's ports. The JMSDF also conducts annual SAREX with the Russian Navy after 1996, although the 2008 SAREX with Russia was postponed due to Russian attacks on Georgia.[39] Exchange port calls between the JMSDF and Chinese Navy were agreed in 2000, but the first call was postponed until 2007 due to the deteriorated bilateral relations under the Koizumi Cabinet.[40] On the other hand, Japan recently strengthened security cooperation with Australia, and both countries announced a joint declaration on security in March 2007. Both navies make mutual port calls and the JMSDF participated in an Australian Navy-hosted multinational exercise in 2008.[41]

Securing sea-lanes

Japan is a trading nation and shipping carries 99.7 percent of the country's overall trade by volume.[42] According to Japanese figures for its maritime seaborne trade in 2008, Asia accounts for 29.8 percent, Oceania 25.4 percent, the Middle East 23.3 percent, North America 7.9 percent, Central and South America 6.8 percent, Europe 3.9 percent, and Africa 2.9 percent.[43] Japan imports most of its raw materials for clothing, food, and housing—for example, 100 percent of its cotton and wool (2008), 86 percent of its wheat (2008), 95 percent of its soybeans (2008), and 70 percent of its timber (2007) are imported—and most of those materials are imported from the Asia-Pacific region.[44] Japan's major markets are also in the Asia-Pacific. The Asia-Pacific region received more than 50 percent of Japanese exports by value in 2008, with North America receiving about 18 percent and Western Europe about 13 percent.[45]

Japan enjoyed rapid economic growth in the 1960s and came to import 80 percent of oil from the Middle East by 1970, with oil supplying 80 percent of Japan's energy needs. Faced with the two oil crises of the 1970s, Japan made every effort to reduce its dependence on the Middle Eastern oil. However, China, from which Japan imported oil, became a net oil importer in the 1990s and, as a result, Japan's dependence on the Middle East oil is increasing again and this trend is expected to continue.[46] Japan's energy self-sufficiency remains as low as 4 percent (16 percent if nuclear power is included). In 2003, oil accounted for 50 percent of Japan's total energy supply, coal for 20 percent, natural gas for 14 percent and nuclear power for 9 percent.[47] In FY 2007, Japan imported 99.6 percent of its oil, 100 percent of its coal, and 96.4 percent of its natural gas from overseas. With regard to suppliers, almost all coal and about 65 percent of liquid natural gas (LNG) came from the Asia-Pacific in FY 2007, while about 88 percent of oil (and 20 percent of LNG) came from the Middle East.[48]

Japan mainly imports its key energy resources from the Asia-Pacific region, with petroleum being the exception, which Japan needs to import from the Middle East through long and dangerous sea-lanes. The maritime highway along the Eurasian rim literally constitutes the lifeline of the Japanese economy. This maritime highway beyond the TGT sea area can be divided into three sea areas: Southeast Asian waters (the South China and the Andaman seas), South Asian waters (Bay of Bengal and the Arabian Sea), and the Persian Gulf. There are two choke points on this maritime highway: the Straits of Malacca and Singapore (SoMS) and the Strait of Hormuz. Different measures are necessary to meet the challenges in those three sea areas.

Japan's contributions to safety and security in Southeast Asian waters

Southeast Asian waters are critically important for the world's shipping. At the same time, tension in this sea area is increasing over navigational rights, boundary delimitation, resources, offshore territories, and environmental concerns.[49] This sea area is a hot spot for piracy and armed robbery, and potentially also for terrorism.[50] Japan has a special interest in maintaining good order at sea in Southeast Asian waters, especially in the SoMS—the shortest sea route between the Gulf suppliers and the Asian markets such as Japan, China and South Korea with an estimated 15 million barrels per day flow in 2006.[51] If the straits were blocked, nearly half of the world's shipping fleet would be required to reroute around the Indonesian archipelago through Lombok Strait, located between the islands of Bali and Lombok, or the Sunda Strait, located between Java and

Sumatra.[52] For example, it is estimated that the alternative route via Lombok would take three more days and cost about an additional $300,000.[53]

Since it was the principal user of the straits, Japan took the initiative to improve safety in these waters after due consultation with the coastal states of Malaysia, Indonesia and Singapore. Japan began operating 200,000-tonne tankers in the 1960s and 300,000-tonne (very large crude carriers, VLCC) and 400,000-tonne (ultra-large crude carriers, ULCC) tankers in the 1970s. However, because in those days navigation in the straits depended on pre-WWII charts and aids to navigation, it was necessary to update the old charts and navigation aids for large vessels. Subsequently, the Nippon Foundation and other Japanese private organizations established the Malacca Strait Council in 1969, which has so far conducted hydrographic surveys, chart compilation, wreck removal, dredging, installation and replacement of aids to navigation, donation of buoy tenders, oil spill countermeasures, and so on—a total contribution of 16.1 billion JPY (US$150 million), with the Nippon Foundation covering three-quarters of the cost.[54] The Japanese private sector also contributed 400 million JPY to set up a revolving fund with the littoral states in 1981 to combat oil spills in the straits. The Japanese private sector also initiated the formation of the Oil Spill Preparedness and Response (OSPAR) Team.[55]

As other East Asian economies, such as China and the Republic of Korea, rapidly develop, traffic volume in the straits will increase and vessels will become larger and faster. This situation requires further navigational safety measures beyond the capacity of the coastal states. Therefore, the coastal states, in cooperation with the International Maritime Organisation (IMO), held a series of international conferences after 2005 to discuss navigational safety and environmental protection measures in the straits based on the United Nations Convention on the Law of the Sea Article 43, which calls for cooperation between coastal and user states of straits used for international navigation. Accordingly, the IMO meeting in Singapore in 2007 agreed on a Cooperative Mechanism to facilitate dialog and cooperation among coastal and user states and, more importantly, user industries.[56] Again, the Japanese private sector, notably the Nippon Foundation, played a unique role not only by making financial contributions but also by introducing the concept of Corporate Social Responsibility (CSR) as a rationale for voluntary contribution by user industries.[57]

The Cooperative Mechanism consists of a Cooperative Forum, a Project Coordination Committee, and an Aids to Navigation Fund. There are six projects to be conducted:

1 Removal of wrecks in the TSS (supported by India)
2 Cooperation and capacity building on hazardous and noxious substance preparedness and response (supported by China, US, and Australia)
3 Demonstration of Class B AIS transponder on small ships (supported by Japan, the Republic of Korea (ROK), and Australia)
4 Installation of a tide, current, and wind measurement system (India, China, and the United States)

5 Replacement and maintenance of aids to navigation (Japan, ROK, and the UAE)
6 Replacement of aids to navigation destroyed or damaged by the tsunami in December 2004 (supported by China)

The Aids to Navigation Fund was established in April 2008 and the first Cooperation Forum followed in May 2008. User states and user industries contribute money to the fund on a voluntary basis. The estimated FY 2009 budget for the fund is US$8 million, with the Nippon Foundation pledging US$2.5 million, the Middle East Navigation Aids Service (MENAS) US$1 million, Greece US$1 million, and the Japan Shipowners' Association US$0.7 million (5.2 million in total) and the gap will be filled by the coastal states. However, it is imperative to secure more voluntary contributions from the users.[58]

Japan also contributed to maritime security measures in the Strait of Malacca. After the Japanese cargo ship, *Alondra Rainbow*, was hijacked by pirates in the straits in October 1999, Japan took the initiative to establish a multilateral framework to deal with piracy in the region. Japan hosted a series of international anti-piracy efforts inviting regional law enforcement agencies, maritime policy agencies, IMO, and shipowners. Those efforts included the Regional Conference on Combating Piracy and Armed Robbery against Ships (2000), the Mission for Combating Piracy and Armed Robbery against Ships (2000), and the Asian Cooperation Conference on Combating Piracy and Armed Robbery against Ships (2001). These initiatives were supported financially by the Nippon Foundation. A product of this multilateral approach was the ReCAAP (Regional Cooperation Agreement on Combating Piracy and Armed Robbery against Ships) in 2004, the first inter-governmental anti-piracy agreement adopted by 16 regional countries, including Japan, the ROK, China, India, and Association of Southeast Asian Nations (ASEAN) member countries. ReCAAP entered into force in 2006 and an Information Sharing Center was established in Singapore.[59]

At the same time, Japan has contributed to capacity building in coastal states. The JCG, in cooperation with the Japan International Cooperation Agency (JICA), provided assistance for the establishment of regional law enforcement entities, such as the Malaysia Maritime Enforcement Agency (MMEA) and the Indonesian BAKORKAMLA, a law enforcement coordination body.[60] The JCG also initiated the annual Heads of Asian Coast Guard Agencies Meeting, financially supported by the Nippon Foundation and the Japan Association for Marine Safety.[61] Japan provided three patrol boats to the Indonesian Marine Police in 2006.[62] The Nippon Foundation also provided a training ship to the MMEA in 2006.[63] The JCG took the lead in organizing the annual Head of Asian Coast Guard Agencies Meeting after 2004, inviting 18 Asian countries, including ASEAN member countries to enhance response capabilities for anti-piracy and counter-terrorism.[64]

Japan's contribution to the navigational safety, environmental protection, and maritime security in the Straits of Malacca is unique. Respecting the sovereignty of coastal states, Japan has taken multilateral approaches in accordance with the law of the sea. For navigational safety and environmental protection, Japan initiated a mechanism that invites every stakeholder to participate. For maritime security, Japan focused on information sharing and regional capacity building. The most unique feature is the public–private partnership. The Japanese private sector has provided valuable knowledge, ideas, and financial assistance.

Japan's activities in South Asian waters

South Asian waters face many challenges. Multinational counter-terrorism and counter-piracy operations are conducted in the western part. Tension between India and Pakistan remains. Proliferation is a great concern in this sea area. The Bay of Bengal is still a piracy hot spot. China is increasing its presence in this sea area as part of what is sometimes called "the string of pearls" strategy, and rivalry between India and China is a growing concern.[65]

To secure its long sea-lanes, the JMSDF envisions an engagement strategy under which it actively participates in maritime security initiatives and builds trust with like-minded navies in the areas of Japan's vital sea-lanes. The JMSDF also prepared a contingency response strategy under which it sends its fleet to troubled waters and/or cooperates with like-minded navies based on mutual trust.[66] As discussed above, the JCG plays greater role in Southeast Asia, but the JMSDF plays the main role in the sea areas beyond the Strait of Malacca.

Japan contributed to Operation *Enduring Freedom* in the Indian Ocean between December 2001 and January 2010, conducting refueling mission for the coalition counties engaged in the maritime interdiction operation.[67] Japan supplied 490,000 kiloliters of fuel in total—worth about US$210 million—to vessels from 11 countries, including the United States, the United Kingdom, France, and Pakistan, on 794 occasions between December 2001 and November 2007.[68] Japan provided 27,000 kiloliters of fuel on 144 occasions between February 2008 and January 2010.[69] This refueling mission was the first long-term over-the-horizon operation for the JMSDF. It contributed to regional stability, thereby securing Japan's vital sea-lanes. However, the Democratic Party of Japan, which took control of the government in August 2009, insisted that it would not continue the refueling after January 2010 but would instead provide "civil assistance" to the people in Afghanistan.[70]

Counter-piracy in the Gulf of Aden, where 2,000 Japanese-related ships pass, is another over-the-horizon mission for the JMSDF and the first JMSDF–JCG joint operation. Given the rapidly growing number of piracy incidents off the coasts of Somalia, Japan sent two JMSDF destroyers to the Gulf of Aden to escort Japanese-related ships in March 2009 and two P-3C patrol aircraft in May 2009 under specific maritime security orders. Under maritime security orders, the JMSDF can protect only Japanese-related ships and its rules of engagement are restrained—the use of force is allowed only for emergency evacuation and self-defense.[71] To deal with piracy threats more properly, Japan enacted the Law on Punishment of and Measures against Acts of Piracy in June 2009.[72] Under this law, the JMSDF can protect any ship regardless of its nationality and fire guns to stop any suspicious ship.[73]

Japan places great significance on its partnership with India for meeting challenges in the Northern Indian Ocean. Japan and India have been promoting a strategic global partnership since 2006 and made a joint security declaration in 2008. Exchanges between navies, defense policy planners, and coast guards are frequent. The JMSDF conducted its first trilateral combined exercise with Indian and American counterparts in April 2007. The JMSDF also participated in Exercise Malabar 07-2 in the Bay of Bengal in September 2007 and in Exercise Malabar 09 off Okinawa in April 2009.[74] Even after the change of government, Japan announced the defense cooperation action plan, focusing on maritime cooperation, with India in December 2009.[75]

Japan and the Persian Gulf

Located between Oman and Iran, the Strait of Hormuz connects the Persian Gulf with the Indian Ocean. An average of about 140 tankers carrying 16.5 to 17 million barrels of crude oil, roughly 40 percent of all oil traded by sea (or 20 percent of oil traded worldwide), pass through the strait every day.[76] Currently, three-quarters of all Japan's oil needs pass through this strait.[77] Closure of the Strait of Hormuz would require the use of longer and more expensive alternate pipeline routes across Saudi Arabia to the Red Sea or to Lebanon, or from Iraq to Turkey.[78]

The first oil shock of October 1973 literally came as a shock to the Japanese. Given an Egyptian surprise attack on Israel in October that year, the Nixon Administration supported Israel, and six Arab nations retaliated by denying their oil to the United States and its allies, including Japan, which had no political involvement in Middle East affairs. Due to its heavy dependence on oil from the region, Japan took a more pro-Arab stance to secure its oil supply. After that, Japan's foreign assistance policy began to focus on energy security.[79]

Keeping sea-lanes open is an important aspect of Japan's energy security. At the outbreak of the Iran–Iraq War of 1980–1988, Japan could not evacuate its own citizens in the Gulf and had to ask Turkey to evacuate them from Teheran.[80] During the war, 407 merchant ships were shot in the Gulf (with 335 crew killed and 317 injured). Among them, 18 Japanese ships were hit (with two crew killed and 19 injured). Japan first considered sending minesweepers to the Gulf, which was soon rejected by a cabinet member. Then Japan tried to send JCG patrol boats, but that plan was also rejected by the same cabinet member since he believed that sending patrol boats would be an act of war.[81] Instead, Japan financially contributed to the establishment of the Decca Navigator System in the Gulf.[82]

Japan faced a similar challenge during the Gulf Crisis of 1990. Japan failed to send its troops to the UN multinational forces to punish Iraq for its invasion of Kuwait due to domestic opposition. Instead, Japan made a US$13 billion financial donation by raising taxes at home. That financial contribution was not well appreciated by the international community; on the contrary, it was criticized as "checkbook diplomacy." After the Gulf War ended, Japan decided to send minesweepers to the Gulf, but only reluctantly.[83] This was the first time that Japan had sent its troops overseas since its independence in 1952. A less well-known fact is that Japan transported supplies such as office equipment and four-wheeled vehicles to the Gulf region by Japanese merchant vessels at an early phase of the Gulf Crisis when US troops lacked those supplies.[84]

Fortunately, the Hormuz Strait has never been shut down, although there have always been political, religious, ethnic, and territorial disputes in the region that could obstruct the freedom of navigation. There is currently a possibility that the Iranian nuclear program might invite a preventive or preemptive attack by Israel or the United States. In June 2008, the commander of IRGC warned that if Iran were attacked by Israel or the United States, it would seal off the Strait of Hormuz to disrupt the global flow of oil.[85] In addition, the Gulf has long been a source of potential or actual military conflict between Iran and the United States, with the Iranian Revolutionary Guards Corps (IRGC) boats harassing US Navy ships in the Strait of Hormuz.[86]

Collisions and other maritime accidents are another concern. Recent collisions in the strait include one between the nuclear submarine USS *Newport News* and the M/V *Mogamigawa*, a 300,000-tonne Japanese-flagged very large crude tanker, in January 2007 and one between the nuclear submarine USS *Hartford* and the amphibious transport dock USS *New Orleans* in March 2009.[87] Both cases involved nuclear submarines and the latter case resulted in a spill of 25,000 gallons of diesel fuel. Another nuclear submarine, the USS *Philadelphia*, also collided with the Turkish merchant ship, the M/V *Yaso Aysen*, 30 miles off the coast of Bahrain in September 2005. Given that submarines operate busily in the relatively shallow waters in the Gulf, there will always be a possibility of accidents occurring.

Japan needs to consider what it can do for the Gulf to secure its vital sea-lanes, and Japan's approach to the Strait of Malacca could be applied to the Gulf. Japan contributed to navigational safety, environmental protection, and maritime security in the Strait of Malacca through regional capacity building and public–private partnerships. This is an appropriate approach to such politically sensitive areas as the Persian Gulf.

The basic act and plan on ocean policy and its implications

As the importance of the seas increases for guaranteeing food, natural resources, and energy, as well as shipping and environmental conservation, Japan faces numerous challenges, including environmental problems, severe maritime accidents, piracy, and the infringement of its maritime interests. It was against this backdrop that Japan enacted the Basic Act on Ocean Policy in April 2007. The protection of Japanese maritime interests was the driving force behind the campaign. A series of infringements on Japanese sovereignty at sea by China—including oil and gas development near the median line in the East China Sea, frequent but unreported marine surveys in Japanese EEZs, the violation of Japanese territorial waters by a nuclear submarine, and the denial of a Japanese EEZ around Okinotorishima Island—made Japanese policy makers and media aware of the growing problem. Subsequently, Japanese lawmakers began to take measures to protect Japanese sovereignty and interests at sea. The drafting process of the Basic Act was first initiated by the Japanese private sector and Japanese lawmakers later took over the initiative on a nonpartisan basis—it was a typical example of a public–private partnership.[88]

The Basic Act on Ocean Policy clarifies the responsibilities of the State, local governments, business operators, and citizens. It formulates the Basic Plan with regard to the measures on the seas by establishing the Headquarters for Ocean Policy within the Cabinet Office in order to promote these measures comprehensively and systematically.[89] The Headquarters for Ocean Policy is led by the Prime Minister and the newly established Minister for Ocean Policy. The Basic Act on Ocean Policy outlines six basic policies:

1 Harmonization of the Development and Use of the Sea with the Preservation of the Marine Environment
2 Securing the Safety and Security of the Sea
3 Enhancement of Scientific Knowledge of the Sea
4 Sound Development of Marine Industries
5 Comprehensive Governance of the Sea
6 International Partnership with Regard to the Sea.

Accordingly, the Basic Plan on Ocean Policy was formulated in March 2008. The Basic Plan outlines 12 measures:

1 Promotion of the Development and Use of Marine Resources
2 Preservation of the Marine Environment
3 Promotion of the Development of EEZs and Continental Shelves
4 Securing Maritime Transport
5 Securing the Safety and Security of the Sea
6 Promotion of Marine Surveys
7 Promotion of Research and Development of Marine Science and Technology
8 Promotion of Marine Industries and Strengthening International Competitiveness
9 Comprehensive Management of the Coastal Zones
10 Preservation of the Islands
11 Securing International Coordination and Promotion of International Cooperation
12 Enhancement of Citizen's Understanding of the Sea and Fostering of Human Resources.[90]

The Basic Plan on Ocean Policy stresses the importance of maintaining good order at sea, navigational safety, and disaster relief to secure the safety and security of the seas. Accordingly, Japan introduced a law to regulate navigation of foreign ships in its internal and territorial seas in July 2008 to ensure their innocent passage.[91] Japan also formulated a basic guideline on the preservation and management of remote islands in December 2009, and is now preparing a law covering these activities.[92] The JCG is taking measures, such as the replacement of patrol boats and aircraft and the introduction of a multi-manning system.[93]

One of the most important implications of the Basic Act on Ocean Policy is that it promotes inter-agency coordination and cooperation to deal with maritime challenges. For example, the Basic Plan calls for joint training between the JCG and the JMSDF to deal with spy boats, based on the response manual. The Headquarters for Ocean Policy plays an important role in promoting inter-agency coordination. It prepared the Law on Punishment of and Measures against Acts of Piracy, which prescribes a clearer division of labor between the JCG and the JMSDF.

Conclusion

As discussed, Japan has taken many measures for good order at sea within its borders and beyond. Japan has developed a good model of public–private partnerships and international cooperation for good order at sea in Southeast Asia, which can potentially be applied to such regions as the Persian Gulf or the Horn of Africa. Japan also has developed a domestic mechanism for good order at sea under the Basic Act on Ocean Policy.

However, the fundamental challenge for Japan remains unsettled—how should Japan allocate its scarce sea assets between sea border protection and sea lines of communication (SLOC) protection? The United States provides territorial defense and long-range SLOC protection for Japan under the US–Japan alliance. Nevertheless, the United States alone can no longer provide sufficient security in the vast maritime domain. The very fact that the Western Pacific and the Western Indian Ocean are piracy hot spots despite the US presence shows this. Accordingly, while it lives in a dangerous neighborhood, Japan is required to contribute more toward securing sea-lanes in the Indian Ocean.

The first priority for Japan is therefore to develop a Japanese national fleet plan for a more effective and efficient use of the JCG and JMSDF to protect its vast sea borders and long sea-lanes. For example, both sea services are introducing large ships (Hyuga class helicopter destroyers and Shikishima class patrol ships), but there is no coordination between these two expensive procurement plans, while smaller ships also need to be replaced. Japan also needs to promote public awareness of the importance of good order at sea so that maritime security and safety measures can be sustained. The cancellation of the refueling mission in the Indian Ocean shows that this is necessity.

Epilogue

The year 2010 was a turning point for Japan's maritime security. The Democratic Party's naïve foreign policy that called for an "equal alliance" with the United States damaged the alliance, which had formed the backbone of the country's global positioning for more than a half of a century, and made regional countries worried about the direction of Japan's foreign policy course. The Democratic Party finally canceled the refueling mission in the Indian Ocean in January 2010, while it continued counter-piracy operations in the Gulf of Aden. In the meantime, North Korean sank a South Korean warship in the Yellow Sea in March and China made a demonstration cruise with ten warships through the Miyako Channel in April. When North Korean bombarded a South Korean island in the Yellow Sea in November 2010, China strongly protested the dispatch of the USS *George Washington* to the Yellow Sea for a US–ROK naval drill. The series of events at sea were a wakeup call for Japanese defense planners regarding the importance of maritime security and the US security umbrella.

The National Defense Program Guidelines (NDPG), approved by the Japanese government on 17 December 2010, provide guidance for defense policy and set out the force structure for the next decade.[94] The document, reflecting the changing regional and global security environment, abandoned the long-held "static" defense posture and introduced a new concept of "dynamic defense" that envisions an increased operational level and tempo of the JSDF. Accordingly, the Japanese government has shifted its strategic focus from the north to the south to meet challenges from the rising China, especially its growing naval power. The emphasis on the defense of the Ryukyu island chain and the plan to increase the submarine fleet from 16 to 22 reflected this strategic shift. Given the growing Chinese anti-access/area-denial capabilities, the document also calls for strengthening partnerships with South Korea, Australia, India, ASEAN members, and NATO and to secure the maritime, space, and cyber commons.

In addition, the September 2010 collision between a Chinese trawler and two JCG patrol vessels in Japanese waters off the Senkaku Islands was a reminder of the importance of protecting the nation's waters. Major Japanese political parties now agree that the ability of the JCG to guard Japanese waters needs to be steadily reinforced. The JCG has a plan to construct 22 new patrol boats, including a 6,500-tonne helicopter vessel and six 1,000-tonne cutters, and a two billion JPY upgrade plan for communication systems. In May 2010, Japan enacted a law for the JCG to inspect North Korean ships in the high seas under UNSCR 1874. The Japanese government is also considering a legal framework that enables the JCG to inspect foreign vessels in territorial waters.

The massive earthquake and tsunami that devastated northeastern Japan on 11 March 2011 posed a serious challenge to Japan in terms of maritime security. The JMSDF and the US Seventh Fleet played a central role in disaster relief operation, involving around 70 warships and 200 aircraft in total, and demonstrated alliance solidarity during crisis. On the other hand, China buzzed aircraft around JMSDF destroyers in the East China Sea, while Russia flew warplanes in the vicinity of Japanese territorial airspace to test the alliance posture. Since the post-disaster economic loss is expected to reach astronomical figures, it will now be difficult to fund maritime security-related programs, including shipbuilding for the JMSDF and the JCG. The radiation leak from the Fukushima Nuclear Power Plant is another challenge. On one hand, this will increase the need for fossil fuel and the importance of SLOC security. On the other hand, the radiation leak to the seas might cause marine environmental destruction, thus damaging coastal fishery.

Notes

1 JCG, Kaijo Hoan Repoto 2008 (Japan Coast Guard annual report 2008), www.kaiho.mlit.go.jp/info/books/report2008/top.html.
2 See Ministry of Defense, Nihon no Boei 2009 (Defense of Japan 2009), pp. 55–57, www.clearing.mod.go.jp/hakusho_data/2009/2009/pdf/21010203.pdf.
3 JCG, Kaijo Hoan Report 2007 (Japan Coast Guard annual report 2007), www.kaiho.mlit.go.jp/info/books/report2007/tokushu/p013.html.
4 Oga Ryohei, *Si-re-n no Himitsu: Beiso Senryaku no Hazamade* (The secret of sea-lanes: between Soviet strategies), Tokyo: Chobunsha, 1983, pp. 28–29.
5 Makoto Momoi, "Basic Trends in Japanese Security Policies," in Robert A. Scalapino (ed.), *The Foreign Policy of Modern Japan*, Berkeley and Los Angeles: University of California Press, 1977, p. 362.
6 JCG, Kaijo Hoan Report 2007.
7 Ibid.
8 Office of the Secretary of Defense, US Department of Defense, "Military Power of the People's Republic of China 2007," p. 16.
9 "China's Worries at Sea," *The People's Liberation Daily*, 2 January 2004.
10 Robyn Lim, *The Geopolitics of East Asia: The Search for Equilibrium*, New York: Routledge, 2005, p. 152.
11 See Russell Hsiao, "China's Expanding Naval Presence Troubles Neighbors," *China Brief*, Vol. 8, Issue 3, 31 January 2008.
12 Tomohisa Takei, "Kaiyo Shinjidai niokeru Kaijo Jieitai: JMSDF in the New Maritime Era," *Hato* No. 199, November 2008, pp. 18–19.
13 The Ministry of Defense, Nihon no Boei 2007 (The defense of Japan 2007), www.clearing.mod.go.jp/hakusho_data/2007/2007/html/j3124300.html.
14 Takei, "Kaiyo Shinjidai niokeru Kaijo Jieitai," pp. 18–19, 23–24.
15 Nihon no Boei 2009, pp. 170–171.
16 JCG, Kaijo Hoan Report 2004 (Japan Coast Guard annual report 2004), www.kaiho.mlit.go.jp/info/books/report2004/honpen/hp05030200.html.
17 Kaijo Hoan Report 2008.
18 Ibid. and Kaijo Hoan Report 2007.
19 Kaijo Hoan Report 2007.
20 JCG, Kaijo Hoan Report 2005 (Japan Coast Guard Annual Report 2005), www.kaiho.mlit.go.jp/info/books/report2005/tokushu/p033.html.
21 Leif-Eric Easley, Tetsuo Kotani, and Aki Mori, "Electing a New Japanese Security Policy?: Examining Foreign Policy Visions within the Democratic Party of Japan," *Asia Policy*, No. 9, January 2010, p. 61.
22 Kaijo Hoan Report 2007; Japan concluded bilateral fisheries agreements with Russia (the former Soviet Union) in 1984, with South Korea in 1999, and with China in 2000.
23 JCG, Kaijo Hoan Report 2007.
24 Kaijo Hoan Report 2008.
25 Ibid.
26 Ibid.
27 Ibid.
28 Nihon no Boei 2009, p. 55.
29 James J. Przystup, "Japan–China Relations: New Year, Old Problems," *Comparative Connections*, April 2009, http://csis.org/files/media/csis/pubs/0901qjapan_china.pdf.
30 Martin Fackler, "A Reef or a Rock? Question Puts Japan In a Hard Place; To Claim Disputed Waters, Charity Tries to Find Use For Okinotori Shima," *Wall Street Journal* (Eastern Edition), 16 February 2005, p. A.1.
31 "China's Argument on Japan Island Unacceptable: Fukuda," *Jiji Press*, 23 April 2004, p. 1.

32 Yoshihiko Yamada, *Nihon no Kokkyo* (*Japan's borders*), Tokyo: Shincho Sha, 2005, p. 63.
33 Reactions of China and the Republic of Korea to the submission made by Japan to the Commission on the Limits of the Continental Shelf, www.un.org/Depts/los/clcs_new/submissions_files/submission_jpn.htm.
34 Kaijo Hoan Report 2006.
35 Ibid.
36 The JCG concluded bilateral agreements with South Korea in 1999, with Russian in 2000, and with China in 2001.
37 Kaijo Hoan Report 2006.
38 Ibid.
39 *Yomiuri Shimbun*, 2 September 2008.
40 *Shikoku Shimbun*, 7 June 2008.
41 *Nihon no Boei 2009*, pp. 259–261.
42 Ministry of Land, Infrastructure and Transport of Japan, Kokudo Kotsu Hakusho, White Paper on land, infrastructure, and transport in Japan 2007), 12 May 2008, p. 147.
43 Japan Maritime Public Relations Center (ed.), *Shipping Now 2009–2010*, p. 6, www.jsanet.or.jp/shipping/shipping_txt.html.
44 Ibid, p. 4.
45 Trade Statistics of Japan, www.customs.go.jp/toukei/suii/html/data/y1.pdf.
46 Agency for Natural Resources and Energy, Ministry of Economy, Technology and Industry, *Energy in Japan 2006: Status and Policies*, March 2006, pp. 5, 22, www.enecho.meti.go.jp/topics/energy-in-japan/energy2006E.pdf.
47 Ibid., p. 5.
48 Japan Maritime Public Relations Center (ed.), *Shipping Now 2009–2010*, p. 5, www.jsanet.or.jp/shipping/pdf/shippingnow2009a.pdf.
49 See Clive Schofield and Ian Storey, *The South China Sea Dispute: Increasing Stakes and Rising Tensions*, Jamestown Foundation, November 2009.
50 Takei, "Kaiyo Shinjidai niokeru Kaijo Jieitai," p. 20.
51 Energy Information Administration, US Department of Energy, "World Oil Transit Chokepoints," p. 3, www.eia.doe.gov/cabs/World_Oil_Transit_Chokepoints/pdf.pdf.
52 "World Oil Transit Chokepoints," p. 4.
53 The Institute for Ocean Policy, Kaiyo Hakusho 2005,White Paper on ocean policy 2005, Tokyo: Ship & Ocean Foundation, 2005, p. 99.
54 Ibid, p. 100.
55 Nazery Khalid, "Burden Sharing, Security and Equity in the Straits of Malacca," *Japan Focus*, www.japanfocus.org/-Nazery-Khalid/2277.
56 Ocean Policy Research Foundation, Kaiyo Hakusho 2009, White Paper on ocean policy 2009, p. 68.
57 Ibid., p. 69.
58 Ibid.
59 Ibid., p. 70.
60 Ibid.
61 Ibid., p. 73.
62 Ministry of Foreign Affairs of Japan, "Grant Aid to Indonesia for the Project for Construction of Patrol Vessels for the Prevention of Piracy, Maritime Terrorism and Proliferation of Weapons," 16 June 2006, www.mofa.go.jp/announce/announce/2006/6/0616-3.html.
63 James L. Huffman, "The Nippon Foundation donates Training Ship to Malaysia," The Nippon Foundation, 1 June 2006, www.nippon-foundation.or.jp/eng/news/2006/brief_dtl/2006753/20067531.html.
64 Kaijo Hoan Report 2006.

65 See Robert D. Kaplan, "Center Stage for the Twenty-first Century: Power Plays in the Indian Ocean," *Foreign Affairs*, Vol. 88, No. 2, March/April 2009.
66 Takei, "Kaiyo Shinjidai niokeru Kaijo Jieitai," pp. 18–19, 23–24.
67 *Nihon no Boei 2009*, pp. 242–247.
68 "MSDF Refueling Mission Resumed," *The Japan Times*, 22 February 2008, http://search.japantimes.co.jp/cgi-bin/nn20080222a3.html.
69 Ministry of Defense website, www.mod.go.jp/j/news/hokyushien/jisseki100108.html.
70 *The Associate Press*, 13 November 2009.
71 *Nihon no Boei 2009*, pp. 108–111.
72 English text is available at www.sof.or.jp/en/topics/pdf/09_01.pdf.
73 *Nihon no Boei 2009*, p. 110.
74 Ibid, pp. 262–264.
75 For the text of this action plan, see www.mofa.go.jp/region/asia-paci/india/pmv0912/action.html.
76 "World Oil Transit Chokepoints," p. 3.
77 Ibid.
78 Ibid.
79 Makoto Iokibe (ed.), *Sengo Nihon Gaikoshi* (*Postwar Japanese Diplomatic History*), Tokyo: Yuhikaku, 1999, pp. 163–164.
80 His Highness Imperial Prince Tomohito, "Paragons of Private Diplomacy—A Friendship Borne of the Ocean," *Ocean Policy Research Foundation Newsletter* No. 178, 5 January 2008, www.sof.or.jp/en/news/151–200/178_2.php.
81 *Tokyo Shimbun*, 14 May 2009, p. 3.
82 Ryohei Murata, *Umiga Nipponno Shorai o Kimeru* (*The Seas Determine the Future of Japan*), Tokyo: Seizando Shoten, 2006, p. 233.
83 Ibid., pp. 216–217.
84 Ibid., pp. 218–219.
85 "U.S. Navy Commander Warns Iran: Don't Try Closing Gulf Oil Passageway," *FOX News Online*, 2 July 2008, www.foxnews.com/story/0,2933,374905,00.html.
86 David Isenberg, "A game of chicken in the Persian Gulf," *Asia Times online*, 8 January 2008, www.atimes.com/atimes/Middle_East/JA10Ak05.html.
87 See "Navy says speed of tanker sucked submarine up to surface," *Pilot Online*, 10 January 2007, http://hamptonroads.com/node/205951; and "U.S. Navy vessels in Bahrain for evaluation after collision," *CNN.com*, 21 March 2009, www.cnn.com/2009/WORLD/meast/03/20/navy.vessels.collide/index.html.
88 For the detailed drafting process of the Basic Act on Ocean Policy, see Masahiro Akiyama, "Enacting the Basic Ocean Law: The Process and the Background," a paper prepared for the Institute for International Policy Studies (IIPS) Symposium on Japan as a Maritime Nation, Tokyo, 16 October 2007, www.iips.org/07mar/07marAkiyama.pdf.
89 The English text of the Basic Act on Ocean Policy is available at www.kantei.go.jp/jp/singi/kaiyou/konkyo6.pdf.
90 The English text of the Basic Plan on Ocean Policy is available at www.kantei.go.jp/jp/singi/kaiyou/kihonkeikaku/080318kihonkeikaku_E.pdf.
91 See Headquarters for Ocean Policy's annual report 2009, p. 4, www.kantei.go.jp/jp/singi/kaiyou/annual/H21/H21all.pdf.
92 *Nihon Keizai Shimbun*, 15 January 2010.
93 Kaijo Hoan Report 2008.
94 The English text of the NDPG at the Ministry of Defense website, www.mod.go.jp/e/d_act/d_policy/national.html.

13 South Korea's maritime challenges and priorities

Seokwoo Lee

Introduction

The sea plays an important role in South Korea's economy and security, and thus, making good order at sea is a vital priority for the country. Of particular economic concern are issues such as piracy and armed robbery against ships, and depletion of fish stocks. South Korea has joined various bilateral, regional and international cooperation agreements to address these issues. Moreover, it has territorial disputes with Japan over the Dokdo (Takeshima) Islet and with China over the Ieodo (Suyan) Rock, which has so far led to little progress in maritime boundary delimitation negotiations between South Korea and these two countries.

In terms of security, South Korea is technically still at war with North Korea, since hostilities during the Korean War were only halted by an armistice agreement in 1953. In particular, the issue of North Korea's nuclear weapons program, as well as the unresolved dispute over sea boundaries between the two countries in the West Sea present serious challenges to peace and stability on the Korean Peninsula. After naval skirmishes in the West Sea in 1999, 2002 and 2009, tensions have escalated recently following the sinking of a South Korean navy corvette, the *Cheonan*, in March 2010. Additionally, South Korea's participation in the Proliferation Security Initiative (PSI) has been met with verbal threats of war by North Korea.

The first part of this chapter discusses some of the maritime challenges facing South Korea, with a particular focus on piracy and armed robbery against ships, depletion of fish stocks, the PSI and the recent conflict over the sinking of the *Cheonan*. The second part of the chapter provides the current status of territorial disputes and delimitation issues between South Korea and its neighbors, followed by a brief summary of South Korea's maritime priorities going forward.

Piracy and armed robbery against ships

With more than 99 percent of South Korean trade being transported by sea, the South Korean economy is dependent on secure global sea-lanes for communication.[1]

Furthermore, as the country does not have any domestic production of oil, South Korea is dependent on oil imports, 80 percent of which are transported from the Middle East through two of the world's major oil transit choke points, the Strait of Hormuz and the Straits of Singapore and Malacca.[2] Any disruption of vessels carrying oil to South Korea through these sea-lanes would have a potentially devastating effect on the South Korean economy.[3] At present, the biggest threat to trade and energy flows seems to be piracy and armed robbery against ships. South Korea is actively engaged in regional and international efforts aimed at combating this problem.

South Korea is a contracting party to the Regional Cooperation Agreement on Combating Piracy and Armed Robbery Against Ships in Asia (ReCAAP) and has provided funding and staff to the ReCAAP Information Sharing Center (ISC), which was officially launched in Singapore in 2006.[4] To support the international efforts to combat piracy and armed robbery against ships in the Gulf of Aden and in the waters off Somalia, South Korea joined the Combined Task Force 151 (CTF 151) in 2009.[5]

The ability to dispatch naval vessels to operations in distant locations is the result of the South Korean strategy to transform its navy from a coastal force into a blue-water navy with capacity to protect Korea's global commercial interests and to contribute to maintaining peace around the world.[6] As part of the Defense Reform 2020, the Korean Navy will be reorganized into three fleets, a Submarine Command, an Aviation Command and a Mobile Flotilla (reinforcement). The overall number of vessels will be reduced, but total capabilities will be upgraded with new-generation frigates and Aegis destroyers.[7]

Depletion of fish stocks

The Korean Peninsula has traditionally been blessed with an abundance of rich fishing grounds, created in part by the mixture of warm and cold ocean currents and the particular geography of the Korean coastline.[8] In recent years, however, fish stocks have declined considerably, with total stocks in 2015 projected to be only 39 percent of the levels in 1980. This drastic decrease is caused by a variety of reasons, including overfishing, pollution and climate change.[9] Such depletion of resources not only challenges the South Korean fisheries industry but also poses a serious threat to food security and access to seafood for future generations.

While South Korea has implemented measures to achieve a sustainable use of fishery resources, such as the Total Allowable Catch System (TAC),[10] the depletion of fish stocks is a problem that is being shared by all countries in the region and therefore requires regional cooperation. South Korea has signed bilateral fishery agreements with Japan and China that determine, for example, quotas on each country's allowable catch in the other country's waters.[11] These agreements, however, do not include provisions for a joint fisheries management system, which is essential to deal effectively with the rapid depletion of fish stocks in Northeast Asia.[12]

The PSI

The proliferation of weapons of mass destruction, their delivery systems and related materials remains a major challenge for the international community. Given the volatile situation on the Korean Peninsula and North Korea's withdrawal from the Six Party Talks in 2009, as well as the country's stated intention of carrying on with its nuclear weapons program, South Korea is facing a difficult challenge in terms of its response to the North Korean export of such materials by sea. This issue continues to be a priority and South Korea's membership in the PSI should be seen in this light.

Immediately following North Korea's second round of nuclear tests in May 2009, South Korea decided to become a member of the PSI after previously sending observers to PSI exercises in its role as a like-minded country. A previous North Korean nuclear test in October 2006 had not led to South Korean participation in the PSI due to concerns about the risk of renewed military confrontation with North Korea and the fact that an agreement with similar objectives as the PSI already existed between the two countries, namely the Agreement on Maritime Transportation between the South and the North.[13]

As a consequence of the increased tensions between the two Koreas in the wake of the sinking of the *Cheonan* in March 2010, the South Korean government in June 2010 announced its intention to join the Operational Experts Group (OEG), the steering committee of the PSI, by the end of 2010. In addition, South Korea hosted a PSI workshop for Asia-Pacific member countries in October 2010.[14] These steps indicate that South Korea is preparing to play a key role in sharing intelligence regarding North Korea with the other PSI members and further emphasizes that anti-proliferation remains a key priority for South Korea.

The Northern Limit Line (NLL)[16]

The United Nations Command and the North Korean Army established a Military Demarcation Line on land at the time the Inter-Korean Armistice Agreement was signed on 27 May 1953, but did not extend it into maritime areas. The seaward extension, which became known as the NLL, was drawn by UN Commander General Mark Clarke on 3 August 1958, and is the line of equidistance between the North Korean coastline and five tiny islands (BaengNyengDo, DaeCheongDo, SoCheongDo, YeonPyeongDo and SoYeonPyeongDo) that hug the North Korean coast but are controlled by and claimed by South Korea (see Figure 13.1). Its purpose was to prevent a clash between military vessels and aircraft from both sides, and seems to have been originally designed to prevent South Korean naval vessels and aircraft from going north. It has been challenged by North Korea ever since, because it was declared unilaterally and because North Korea views it as an infringement of its sovereignty and legitimate access to the sea. Because the NLL is not mentioned in the armistice agreement itself, its status and that of the waters around it remain contentious.

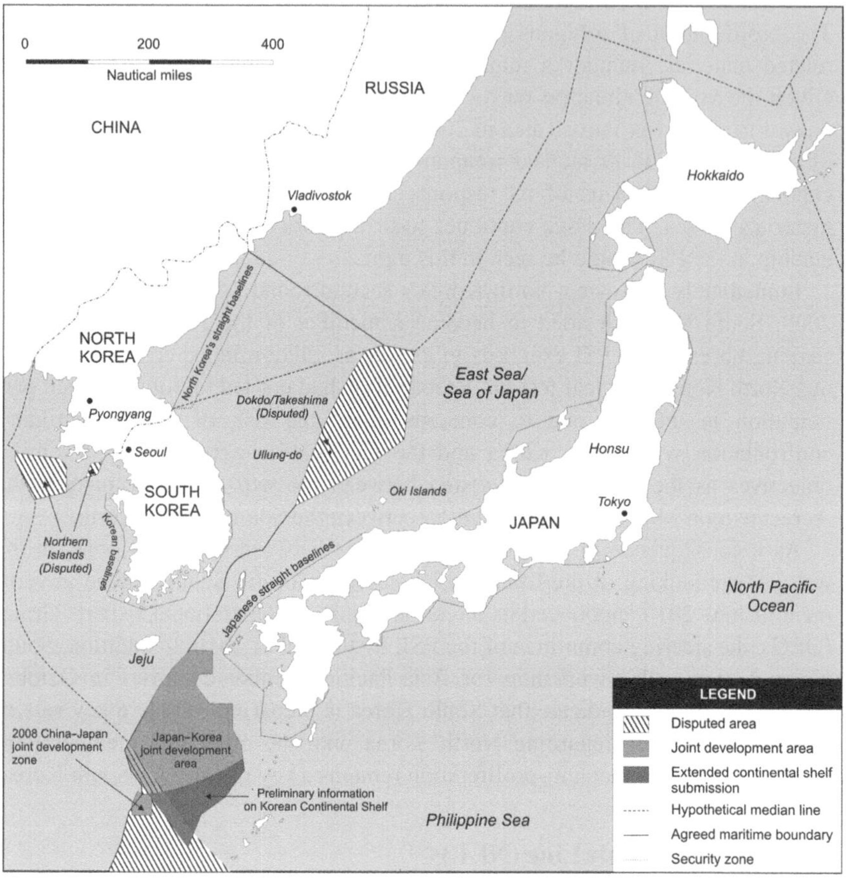

Figure 13.1 Territorial disputes and delimitation issues between South Korea and its neighbours[15] (source: map drawn by I. Made Andi Arsana, Gadjah Mada University, Yogyakarta, Indonesia).

South Korea argues that (1) North Korea did not object to the NLL until October 1973;[17] (2) North Korea implicitly recognized the NLL several times; (3) the 1991 Basic Agreement stipulates (in Article 11) that "the South–North demarcation line and areas for non-aggression shall be identical with areas that have been under the jurisdiction of each side until the present time" and that the Protocol on Non-Aggression states (in Article 10) that

> the South–North sea non-aggression demarcation line shall continue to be discussed in the future. Until the sea non-aggression demarcation has been settled, the sea non-aggression zones shall be identical with those that have been under the jurisdiction of each side until the present time;

(4) the NLL is the legal sea demarcation line between South and North Korea; and (5) the NLL cannot be unilaterally challenged or discussed except in a comprehensive agreement to bring permanent peace to the Korean Peninsula. The United States concurs that the 1992 Basic Agreement between North and South Korea stipulates that both Koreas must respect the line until a new agreement can be reached.

North Korea counters that when the NLL was drawn, the UN command did not inform Pyongyang, which neither acknowledged nor accepted it. It argues that it has challenged the line on many occasions during the past 55 years, particularly as the value of the blue crab catch in the area has become more apparent. It also argues that its vessels have regularly fished in the waters claimed by the South and that since March 1955 it has claimed under customary international law a 12 nautical mile territorial sea from its coast, which extends well south of the NLL. Because the NLL veers sharply to the north after leaving land, Pyongyang claims that it unfairly gives too much ocean space to South Korea.

The NLL has served a useful purpose as a line of military control and should continue in place until the two Koreas can reach agreement to end their state of war. However, if the two Koreas were to normalize their relations fully and accept each other as independent countries, the NLL would probably not stand as a legitimate maritime boundary under the "equitable principles" that have evolved from decisions based on Articles 74 and 83 of the 1982 UN Law of the Sea Convention, because the NLL denies North Korea legitimate access to its adjacent sea areas and is contrary to the principle of "non-encroachment."[18] Further, according to legal precedents and international practice, islands do not have an equal capacity with landmasses to create maritime zones, nor do they command equal strength with an opposing continental area or land mass.[19]

Naval skirmishes in the West Sea (Yellow Sea) and the *Cheonan* incident

Although the NLL has never been accepted by North Korea, there had not been any violent clashes until June 1999, when several North Korean naval vessels crossed the NLL and opened fire against South Korean warships, leading to an armed skirmish. Similar naval incidents occurred in 2002 and 2009, resulting in several dead and wounded sailors on both sides.[20] In addition, North Korea has drawn its own demarcation line, located south of the NLL. After the skirmish in November 2009, the North Korean Army reiterated that it considered this the only valid border and that it would be defended with merciless military measures.[21]

On 26 March 2010, the South Korean corvette, the *Cheonan*, sank near Baengnyeong Island on the South Korean side of the NLL, resulting in the death of 46 sailors out of a total crew of 104. To determine the cause of the sinking, the South Korean government established the Joint Civilian-Military Investigation Group, consisting of South Korean experts as well as international experts from Australia, Sweden, the United Kingdom and the USA. The result of the investigation was released on 20 May 2010, and concluded that the sinking of the *Cheonan* was the result of an explosion caused by a torpedo made in North Korea and fired by a North Korean submarine.[22] North Korea, however, has denied having played any role in the sinking of the *Cheonan*.

Following the findings of the international investigation team, on 4 June 2010 South Korea referred the issue of North Korea's role in the sinking of the *Cheonan* to the UN Security Council, seeking a resolution condemning North Korea. On the international front, however, the South Korean administration has faced an unfavorable attitude from key neighbors, namely China and Russia, who have expressed doubt as to North Korea's culpability for the sinking of the *Cheonan*.[23] Given the Lee administration's efforts over the years to strengthen strategic ties with the United States, it is not surprising that China and Russia are wary of South Korea's efforts to lay the blame on the North. Despite this obvious position, the South Korean government failed to adequately engage both members of the "Permanent Five," necessary to ensure widespread support for Korea's international effort to punish North Korea. Both China and Russia were left out of the Joint Civilian-Military Investigation Group, whose conclusions were called into question by both nations. It was under these circumstances that South Korea sought to bring the *Cheonan* incident to the Security Council, seeking a resolution that would clearly lay state responsibility of the tragedy on North Korea. However, all the South Korean government was able to show for its efforts at the United Nations was a presidential statement from the Security Council that made no mention of North Korea at all. The capacity of such a statement to provide international legal justification for any subsequent South Korean actions against North Korea is doubtful, as it does not reach the level a binding Security Council resolution. To add insult to injury, North Korea claims that the statement of the Security Council absolves it from any responsibility at all and provides a propaganda coup for the Kim Jong-Il regime. While there may have been some in the South Korean Government who desired to show North Korea that there was a price to pay for sinking the *Cheonan*, South Korea's effort to bring the international community to punish North Korea has resulted in failure and has put the South Korean Government in the uncomfortable position of having no apparent exit strategy.

On 23 November 2010, North Korean artillery crossed the NLL, landing on South Korea's Yeonpyeong Island, causing death and injury, and substantial destruction.[24]

Maritime delimitation between South Korea and China in the Yellow Sea[25]

The Yellow Sea (also known as the West Sea) is a semi-enclosed body of water measuring about 520 nautical miles from north to south and about 380 nautical miles from east to west. The total area covered by the Yellow Sea is 400,000 square kilometers, with an average depth of 55 meters and a maximum depth of 125 meters.[26] This section focuses on the unresolved maritime boundary between

South Korea and China, which have both ratified the 1982 United Nations Law of the Sea Convention. Article 57 of the Law of the Sea Convention authorizes each coastal state to declare an exclusive economic zone (EEZ) of 200 nautical miles from the coast or "from baselines from which the breadth of the territorial sea is measured,"[27] but because the Yellow Sea is less than 400 nautical miles wide, none of the coastal states can declare full zones and their claimed EEZs overlap. The extent of the overlap is exacerbated by arguably excessive straight baselines that have been claimed by the coastal countries.[28]

Because the Yellow Sea is rich in natural resources, with the capacity for year-round fishing and an estimated oil reserve that may contain up to ten billion barrels of oil,[29] it has been difficult for the coastal countries to agree on maritime delimitation. Tension over these resources endangers security in Northeast Asia, and conflicts are likely to continue as long as the region's maritime boundaries remain unresolved.[30] South Korea and China have had an awkward relationship during previous centuries,[31] but are cooperating economically at present and it should be possible for these two important countries to reach an agreement on the maritime delimitation of the Yellow Sea.

South Korea has maintained since the 1960s that the most equitable approach to the maritime delimitation in the Yellow Sea is to utilize the equidistance principle, whereby the EEZs of South Korea and China would be delimited at the median line.[32] This position is somewhat inconsistent with South Korea's approach toward its boundary dispute with Japan in the East China Sea, where South Korea argues for the natural prolongation approach,[33] but South Korea explains the difference by referring to the goal of delimitation, which is to reach an "equitable" result. China's approach toward delimitation also has its inconsistencies, because it favors the natural prolongation theory in the Yellow Sea dispute with South Korea but maintains that the equidistance line should divide its boundary with North Korea in the Gulf of Korea and with Vietnam in the Gulf of Tonkin.[34] Perhaps most importantly, the natural prolongation approach does not appear to apply in any significant geographical way to the Yellow Sea, because (unlike the East China Sea, where the seabed drops off sharply at the Okinawa Trough, near the small Japanese islands) the Yellow Sea has a flat, shallow, and relatively featureless sea floor throughout. The sediments do not shift dramatically from clay to sand, but instead make a gradual transition and the sea includes areas where the sediments are mixed.

Maritime delimitation and territorial disputes between South Korea and Japan in the East Sea (Sea of Japan)[35]

Korea regained its independence after World War II, but its sovereignty over Dokdo continues to be challenged by Japan, and the events, decrees and agreements during and after World War II continue to be relevant to this controversy. Dokdo consists of two rocky structures and 32 smaller outcroppings in the East Sea with a combined land area of 0.18 square kilometers. East Island (Dongdo) has a circumference of 1.9 kilometers and West Island (Seodo) has a circumference of 2.8 kilometers.[36] These islets are located 88 kilometers (about 55 miles or 47 nautical miles) from Korea's Ullungdo[37] and are about 158 kilometers (about 99 miles or 86 nautical miles) from Japan's Oki Islands.[38] Korea's claim to Dokdo goes back many centuries and is based on contacts during many previous eras.[39] Japan asserts, on the other hand, that Dokdo was *terra nullius* in 1905 and that Japan acted in accordance with international law in claiming and incorporating the islets into Japanese territory at that time. Korea viewed this initiative as part of Japan's aggressive and illegal expansionism, whereby Japan established a protectorate over Korea in 1905 and then formally annexed Korea in 1910. After World War II, Korea re-established its occupation of Dokdo and has maintained a small contingent of marine guards on the islets during the past half century.

The delimitation of maritime boundaries between South Korea and Japan in the East Sea (or Sea of Japan) and the East China Sea also remains unsettled, except in the southern part of the continental shelf in the East Sea (or Sea of Japan) of South Korea. Prompted by the need for the exploitation of oil on the continental shelf, South Korea and Japan agreed to the joint development of the disputed continental shelf south of Jeju Island in 1974, in addition to delimitation of the continental shelf in the Korea Strait. As with China and Japan, a disputed island, Dokdo (or Takeshima) – which is located 50 nautical miles east of South Korea's Ullung Island and 90 nautical miles north-west of Japan's Oki Islands, and is currently under South Korea's control – lies at the core of the dispute over maritime boundary delimitation between the two countries. Whereas South Korea has argued that the EEZs of both countries should be divided along a median line between Ullung Island and the Oki Islands, Japan claims a median line between Ullung Island and Dokdo, arguing that Dokdo is its own island. Both countries' claims enclose Dokdo within their own EEZs. The recent standoff by the coast guards of the two countries over Japan's attempt to conduct a maritime survey in the disputed waters off Dokdo represents the volatility of maritime issues between the two countries.

South Korea's maritime priorities: the way forward

This chapter discusses the central maritime challenges facing South Korea, including piracy and armed robbery against ships, depletion of fish stocks, the PSI, and territorial disputes and delimitation issues between South Korea and its neighbors. These challenges are so broad in terms of scope and so deep in terms of importance as to put South Korea on notice in terms of its state of preparedness.

The recent skirmishes in the Yellow Sea area between South and North Korea have reshuffled the maritime priorities of South Korea, as North Korea issues now overwhelm other important priorities. The South Korean government should set up guidelines for maritime security, as it is surrounded by neighbors that have unresolved territorial and maritime boundary issues with it. South Korea has to prepare not only for bilateral disputes, but also for bilateral disputes from a multilateral perspective.

Notes

1 Republic of Korea Ministry of Land, Transport and Maritime Affairs, Statistical Yearbook of MLTM (2008).
2 Korea Energy Economics Institute, Energy Statistics 2008, www.kesis.net/flex/eng_main.jsp.
3 Lok Vi Ming and Laura Cheng, "Maritime Insurance against Piracy: A Shield or a Sword?" in Joshua H. Ho (ed.), *Realising Safe and Secure Seas for All: International Maritime Security Conference 2009* (Singapore: Select Books, 2009), pp. 151–152.
4 "The ReCAAP ISC makes further progress and will co-operate with the International Maritime Organization in the effort against piracy in the Western Indian Ocean and Gulf of Aden," ReCAAP ISC Press Release, 27 February 2009, www.recaap.org/news/pdf/press/2009/Press%20Release-3GC%20Mtg.pdf.
5 John Fage, "CTF Strengthens Partnerships, Stresses Cooperation," *navy.mil* (official Website of the United States Navy), 4 June 2009, www.navy.mil/search/display.asp?story_id=45960.
6 "Lee backs plan for blue-water navy," *Republic of Korea Navy* article, 25 March 2008, www.navy.mil.kr/bbs/articleView.action?boardId=1070&articleId=2903&page=1.
7 Keith Jacobs, "The ROK Navy: Towards a Regional Force Status," *Military Technology: MILTECH* (10), 2007, pp. 96–97.
8 Food and Agriculture Organization of the United Nations, Fishery and Aquaculture Country Profiles: Republic of Korea, www.fao.org/fishery/countrysector/FI-CP_KR/en.
9 Sang-Go Lee, "Rebuilding Fish Stocks in Korea: A National Comprehensive Approach," OECD document, www.oecd.org/dataoecd/20/43/43017813.pdf.
10 Jeong-Gon Ryu, Jongoh Nam and John M. Gates, "Limitations of the Korean conventional fisheries management regime and expanding Korean TAC system toward output control systems," *Marine Policy* 30 (5), 2006, pp. 510–522.
11 Kunwoo Kim, "Korea-Japan Fish Dispute," *ICE Case Studies*, 23 April 2002, http://www1.american.edu/ted/ice/korea-japan-islands.htm.
12 San-Go Lee, "Rebuilding Fish Stocks in Korea."
13 Suk Kyoon Kim, "Korean Peninsula Maritime Issues," *Ocean Development & International Law* 41(2), 2010, pp. 179–180.
14 Sang-ho Song, "Seoul seeks to play increased role in PSI," *The Korea Herald*, 21 June 2010.
15 The author would like to express his gratitude to Clive Schofield, Director of Research and Queen Elizabeth II Research Fellow at the Australian National Centre for Ocean Resources and Security (ANCORS), University of Wollongong (Australia), and Andi Arsana, Lecturer and Researcher in the Department of Geodetic Engineering, Gadjah Mada University (Indonesia), for their work in producing the map that appears in this article, which originally appeared in Seokwoo Lee and Hee Eun Lee (eds), *Dokdo: Historical Appraisal and International Justice* (Brill/Martinus Nijhoff Publishers, 2011), p. xi. The map was drawn by I. Made Andi Arsana, Gadjah Mada University, Yogyakarta, Indonesia.
16 See Jon M. Van Dyke and Seokwoo Lee, "The Maritime Boundaries of North Korea in the Yellow Sea" (forthcoming publication).
17 Republic of Korea Ministry of National Defense, The Republic of Korea Position Regarding the NLL, August 2002: "North Korea had observed the NLL for a couple of decades until it challenged the line in the wake of a series of clashes in the West Sea (or Yellow Sea) in 1973." Suk Kyoon Kim, "Understanding Maritime Disputes in Northeast Asia: Issues and Nature," *International Journal of Marine & Coastal Law* (23), 2008, p. 220.
18 This principle is stated explicitly in Article 7(6) of the United Nations Convention on the Law of the Sea, 10 December 1982, UN Doc. A/CONF.62/122, reprinted in 21 I.L.M.

1261 (1982), which says that no state can use a system of straight baselines "in such a manner as to cut off the territorial sea of another state from the high seas or an EEZ."

19 Islands can generate maritime zones (Article 121 of the Law of the Sea Convention, ibid), but they do not generate full zones when they are opposite or adjacent to continental land areas or substantially larger islands. This conclusion has been reached consistently by the International Court of Justice and arbitral tribunals, e.g., North Sea Continental Shelf Case (*Fed. Rep. of Germany* v. *Denmark & Netherlands*), 1969 I.C.J. 3, para. 101(d); Arbitration Between the United Kingdom of Great Britain and Northern Ireland and the French Republic on the Delimitation of the Continental Shelf (1977–78), 18 I.L.M. 397 (1979); Case Concerning the Continental Shelf (*Tunisia* v. *Libya*), 1982 I.C.J. 18; Continental Shelf (*Libya* v. *Malta*), 1985 I.C.J. 13; Case Concerning Delimitation of the Maritime Boundary in Gulf of Maine Area (*US* v. *Canada*), 1984 I.C.J. 246; Delimitation of the Maritime Boundary Between Guinea and Guinea-Bissau, 25 I.L.M. 252 (1986); Case Concerning Delimitation of the Maritime Delimitation in the Area Between Greenland and Jan Mayen (*Denmark* v. *Norway*), 1993 I.C.J. 38; Delimitation of the Maritime Area Between Canada and France (St. Pierre and Miquelon), 31 I.L.M. 1149 (1992); the Eritrea–Yemen Arbitration, www.pca-cpa.org (1998–1999); Qatar-Bahrain Maritime Delimitation and Territorial Questions, 2001 I.C.J. 40; Maritime Delimitation in the Black Sea (*Romania* v. *Ukraine*), ICJ, 3 Feb. 2009.

20 Sang-Hun Choe, "North Korea Threatens to Fire into Disputed Waters," *New York Times*, 22 December 2009, www.nytimes.com/2009/12/22/world/asia/22korea.html.

21 Suk Kyoon Kim, "Korean Peninsula Maritime Issues," pp. 171–173.

22 The Joint Civilian–Military Investigation Group, "Investigation Result on the Sinking of ROKS 'Cheonan,'" *globalsecurity.org*, 20 May 2010, www.globalsecurity.org/military/library/report/2010/100520_jcmig-roks-cheonan/100520_jcmig-roks-cheonan.pdf.

23 Ji-Hyun Kim, "Seoul awaits U.N. decision after summit", *The Korea Herald*, 29 June 2010, p. 2.

24 "North Korean Artillery Hits South Korean Island", *BBC News*, 23 November 2010, www.bbc.co.uk/news/world-asia-pacific-11818005.

25 See Jon M. Van Dyke & Seokwoo Lee, "Maritime Delimitation Between China and South Korea in the Yellow Sea" (forthcoming publication).

26 See e.g., Ji Guoxing, Maritime Jurisdiction in the Three China Seas: Options for Equitable Settlement, Institute on Global Conflict and Cooperation (Working Paper) (1995), p. 4, http://igcc.ucsd.edu/pdf/policypapers/pp.19.pdf and www.ciaonet.org/wps/guj01/.

27 United Nations Convention on the Law of the Sea, see note 18, Art. 76(1).

28 The baseline claims are discussed in Jon M. Van Dyke and Seokwoo Lee, "The Straight Baseline Claims of the Three Coastal Countries Bordering the Yellow Sea" (publication forthcoming).

29 Ji Guoxing, see note 26, p. 4; Douglas M. Johnston and Mark J. Valencia, *Pacific Ocean Boundary Problems – Status and Solutions* (1991), pp. 115–117 (describing the hydrocarbon situation as it was then understood); Mark J. Valencia, "International Conference on the Yellow Sea", *East–West Environment and Policy Institute Occasional Paper No. 3*, 1987.

30 Ji Guoxing, "Sino-Japanese Jurisdictional Delimitation in East China Sea: Approaches to Dispute Settlement", in Seoung-Yong Hong and Jon M. Van Dyke (eds), *Maritime Boundary Disputes, Settlement Processes, and the Law of the Sea* (Leiden: Koninklijke Brill NV, 2009), pp. 77–105.

31 See e.g., Michael J. Seth, *A Concise History of Korea: From the Neolithic Period Through the Nineteenth Century* (Lanham, MD: Rowman & Littlefield Publishers, Inc., 2006); Bruce Cummings, *Korea's Place in the Sun:* A *Modern History* (New York: W.W. Norton, 1997).

32 Choon-Ho Park, "Sea Bed Boundaries in the Yellow Sea", www.wilsoncenter.org/topics/docs/Choon-Ho_Park_2_.pdf, p. 2; Choung Il Chee, *Korea and International Law* (1993), p. 14, stating, "Use of the median line solution by the ROK in the Yellow Sea and part of the East China Sea is entirely in line with the customary rule of international law."
33 Mark J. Valencia, "East China Sea Dispute: Context, Claims, Issues, and Possible Solutions", *Asian Perspective* (31), 2007, p. 144.
34 Choon-Ho Park, "Oil Under Troubled Waters: The Northeast Asia Sea Bed Controversy", *Harvard International Law Journal*, 14, 1973, p. 226; Ji Guoxing, see note 26, p. 12. Vietnam and China reached agreement on the maritime delimitation in the Gulf of Tonkin in 2004. See Nguyen Hong Thao, "Maritime Delimitation and Fishery Cooperation in the Tonkin Gulf", *Ocean Development & International Law*, 36, 2005, pp. 25–44.
35 Seokwoo Lee and Jon M. Van Dyke, "The 1951 San Francisco Peace Treaty and Its Relevance to the Sovereignty of Dokdo", *Chinese Journal of International Law*, 9, 2010, pp. 741–762.
36 Republic of Korea Ministry of Maritime Affairs and Fisheries, "Beautiful Island, Dokdo" (2000).
37 Ibid, p. 10.
38 J.R.V. Prescott, "Maritime Jurisdiction in East Asian Seas", *East–West Environment and Policy Institute Occasional Paper No. 4*, 1987, p. 48.
39 See Jon M. Van Dyke, "Legal Issues Related to Sovereignty Over Dokdo and Its Maritime Boundary", *Ocean Development & International Law* (38), 2007, pp. 157–224.

Part IV

Maritime challenges and priorities for the rest of the Indo-Pacific

14 America's maritime challenges and priorities

The Asian dimension

*James Kraska**

Introduction—America's strategic approach to sea power

The goal of contemporary American sea power is to protect the global maritime system more so than the US homeland proper. Whether this approach is wise and visionary or foolish and illusory, it now colors US maritime strategy as much as it shapes American national defense policy. Compared with any other nation, the United States inures disproportionate benefits, as well as absorbing disproportionate costs, in pursuit of this grandiose goal. The US Sea Services—the Coast Guard, Marine Corps and the Navy—work in tandem to maintain America's leadership role in global maritime security. These forces are combined with a network of friends, allies and partner nations that bring naval and joint forces to the table—with the goal of strengthening the cause of liberal internationalism with both military forces and political authority. These friends and allies, however, also sometimes dilute systemic stability in Asia through "free riding" or an overreliance on American power to keep the peace. Some partner states also attempt to steer Washington toward courses of action that strengthen their hand in local, internecine political disputes and fairly inconsequential bilateral squabbles with neighboring states. Involvement in trying to mediate local quarrels between friendly states drains US attention from shoring up systemic security, as well as earning enmity from both antagonists. The American approach attempts to navigate these challenges, mostly through a strategy that co-opts friends and allies into a Global Maritime Partnership. The idea of a global maritime partnership is the foundation of the principle strategy document of the US Sea Services, "The Cooperative Strategy for 21st Century Seapower," released in 2007.

The contemporary maritime security environment tests the famous exclamation of the late Chairman Mao Zedong that, "Political power comes out of the barrel of a gun." At sea, this power comes out of the capabilities of the naval fleet—sea power. Sea power is a cornerstone of globalization in a way that land power and air power are not, for the simple reason that globalization is made possible only through usage of the sea.[1] More than 90 percent of world trade travels by sea, the world's greatest highways. The world's oceans are interconnected, forming one vast world ocean that links the continents.

Sea power includes the underwater, surface and aerospace and cyberspace capabilities of the navy, the integrated air-ground combat and logistics elements of the Marine Corps and the littoral civil and law enforcement capabilities of the Coast Guard. The maritime force resident in these three armed forces has both a speed and weight advantage over any other national instruments of force—land forces are limited to movement by roads through contiguous territory; aircraft, while more mobile than ships, have precious little payload and sustainability and are subject to the political vagaries of forward bases and overflight rights to sustain an effective operational tempo. Persistence and sustainability—what the Coast Guard calls "endurance," is the crowning capability of the sea services. If there is an aircraft overhead, it won't be there for long. The farther an airplane travels from its shore-based airfield, the less time it has on station. It is exceedingly difficult to maintain constant overhead coverage of an area from very long distances, and the capabilities of aircraft are severely limited to gathering intelligence or dropping bombs. Ships, however, can loiter offshore essentially indefinitely, and become seamlessly linked to the land through amphibious and expeditionary air and land capabilities. During the Vietnam War, for example, the United States maintained a continuous aircraft carrier presence in the Gulf of Tonkin for years. Capable of executing the entire spectrum of missions, from humanitarian assistance and disaster relief to major combat operations, today's US fleet is the most versatile element of national military power.

After World War II, Sir Winston S. Churchill expressed the commonly held belief that in the future mastery of the air would be the supreme expression of military power, and that fleets and armies would be subordinate.[2] This bold statement, made at the formation of the nuclear age, seemed immutable, but we now know that aircraft dominate the one dimension—airspace—that has no population or resources, and therefore is mostly devoid of politics. Aircraft cannot take and hold territory, help to establish and build government and civil society, maintain the peace or keep order. Thus, even when it comes to projecting power ashore, sea power is the most useful device in the toolkit. In an increasingly interconnected and transcontinental world, naval forces constitute the preeminent currency of contemporary military power.

The American maritime experience

Since its independence in the late eighteenth century, the United States has been a maritime nation, with one eye on the frontier and the other gazing seaward. Blessed with good governance and the resources of a virgin continent, the original 13 colonies prospered under the omnipresent protection of the Royal Navy. The country was reliant on the Atlantic Ocean for trade with Europe. As an independent nation, the young republic championed freedom of the seas to ensure economic prosperity and continental security. To underscore the importance of freedom of navigation in the American psyche, it is instructive to recall that the United States fought its first, second, third and fourth wars as an independent country in large part over the issue of freedom of the seas. The first war, the Quasi-War of 1798–1800, was fought with France over the issue of free transit of US vessels, which were regarded by Paris as supporting the British war effort against France. Likewise, the Barbary Wars—the first in 1801–1805 and the second in 1815–1816—were fought against the Ottoman principalities of North Africa over the issue of maritime piracy attacks against US commerce. Finally, the war of 1812 against the British Empire was fought largely over the issue of impressment of American seafarers into the Royal Navy.

During much of the nineteenth century, the concepts of the Monroe Doctrine and hemispheric defense dominated the American strategic thinking, even as transatlantic trade ballooned. However, the rise of the US Navy in the late-nineteenth century was dramatic. In 1883, the US Navy ranked twelfth among the world's fleets; by 1906, it was second in size only to the British Royal Navy.[3] The United States entered into naval preeminence with the circumnavigation of the planet by the Great White Fleet under President Theodore Roosevelt between 1907 and 1909. The force consisted of four squadrons of four battleships, plus escort and support vessels. The Great White Fleet was a precursor to innumerable forward presence naval missions, demonstrating the ability of the nation to project ready combat power throughout the globe.

For the past one hundred years, the US command of the oceans commons has meant that the nation has the capability to quickly bring forces to bear at virtually any point on the planet (see Figure 14.1).[4] Maritime mobility on the surface of the ocean, in the air and under the water remains the cornerstone of American military power.[5] By 1950, the nation was unique in this regard, and assuring access to the oceans and preserving the freedom to conduct naval operations remained a key tenet of America's deterrent strategy.[6]

The oceans are the world's largest maneuver space, and in recent decades the United States exercised maritime mobility to outflank its enemies at Inchon in Korea, topple a rogue regime in Grenada and sustain huge ground armies indefinitely in Vietnam and twice in Iraq. The unique capability to rapidly project decisive power to any corner of the world produced a distinctively American form of conventional and nuclear power.[7]

Although by the late 1970s, freedom of navigation was engraved in the draft negotiating text at the Third United Nations Conference on the Law of the Sea, numerous coastal states continued to assert excessive maritime claims. The United States maintained economic and military dependence on global access to the world's oceans, and joined with the Union of Soviet Socialist Republics and other maritime powers in ensuring that the 1982 UN Convention on the Law of the Sea (UNCLOS) would reflect a liberal oceans order that protected freedom of navigation. In the face of expanding illegal coastal state maritime claims, however, in 1979 President Jimmy Carter launched the Freedom of Navigation (FON) program. The FON program coordinated naval air and surface operations with US diplomacy to tangibly demonstrate US non-acceptance of excessive coastal state maritime claims.

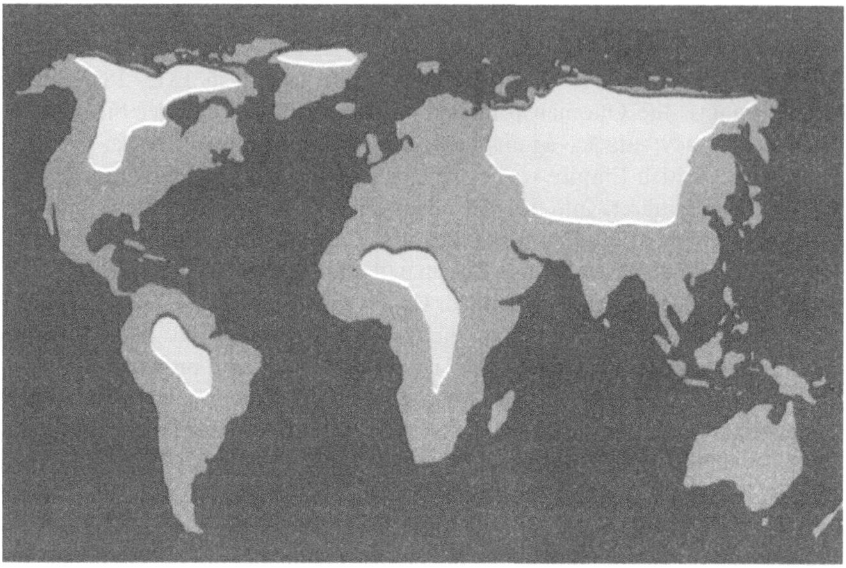

= Within 650 nautical miles of coastal region, the striking range of US Naval Forces

Figure 14.1 Terrestrial regions within the striking range of US Naval Forces.

Contemporary policies and priorities

During the 1980s, the United States pursued a high seas "maritime strategy," in which aircraft carriers and nuclear-powered submarines plied the oceans preparing for blue-water pitched battles against the Soviet Navy. No sooner was the Berlin Wall torn down than the United States and other countries became engulfed in peacekeeping, then peace enforcement, first in Somalia and then elsewhere. The experience in Somalia in the early 1990s made American strategists realize that the littoral regions were the new fulcrum for geopolitics. Throughout the world, most of the population, and political and economic centers of power, were situated along the shore and coastal zones. Similarly, coastal waters contained the world's richest fisheries, as well as the greatest density of vessel traffic. The first post-Cold War national security document to recognize these changes was *From the Sea*, the Department of the Navy white paper released in September 1992.[8] The focus of *From the Sea* was on joint, expeditionary forces operating forward from the sea and projecting power through the coastal zone and onto the shore.

After the attacks of 9/11, the United States spent half a decade rethinking maritime strategy, and the result was a greater focus on maritime homeland security in the domestic setting, and a refocus on multilateral cooperation in the international setting. The attacks on the Twin Towers and the Pentagon raised the specter that the oceans would be used by al-Qaeda or other extremists to stage a spectacular and catastrophic attack on the United States. Potential scenarios included exploding a liquefied natural gas (LNG) tanker in a congested, urban harbor, such as Boston, or ramming and toppling a landmark bridge, such as the Golden Gate Bridge, with an explosive-laden vessel. Al-Qaeda has already demonstrated a capacity to inflict devastating attack in the maritime domain, having successfully attacked the USS *Cole* in the port of Aden, Yemen in 2000, almost sinking the massive warship. The organization struck again in 2003, damaging the French-flagged crude carrier M/V *Limburg*, which was carrying 400,000 barrels of oil in the Gulf of Aden off the coast of Yemen. Similarly, on 28 July 2010, the Japanese oil supertanker *M. Star* was attacked while transiting the Strait of Hormuz off the coast of Oman and the United Arab Emirates by the Abdullah Azzam Brigades, an al-Qaeda-linked group based in Lebanon.

In order to forestall such attacks, the United States launched a renaissance in multilateral diplomacy to expand global maritime security, principally working through the International Maritime Organization (IMO) in London. This legalistic approach is a natural recourse for the United States, which was founded on the precept that the country was, "a nation of laws, not men." The United States was the leader in developing the post-World War II international legal order, and is comfortable dissecting, capturing and converting political conflicts into legal issues that can be negotiated and resolved. The multilateral approach produced a long line of treaties, agreements and partnerships to enhance maritime security—an effort to protect the global maritime system, rather than simply guarding the maritime approaches to the United States. These efforts have included extensive revisions to the 1974 Safety of Life at Sea Convention (SOLAS), focusing on universal maritime security standards in the International Ship and Port Facility Security (ISPS) Code and global maritime domain awareness (MDA) initiatives, such as the ubiquitous Automatic Identification System (AIS) and the nascent Long-Range Identification and Tracking (LRIT) system.

First, the United States and other nations proposed updating the 1974 SOLAS with the comprehensive ISPS Code, which was adopted at the IMO in order to develop a worldwide public–private partnership for maritime security. The ISPS Code was designed to enable national governments to maintain better oversight of their commercial shipping and port facility industries. As a work in progress, the ISPS Code already applies to 158 states, accounting for over 99 percent of the world's merchant fleet gross tonnage. Many of these nations are still implementing the new security measures, however. By promulgating a framework for standardizing and evaluating maritime risk, the ISPS Code is helping governments and industry to synchronize security within nations and across continents.

Another set of SOLAS amendments has also enhanced the security of the global cargo chain by bringing greater transparency to the maritime domain. The United States generally supports MDA, VHF and satellite communications technologies and information sharing that helps to provide maritime situational awareness to governments, naval forces and law enforcement. By better understanding where legitimate shipping is located, states can focus scarce resources on anomalous contacts and sort civil commerce from suspicious activity. Two systems for collecting and sharing information are attached to the SOLAS Convention—AIS and the emerging, satellite-based LRIT system. The systems are complementary, but with AIS developed from open-architecture VHF-band communications, it has substantial limitations. By way of developing a next-generation approach to maritime situational awareness, the US led the adoption of LRIT at the IMO in May 2006. LRIT is an additional amendment to SOLAS Chapter V. More secure than AIS and favored by the US Coast Guard, LRIT is a global, satellite-based vessel identification system. When fully operational, the system will make information on vessel location and identity available worldwide. Although MDA systems can promote maritime security, the systems can also be misused, by either states or non-state actors.[9] Consequently, MDA is not an unmitigated international public good and its application must be carefully calibrated with friends, allies and partner nations. Furthermore, AIS and LRIT only apply to larger vessels with a displacement of 300 tons or more and on international voyages, while ignoring the greatest threat to ships from terrorism—the enormous number of small boats throughout the world.

Concurrently, the United States worked with a small core of partner nations to participate in the Proliferation Security Initiative (PSI). Speaking in Kraków, Poland, in May 2003, President George W. Bush unveiled the PSI as a partnership activity to counter proliferation and trafficking of weapons of mass destruction (WMD) in accordance with international law and under the guidance of a set of interdiction principles. Originally, 11 core members launched the initiative. Now more than one hundred states have joined the informal network to work together in a more coordinated and effective manner, and the PSI was endorsed by the former UN Secretary-General.[10] Participants in the PSI include some of the nations with the largest shipping registries in the world, such as Panama, Liberia and Malta. Nine states have signed PSI ship-boarding agreements with the United States.[11] The agreements do not constitute blanket authority by one state to board the vessel of the other, but they offer a mechanism for expedited review by the flag state of requests to board, and some of the agreements provide for presumed consent if a request is not denied by the flag state or registry is not confirmed within a few hours.

Only months after PSI began, British and American intelligence services discovered that the German-registered vessel BBC *China* was transporting uranium-enrichment equipment from Malaysia to Libya, via Dubai. With the consent of the German government, the vessel was diverted to the Italian port of Taranto, where Italian authorities searched the ship and seized centrifuge materials, which were not listed on the cargo manifest. Two months later, Libya announced that it was abandoning its ambition to develop a uranium-enrichment capability.[12] The BBC *China* interdiction has been followed by additional PSI successes, conducted quietly to avoid attention.[13] Efforts by Iran to procure goods for its nuclear program have been disrupted, and an undisclosed country in another region of the world has been prevented from receiving equipment for a ballistic missile program.[14]

Seven months after the introduction of the PSI, the UN Security Council adopted a historic resolution under Chapter VII of the UN Charter to address terrorism and the maritime transport of WMD. Unanimously adopted in April 2004, Resolution 1540 is binding on all nations under Article 49 of the UN Charter. The resolution asserts that proliferation of WMD to non-state actors constitutes a threat to international peace and security within the meaning of Article 39 of the UN Charter and promulgates new rules to address that threat.[15] The resolution calls on all states to take cooperative action to prevent trafficking in WMD and offers a new foundation for counter-proliferation in international law.

As a complement to Resolution 1540 and reflecting the philosophy of the PSI, in 2005 the US and other countries working at the IMO successfully adopted two major protocols to the 1988 *Achille Lauro* convention. The amendments represent a breakthrough in maritime security cooperation, updating the 1988 Convention on the Suppression of Unlawful Acts against the Safety of Maritime Navigation (SUA) for the post-9/11 era.[16] The original SUA treaty was crafted as a response to the hijacking of the cruise ship *Achille Lauro* in 1985. Following the attack on the Italian-flagged vessel by Palestinian terrorists and the subsequent brutal murder of a disabled American passenger, Leon Klinghoffer, Austria, Egypt and Italy proposed that the IMO prepare a convention on crimes against the safety of maritime navigation. The goal was to create a comprehensive new set of rules to ensure cooperation among states for the suppression of unlawful acts at sea. The IMO promptly drafted a treaty, and in 1988 a conference in Rome adopted the SUA Convention. The SUA Convention provides a framework for states to cooperate in cases in which armed groups seize "control over a ship by force or threat thereof or any other form of intimidation" (Article 3), or commit acts of violence against persons on board ships and participate in the "placing of devices on board a ship that are likely to destroy or damage it." The treaty obligates contracting governments either to extradite or prosecute offenders.

On 8 November 2005, the IMO reported in SUA.1/Circular 79 that there were 156 states are party to the SUA Convention, and these states represented 94.62 percent of the world's merchant shipping tonnage. Building on the momentum of the PSI, the United States proposed a package of counter-terrorism provisions for the 1988 SUA Convention. In 2005, a diplomatic conference at the IMO adopted two protocols to the SUA Convention, one on strengthening the rules for the safety of vessels and the other on enhancing efforts to ensure the safety of fixed platforms on the continental shelf. Article 3*bis* of the 2005 protocols added several new offenses, including attempts to intimidate a population or compel a government or an international organization to "do or abstain from any act." Specifically, the 2005 protocols criminalize such perilous activities as using any explosive, radioactive material or a biological, chemical, or nuclear weapon on or against a ship; knowingly transporting such material on a ship; or operating a ship in a manner that causes death or serious injury or damage. The protocols also prohibit the transport of "dual use" or source materials that might find their way into chemical, biological or nuclear weapons.

After Pyongyang's nuclear test of 14 October 2006, the UN Security Council adopted Resolution 1718.[17] Security Council Resolution 1718 reiterates that WMD proliferation poses a threat to international peace and security, and it calls upon all states to prevent North Korea from obtaining material that would support its nuclear, WMD or missile programs, or even replenish the country's stock of conventional weaponry. Similarly, Resolution 1874 of 12 June 2009 was also adopted under Chapter VII of the UN Charter and imposed a total embargo on arms exports from North Korea and significantly expanded the ban on arms imports by creating a new framework of inspections. Similarly, there are five UN Security Council resolutions addressing Iran's effort to develop nuclear weapons and missile delivery technology. Resolution 1803 of 3 March 2008 calls for cargo inspections of aircraft and vessels traveling to and from Iran, owned by Iran Air Cargo and the Islamic Republic of Iran Shipping Line, provided there are reasonable grounds to believe the ships or aircraft are carrying technology related to the development of nuclear weapons. Follow-on resolutions include Resolution 1887 of 24 September 2009 and Resolution 1929 of 9 June 2010.

With multilateral efforts such as the PSI, resolutions 1540, 1718, 1803, 1874 and the amended SUA Convention, US policy is to broaden and develop the global legal and policy framework against proliferation of WMD and terrorism. The SUA protocols, which are binding treaty obligations, may end up eclipsing the informal PSI, notwithstanding the value of an interlocking network of formal and informal arrangements. First, the era of "coalitions of the willing" may be coming to a close, the concept having been badly bruised by the coalition experience in Iraq. For all the groundbreaking (and frankly astonishing) successes of the PSI, some countries are wary of its informal nature and process. Second, shipping commerce is a global industry, one that relies on a common framework of international conventions and treaties; the industry can operate efficiently only when regulations applicable to a particular ship are identical at the port of departure, on the high seas and at the port of arrival. Since the PSI focuses on enlarging national authorities rather than global rules, it is more likely to inadvertently create a web of national laws that may be inconsistent with one another. A standardized international legal regime, such as the framework in SUA, ultimately may prove more attractive. The shipping industry, in particular, is hopeful that the standardized rules contained in the amended SUA 2005 will attract widespread support and enter into force quickly.

At home, the United States also set about developing updated maritime security policy guidance that would focus the nation toward defeating irregular threats from the sea. The 2005 *National Strategy for Maritime Security* (NSMS) sets forth a symbiotic relationship between maintaining maritime security and coastal state jurisdictional prerogatives offshore, suggesting that both maritime security and freedom of the seas are dependent on one another: "Maritime security is required to ensure freedom of the seas; facilitate freedom of navigation and commerce; advance prosperity and freedom; and protect the resources of the ocean."[18] In the strongest representation of any contemporary national-level document in the United States or overseas on the issue of freedom of the seas, the NSMS states that

> [t]hree broad principles provide overarching guidance to this *Strategy*. First, *preserving the freedom of the seas is a top national priority*.[19] The free, continuing, unthreatened intercourse of nations is an essential global freedom and helps ensure the smooth operation of the world's economy.[20]

Maintaining a stable regime that ensures global maritime maneuverability and mobility also is a cornerstone of the nation's global security posture. The 2008 Department of Defense *Capstone Concept for Joint Operations* describes the new ocean operating environment:

> Foreign sensitivities to U.S. military presence have steadily been increasing.... Diminished access will complicate the maintenance of forward presence, a critical aspect of past and current U.S. military strategy, necessitating new approaches to responding quickly to developments around the world as well as more robust exploitation of existing U.S. advantages to operate at sea and in the air, space and cyberspace. Assuring access to ports, airfields, foreign airspace, coastal waters and host-nation support in potential commitment areas will be a challenge and will require active peacetime engagement with states in volatile areas. In War, this challenge may require forcible-entry capabilities designed to seize and maintain lodgments in the face of armed resistance.

The cooperative strategy

The armed forces provide further fidelity to the nation's cooperative and collaborative approach to maritime security. "The old Maritime Strategy focused on sea control," Chairman of the Joint Chiefs of Staff Admiral Michael G. Mullen explained, while the new one must recognize that the "economic tide of all nations rises—not when the seas are controlled by one—but rather when they are made safe and free for all." The 2008 *National Defense Strategy*, however, stated: "For more than sixty years, the United States has secured the global commons for the benefit of all," and the challenge is to reconcile American sea power to a cooperative paradigm.[21]

At the 2005 International Sea Power Symposium, then Chief of Naval Operations Admiral Mullen observed that all of the world's regions shared a common set of challenges—maritime piracy, trafficking and terrorism. The world is not simply a collection of regions or an assortment of theaters of operations. The world's oceans interconnect the globe. The idea that the United States is best served by a maritime strategy that encompasses the globe culminated in release of the *Cooperative Strategy for Maritime Security for the 21st Century* (CS 21) in 2007. The cornerstone of the new strategy is deepening cooperation and coordination at sea:

> Sea power in this century cannot be harnessed by a single nation acting alone. If we are to build a fleet for the future capable of keeping pace with globalization, we must leverage the capacity of our partners with common interests. The positive potential of sea power and freedom of the seas can only be achieved through a collective and cooperative approach focused on international rule of law and freedom of the maritime commons.[22]

Implementation of the CS 21 reflects a shift in theoretical approach to sea power in the United States away from the concept of command of the sea, the linchpin of geostrategist Alfred Thayer Mahan, and toward the notion of control of the sea, a concept much more related to constabulary maintenance of the oceans, and which was promoted by British historian Sir Julian S. Corbett. Faced with fiscal realities and a declining force structure, as well as the goal of shoring up the international system and spreading the burden of maintaining order, CS 21 seeks to leverage the power of other nations in the fight to maintain a stable global maritime system. The strategy, which was signed by the Commandant of the US Marine Corps, the Commandant of the US Coast Guard and the Chief of Naval Operations, co-opts and leverages the supportive work of America's friends, allies and partners throughout the world. Embodying the notion that no nation can do it alone, CS 21 calls for even greater collaboration at sea in the years ahead.

The spectrum of naval operations

Below the national and cabinet department-level strategy documents, the US Navy and Marine Corps have developed service-specific strategies. The *Naval Operation Concept* (*NOC*) serves as the "commander's intent" of the Chief of Naval Operations and the Commandant of the Marine Corps to provide essential principles for missions at sea. The NOC sets forth the goal for the Department of the Navy to "secure strategic access," in order to "retain global freedom of action" by ensuring that "key regions, lines of communication and the global commons remain accessible to all."[23] One of the newest naval missions, for example, is the operation of Aegis destroyers that have ballistic missile defense (BMD) capability, assigned to loitering stations off the coasts of North Korea, and Iran. These warships require the exercise of the right of freedom of navigation in order to maintain the flexibility to modify location at will.

Naval forces depend upon global strategic mobility and tactical maneuverability to conduct the spectrum of sea–air–land operations in pursuit of the national interest. Missions include operating the most survivable components of nuclear deterrence, which are ballistic missile submarines (SSBNs). Global mobility is essential for conventional global strike, anti-air warfare, air defense, information operations, direct attack with missiles, naval gunfire, humanitarian assistance and disaster relief,[24] homeland security,[25] amphibious and expeditionary operations in littoral areas,[26] insertion of special operations forces (SOF) for missions such as counterinsurgency and counter-terrorism,[27] constabulary functions and maritime security operations such as counterdrug operations[28] and piracy suppression, counter-proliferation operations such as the PSI, the exercise of the right of approach, maritime interception operations (MIO) and visit, board, search and seizure (VBSS), naval control and protection of shipping (NCAPS) and the protection of sea lines of communication (SLOC), sea control, anti-access and area-denial strategies such as marine mines, civil-military affairs, security cooperation and capacity-building, peacekeeping and peace enforcement, and forward presence.[29]

Does the nation have a sufficiently large force structure to accomplish this extensive mission set? Composed of surface warships, submarines, aircraft and outer space and cyberspace assets, the US Navy operates the largest fleet in the world. Uniquely capable, the US Navy has decades of experience in projecting and sustaining expeditionary power to virtually any point on the globe. Furthermore, the US Naval Force is supported and complemented by joint and interagency forces—and increasingly—combined forces from partner nations.

However, the commitment of the United States to maintain its position of naval superiority is now in doubt, with particular implications for Asia. The ephemeral 313-ship force structure is unlikely to be achieved, and even that is one-third too small. The goal is to grow the fleet to a size that includes 11 aircraft carriers, 88 cruisers and destroyers, 48 submarines, 55 littoral combat ships and 31 amphibious warfare ships. But even if this is achieved, these forces will be spread thinly throughout the world. The ships already juggle a bewildering, multi-tasked schedule in every theater.

At the same time, the threats in the maritime domain include conventional naval forces and the prospect of major combat operations, as well as irregular threats from pirates, terrorists and smugglers. New threats call for new strategies. The cornerstone of the new strategy is that the oceans are secure—and nations are safer and more prosperous—not when the seas are controlled by one nation, but rather when they are made safe and free for all.[30] The common interests and the capabilities of partner nations are leveraged in an effort to promote the interests of the international community, achieving a collective and cooperative approach focused on the rule of law, security and freedom of the maritime commons.[31] CS 21 hopes to alleviate some of the stress on the US fleet by incorporating foreign naval capabilities into a common project to protect a world order of the oceans. To some extent, these efforts have paid off, particularly on the lower-end of mission sets, such as counter-piracy. But few nations can add substantial, ready combat power at the higher end of the conflict spectrum—and those with the fleets most capable, such as Japan, France and the United Kingdom—face considerable legal and political obstacles to employing their forces on behalf of American interests.

The Asian-Pacific challenge

The Pacific Ocean is the world's largest: its 169 million square kilometers cover 46 percent of the world's oceans and 30 percent of the surface of the globe. The

Indian Ocean, the third largest in the world, covers 73 million square miles, or about 20 percent of the world's oceans. Together, these two vast bodies of water account for two-thirds of the seas on the planet, underscoring the geostrategic tyranny of time, distance and space that makes the Asia-Pacific principally a maritime theater. The Strait of Malacca is the most important strategic strait in the world.

The Asia-Pacific is perhaps the most dynamic and culturally diverse region in the world, containing more than 50 percent of the world's population and three thousand different languages. India is the world's largest democracy and Indonesia is the largest Muslim-majority nation. The region is home to all of the world's largest militaries, which include the United States, China, Russia, India, South Korea and North Korea. The United States has formal security treaties with five allied nations in Asia, including Japan, Korea and Australia. Ten of the 14 smallest economies in the world are in the region, situated near China and Japan, which have the second and third largest economies on Earth. One-third of US two-way trade in goods is with nations in the region—valued at US$1 trillion annually, and almost all of it is transported by sea. Until 1985, the port of New York and New Jersey was the largest container shipping port in the world. Today, of the top ten largest ports in the world, seven are in Asia.[32] More remarkable, however, is that six of the top 12 largest ports in the world are in China (including Hong Kong)—seven, if you count Taiwan. Los Angeles—the largest port not only in North America, but in the Western Hemisphere, is only 13th on the list of the world's largest ports.

The United States is a Pacific nation, sharing the destiny of the region with the nations of Asia, Australia and the subcontinent. With territories stretching from Guam to the Hawaiian Islands to Alaska and the West Coast of the United States, the security of the nation is intertwined with the stability of the region. American naval interests in the Asia-Pacific are oriented toward the maintenance of a secure, peaceful and prosperous regional state system. In order to help maintain order in Asia, the US joint force is led by the US Seventh Fleet. Embarked on board USS *Blue Ridge* (LCC 19), forward deployed to Yokosuka, Japan, the US Seventh Fleet is America's largest numbered fleet and primary sea power presence in the Western Pacific. Comprised of 40,000 sailors and Marines, 60–70 ships and 200–300 aircraft, Seventh Fleet is organized around the USS *George Washington* (CVN 73) aircraft carrier strike group in Yokosuka, an expeditionary strike group headquartered in Okinawa, which includes the USS *Essex* (LHD 2) amphibious assault ship, forward deployed to Sasebo, Japan, coupled with the Third Marine Expeditionary Brigade, when acting as Landing Force, Seventh Fleet. This is a "ready power for peace." While the force is impressive in its combat power and deterrent capability, it has experienced a relative decline over the past 20 years in its ability to maintain a decisive presence in the region. With the rapid expansion and modernization of regional naval powers, particularly China, the US Seventh Fleet is stretched thin.

In the maritime Asia-Pacific, the declining US force structure has particular resonance. Unlike Europe, which has come together in economic and political integration, the Asia-Pacific region is fraught with old animosities and new instabilities. Regional threats include a divided Korean peninsula in Northeast Asia, a nuclear rivalry between India and Pakistan on the South Asian subcontinent and potential instability in Indonesia in Southeast Asia. The rise of Chinese economic and military power, the proliferation of high-technology conventional weapons and nuclear weapons and flourishing international criminal enterprises threaten the stability and prosperity of the region.

The requirement to ensure access to the sea-lanes in the Pacific and Indian Oceans is particularly acute. The imperative for preserving the right of the international community to enjoy the internationally lawful uses of the sea is pushing up against a concerted effort on the part of some Asian coastal states to appropriate ocean areas and airspace into national waters. China is most aggressively pursuing this strategy as part of a campaign of regional intimidation and domination. The US Pacific Command strategy, for example, states, "Freedom of movement in and secure access to all domains for all nations is quintessential to a healthy and prosperous region."[33] At the same time, the US Pacific Command has indicated that it "will not permit conditions which impede such movement and access; nor will we tolerate disruptions to global supply chains or threats to lines of communication and commerce."[34]

The US Navy also serves a diplomatic function, and the United States is committed to the diplomatic project, begun by President Woodrow Wilson, of peacefully promoting democracy as a bipartisan goal of US security policy in the belief that democratic nations are more peaceful, verdant and prosperous. This belief flows from the Western intellectual tradition that mankind is endowed by Nature and his Creator with certain inalienable rights, and that those rights are most effectively enforced in the form of civil liberties and civil rights enforceable against the state. Consequently, the greatest non-state threats to American interests in the Asia-Pacific are corruption, organized crime and violent Islamist extremism that promotes disorder, disrupts stability, and opposes freedom. The immense expanse of sea and complex littoral marine environment makes Asia ripe for exploitation by subnational groups that erode the rule of law and undermine democracy.

In terms of human life, the most costly event in memory was the devastating 9-magnitude Sumatra tsunami that struck the Indian Ocean on 26 December 2004. An estimated 230,000 people were killed, 168,000 in Indonesia alone. Other environmental risks to the region include pandemic, famine and drought, earthquakes, volcanoes, typhoons and cyclones. The amphibious-expeditionary navy is the quickest and most capable first responder to such events. Operation *Unified Assistance* involved 20 US naval vessels to deliver supplies to the survivors of the 2004 tsunami. Poor environmental stewardship and marine resource mismanagement, illegal, unreported and unregulated (IUU) poaching of fisheries in archipelagic waters and the exclusive economic zone (EEZ) of coastal nations deprives economies of wealth and governments of tax revenue. An effective response to natural disasters and humanitarian crises is an essential component in stability operations and the promotion of democracy.

The United States also seeks to dissuade potentially hostile powers, deter war and preserve the peace in Asia. In particular, the state sponsorship of terrorism and the proliferation of nuclear, chemical and biological WMD is destabilizing to the region. Finally, conventional or traditional threats include large and disproportionate investments in advanced weapons and rapid military expansion and the pursuit of sensitive and asymmetric weapons, such as cyber-warfare capabilities, anti-ship cruise missiles, ballistic missiles and space weapons.

Faced with this dark menu of conventional and irregular threats, it is clear that the tasks ahead are too great for any single nation. The United States has set forth large, even magnanimous goals for maritime security and stability in the Asia-Pacific—goals that are far in excess of the nation's capabilities. In an effort to energize others to share the burden, US naval forces seek to work with and complement the capabilities of an influential group of friends, allies and partner nations—an extended network of regional states with varying levels of military and political commitment and a union of interests to keep the peace. Foremost among these front line states are the countries with which the United States has a formal security alliance—Japan, India, South Korea, Australia, Singapore and Thailand. In December 2010, Japan released a new defense plan to acquire five submarines, three destroyers, 12 fighter jets, ten patrol planes and 39 helicopters.[35]

The Kokoda Foundation, a think tank in Australia, released a report on 5 February 2011 that called the scale and pace of China's military expansion the "most serious challenge to Australia, the United States and their allies and friends in the Western Pacific since the Second World War." As a result, the principal author of the report, Ross Babbage, recommends the nation acquire 12 nuclear-powered submarines by 2020.[36] As it is, Australia will spend as much as US$279 billion over the next 20 years on new submarines, warships and fighter jets—the largest expansion in the nation's defenses since 1945.[37] Tiny Singapore is adding two submarines in the coming years, as is Malaysia and Indonesia.[38] South Korea and Vietnam are set to acquire six new submarines each by 2020.[39] These nations bring an array of political and military capabilities and power to the table and each represents a force for military stability in an uncertain region. Nobody wants to say that the defense build-up is aimed at containing China, but the breakneck pace of Chinese military expansion has caused concern in every nation from the Arabian Sea to the Western Pacific. China will play an increasingly influential role in Asia and in the world. It is unclear whether Beijing can manage a "peaceful rise," or will be tempted to misuse its power in a manner that ignites fear and further alienates surrounding countries. Over the past decade, China has increased defense spending by an average of 16 percent per year—and now has not only a booming economy, but the second highest defense budget in the world.[40] China can afford both guns and butter. Beijing hides the true level of its military spending, and the lack of transparency has raised concerns in the region because Beijing faces no external threats. The People's Liberation Army Navy (PLA Navy) has been a principal beneficiary of massive new spending, swallowing 30 percent of the defense budget. By 2009, the PLA Navy was building super-quiet air-independent propulsion (AIP) submarines that are reportedly stealthier than US fast-attack nuclear boats. The US Congressional Research Service predicts that in 2010 China's submarine force will be almost double the size of the US submarine force and that the entire PLA Navy will surpass the size of the US fleet by 2015.[41] China is also building a new generation of large destroyers and has embarked on an aircraft carrier program. China's development of the DF-21 anti-ship ballistic missile (ASBM) could be the most alarming development, shifting the naval balance of power in Asia in China's favor.

China's ascendency in naval power and maritime shipping means that the we are on the cusp of a mega-trend in global sea power, potentially as significant as the rotation of naval leadership from Spain to the Dutch Republic, as monumental as the rivalry between England and France, and no less a harbinger of the future than Japan's defeat of the Czar's fleet in the Tsushima Straits in 1905. Deterrence is a combination of willpower and capability, and American political resolve is prone to be inconsistent. This does not suggest a dramatic naval encounter, but rather a slow but inexorable gravitation of Asian leadership from the US anchor in the West to the Chinese anchor in the East. This mighty shift promises to upend the security architecture in Asia, compelling some nations to divide their reliance for sea-lane security—and hence their maritime loyalties—between the Seventh Fleet and the PLA Navy. While the changes are manifest in observable adjustments in naval power, the effects will arise in the political sphere. India and Japan, in particular, remain especially watchful. To the extent that China rattles its saber, Delhi and Tokyo will closely embrace the United States in a deterrent triad that encircles China. If China embarks on a course to bully the region, it will find itself checked and balanced by a stronger India–Japan–United States axis of democratic states.

Conclusion—is there really a new naval paradigm?

Will the United States and its friends and allies be able to develop and nurture a global maritime partnership that can preserve order in the Asia-Pacific? Will other nations, including Japan, India and Australia, let alone the Russian Federation and China, participate in such a project—employing their naval strength on behalf of a broadly defined and American-led enterprise to ensure security of the sea-lanes? Only time will tell, although there is some room for optimism as well as doubt. Nations have committed resources in several instances toward maintaining law and order at sea. The international community came together spontaneously to cooperate during both the aftermath of the 26 December 2004 Asian tsunami and the massive sealift of civilians and non-combatants from the "Summer War" in Lebanon in 2006. In each case, naval forces from a variety of nations came together in a maritime partnership to engage in an effective humanitarian and maritime constabulary operation.

On the diplomatic front, the efforts of the IMO are paying off, and nations have been successful in developing a mutually agreeable framework for ensuring maritime safety and security. Nowhere have these efforts been more productive than in developing an international regime to address the threat of maritime piracy off the coast of Somalia. Working in conjunction with the World Food Program (WFP), the IMO was the first UN agency to initiate a call to action against the emerging threat of maritime piracy in the Horn of Africa. In November of 2005 and 2007, the IMO Assembly adopted major resolutions on suppressing maritime piracy, which were the earliest calls for action by the UN Security Council.[42] Subsequent pleas by the secretaries-general of the IMO and the WFP for UN Security Council action have produced a bevy of five UN Security Council resolutions under Chapter VII of the UN Charter. These resolutions have authorized states to work in conjunction with governing leaders inside Somalia to conduct counter-piracy operations inside the country's territorial sea and, if necessary, on its land territory.

Two dozen countries have deployed warships to the region to fight piracy, including Singapore, South Korea, Australia, Japan, Pakistan, India, China and even Iran. Working through a loose-knit collection of task forces, the European Union, North Atlantic Treaty Organisation (NATO) and the Commander, Maritime Forces—a position held by Commander, Naval Forces, US Central Command—have coordinated this armada. The threat of maritime piracy in the Horn of Africa is the first opportunity to implement the CS 21 in actual operations. Cooperatively confronting piracy in East Africa has begun to strengthen relationships among states in the region, and between them and maritime powers and shipping nations. Still, there is some room to pause and wonder whether the success in assisting tsunami victims or fostering cooperation for counter-piracy operations can be replicated—or even sustained—when it comes to responding to an actual naval threat in the Pacific Ocean. A number of nations, such as Japan, appear to have responded to the counter-piracy mission because the imprimatur of the UN Security Council was stamped on the operation. Others, like China, relish the opportunity to display newly fashioned blue-water capabilities. Still others, including some European nations, hope the effort polishes the maritime reputation of international organizations, such as NATO and the EU. It is unclear to what extent any of these nations can cooperate against a higher-order maritime threat, such as a naval threat emanating from the always unpredictable North Korea or to counter Chinese naval aggression against Taiwan or against a neighbor in the East China Sea or Spratly or Paracel Islands. Alliance cohesion is always open to question in time of great crisis or warfare, but it is uncertain whether the maritime partnerships that are being forged can address even lower order threats, such as Islamic terrorists in the Philippines or Indonesia. In the end, we can accept the benefits of cooperation against maritime piracy, while realizing that the special circumstances for naval collaboration off the coast of Somalia may be difficult to reproduce in other situations. Ironically, the ability of the United States to maintain cohesion and lead an effective coalition of friends, allies and partners in Asia, including Japan, Singapore, India, South Korea and Australia, encourages rather than discourages the growth of stronger naval capabilities in the region. Only when the regional states are vested in stability and have a role in preserving it will they serve as deterrents to threats larger than piracy.

Notes

* The views presented do not reflect the official policy or position of the US Navy or the Department of Defense.

1 Geoffrey Till, *Seapower: A Guide for the Twenty-First Century*, 2nd edn (Abingdon and New York: Routledge, 2009), p. 6.

2 Geoffrey Till, "Making Waves—Naval Power Evolves for the 21st Century," *Jane's Intelligence Review*, November 2009, p. 12.

3 Robert Work, *Thinking about Seabasing: All Ahead Slow* (Washington, DC: Center for Security and Budgetary Assessments, 2006), p. 25.

4 Barry Posen, "Command of the Commons: The Military Foundations of U.S. Hegemony," *International Security*, 5(46), Summer 2003, p. 8.

5 Ibid.

6 "An Interview with Admiral Mike Mullen, Chief of Naval Operations", *Surface Sitrep*, Department of the Navy, Winter 2007, www.navy.mil/navydata/cno/mullen/Surface_Sitrep_Winter_2007.pdf.

7 Sean O'Keefe, Secretary of the Navy, Admiral Frank B. Kelso, US Navy, and General C.E. Mundy, Jr., US Marine Corps, "From the Sea: Preparing the Naval Service for the Twenty-first Century," in John B. Hattendorf (ed.), *U.S. Naval Strategy in the 1990s: Selected Documents 92*, 30 September 1992, www.globalsecurity.org/military/library/policy/navy/fts.htm.

8 Ibid.

9 See James Kraska, "The Dark Side of Maritime Domain Awareness," *U.S. Naval Institute Proceedings*, December 2009, pp. 56–61; and James Kraska and Brian Wilson, "Off course: The Dark Side of Tracking All Shipping – Pirates Can Do It Too," *Armed Forces Journal*, November, 2009, pp. 27–29, 40–41.

10 *The UN Secretary-General's High Level Panel on Threats, Challenges and Change – Final Report: A More Secure World: Our Shared Responsibility, UN Doc. A/59/565* (New York: 1 December 2004), p. 45, para 132.

11 The nine nations are Bahamas, Belize, Croatia, Cyprus, Liberia, Malta, Marshall Islands, Mongolia and Panama.

12 Robin Wright, "Ship Incident May Have Swayed Libya," *Washington Post*, 1 January 2004, p. 18.

13 "State's Joseph Urges 'Diplomacy of Action' against WMD Threat, in Singapore, Outlines U.S. Counter-proliferation Strategy," *Joint Efforts*, 17 August 2005, America.gov. Robert Joseph is Under Secretary of State for Arms Control and International Security.

14 Ibid.

15 UN Doc. S/Res/1540 (2004).

16 *United Nations Convention for the Suppression of Unlawful Acts against the Safety of Maritime Navigation, 1988*, 1678 UNTS 221, 27 Int'l Legal Mat. 668 (1988), entered into force 1 March 1992.

17 UN Doc. S/Res/1718 (2006).

18 *NSMS* (The White House, September 2005), p. 2, www.whitehouse.gov/homeland/4844-nsms.pdf.

19 Ibid, p. 7. Italics in original. The author was the lead for the US armed forces during completion of the *NSMS* in 2005 when the document was released by the White House.

20 Ibid.

21 Robert M. Gates, *National Defense Strategy of the United States 2008* (2008), p. 16.

22 Statement of Admiral Michael G. Mullen, Chief of Naval Operations before the Senate Armed Services Committee, 29 March 2007, www.jag.navy.mil/documents/testSASC_CNO_FY08_Posture_Hearing_final.pdf.

23 Admiral Michael G. Mullen and General Michael G. Hagee, *Naval Operations Concept 2006* (2006), pp. 7–8, 33–36. The "global commons" includes "international waters, airspace, space, cyberspace."

24 Ibid, pp. 12–13.
25 David Longshore, "American Naval Power and the Prevention of Terror," Homeland Security Affairs, Summer 2005, www.hsaj.org/pages/volume1/issue1/pdfs/1.1.6.pdf.
26 Mullen and Hagee, *Naval Operations Concept*, pp. 9, 13. "Littoral" areas are those areas both seaward of the open ocean to the shore that must be controlled to conduct effectively operations ashore, as well as those areas inland and adjacent to the shore that can be supported from the sea. See also Andrew Scutro, "Navy and Marine Corps Plan Together for Future," *Navy Times*, 18 September 2006, p. 18.
27 Mullen and Hagee, *Naval Operations Concept*, pp. 20–21.
28 See, James Kraska, "Counterdrug Operations in U.S. Pacific Command," *Joint Force Quarterly 81*, Winter 1997–1998.
29 Captain Wayne P. Hughes, *Fleet Tactics and Coastal Combat*, 2nd edn, 2000, p. 35.
30 Robert M. Gates, *National Defense Strategy*, June 2008, p. 16.
31 Subcommittee on Defense, Senate Committee on Appropriations, 27 March 2007.
32 The 13 largest ports in the world are Singapore, Shanghai, Hong Kong, Shenzhen, Busan, Rotterdam, Dubai, Kaohsiung, Hamburg, Qingdao, Ningbo, Guangzhou and Los Angeles. See Jim Wong and Andrew Lee, "Ranking of Top 30 Global Container Port Hubs," *Ships/Container Shipping Asia*, Transport & Logistics, Nomura Securities, Nomura International (Hong Kong) Ltd., Exhibit 65, 28 October 2009, p. 37.
33 *U.S. Pacific Command Strategy*, April 2009, p. 7.
34 Ibid.
35 Amol Sharma, Jeremy Page, James Hookway and Rachel Pannett, "Asia's new Arms Race," *The Wall Street Journal*, 12 February 2011, p. C1.
36 Greg Sheridan, "Time to Beat China at its Own Game," *The Australian*, 5 February 2011 (an analysis of Ross Babbage's paper, "Australia's Strategic Edge in 2030").
37 Amol Sharma, Jeremy Page, James Hookway and Rachel Pannett, "Asia's new Arms Race," *The Wall Street Journal*, 12 February 2011, p. C1.
38 Ibid.
39 Ibid.
40 Xiaoxiong Yi, "The Chinese Navy is Going Blue Water," *Lancaster Eagle Gazette*, 4 November 2009.
41 The American Shipbuilding Association, which represents the six US shipyards that build the Navy's larger warships, states that by 2010, China's submarine force will be nearly double the size of the US submarine fleet. By 2015, the PLA Navy will be larger than the US Navy. Anne Plummer, "Republican Senators Concerned About Timing of Nay Force Reduction Plans," *Congressional Quarterly Today*, 9 March 2005. See also Ronald O'Rourke, *China Naval Modernisation: Implications for U.S. Navy Capabilities – Background and Issues for Congress* (Congressional Research Service Report, 18 November 2005).
42 IMO Res. 979(24), Piracy and Armed Robbery against Ships in Waters off the Coast of Somalia, 23 November 2005 and IMO Res. 1002(25), Piracy and Armed Robbery against Ships in Waters off the Coast of Somalia, 29 November 2007.

15 Australia's maritime challenges and priorities

Recent developments and future prospects

Robin Warner

Introduction

Australia, with its lengthy coastline, vast maritime jurisdiction and multiple offshore territories, undoubtedly fits the description of a maritime nation,[1] but it was not until the issue of Australia's Oceans Policy in 1998 that a comprehensive statement of Australia's maritime challenges and priorities emerged at the Federal Government level.[2] The Oceans Policy articulated a diverse array of challenges and priorities relating to Australia's maritime interests, including the conservation of marine biological diversity, the maintenance of ecologically sustainable fisheries, the prevention of marine pollution, the development of the offshore petroleum and minerals industry, the definition of Australia's maritime jurisdiction and the protection of Australia's national interests both within and beyond Australian maritime jurisdiction.[3] In addition to these fundamental maritime challenges and priorities, the Oceans Policy highlighted some emerging challenges, such as improving and disseminating our knowledge of the role of the oceans in climate change and developing, using and exporting Australia's ocean energy resources.[4] To tackle all these challenges and priorities in a balanced and effective manner, the Oceans Policy identified the need for integrated ocean planning and management, and nominated specific responses for particular sectors of ocean activity. Thirteen years on from the Oceans Policy, it is timely to reassess some key maritime challenges and priorities identified in that document to determine their relevance to the current strategic and political environment for Australia and the Asia-Pacific region. This chapter will examine a selection of these maritime challenges and priorities, their applicability to Australia's current geostrategic circumstances and some recent developments in responding to them.

Identifying Australia's maritime challenges and priorities

Australia's Oceans Policy had the ambitious objective of setting in place the framework for integrated and ecosystem-based planning and management for all of Australia's marine jurisdictions, which would be implemented through the development of Regional Marine Plans based on large marine ecosystems and intended to be binding on all Commonwealth agencies with responsibilities in the marine environment.[5] It set out broad goals for the care, understanding and use of Australia's oceans. These included:

- The exercise and protection of Australia's rights and jurisdiction over offshore areas, including offshore resources;
- Meeting Australia's international obligations under the United Nations Convention on the Law of the Sea (UNCLOS) and other international treaties;
- Understanding and protecting Australia's marine biological diversity, the ocean environment and its resources, and ensuring ocean uses are ecologically sustainable;
- Promoting ecologically sustainable economic development and job creation;
- Establishing integrated oceans planning and management arrangements;
- Accommodating community needs and aspirations;
- Improving Australia's expertise and capabilities in ocean-related management, science, technology and engineering;
- Identifying and protecting Australia's natural and cultural marine heritage;
- Promoting public awareness and understanding of the oceans.[6]

While the overarching vision of integrated oceans management for Australia's offshore marine environment has been modified since the issue of the Oceans Policy, the policy did perform the important initial function of expounding the major maritime challenges confronting Australia in 20 areas of oceans planning and management, together with proposed responses.[7] It identified the need for specific action under several broad headings including ocean uses and impacts, protecting national interests and understanding the oceans.

The second volume of Australia's Oceans Policy enumerated measures to address Australia's maritime challenges in specific sectors of ocean activity under the broad headings identified in the first volume of the policy. Governmental responses to Australia's maritime challenges since the Oceans Policy have tended to occur within specific sectors of ocean activity rather than being prompted by the regional marine planning process initiated by the Oceans Policy or its successor, the marine bioregional planning process being implemented under the Environment Protection and Biodiversity Conservation Act 1999. While some sectors have adopted a more integrated approach to oceans management, cross-sectoral cooperation in oceans management is still developing within Australia's maritime jurisdiction.[8] Subsequent sections of this chapter will analyse key challenges identified in the Oceans Policy, projected responses and recent developments in addressing these challenges.

Defining and describing Australia's maritime jurisdiction

Critical factors in managing Australia's offshore areas are the clear definition of the extent of Australia's maritime jurisdiction and understanding the physical nature of the marine areas under Australian jurisdiction. The Oceans Policy characterized this challenge as defining, describing and documenting the physical, geological and chemical attributes of the marine areas under Australian jurisdiction, including the continental shelf and the physical and chemical structure of the adjacent oceans.[9] Australia ratified the United Nations Convention on the Law of the Sea (UNCLOS)[10] in 1994, assuming a wide range of international legal obligations in relation to its offshore areas. One of the major achievements of the UNCLOS was to provide clearly defined maximum limits for offshore jurisdictional zones, including the territorial sea, the contiguous zone, the exclusive economic zone (EEZ) and the continental shelf. Australia had already claimed a 12 nautical mile territorial sea in 1990 and a continental shelf based on earlier criteria in the 1958 Geneva Convention on the Continental Shelf.[11] In 1994, Australia claimed a contiguous zone adjacent to its territorial sea out to the maximum limit of 24 nautical miles provided for in the UNCLOS.[12] Australia's EEZ was also proclaimed in 1994 out to the maximum limit provided for in the UNCLOS of 200 nautical miles from the territorial sea baseline.[13]

The Oceans Policy noted that technical advice and information on mapping, seafloor morphology, geology and resource potential were required to support Australia's claim for a legal continental shelf extending beyond the EEZ under the provisions of the UNCLOS and to support Australia's negotiations on maritime boundaries with adjacent countries.[14] Geoscience Australia and its predecessor agencies, the Australian Geological Survey Organisation (AGSO) and the Australian Survey and Land Information Group (AUSLIG), have continued to meet this challenge as evidenced by the endorsement of Australia's recommendations for the outer limits of nine of the ten areas of its extended continental shelf claim by the Commission on the Limits of the Continental Shelf (CLCS) in April 2008[15] and successful maritime delimitation negotiations with New Zealand in 2004 since the Oceans Policy was issued.[16] The scientific data gathered by agencies such as Geoscience Australia on the physical, geological, oceanographic and chemical aspects of the water column and the seabed has also been vital in meeting other challenges within Australia's marine areas, such as conservation of marine biodiversity, ecologically sustainable fisheries exploitation and the development of Australia's offshore petroleum and minerals industry.

Managing rights and responsibilities on Australia's extended continental shelf

The sustainable management of Australia's extended continental shelf will present enormous challenges. The extended continental shelf, located beyond 200 nautical miles (up to a maximum of 350 nautical miles or 100 nautical miles from the 2,500 metre isobath) from the coast of Australia and its offshore territories encompasses an area of 2.56 million square kilometres or around a third of the land mass of continental Australia.[17] Extended continental shelf areas contain a cornucopia of non-living resources, with the most obvious being seabed oil and gas but also including manganese nodules, polymetallic sulphides, gas hydrates and phosphorates.[18] There are also valuable living resources on the shelf, including sedentary species such as trochus shell and beche-de-mer (sea cucumber).[19] The relatively shallow depths of many parts of the extended continental shelf make exploitation of the living resources practical and attractive to both authorized and illegal fishers. Valuable marine genetic resources with proven medical, pharmaceutical and industrial benefits have been discovered at seabed features such as hydrothermal vents and cold seeps and are already supporting a thriving international bioprospecting industry.[20] The catalogue of potential resources that could be derived from Australia's extended continental shelf areas may well be incomplete because scientists are still in the process of researching these areas. International acknowledgement of Australia's claim to the substantial resources bound up in these remote areas is only the first step in realizing this bounty. To exploit these resources, Australia and its exploitation contractors will have to grapple with multi-objective management in a complex legal, investment and operating environment.

All areas of Australia's extended continental shelf lie far beyond its territorial sea limit of 12 nautical miles beneath vast tracts of high seas water column. Under international law the high seas are not owned by any state.[21] This means that vessels and aircraft of all states can exercise a wide array of freedoms in these areas, including freedoms to navigate, to conduct marine scientific research, lay submarine cables and pipelines and, subject to limited conservation and management measures imposed by some regional fisheries management organizations, the freedom to fish.[22] Under the relevant provisions of the UNCLOS, Australia's exploitation of the extended continental shelf must not infringe or interfere with navigation and the other rights enjoyed by the global community in these areas.[23] The siting of installations to drill for hydrocarbons or mine seabed minerals on the extended continental shelf will need to take account of established shipping routes in the area, the location of submarine cables and pipelines, and the existence of equipment related to marine scientific research on the seabed. The potential for disputes arising between Australia and other states with interests in the water column above Australian extended continental shelf exploitation sites cannot be discounted and will have to be factored into investment decisions.

Investors in exploitation activities on the extended continental shelf also face the prospect of some of their profits being surrendered because Australia is obliged to make annual payments or contributions in kind for all production at an extended continental shelf site after the first five years of production at that site.[24] The payments are made to the International Seabed Authority (ISA), the supranational body established under the UNCLOS to administer the exploitation of deep seabed minerals beyond national jurisdiction. The ISA will distribute payments to states that have ratified the UNCLOS, taking into account the interests and needs of developing states.[25] The proportion of profits to be remitted to the ISA is not inconsiderable, commencing at 1 per cent of the value or volume of production at the site in the sixth year of production and increasing by 1 per cent for each subsequent year until the twelfth year of production and remaining at 7 per cent in subsequent years.[26]

There will be significant logistical and security challenges involved in establishing and protecting exploitation activities on Australia's extended continental shelf. Offshore installations located in remote extended continental shelf areas could be vulnerable to attack by terrorists and more susceptible to the severe weather events that are predicted in connection with climate change. The illegal exploitation of Australia's extended continental shelf resources is a real threat. To counter this threat, more surveillance and enforcement patrols will be necessary. Australia has limited resources to conduct comprehensive surveillance and monitoring of its EEZ out to 200 nautical miles from its coastline, let alone scanning activities occurring beyond this limit.[27] Experience garnered from enforcing Australia's fisheries legislation in waters surrounding remote offshore territories, such as Heard Island and the McDonald Islands, foreshadows some of the jurisdictional dilemmas and practical difficulties that may be encountered by maritime enforcement units. Two foreign vessels suspected of illegal fishing in these remote waters were only apprehended in waters south of South Africa after lengthy hot pursuits across thousands of miles of ocean.[28] In addition, the extended continental shelf areas around Heard Island and the McDonald Islands fall within the Antarctic Treaty area and contractors in these areas will be subject to the stringent environmental protection provisions of the Madrid Protocol to the Antarctic Treaty.[29] Distinguishing between legitimate marine scientific research activities conducted from foreign vessels on Australia's extended continental shelf and illegal foreign bioprospecting for marine genetic resources will be an ongoing enforcement challenge because the two activities are closely intertwined.[30]

Other global governance imperatives related to the protection of the high seas marine environment and its biodiversity are relevant to extended continental shelf areas. The international community has been discussing the conservation of high seas biodiversity in a Working Group established by the United Nations General Assembly (UNGA) and considering a range of options for more effective biodiversity conservation.[31] These include developing environmental impact assessment and strategic environmental assessment guidelines for all activities, plans and programmes affecting high seas areas and options for marine spatial management in environmentally sensitive high seas areas.[32] The introduction of high seas biodiversity conservation measures in extended continental shelf areas may impose some constraints on resource exploitation. Policy makers, scientists and industry players eager to explore and take advantage of the potential resource bounty on Australia's extended continental shelf will have to come to terms with operating in a complex environment influenced by both national and international regulations.

Protecting Australia's national interests at sea

The protection of Australia's interests at sea is a multifaceted challenge that ranges from preventing potential aggressors crossing Australia's maritime approaches and deterring criminal activity in Australian offshore zones to supporting regional and global security initiatives that help maintain freedom of use and access to the oceans for vessels worldwide. The Australian Defence Force (ADF) is the primary government organization responsible for meeting this challenge although other government agencies such as Customs, Australian Fisheries Management Agency (AFMA), Immigration, Australian Quarantine Inspection Service, Australian Federal Police and state police services also contribute. The Oceans Policy listed projected responses to this challenge that have evolved in recent years as a result of specific threats such as the increase in people smuggling in Australia's northern sea approaches and illegal fishing to the north of Australia and in the offshore zones of its sub-Antarctic islands in the Southern Ocean.[33] Initiatives have been taken at national, regional and global levels to protect Australia's national interests at sea.

National initiatives

One response highlighted in the Oceans Policy was a full contribution by the ADF to the National Surveillance Programme managed by Coastwatch.[34] This programme, originally coordinated by Coastwatch and involving a range of Commonwealth Government agencies, has now been replaced by Border Protection Command, a joint ADF and Customs organization that draws on ADF and Customs assets to perform surveillance and enforcement tasks in Australia's offshore zones.[35] The Oceans Policy also foreshadowed the development of an integrated surveillance system combining all surveillance sources in a single system to provide continuous real-time, all-weather detection and identification of aircraft and ships in Australia's maritime approaches.[36] The Australian Maritime Identification System (AMIS), introduced in February 2005, is an important component of this system with the objective of providing enhanced maritime domain awareness of shipping and other activity in Australia's offshore zones to Border Protection Command.[37] AMIS operates through the phased request of positional information from non-Australian flagged vessels seeking to enter Australian ports. Up to 1,000 nautical miles or 48 hours steaming time from the Australian coast, Australian authorities request advanced arrival information from International Ship and Port Security Code (ISPS) vessels whose next port of call is Australia. This information on ship identity, crew, cargo, location, course, speed and intended port of arrival is already collected for Australian Customs and ISPS purposes. Up to 500 nautical miles or 24 hours steaming time from Australia, information is sought on a voluntary basis on the identity, course and speed of vessels intending to transit Australia's EEZ or territorial sea.[38]

The Oceans Policy flagged the need to develop Australia's ability to defeat threats in its sea and air approaches by expanding its submarine capabilities and making cost effective investments in the defensive and offensive capabilities of its fleet of surface combatants.[39] The plans for naval force modernization announced in Australia's 2009 Defence White Paper reflect recent developments in addressing this challenge, although their realization will occur over a lengthy time frame and will be subject to fluctuations in the national budget and the ability to achieve projected savings by defence organization. The white paper recognizes that

> major surface combatants (destroyers and frigates), submarines and other naval capabilities, supported by air combat (for air superiority and maritime strike) and maritime surveillance and response assets are necessary to establish sea control, and to project force in [Australia's] maritime environment (including for the purposes of maintaining freedom of navigation, protecting our shipping, and lifting and supporting land forces).[40]

In acquisition terms, the white paper announces that by the mid-2030s the government will double the size of the submarine force with 12 more capable submarines to replace the current fleet of six Collins Class submarines and replace the current Anzac class frigate with a more capable Future Frigate with optimal capabilities for anti-submarine warfare.[41] The rationale provided for the acquisition of the augmented submarine force is that future strategic circumstances in the region and beyond will necessitate

> a substantially expanded submarine fleet in order to sustain a force at sea large enough in a crisis or conflict to be able to defend Australia's approaches (including at considerable distance from Australia), protect and support other ADF assets and undertake other strategic missions where the stealth and operating characteristics of highly capable advance submarines would be crucial.[42]

The white paper also emphasizes the deterrent value of such a submarine force for potential adversaries.[43]

The ability of Australia's maritime surveillance and enforcement resources to respond to illegal activity within Australia's offshore zones, including illegal foreign fishing, customs and quarantine offences and drug trafficking, will be further enhanced by the proposed consolidation of maritime law enforcement powers in a single Commonwealth statute. In September 2009, the Australian Government announced the introduction of a Maritime Powers Bill in 2010 to provide a uniform set of maritime enforcement powers. The proposed Maritime Powers Bill will consolidate the wide array of maritime law enforcement powers contained in 38 separate pieces of Commonwealth legislation by:

- Establishing comprehensive powers on interdiction, boarding, search, seizure and retention of vessels;
- Ensuring a common enforcement approach to promote coordination between agencies;
- Creating a mechanism to implement and enforce international agreements that have a maritime aspect.[44]

Regional and global initiatives

Collaboration with regional and global partners in implementing oceans management regimes was identified in the Oceans Policy as a key challenge and critical to protecting Australia's national interests at sea, as well as those of the global community.[45] Since the Oceans Policy was issued, Australia has made considerable progress in establishing both ad hoc and ongoing cooperation arrangements with regional and global partners to combat criminal activity at sea. Examples of this are evident in the spheres of illegal foreign fishing, people smuggling and counter-piracy operations.

Since 1997, the Australian Government has mounted a concerted challenge to foreign fishing vessels (FFVs) fishing illegally in the EEZ off its sub-Antarctic territories, Heard Island and the McDonald Islands. Addressing this challenge has entailed operational responses and legal developments that involve the broadest interpretation of the current international framework for maritime law enforcement. The primary target species for illegal fishers in these waters has been the Patagonian toothfish. Australian fishermen began fishing for this species off Heard Island and the McDonald Islands in 1997 and unlicensed FFVs were also operating in the area.[46] Most of these were registered under the flag of convenience states that maintained very limited control over their activities.[47] Lucrative potential returns made these waters an attractive prospect for the FFVs. Initially, enforcement was hampered by FFVs contacting each other to report on the location of enforcement vessels, and the extreme weather conditions and long transit times for enforcement vessels to reach the Heard and McDonald Islands.[48]

The Australian Navy conducted its first enforcement operation in the Heard and McDonald Islands area in October 1997, arresting two FFVs, the *Aliza Glacial* (Panama registered) and the *Salvora* (Belize registered).[49] Since 1997, six further FFVs have been arrested with two, the *South Tomi* (Togo registered) and the *Viarsa* (Uruguay registered), being apprehended in waters south of South Africa following lengthy hot pursuits by the civilian patrol vessel *Southern Supporter* in 2001 and 2003.[50] Following the *Viarsa* hot pursuit, the Australian Government announced that it would initiate full-time armed patrols to the Southern Ocean to meet the escalating threat of illegal fishing. A full-time contracted vessel, the *Oceanic Viking*, capable of operating all year round in almost any weather conditions, was chartered to undertake fisheries and customs patrols.[51]

Strengthened bilateral cooperation has also played an important role in addressing this significant maritime challenge. Australia and France concluded an agreement on cooperation in their adjacent EEZs in the Southern Ocean in 2003.[52] The treaty provided a framework to enhance the cooperative surveillance of FFVs in the neighbouring territorial seas and EEZs of Australia and France's sub-Antarctic islands. It enables the exchange of information about the location, movements and other details of vessels suspected of fishing illegally to facilitate operational responses, logistical support in the conduct of hot pursuits and the undertaking of cooperative research on marine living resources.[53] There is also provision for surveillance of each party's maritime zones with the consent of the relevant coastal state.[54] It establishes a consent regime allowing for the continuation of hot pursuit into the other party's territorial sea provided the other state is informed and no physical law enforcement or coercive action is taken against the pursued vessel during this phase of the hot pursuit.[55] Under the 2003 Treaty, practical cooperation has taken place with Australian customs and fisheries officers taking part in French patrols and French enforcement officials participating in Australian patrols. Cooperative activities have also included establishment of a shared register of FFVs licensed to fish in French and Australian waters and exchange of information on suspected illegal FFVs.[56]

In 2007, Australia and France extended their cooperation with the conclusion of a further bilateral agreement on the cooperative enforcement of fisheries laws in the maritime zones adjacent to their sub-Antarctic islands.[57] The 2007 Treaty formalizes cooperative enforcement of the two states' fisheries laws allowing each party's enforcement officers to apprehend alleged FFVs in the other's adjacent EEZs.[58] Setting aside the clear practical advantages of the 2003 and 2007 treaties in enhancing cooperative maritime surveillance and enforcement for Australia and France in the Southern Ocean, the treaties' provisions on hot pursuit raise a number of questions concerning their consistency with relevant UNCLOS provisions. Key provisions in the 2003 and 2007 treaties authorize each state's enforcement vessels to maintain hot pursuits through each other's maritime zones in the area of cooperation including through each other's territorial seas.[59] Article 111(3) of the UNCLOS provides that the right of hot pursuit ceases as soon as the ship pursued enters the territorial sea of its own or a third state. A literal reading of this provision would appear to preclude French enforcement vessels or Australian enforcement vessels from continuing a hot pursuit through the other's territorial sea. In support of the legitimacy of the 2003 and 2007 treaty provisions on hot pursuit, however, is the argument that the treaty partners have consented to the continuation of such a hot pursuit and the pursuing vessel would not therefore be infringing on the sovereignty of the coastal state. The critical question in any subsequent prosecution of a FFV, however, would be whether a hot pursuit through the territorial sea of a third state is consistent with Article 111(3) of the UNCLOS and whether it could be challenged as an invalid exercise of the right of hot pursuit by the flag state of the pursued vessel. Notwithstanding this legal ambiguity, the measures taken by Australia in cooperation with France over recent years to counter illegal fishing in the Southern Ocean appear to have resulted in the successful deterrence of illegal fishers in this area of Australia's maritime jurisdiction.

The resurgence of people smuggling in the water gap between Indonesia and Australia in 2008 and 2009 has heightened the need for continued and enhanced cooperation between Australia and Indonesia to apprehend vessels carrying asylum seekers and to investigate and prosecute offenders.[60] Addressing this challenge entails both maritime and terrestrial dimensions. In the framework for security cooperation contained in the Agreement between the Republic of Indonesia and Australia on the Framework for Security Cooperation (Lombok Treaty) of

November 2006, which entered into force on 7 February 2008, law enforcement cooperation has been elevated to the same level as more traditional security concerns, such as defence and counter terrorism.[61] In this treaty, Indonesia and Australia have agreed to deepening and expanding their bilateral cooperation at multiple levels to prevent, respond to, investigate and prosecute transnational crimes such as people-smuggling.[62] At the ninth Australia–Indonesia Ministerial Forum in 2008, ministers released a Joint Statement on people-smuggling and trafficking in persons that reaffirmed their continuing commitment to combating people-smuggling and trafficking in persons and to cooperating with source, transit and destination countries.[63] They agreed to enhance their bilateral cooperation through increased operational assistance and information sharing, and exploring measures to strengthen their respective domestic legal frameworks consistent with the relevant international instruments.[64]

The forum nominated to achieve this objective is the Bali Process on People Smuggling, Trafficking in Persons and Related Transnational Crime, co-chaired by Australia and Indonesia, and involving more than 50 countries from the Asia-Pacific region and beyond, as well as international organizations such as the UN High Commissioner for Refugees and the International Organization for Migration.[65] The inception of the Bali Process in February 2002 was a response to the last spike in people-smuggling operations between Indonesia and Australia.[66] In its first few years, the Bali Process established a range of multilateral initiatives between member countries to combat people-smuggling, and involved operational and policy officials from police, immigration, justice and development agencies.[67] Many of these initiatives were centred on implementing the Protocol against the Smuggling of Migrants by Land Sea and Air supplementing the UN Convention against Transnational Organized Crime (People Smuggling Protocol), which is intended to prevent and combat people-smuggling as well as promoting cooperation among state parties to protect the rights of smuggled migrants.[68] The early momentum of the Bali Process, with two ministerial meetings in 2002 and 2003 and a series of regional capacity building activities, produced some very positive results including enhanced police-to-police cooperation, people-smuggling legislation in some countries that had not previously criminalized this conduct, and improved border control and document identification systems.[69] The initial enthusiasm for the people-smuggling aspects of the process diminished from 2004, however, as people-smuggling voyages between Indonesia and Australia lessened and the focus of the process focused more on measures to combat trafficking in persons.[70]

The Bali Process was re-invigorated at a third ministerial meeting held in April 2009 where the co-chairs' statement re-emphasized the original objectives of the process and acknowledged some additional incentives for the resurgence of people-smuggling, including the global financial crisis and the intensification of conflicts within and beyond the region.[71] The ad hoc groups formed to implement earlier Bali Process initiatives have been re-established and tasked with developing practical outcomes at the operational level to assist countries in mitigating increased irregular population movements, enhancing information sharing agreements between most affected countries and reporting back to the co-chairs of the process with concrete recommendations to inform future regional cooperation on people-smuggling and trafficking in persons.[72] One area that the Bali Process has not yet addressed is the possibility of cooperative maritime surveillance and enforcement agreements between neighbouring countries to detect and apprehend people-smuggling boats. Precedents for this type of cooperation exist in the illegal fishing arena between Australia and France in the Southern Ocean and between some Pacific island states. The Bali Process has now entered a more mature phase in which it appears that it will go beyond fundamental capacity building and prevention to developing specific measures to address people-smuggling problems at the request of the most affected states.[73] A tailored solution for cooperative detection and apprehension of people-smuggling boats between Indonesia and Australia is a potential product of this re-invigorated process.

At a global level, Australia is also contributing to counter-piracy operations in the Horn of Africa region that underpin the freedom of access of all vessels to transit these parts of the ocean unimpeded. A surge in piracy and armed robbery against shipping off the Horn of Africa since late 2008 by Somali pirates has prompted unparalleled cooperation between concerned states who have despatched warships to patrol the Gulf of Aden and waters off the coast of Somalia.[74] The Horn of Africa contains some of the world's most heavily travelled shipping routes with some 33,000 ship transits annually through the Red Sea choke point of the Bab-al-Mandeb Strait, mainly en route to and from the Suez Canal.[75] In 2008, there was a large increase in piracy and armed robbery attacks against ships transiting the Horn of Africa region, with 111 attacks against ships and 42 successful hijackings.[76] The trend continued in 2009 and 2010, with 47 successful hijackings in 2009 and 49 in 2010 and the pirates range extending beyond the coast of Somali and the Gulf of Aden into the western Indian Ocean. Piracy incidents have included attacks on a wide array of vessels ranging from traditional dhows, yachts and fishing trawlers to super tankers, passenger cruisers and other large trading vessels.[77]

The global response to the piracy incidents off the Horn of Africa has encompassed a variety of measures. A series of Security Council Resolutions have been passed under Chapter VII of the United Nations Charter authorizing member States of the UN to act against the piracy attacks. Initially Resolution 1816 of 2 June 2008 authorized member states cooperating with the Somali Transitional Federal Government to enter the territorial waters of Somalia and to use "all necessary means" to repress acts of piracy and armed robbery at sea in a manner "consistent with the relevant provisions of international law".[78] In passing this resolution, the Security Council had clearly taken into account the unstable political conditions in Somalia and its inability to undertake maritime law enforcement in waters under its jurisdiction and beyond. Security Council Resolution 1838 of 7 October 2008 reinforced Resolution 1816 and called upon "all States interested in the security of maritime activities to take part actively in the fight against piracy on the high seas off the coast of Somalia, in particular by deploying naval vessels and military aircraft".[79] In a further Resolution 1851 of 16 December 2008, the

Security Council encouraged states to establish an international cooperation mechanism to act as a common point of contact among them on all aspects of the fight against piracy off Somalia.[80] Subsequent resolutions, particularly Resolution 1918 of 27 April 2010, have expressed concern that the failure to prosecute those responsible for piracy has undermined anti-piracy efforts by the international community.[81] Resolution 1950 of 23 November 2010 re-authorized states to intervene in acts of piracy by Somali pirates at sea for a further period of 12 months.[82] It expressed ongoing concern at the threat of piracy and armed robbery at sea and noted that this threat now extended beyond Somalia to the western Indian Ocean and that children were involved. Member states were urged to improve the capacity of authorities in Somalia to prosecute those planning and undertaking attacks, to determine jurisdiction and to criminalize piracy under their domestic laws.

The principal global response to piracy off the Horn of Africa has been a naval one. Warships from the United States, Canada, a number of European states, Russia, India, China, Japan and, more recently, Australia are now or have recently been active in the waters off the Horn of Africa.[83] Within the region, anti-piracy efforts are coordinated and information is shared under the Code of Conduct concerning the Repression of Piracy and Armed Robbery against Ships in the Western Indian Ocean, concluded in Djibouti in January 2009.[84] Several concurrent naval operations are taking place in the region. In October 2008, NATO launched a counter-piracy operation called *Allied Provider*, which was succeeded on 17 August 2009 by Operation *Ocean Shield*.[85] In December 2008, the European Union initiated Operation *Atalanta*, which includes warships from ten countries, and in January 2009 the United States established Combined Task Force (CTF) 151, which now includes a warship from the Australian Navy on an as-required basis.[86] To enhance protection of shipping in the heavily transited Gulf of Aden area, a Maritime Security Patrol Area (MSPA) has been defined to provide a common system of reference that allows navies patrolling the area to de-conflict their activities. Running through the MSPA, an Internationally Recommended Transit Corridor (IRTC) has been established and group transits of shipping through the IRTC are protected by ships from CTF 151, NATO and European Naval Forces (EUNAVFOR).[87]

The naval response to piracy off the Horn of Africa, of which Australia is a part, has assisted in maintaining a degree of maritime security and freedom of access for shipping in the region but has not curbed or significantly decreased the number of piracy attacks on shipping in the region or addressed the root cause of the problem, which lies in the lack of governance, political instability and poverty rife in Somalia itself. A particular problem that participating Australian Navy vessels face in contributing to these operations is the dilemma of what to do with captured Somali pirates. As there is no functioning central government operating in Somalia, pirates cannot be handed over to Somali authorities for investigation and prosecution. Although they could be tried under Australian law, detaining and transporting them to Australia for trial would represent a considerable burden on the government's resources. Although some states participating in the naval patrols off the Horn of Africa have negotiated transfer agreements with countries in the region, such as Kenya, to accept the pirates for investigation and prosecution, Australia has been unable to secure such an agreement thus far.[88] All these factors militate against states in Australia's circumstances taking criminal justice action against apprehended pirates and have led to the adoption of a catch and release policy in which the pirates' weapons are confiscated and the pirates themselves are released.[89] Australia's contribution to this global maritime challenge, while beneficial in maintaining a degree of security for shipping transiting these areas, falls short of establishing a substantial deterrent to this form of criminal activity at sea.

Maintenance of regional and global maritime security, as well as security and integrity of resources in Australia's own offshore zones, will require ongoing extension and development of existing frameworks for cooperative maritime surveillance and enforcement across national boundaries and on the high seas. Future maritime challenges for Australia in conjunction with global and regional partners may include surveillance and enforcement operations related to high seas fishing of highly migratory stocks and straddling stocks, and collaborative monitoring of other high seas activities, such as marine genetic resource exploitation, climate change mitigation activities and dumping operations by ships, in order to prevent adverse impacts on high seas biodiversity and to maintain high seas resources for current and future generations.

Understanding the oceans and their relationship to the global climate

Australia's Oceans Policy anticipated the global preoccupation with mitigating and adapting to the adverse effects of human-induced climate change and the need to understand the role of the oceans in that process. The challenge articulated in relation to climate change and variability was to improve and disseminate Australia's knowledge of the oceans in climate change, including sea level rise and the uptake of carbon dioxide.[90] The Oceans Policy also recognized that, where possible, Australia should identify alternative energy sources, including ocean-based energy, and investigate the potential for using the ocean's capacity to absorb greenhouse gases.[91] In relation to ocean-based energy sources, the policy encouraged the development, use and export of Australia's ocean energy resources, technology and expertise to their full commercial potential within the limits of ecological sustainability and identified five potential ocean-based energy sources: wind, tidal, wave, ocean thermal and ocean currents.[92] Australia's vast maritime jurisdiction represents an enormous asset in responding to climate change and variability. However, national development of ocean-based energy sources and climate change mitigation activities associated with the ocean is still at an early stage.

Ocean based energy sources in Australia

The Intergovernmental Panel on Climate Change (IPCC)'s Fourth Assessment Report states that the potential marine energy resource of wind-driven waves, gravitational tide ranges, thermal gradients between warm surface water and cooler water at depths of over 1,000 metres, salinity gradients and marine currents is huge but what is currently exploitable, based on the economic potential of these energy sources, is low.[93] The report recommends the rapid development of renewable energy technologies to eventually overtake fossil fuel energy sources.[94] In order to maximize the potential of these new technologies, sustained government support and supportive regulatory frameworks will be necessary over the coming decades. In its statements on renewable energy targets, the Australian Government has committed itself to ensuring that 20 per cent of Australia's electricity supply comes from renewable energy by 2020.[95]

Australia has suitable climates for wave energy, particularly off the coast of Western Australia. In an article on climate change and renewable energy from the ocean and tides, David Leary and Miguel Esteban describe the pre-commercial wave energy projects being undertaken by three companies off the Australian coastline.[96] The Western Australian company, the Carnegie Corporation, has developed the CETO wave power converter which produces high pressure seawater from the power of waves, which is used to power onshore turbines that produce electricity. Commercial testing of the CETO apparatus was completed in 2009 and the construction of a commercial scale plant is due for completion and connection to the electricity grid by 2013.[97] Another company, Biopower Systems, was planning to pilot wave power apparatus on King Island and Flinders Island in conjunction with Hydro Tasmania in 2009.[98] Oceanlinx redeployed its pilot wave energy device at Port Kembla on the New South Wales coast south of Sydney during 2009.[99] A major hurdle for all these projects is the attraction of sufficient ongoing investment to become viable commercial operations and finding suitable locations for the deployment of wave energy devices that accommodate other ocean uses in the relevant areas and are approved by government authorities.

Climate change mitigation options involving the ocean

The capacity of the ocean to act a storage receptacle and to absorb rising levels of carbon dioxide in the atmosphere has been the focus of a number of activities designed to mitigate the adverse effects of climate change on the environment. As the impacts of climate change begin to be felt, states and policy makers are turning to marine geo-engineering schemes as part of the solution. Used irresponsibly, ocean-based climate change mitigation options could have catastrophic consequences for the marine environment.[100] For this reason, regulatory frameworks subjecting such activities to environmental safeguards are growing in importance.

One of the earliest climate change mitigation schemes associated with the ocean involves the permanent sequestration of carbon dioxide emissions from large point sources, such as fossil fuel-fired power plants, steel works and fuel processing plants, into sub-seabed geological formations.[101] The process involves separating carbon dioxide from flue gases and pressurizing it for transport by pipeline or vessel to a sub-seabed storage site such as depleted oil or gas fields or deep subterranean and subsea saline aquifers.[102] The principal risk associated with carbon dioxide disposal in the sub-seabed is the potential for leakage of carbon dioxide and any other substances in the carbon dioxide stream, such as heavy metals, into the marine environment either during transport to a storage site or during storage.[103] Considerable research has been undertaken by states and corporations in developed countries to assess and minimize the risks associated with sub-seabed sequestration of carbon dioxide and this method of disposal is being implemented in a number of projects around the world.[104]

Australia is one of the first countries in the world to legislate for offshore carbon capture and storage. The Offshore Petroleum Amendment (Greenhouse Gas Storage) Act 2008 aims to provide certainty for operators regarding access and title to offshore greenhouse gas storage formations while also ensuring that such storage is safe and secure. Actual greenhouse gas injection will be regulated through an injection licence requiring a comprehensive site plan.[105] At the end of an injection site's life, decommissioning reports must be submitted to the appropriate minister together with suggestions for monitoring, measurement and verification. The holder of a licence will not be free of statutory liability until a site-closing certificate has been issued. The requirement for a site-closing certificate includes a thorough assessment of the migratory behaviour of the injected greenhouse gas.[106] As a result of amendments to the bill in the senate, the Act contains a provision on transfer of long-term liability from the operator to the government at the end of a closure assurance period, which is to be a minimum of 15 years. The Act also includes a 20-year sunset period on the proponent's liability for damages.[107]

The IPCC's Fourth Assessment Report acknowledges that fertilization of the oceans may also be a strategy for removing carbon dioxide from the atmosphere.[108] The process of open ocean fertilization uses iron and other micro nutrients to increase phytoplankton growth in areas of the ocean deficient in iron and other nutrients in order to promote further drawdown of photosynthesized carbon into the deep ocean.[109] The Southern Ocean is one of the areas of the ocean that is iron deficient.[110] There are a variety of risks and uncertainties associated with open ocean fertilization that have excited concern among scientists and environmentalists. The effects of stimulating phytoplankton growth on other marine organisms and ecosystems are poorly understood.[111] Increased phytoplankton growth may boost the production of other greenhouse gases, such as nitrous oxide, thereby neutralizing the positive effects of carbon dioxide drawdown, and the sinking of phytoplankton blooms into the deep ocean may reduce oxygen levels at these depths with adverse consequences for fish and other marine organisms.[112] The sustainability of open ocean fertilization has also been called into question on the basis of the lengthy time-frames and huge quantities of iron or other nutrients required for the process to have any positive effects.[113]

Guidelines for assessing the impact of ocean fertilization experiments on the marine environment have been developed by the Scientific Groups of the London Convention and Protocol.[114] The risk assessment framework on ocean fertilization takes a risk analysis approach to the decision to approve ocean fertilization experiments as legitimate scientific research. The framework provides that a decision to approve ocean fertilization and to determine that it is legitimate scientific research that is not contrary to the aims of the London Convention and Protocol should ensure that the scientific objectives of the experiment can be met and that, as far as practicable, environmental disturbance and detriment are minimized and benefits are maximized. The proponent of an ocean fertilization experiment must prepare an impact hypothesis that forms the basis for impact monitoring. Now that the risk assessment framework has been endorsed by the London Convention and Protocol Parties, it opens the way to ocean fertilization experiments on a larger scale in waters within and beyond national jurisdiction. For ocean fertilization experiments under Australian national jurisdiction or control, the challenge will be to put in place sufficiently rigorous environmental safeguards to prevent adverse impacts on the marine environment of Australia's offshore zones, including those around its sub-Antarctic islands.

Conclusion

This chapter has examined a selection of Australia's maritime challenges and priorities through the prism of Australia's 1998 Oceans Policy, the first comprehensive Commonwealth Government policy statement on ocean-related issues. The Oceans Policy described a complex and multifaceted set of challenges and projected responses, with the ultimate objective of achieving integrated, ecosystem-based management for marine areas under Australian national jurisdiction. Analysis of three policy areas highlighted in the Oceans Policy, defining Australia's maritime jurisdiction, protecting Australia's national interests at sea and understanding the oceans and their relationship to global climate, reveals that although some of the challenges identified in the Oceans Policy have been successfully addressed, others will require ongoing commitment, and others still have evolved into more urgent and substantial challenges. Australia has reached an advanced stage in defining its maritime boundaries, having negotiated delimitation agreements or joint resource development arrangements with all its neighbouring states. The challenge now lies in conserving, managing and exploiting the resources and biodiversity in all of the areas under its national jurisdiction in an ecologically sustainable manner. As Australia is an island continent with an extensive coastline, significant offshore territories and enormous areas of ocean under its national jurisdiction, the task of protecting its national interests at sea is constant and daunting in its complexity. Maintaining border security and combating the poaching of Australia's fisheries by FFVs have been the focus of significant government policy initiatives, resource investment and legislative action in the years since Australia's Oceans Policy was issued. While these challenges will continue to absorb Australian Government resources for the foreseeable future, positive developments have occurred in cooperative maritime surveillance and development with neighbouring states, such as France, in the Southern Ocean and in criminal justice cooperation links with Indonesia. Finally, Australia is just beginning to address the emerging challenge of harnessing the oceans to combat climate change with the development of technology and regulatory frameworks for ocean-based energy and offshore carbon capture. The addition of new areas of maritime jurisdiction in the form of the extended continental shelf, the presence of ongoing threats to Australia's resource and border security represented by illegal fishers and people smuggling operations, and the considerable investment required for ocean-based technology to combat climate change highlights the need for a comprehensive reassessment of the challenges and priorities outlined in Australia's Oceans Policy in the near future.

Notes

1 Vivian Louis Forbes, "Australia's Maritime Space: Conflict and Cooperation", in Dennis Rumley, Vivian Louis Forbes and Christopher Griffin, *Australia's Arc of Instability: The Political and Cultural Dynamics of Regional Security* (Springer: Dordrecht, 2006), p. 23, notes that Australia has a coastline of approximately 69,650 km in length, including the coastlines of some 12,000 adjacent islands; Clive Schofield, Martin Tsamenyi and Mary Ann Palma, "Securing Maritime Australia: Developments in Maritime Surveillance and Security", *Ocean Development and International Law*, 39 (1), 2008, p. 94.

2 Commonwealth of Australia, *Australia's Oceans Policy* (Canberra: Environment Australia, 1998), p. 9, www.environment.gov.au/coasts/oceans-policy/publications/pubs/policyv1.pdf.

3 Ibid.

4 Ibid., Vol. 2, pp. 23, 34.

5 Ibid., Vol. 1, p. 11.

6 Ibid., Vol. 1, p. 6.

7 See the description of Marine Bioregional Planning, www.environment.gov.au/coasts/mbp/index.htm, which has replaced the original concept of Regional Marine Plans set out in the *Oceans Policy*.

8 Enhanced cooperation between Commonwealth Government agencies involved in maritime law enforcement has been achieved through initiatives such as the Border Protection Command discussed later in this chapter.

9 *Oceans Policy*, Vol. 2, p. 29.

10 United Nations Convention on the Law of the Sea, opened for signature 10 December 1982, 1833 UNTS 3 (entered into force 16 November 1994).

11 G. Evans and M. Duffy, "Australia Extends Territorial Sea", *Australian Foreign Affairs and Trade* (November 1990), p. 816; R.D. Lumb, "Australian Coastal Jurisdiction", in K.W. Ryan (ed.), *International Law in Australia*, 2nd edn (North Ryde, NSW: Law Book Co., 1984); M. Landale and H. Burmester, "Australia and the Law of the Sea: Offshore Jurisdiction", in Ibid.

12 D.R. Rothwell, "The Legal Framework for Ocean and Coastal Management in Australia", *Ocean and Coastal Management*, 33 (1), 1996, p. 41.

13 Ibid.

14 *Oceans Policy*, Vol. 2, p. 29.

15 Commission on the Limits of the Continental Shelf, *Statement by the Chairman on the Limits of the Continental Shelf on the progress of the work of the Commission – Twenty First Session*, UN Doc CLCS/58, 25 April 2008, http:www.un.org/Depts/los/clcs_new/commission_documents.htm#Statements%20by%20the%20Chairman%20of%20the%20Commission.

16 Treaty between the Government of Australia and the Government of New Zealand establishing Certain Exclusive Economic Zone and Continental Shelf Boundaries, opened for signature 25 July 2004, (2006) ATS 4 (entered into force 25 January 2006).

17 Geoscience Australia, *Find out More about Law of the Sea*, www.ga.gov.au/oceans/mc_los_More.jsp; see note 15.

18 Bramley J. Murton, "A global review of non-living resources on the extended continental shelf", *Revista Brasileira de Geofisica* 18 (3), 2000, www.scielo.br/scielo.php?pid=S0102-261X2000000300007&script=sci_arttext&.
19 Justin Healey (ed.), *Marine Conservation: Issues in Society*, Vol. 297 (Thirroul, NSW: The Spinney Press, 2009), ch. 1.
20 Joanna Mossop, "Protecting Marine Biodiversity on the Continental Shelf", *Ocean Development and International Law*, 38 (3), 2007, pp. 284–285.
21 UNCLOS, Article 89.
22 UNCLOS, Article 87(1).
23 UNCLOS, Article 78(2).
24 UNCLOS, Article 82(1).
25 UNCLOS, Article 82(4).
26 UNCLOS, Article 82(2).
27 Schofield *et al.*, see note 1, p. 94.
28 E.J. Molenaar, "Multilateral Hot Pursuit and Illegal Fishing in the Southern Ocean: The Pursuits of the Viarsa I and the South Tomi", *International Journal of Marine and Coastal* Law, 19 (1), 2004, pp. 19–42; Warwick Gullett and Clive Schofield, "Pushing the Limits of the Law of the Sea Convention: Australian and French Cooperative Surveillance and Enforcement in the Southern Ocean", *The International Journal of Marine and Coastal Law*, 22 (4), 2007, p. 551.
29 Julia Jabour, "The Australian continental shelf: Has Australia's high latitude diplomacy paid off?", *Marine Policy* 33 (2), 2009, p. 431.
30 D. Farrier and L. Tucker, "Hitching the Conservation Cart to the Bioprospecting Horse", *Ocean Development and International Law*, 32 (3), 2001, pp. 213–214, defines bioprospecting as "the collection of small samples of biological material for screening in search for commercially exploitable biologically active compounds or attributes such as genetic information".
31 The United Nations Ad hoc Open-ended Informal Working Group to study issues relating to the conservation and sustainable use of marine biological diversity beyond areas of national jurisdiction met three times, in 2006, 2008 and 2010. The Reports of the Co-Chairpersons are available online at www.un/org/Depts/los/biodiversityworkinggroup/biodiversityworkinggroup.htm; Rosemary Rayfuse and Robin Warner, "Securing a Sustainable Future for the Oceans Beyond National Jurisdiction: The Legal Basis for an Integrated, Cross-Sectoral Regime for High Seas Governance for the 21st Century", *The International Journal for Marine and Coastal Law*, 23 (3), 2008, pp. 403–407.
32 In recent years, several initiatives have been taken by the international community to establish best practice scientific and technical guidelines for Energy Information Administration (EIA) and South-East Asia (SEA) of activities affecting marine areas beyond national jurisdiction. The issue has been discussed in the United Nations Ad hoc Open-ended Informal Working Group to study issues relating to the conservation and sustainable use of marine biological diversity in areas beyond national jurisdiction (BBNJ) working group, where there has been consistent support among member states for further development of the scientific and technical guidance required to conduct EIAs and SEAs of activities with significant impacts on marine areas beyond national jurisdiction through the Convention on Biological Diversity Conference of the Parties (CBD COP). To facilitate cooperation, COP 9 decided to convene an expert workshop in November 2009 to discuss scientific and technical aspects relevant to EIA and SEA of activities affecting marine areas beyond national jurisdiction and to build on sectoral, regional and national EIA and SEA frameworks. The tenth meeting of the COP CBD in October 2010 considered the Expert Workshop Report and approved the revision of the CBD Voluntary Guidelines on EIA and the draft Guidance on SEA to take into account the conclusions of the Expert Workshop Report on EIAs and SEAs related to marine areas beyond national

jurisdiction. The revised guidelines will be submitted to a future meeting of the Subsidiary Body on Scientific, Technical and Technological Advice (SBSTTA) prior to the eleventh meeting of the COP CBD in 2012; R. Warner, *Protecting the Oceans beyond National Jurisdiction* (Leiden: Martinus Nijhoff, 2009), pp. 214–215.

33 *Oceans Policy*, Vol. 2, p. 37.
34 Ibid., p. 38.
35 See Border Protection Command website, www.bpc.gov.au/default.asp.
36 *Oceans Policy*, Vol. 2, p. 38.
37 Border Protection Command website, *Australian Maritime Information Fusion Centre*, www.bpc.gov.au/site/page5783.asp.
38 Ibid; Schofield *et al.*, note 1, pp. 103–104.
39 *Oceans Policy*, Vol. 2, p. 38.
40 Department of Defence, *Defending Australia in the Asia Pacific Century: Force 2030*, www.defence.gov.au/whitepaper/docs/defence_white_paper2009.pdf, p. 60, para. 8.19.
41 Ibid., p. 64, para. 8.39.
42 Ibid., p. 64, para. 8.40.
43 Ibid.
44 Attorney General for Australia, *Reform of Maritime Enforcement Legislation*, www.AttorneyGeneral.gov.au/www/ministers/mclelland.nsf/Page/MediaReleases_2009_Third Quarter_15September2009-ReformofMaritimeEnforcementLegislation.
45 *Oceans Policy*, Vol. 2, p. 38.
46 Gullett *et al.*, see note 28, p. 550.
47 Ibid.
48 Ibid.
49 Australian Navy, "RAN Activities in the Southern Ocean", *Semaphore*, Newsletter of the Sea Power Centre, Australia, Issue 18, October 2006, www.navy.gov.au/Publication:Semaphore__Issue_18,_2006.
50 Gullett *et al.*, see note 28, p. 551.
51 Ibid., pp. 556–557.
52 *Treaty between the Government of Australia and the Government of the French Republic on Cooperation in the Maritime Areas adjacent to the French Southern and Antarctic Territories (TAAF), Heard Island and the McDonald Islands*, opened for signature 24 November 2003, (2005) ATS 6 (entered into force 1 February 2005) (*2003 Treaty*).
53 *2003 Treaty*, Articles 3(3), 3(5), 5(1)(a) and Annex II.
54 *2003 Treaty*, Articles 1 and 3.
55 *2003 Treaty*, Article 4.
56 Australian Customs and Border Protection Service, *Enforcement Operations in the Southern Ocean*, www.customs.gov.au/webdata/resources/files/FS_Enforcement_Operations_in_the_SO1.pdf; Gullett *et al.*, see note 46, p. 560.
57 *Agreement on Cooperative Enforcement of Fisheries Laws between the Government of Australia and the Government of the French Republic in the Maritime Areas Adjacent to the French Southern and Antarctic Territories, Heard Island and the McDonald Islands*, opened for signature 8 January 2007, (entered into force 7 January 2011), www.info.dfat.gov.au/Info/Treaties/treaties.nsf/AllDocIDs/A357911148DOF38CA257IDC000D800A(.
58 *2007 Treaty*, Articles 3 and 4.
59 See notes 54 and 57.
60 Parliamentary Library, *Budget 2009–10: Immigration. Border Protection and combating people smuggling*, www.aph.gov.au/library/Pubs/RP/BudgetReview2009–10/Immigration_BorderProtect.htm.
61 *Agreement between the Republic of Indonesia and Australia on the Framework for Security Cooperation*, opened for signature 13 November 2006, [2008] ATS 3 (entered into force 7 February 2008) (*Lombok Treaty*), Article 3.

62 Ibid.
63 Australian Minister for Foreign Affairs, *Joint Ministerial Statement Australia-Indonesia Ministerial Forum – People Smuggling*, www.foreignminister.gov.au/releases/2008/9_aimf_statement.pshtml.
64 Ibid.
65 Bali Process, www.baliprocess.net/.
66 Bali Process, *About the Bali Process*, www.baliprocess.net/index.asp?pageID=2145831401.
67 Ibid.
68 *Protocol against the Smuggling of Migrants by Land, Sea and Air Supplementing the United Nations Convention against Transnational Organized Crime*, opened for signature 12 December 2000, [2004] ATS 11 (entered into force 28 January 2004) (*People Smuggling Protocol*).
69 See note 65.
70 Ibid.
71 Bali Process, *Co-Chairs Statement Third Regional Ministerial Conference on People Smuggling, Trafficking in Persons and Related Transnational Crime*, Bali Indonesia, 14–15 April 2009, www.baliprocess.net/files/CO%20Chairs%20Statement%20BRMC%20III_FINAL.doc.
72 Ibid., paras. 26–28.
73 Ibid., paras. 25–26.
74 NATO Parliamentary Assembly, "The Growing Threat of Piracy to Regional and Global Security", *Committee Report 169 CDS 09 E*, 2009 Annual Session, para. 72, www.nato-pa.int/Default.asp/SHORTCUT=1770.
75 "FACTBOX: Ships held by Somali Pirates", *Reuters*, 17 November 2009, www.reuters.com/article/world/News/idUSTRE5AG1UV20091117?.
76 Alison Bevege, "NATO warship hunts Somali pirates, escorts food aid", *Reuters*, 12 June 2009, www.reuters.com/article/latest/Crisis/idUSLC801321.
77 See note 74.
78 United Nations Security Council Resolution 1816 (2008), S/RES/1816 (2008), 2 June 2008, www.un.org/Docs/sc/unsc_resolutions08.htm.
79 United Nations Security Council Resolution 1838 (2008), S/RES/1838 (2008), 7 October 2008, www.un.org/Docs/sc/unsc_resolutions08.htm.
80 United Nations Security Council Resolution 1851 (2008), S/RES/1851 (2008), 16 December 2008, www.un.org/Docs/sc/unsc_resolutions08.htm.
81 United Nations Security Council Resolution 1918 (2010), S/RES/1918 (2010), 27 April 2010, www.un.org/Docs/sc/unsc_resolutions10.htm.
82 United Nations Security Council Resolution 1950 (2010), S/RES/1950(2010), 23 November 2010, www.un.org/Docs/sc/unsc_resolutions10.htm.
83 See note 74, para. 72.
84 International Maritime Organization (IMO), *Piracy in waters off the coast of Somalia*, www.imo.org/home.asp?topic_id=1178.
85 See note 74, para. 71.
86 Ibid., paras. 64, 67.
87 Ibid., para. 73.
88 Douglas Guilfoyle, "The Legal Challenges in Fighting Piracy", 16 April 2009, www.clingendael.nl/cscp/events/20090708_note_guilfoyle.pdf.
89 Kathryn Westcott, "Pirates in the Dock", *BBC News*, 21 March 2009, http://news.bbc.co.uk/2/hi/africa/8059345.stm; Frances Njubi Nesbitt, "Antipiracy Campaign Hijacks International Law", *The Zeleza Post*, 9 April 2009, http://zeleza.com/blogging/african-affairs/antipiracy-campaign-hijacks-international-law.
90 *Oceans Policy*, Vol. 2, p. 34.
91 Ibid.
92 Ibid., p. 23.

93 IPCC, IPCC Fourth Assessment Report (2007), www.ipc.chpublications_and_data/ar4/wg3/en/ch4-ens4–3–3–8.html.

94 Ibid., sect. 4.3.

95 Department of Climate Change, *Renewable Energy Target*, www.climatechange.gov.au/government/initiative/renewable-target.aspx.

96 David Leary and Miguel Esteban, "Climate Change and Renewable Energy from the Ocean and Tides: Calming the Sea of Regulatory Uncertainty", *The International Journal of Marine and Coastal Law*, 24 (4), 2009, pp. 617–651.

97 Ibid., p. 621; Carnegie Wave Energy Limited, *Projects*, www.carnegiecorp.com.au/index.php?url=/projects.

98 Ibid., pp. 621–622; Biopower Systems, *Projects*, http://biopowersystems.com/projects.php.

99 Ibid., p. 622; Oceanlinx, *Current Projects*, www.oceanlinx.com/index.php/current-projects.

100 Tony Koslow, *The Silent Deep* (Sydney, Australia: UNSW Press, 2007), pp. 159–160; Karen N. Scott, "The Day after Tomorrow: Ocean CO_2 Sequestration and the Future of Climate Change", *Georgetown International Environmental Law Review*, 2005, pp. 18, 58.

101 See Koslow, note 98, p. 157; IMO Press Briefing 5, www.imo/org/Safety/mainframe.asp?topic_id=1472&4doc_id=7772.

102 See Scott, note 98, p. 60; Ann Brewster Weeks, "Sub Seabed Carbon Dioxide Sequestration as a Climate Mitigation Option for the Eastern United States: A Preliminary Assessment of Technology and Law", *Ocean and Coastal Law Journal*, 12 (2), 2007, p. 252.

103 Juan C. Abanades, *et al.*, *IPCC Special Report on Carbon Dioxide Capture and Storage* (Cambridge: Cambridge University Press, 2005), p. 18; Koslow, note 98, p. 160.

104 See Scott, note 98, p. 60; Weeks, note 100, pp. 252–253.

105 Department of Resources, Energy and Tourism, *CCS Legislation*, www.ret.gov.au/resources/carbon_dioxide_capture_and_storage/Pages/CCS_legislation.aspx.

106 Ibid.

107 Ibid.

108 See note 91, sect. 11.2.2.

109 See Koslow, note 98, pp. 157–158; Rosemary Rayfuse, Mark Lawrence and Kristina Gjerde, "Ocean Fertilization and Climate Change: The Need to Regulate Emerging High Seas Uses", *The International Journal of Marine and Coastal Law*, 23 (2), 2008, pp. 6–7.

110 See Koslow, note 98, p. 158.

111 See Rayfuse *et al.*, note 107, pp. 8–9; Koslow, note 98, p. 159; Scott, note 98, pp. 87–88.

112 See Rayfuse *et al.*, note 107, p. 10; Paul Johnston, David Santillo, Ruth Stringer, Rémi Parmentier, Bill Hare and Martina Krueger, *Ocean Disposal/Sequestration of Carbon Dioxide from Fossil Fuel Production and Use: An Overview of Rationale, Techniques and Implications*, Technical Note 01/99, 4 March 1999, pp. 24–25.

113 See Koslow, note 98, p. 159; Rayfuse *et al.*, note 107, p. 9; Tatjana Rosen, "Open Ocean Fertilization," in Cutler J. Cleveland, *Encyclopaedia of Earth* (Washington, DC: Environmental Information Coalition, National Council for Science and the Environment, 2007), www.eoearth.org/article/Open_ocean_iron.fertilization.

114 P. Verlaan, "Current Legal Developments. London Convention and London Protocol", *International Journal For Marine and Coastal Law*, 26, 2011, p. 187: The Thirty Second Consultative Meeting of the London Convention Parties and the Fifth Consultative Meeting of the London Protocol Parties held from 11 to 15 October 2010 adopted the Assessment Framework For Scientific Research involving Ocean Fertilization.

16 Maritime challenges and priorities in Asia

An Indian perspective

Prabhakaran Paleri

The maritime challenges that India faces are similar to those of other nations. It is the threat factor that varies. India has always been a threat attractor. The country has sufficient security forces and agencies, and a stable governmental system. However, its maritime governance will require systematic orientation of policies and practices if the country is to face challenges at sea and from the sea. The chapter examines India's perspectives against this background.

Although the global perspective of the ocean is changing, there is a certain degree of invariance[1] in the challenges and imperatives that nations face at sea. The lack of variance is obvious in both military and non-military statements that determine the strategic context. The current challenges are more or less at invariance with those of the past. In other words, they remain unaltered. They include the possibility of military intervention under the conditions of the laws of war or otherwise,[2] unlawful activities such as terrorism and piracy, and the destructive forces of nature that may cause mayhem in national governance. It is the approaches of the nations that may differ as time passes. Perhaps the greatest challenge that nations and other geostrategic entities face is in fine-tuning their maritime interests and their approaches to policy. This fault-line in national maritime thinking and approach is evident when incidents, such as the Mumbai massacre of 26 November 2008[3] or the escalation of piracy around the Horn of Africa, are dissected on the analyst's table.

Maritime challenges affect every geostrategic entity. The author has identified 272 geostrategic territorial entities, comprising landlocked, coastal and island states and their island territories, in a global perspective in a study carried out in 2008.[4] Such an investigation was necessary to understand the gravity of maritime challenges and their impact on the entities identified. Of these, 192 were members of the United Nations. Irrespective of their geostrategic distinctiveness, every entity, including those that are landlocked, faced the impact of maritime challenges. Some of the landlocked entities also have maritime military and non-military forces. Many of these entities are active and participating members of international maritime organisations or parties to maritime agreements out of sheer necessity. This speaks volumes about the appreciation of these countries about the impact of maritime challenges on their national security matters.

Demanding challenges

Asia faces demanding challenges within the maritime scenario of the Pacific Ocean and the Indian Ocean. Often it is not easy to appreciate the changing trends and this can become a constraint for problem solving. Besides, governments view these challenges against their exclusive national security perspectives. The dichotomy begins from such an appreciation. Collectivism should spring from priorities based on overall regional interests, which should ideally synchronise with national interests. Often this may not be the case. However, Asia, as a region, has shown glimpses of a collective mindset at least in select pockets, like the Association of Southeast Asian Nations (ASEAN), or in some particular type of issue, such as global climate change forums. From such outlying appreciation of the collective political psyche of the region, it can be deduced that Asia has the capability and inductive mindset for initiating cooperative approaches to face the maritime challenges.[5]

The maritime dimension of Asia is vital in the quest to appreciate the challenges the region faces. Asia is a distinctively maritime region sitting astride strategic choke points. However, the perception of each entity about their own maritime domain is naturally different. The challenges within this domain may spring from military and non-military sources. Most of the nations of the region are inheritors of a violent and volatile past, and there are unresolved issues carried forward from earlier periods.

Foremost among the appreciated challenges are territorial disputes. Often these disputes are quoted as potential flash points, but nations have shown considerable political maturity in handling them. There are recent instances of favourable approaches in settling territorial disputes under bilateral consensus without the use of force. This is an encouraging trend in the region's geopolitical scenario. However, there are still far too many issues that could invite all out wars in the region if the delicate geopolitical balance is breached by unforeseen circumstances, including disputes over land. Any such conflict could break into the maritime domain of the region, paralysing good order and discipline with far-flung repercussions. The military doctrines of many nations are being revised under the possibility of future conflicts. Some even consider multi-front conflicts as a possibility. The world over, military preparedness refuses to take a back seat in spite of a much-touted aversion to war among the international community. It is no different in Asia. Hence, military conflict is a perceived possibility even under geostrategic restraint by mature ideologies. The greatest maritime challenge faced by the region is the prospect of interstate warfare with a significant maritime dimension.

The Indian perspective

India is geostrategically located on an open roadstead in the Indian Ocean, and its socio-economic and political fabric is highly influenced by the ocean around it. India has been a serious threat attractor since early times. The threat factor has always remained embedded in India's tryst with destiny even after independence and shows no sign of waning. The 2008 Mumbai massacre is the latest incident where India had to face unexpected challenges. In an incident across the land border in January 2010, three *fidayeen* blasted into a hotel in Lal Chowk in Srinagar and held people hostage in a Mumbai-model attack.

The overall Indian threat factor rises beyond the classification of challenges. When a country is targeted internally or externally by terrorists and insurgents, it becomes a perfect threat attractor. Assessing the threat factor beyond the normal, therefore, becomes extremely important. When the apparent threat perception rises above the perceived normal, the country gets into a dilemma of sorts about managing the strategic deficit in handling situations. This, perhaps, is the greatest challenge India faces today. The country, therefore, has to upgrade its capabilities to meet the deficit in facing its challenges with a forward-looking perspective. India's political establishment is conscious of this. The question is, 'How prudent will India's politicians and political establishment be in appreciating the situation and upgrading the preparedness level to face these challenges?'

India is a mature and responsible state. This statement is validated by the Constitution of India and the nation's geostrategic endeavours for systemic growth. Ironically, the country has a long history of violence and a restive appearance. That is a paradox under which India strives and moves with a Zen-like calm. India faces similar maritime challenges to many other countries in a volatile world: India has maritime disputes with two of its seven maritime neighbours; terrorism and insurgency in India have their supply chains extending to the ocean; and almost every conceivable unlawful activity can be seen in India's waters and their adjacent neighbourhood. The possibility of the continued existence of such unlawful activities and cross border conflicts is very real in the geostrategic context of India.

It is natural for any country, therefore, to feel the need for military and non-military preparedness at a basic level in its doctrine. Such an approach calls for effective coordination between the military and non-military forces in appropriate areas and through an appropriate security doctrine. Under such conditions, the country's armed forces need to identify the key areas in their respective fields of expertise. India may, therefore, have to prepare for military operations, asymmetric and sub-conventional threats (including weapons of mass destruction (WMD), terrorism, insurgency, cyber-attacks), strategic reach and out-of-area capabilities, independence and operational synergy with other forces, and law enforcement capabilities, in addition to gaining a technological edge in these activities. The maritime domain of India is an important arena for all these activities.

Most of the challenges can also be handled without the use of force under effective diplomacy, bilateral and multilateral coordination, and cooperation with willing partners. India continues to thrive on proactive diplomacy through mutual trust and understanding with its neighbours and other outreach countries. However, the success of these efforts will be in their acceptance by concerned parties. Diplomacy may be a slow process, but it is much ahead of war and conflict as a choice. India will be able to tackle the issues with the wholehearted support of like-minded neighbours and other global partners.

Maritime challenges to India

Maritime challenges to India are to be identified from various sources, including the documented databases of intelligence and enforcement agencies, indeterminate alarms raised under apprehensions and assumptions, and the hidden challenges that may emerge without warning. According to the constitution, the interests of the centre, states and union territories are important for facing these challenges. All must deal with constitutionally authorised forces and legislative measures. The Constitution of India has been framed to meet the varied demands of the states and the union territories with the centre at the apex under the freedom of independent governance.

In the geopolitical context, an outreach of power and influence, especially in maritime affairs, can be interpreted as hegemonic. Since ancient times, maritime supremacy has not been India's forte and this was considered a weakness by many analysts within the country. India certainly was not heir to maritime supremacy in the old world, according to the perceived meaning of the term. It is true that mediaeval India yielded to the maritime supremacy of alien invaders. This may be because the interests of peninsular India in its maritime domain remained inward looking towards matters specific to India. Generally, India did not aim for maritime supremacy and its propensity to do so was judiciously absent. The so-called command of the sea, therefore, was set aside as a policy except in a limited way. Efforts in this direction will involve all the ingredients for maximising maritime security as demanded by each situation: these include suppressing unlawful activities.

Far too many unlawful activities fall under the documented database of intelligence and enforcement agencies. According to the database of the Indian Coast Guard, these include:

- Illegal, unregulated and unreported (IUU) fishing
- Contraband smuggling
- Violence at sea involving alien vessels and forces
- Drug trafficking
- Oil pollution
- Marine wildlife violations
- Armed robbery
- Piracy
- Illegal immigration
- Human trafficking
- Hostage taking
- Terror strikes and terror logistics supply
- Illegal marine survey
- Crime at sea in merchant vessels
- Maritime fraud
- Espionage and insurgency support.

The hidden challenges are those that can disrupt the government and the enforcement machinery. The Mumbai massacre of 2008 was one such incident that came out of the blue. Following the incident, the government and the entire enforcement machinery woke up from their limbo, although there were reports that the intelligence agencies had warned the government of the impending terror catastrophe. The incident changed the law enforcement policies of the government. However, their effectiveness is yet to be seen. In reality, the hidden challenges are packaged in surprise and could turn out to be cataclysmic. Most are not considered critically and anticipated to enable early action. The aim is to bring hidden issues to the fore using intelligence and analysis, and to prepare for them. This cannot be handled by hasty over-the-counter prescriptions. Every nation, especially threat attractors, has to understand this.

Responsibilities and requirements

The suppression of unlawful activities at sea or from the sea requires competent forces and agencies and an efficient maritime administration, supported by well-framed laws and an expeditious judicial system. India has regulations for maritime enforcement from different departments, including the navy, the coast guard, the customs, the police and the mercantile marine department, as well as agriculture, forest, environmental, mining, and state and union territory agencies. In addition, there are intelligence agencies to provide input. Various regulatory measures are in force and the entire enforcement machinery of the nation is within a large system of government.

Multiple agencies are often seen as having a functional overlap. It need not be so, but depends on their usage and the policies of the government. Multiple agencies can be used very effectively to maximum result in the most cost-effective and constitutionally acceptable manner under mature governance. Multiple agencies can also provide the desired flexibility and focussed attention on key issues that assist for a nation like India in establishing rule of law. They need to be managed appropriately under freedom of performance and organisational identity. This is possible only by ensuring maximum accountability. In a linear programming model, this means maximising the returns from each agency through its accountability for its role by minimising the cost of governance. This could be done either jointly or independently. Therefore, the efficacy of multiple agencies lies in the stratagem of governance in utilising them in their respective roles.

Among the forces and agencies, the navy was previously involved in the interdiction of law violators, with the support of the Union Ministry of Home Affairs and the Central Board of Excise and Customs of the Ministry of Finance (Department of Revenue and Banking). The navy is the only force expected to have the capability for the effective blockade of the waters and to safeguard India's sovereign interests and integrity during times of war. However, a country's navy should not end up as a law enforcement agency in the constabulary garb, and ultimately become a coast guard. Diverting the into these enforcement roles can blunt its cutting edge for war.

The primary law enforcement agency at sea should be the coast guard, which should be developed accordingly with sufficient freedom under absolute accountability. The role of the Indian Coast Guard is well articulated in its charter under the Coast Guard Act, 1978. The duties and functions of the coast guard are universal and specific to law enforcement and service. The Indian Coast Guard is constitutionally chartered to perform the duties and functions 'as it thinks fit' and 'without duplication of effort'. Its accountability derives from this statement. The coast guard is notified as the lead intelligence agency (LIA) for coastal security.[6] By its charter, it is also the national agency for offshore security, maritime search and rescue, and marine environmental security. The coast guard is not an agency for investigating for unlawful activities at sea or from the sea except with respect to centrally controlled fisheries in India. Its absence of investigative powers could be seen as a lacuna. However, opinions vary. Furthermore, the capability of the Indian Coast Guard to establish the rule of law at sea is yet to be assessed firmly.

The police force is the universal law enforcement agency applicable to the centre, states and union territories in accordance with the constitution. In the wake of the 1999 Kargil conflict,[7] the Government of India decided to create exclusive marine police forces for the coastal states and union territories to improve the containment of unlawful activities at sea and from the sea, especially 'crimes at sea' (i.e. crimes committed on board ships and other vessels or platforms), by enhancing investigative enforcement and judicial procedures. The coastal states and union territories are slowly establishing marine police forces in India.

The customs marine organisation was formed prior to the coast guard – on 2 August 1974 – to interdict smugglers in Indian customs waters at a time when India faced serious problems with the parallel economy aided by maritime smuggling. In the early periods, the organisation was effective within the contiguous zone. However, although the organisation has gained maritime experience, it is handicapped by obsolescence and a lack of capacity. There are currently efforts to revive the organisation.

Fisheries operations are carried out by state and union territory fisheries and marine enforcement forces within the territorial sea. The states and union territories have their own marine fisheries regulation acts, but they lack the force and the expertise to enforce them. Central government regulates fisheries in the exclusive economic zone (EEZ) with the help of the coast guard. The mercantile marine department (MMD), under the directorate general of shipping, engages the maritime administration through its principal officers and surveyors. Under the central, states, and union territory administrations, the pollution control boards (PCB) and wild life wardens are expected to ensure environmental and wild life legislation even at sea. Furthermore, the mining safety agencies are endorsed with mine safety regulations for exploration of minerals, including those at sea. However, all these forces and agencies have their limitations. They require assistance from the coast guard or the navy when the situation becomes exacerbated.

Laws and regulations

According to their charters, the law enforcement forces and agencies are empowered under various legislations to suppress unlawful activities. The important central laws include:

- Indian Penal Code, 1860
- The Passport (Entry into India) Act, 1920
- The Emigration Act, 1922
- The Regulation of Foreigners Act, 1939
- The Foreigners Act, 1946
- The Merchant Shipping Act, 1958
- The Arms Act, 1959
- The Customs Act, 1962
- The Passport Act, 1967
- The Unlawful Activities (Prevention) Act, 1967
- The Indian Wildlife (Protection) Act, 1972
- The Code of Criminal Procedures, 1973
- The Territorial Waters, Continental Shelf, Exclusive Economic Zone and Other Maritime Zones Act, 1976
- The Coast Guard Act, 1978
- The National Security Act, 1980
- The Maritime Zone of India Act, 1981
- Maritime Zones of India (Regulation of Fishing by Foreign Vessels) Act, 1981
- The Narcotic Drugs and Psychotropic Drugs Act, 1985
- The Environment Protection Act, 1986
- The Foreign Exchange Management Act, 1999
- The Suppression of Unlawful Activities against Safety of Maritime Navigation and Fixed Platforms on Continental Shelf Act, 2002
- The Offshore Area Minerals (Development and Regulation) Act, 2002
- The National Investigation Agency Act, 2008.

The importance and relevance of the central, state and union territory acts and regulations depend upon their 'enforcement friendliness'. Here the term 'enforcement friendly' means (1) the existence of legislation that clearly depicts the unlawful activities and punitive measures that serve the purpose of deterrence; (2) clarity of jurisdiction; (3) the absence of limitations or constraints in enforcing legislation under intent; (4) the expediency of the judicial system; and (5) being resistant to abuse. The enforcement friendliness of a legislation has also to be viewed against the fact that while legislation is frozen on the date of its enactment, the unlawful activity can take different turns to slip through unforeseen loopholes in the legislation. This is an aspect that the legislators have to anticipate by observing trends in unlawful activities. Drafting and enacting legislation that will remain balanced at all times within the level of absolute enforcement friendliness is a difficult task. In spite of the extent of existing legislation, the enforcement agencies had to invoke the provisions of the Admiralty Offences (Colonial) Act, 1849 and the Admiralty Jurisdiction (India) Act, 1860 in the case of the pirated vessel MV *Alondra Rainbow* in November 1999.[8] The case also needed the support of the provisions of the United Nations Convention on the Law of the Sea (UNCLOS), 1982. There have been other cases of lapses and the repeal of acts. These are examples of 'enforcement unfriendly' laws and indicate that law alone cannot be a solution for serious problems like terrorism or insurgency.

Exercising jurisdiction for law enforcement is a difficult task. The maritime dimension of India comprises its designated maritime zones. India's legal maritime zones are articulated in the Territorial Waters, Continental Shelf, Exclusive Economic Zone and Other Maritime Zones Act, 1976 of India. There are provisions in international law for identifying and managing maritime zones. A state should be clear about its maritime zones and the national interests within them at any given time for ocean-specific decision-making.

India ratified UNCLOS on 29 June 1995. Thus, India can make its imperatives clear in the ocean without violating the ratification or the provisions of customary international law. Designating maritime zones is not related to attempts at maritime supremacy or hegemonic dominance; it is for law enforcement in the national interest of a state within the provisions of national and international laws. India's command over the maritime zones with respect to the legal authority therein under national and international laws should be clear and without ambiguity in the geostrategic context. This is the goal of an enforcement regime.

Maritime zones

India has accepted the maximum allowed range – 12 nautical miles – for the territorial sea to which its sovereignty extends. The coastal states and union territories should see the territorial waters as an extension of their jurisdictional limits for exploitation and law enforcement. This is a major activity for them. They need adequate machinery – including police and fisheries, environmental and intelligence agencies – competent to safeguard their interests in the adjacent territorial sea. However, the capability of Indian coastal states and union territories to enforce the rule of law in the territorial waters is grossly inadequate.

Waters on the landward side of the baseline of the territorial sea form part of the internal waters of any country. However, the regime for inland waters may be different from that of the legally demarcated maritime zones in the ocean and identifying the inland 'maritime' zones is an interesting exercise for any country. Inland waters are called *internal waters* under UNCLOS, which provides that inland waters that are navigable from and into the sea are to be treated as maritime zones, along with the ports and harbours in the chain. India has such navigable waters. It is imperative at this stage to define the land terrain at the interface of the sea and land – this is the coastal zone and is another vital area when dealing with unlawful activities.

The term 'high seas' refers to all parts of the sea that are not included in the EEZ, in the territorial sea or the internal waters of a state, or in the archipelagic waters of an archipelagic state,[9] in which no nation can exercise sovereign rights. This area is reserved for peaceful purposes and is open to all states including landlocked states. Every state has the freedom of navigation, overflight, laying undersea cables and pipelines, constructing artificial islands and other installations permitted under international law, fishing and scientific research, subject to the provisions of the convention. The principle of *high seas* or *mare liberum* is applicable here. However, the high seas can be used for unlawful activities according to the innovative acuity of the perpetrators. Unauthorised broadcasting, piracy and illicit traffic in narcotic or psychotropic substances are included. According to international law, states are expected to cooperate in suppressing these activities. It is important to see that this aspect does not remain as an expression of fancy in the texts of the conventions lest the perpetrators of unlawful activities should take advantage of the 'freedom' of the high seas.

Immediately adjacent to the territorial waters of a state is the less well known and understood *contiguous zone*,[10] which has a maximum limit of 24 nautical miles from the baseline from which the territorial sea is measured. India has claimed the full extent of its contiguous zone. The central government exercises powers in this area and may take measures related to immigration, sanitation, customs and other fiscal matters by notification.

The *exclusive economic zone*, widely known as the EEZ, is an area beyond and adjacent to the territorial sea subject to the specific legal regime established in Part V of UNCLOS. Establishment of the EEZ by a state should in no way infringe upon the rights and freedoms of other states governed by UNCLOS. The breadth of the EEZ is limited to 200 nautical miles from the baseline from which the territorial sea is measured. Each country has such rights as are applicable to the continental shelf and other such rights as are recognised by international law. As per the convention, India has sovereign rights for exploring and exploiting, conserving and managing natural resources, whether living or non-living of the waters superjacent to the seabed and of the seabed and its subsoil and with regard to other activities for the economic exploitation of the zone, such as the production of energy from sea water, current and winds. India has jurisdiction for the establishment and use of artificial islands, installations and structures, for marine scientific research, for the protection and preservation of the marine environment, and other rights and duties as provided in the convention with due regard to the rights and duties of other states, and has to act in a manner compatible with the provisions therein. India's rights with respect to the seabed and subsoil are in accordance with Part VI of the convention that deals with the continental shelf. The EEZ is a vital maritime zone with an extraordinary jurisdiction under international law. It provides a great potential for resource exploitation in the water column, the seabed and its subsoil for India. However, along with its benefits, the EEZ is also a threat attractor of varying sensitivity.

The *continental shelf* is a primary maritime area forming the extended perimeter of the continent and the associated coastal plain. It comprises the seabed and the subsoil of the submarine areas that extend beyond the limits of the territorial waters throughout the natural propagation of its land territory to the outer edge of the continental margin, or to a distance of 200 nautical miles from the base line where the outer edge of the continental margin does not extend to that distance.

In addition, the government may by notification declare certain waters as *historic waters*, and specify the limits adjacent to its land territory. The sovereignty of India shall extend, and always extended, to these waters, the seabed, the underlying subsoil and the airspace over such waters up to the notified limit. The waters in the Palk Strait, Palk Bay and Gulf of Mannar between India and Sri Lanka were declared as historic waters on 15 January 1977.

The world maritime trade moves through sea lines of communication (SLOC). The obligation of a coastal state to keep the SLOC around it safe for navigation is coordinated by a designated nation on the rim. India is one of the navigational area coordinators and the hydrographic department of the Indian Navy issues navigational warnings and notices in this area.

In most of cases, unlawful activists deviate from recognised SLOCs and proceed with stealth towards their destination or target. In a research study by the author, these routes are termed the sea-lanes of traffic (SLOT),[11] more or less the hidden highways at sea used for unlawful activities. It is necessary for India to map the SLOTs around it for enforcement and security operations with respect to each unlawful activity, but presently this is not done. Most SLOTs are in the territorial waters of a coastal state and it is easy to slip into them from bordering states with adjacent land and maritime borders. Often the coastal state or the landing point or area in the coastal state need not be the target, but it has the responsibility to ensure the waters around it are safe. The territorial waters of India should be sanitised by the enforcement regimes of the respective coastal states and union territories either independently or jointly with the central enforcement forces and agencies. This is important for effectiveness in operation. The entire water body around India's mainland as well as islands can be utilised as SLOTs and maritime intelligence is vital to monitor this area. Close to the shore, SLOTs converge towards temporary or permanent landing sites or rivers and creeks, and may continue inland through internal waters.

The maritime dimension of India is asymmetrical to that of its neighbours. India has signed 12 maritime boundary agreements with five out of seven of its maritime neighbours, and all its maritime neighbours have ratified UNCLOS, except for Thailand. The attitudes and external and internal policies of maritime neighbours and more distant countries will have a direct bearing on the issues India will face in its maritime zones, and unlawful activities will form a major part of these. India has the fifteenth largest coastline in the world and large maritime zones in the Indian Ocean, with an equivalent ocean property[12] to govern and strategic interests to manage. A brief summary of India's overall maritime dimensions is given in Table 16.1.

Table 16.1 The maritime dimensions of India

Area		*Dimensions*
1	Coastline	
	Mainland	5,422.6 km
	Lakshadweep	132 km
	Andaman and Nicobar Islands	1,962 km
	Total	7,516.6 km
2	Internal waters linked to sea for navigation	Gulf of Kachch, Gulf of Khambhat, Hooghly River, navigable channels linking ports
3	Territorial waters	
	Distance from baseline	12 nm
	Area	155,889 km^2
	Perimeter	8,682 km
4	Contiguous zone	
	Distance from baseline	24 nm
	Perimeter	9,315 km
5	Exclusive Economic Zone	
	Distance from baseline	200 nm
	Area	2,013,410 km^2
6	Historic waters	Palk Strait, Palk Bay, Gulf of Mannar
7	Legal Continental Shelf	
	Expected additional area	530,000 km^2
8	Search and Rescue Region	
	Area	4,600,000 km^2
9	Deep sea-bed mining	
	Area	150,000 km^2
	Distance from mainland	1,080 nm due south from Cape Comorin
10	Antarctica	First station was established in 1983
11	Major ports	12
12	Minor ports	184
13	Private ports	2
14	Islands	1,197
	Lakshadweep	11 inhabited
	Andaman and Nicobar	16 uninhabited
	Near shore – mainland	36 inhabited (24 in Andaman, 12 in Nicobar)
		536 uninhabited
		447 west
		151 east

Conclusion

The maritime problems that India faces will vary in degrees to all ranges and levels of possible unlawful activities that exist at present and are possible in the future. It is from this perspective that the state of preparedness of India has to be visualised. India needs the capability to constitutionally enforce the rule of law at sea. The capability of a nation depends on the capacity[13] of its forces and the legislative acuity in handling the issues. India needs to constantly review and upgrade its capacity as the challenges at sea and from the sea show up under varying circumstances.

Notes

1 A term used by the author in his book, *National Security: Imperatives and Challenges* (New Delhi: Tata McGraw Hill Publishing Ltd, 2008), to explain the relatively unchanging nature of the human system.

2 Military intervention can be declared or undeclared. In the case of containing terrorism and handling unlawful combatants, the application of laws of war is debatable.

3 The terrorists allegedly came by sea from Karachi to Mumbai on 26 November 2008. A total of 173 people were reportedly massacred and 308 wounded in ten different locations in Mumbai where the terrorist went on a on a coordinated killing spree, www.Wikipedia.org.

4 P. Paleri, *Coast Guards of the World and Emerging Maritime Threats* (Tokyo: Ocean Policy Research Foundation, 2009), Table 1.8, pp. 34–42, www.sof.or.jp/en/report/pdf/200903_ISSN1880–0017.pdf.

5 The author's perception through research as a visiting research fellow at the Ocean Policy Research Foundation, Tokyo, June–November 2008, and a senior research fellow at RSIS, NTU, Singapore, January–March 2009.

6 It is the opinion of the author that the term 'coastal security' is a misnomer, since the maritime borders cannot be equated to land borders. 'Maritime border security' is a better term, based on the principles of maritime jurisdiction under international law.

7 The 1999 Kargil War took place between 8 May, when Pakistani forces and Kashmiri militants were detected atop the Kargil ridges in the disputed Kashmiri territory, and 14 July, when both sides had essentially ceased military operations. See '1999 Kargil Conflict', *GlobalSecurity.org*, www.globalsecurity.org/military/world/war/kargil-99.htm.

8 *The State v/s 15 Accused (named)* (2000, Sessions Case no. 197 in the Court of Sessions for Greater Mumbai, Mumbai, India).

9 UNCLOS Article 86.

10 UNCLOS Article 33.

11 P. Paleri, *Role of the Coast Guard in the Maritime Security of India*, 2nd edn (New Delhi: Knowledge World, 2007), p. 120.

12 Paleri, *Role of the Coast Guard in the Maritime Security of India*, pp. 108–109. Ocean property is a concept identified by the author in a research project and first published in the book. The collective term in line with the geoproperty concept comprises four elements, ocean resources, ocean advantage, oceanic islands and ocean environment, the maximisation of which will lead to the maximisation of maritime security. Every nation has to understand the quantum of its ocean property and use it to its maximum advantage.

13 The 'capacity' of a force is an oft-quoted term, which could be used on various occasions under differing meanings. This study assumes that the government, by formally designing and creating the force, also ensures that it will have the 'capacity' to perform its duties and functions. To that extent the capacity of a force means, personnel quality standards (PQS), professional competence of the organisation to perform its duties and functions assigned under the act, organisational acuity and zeal, authority and accountability, force level, compatibility of weapons and sensors with the assigned role, supporting legislations for enforcement, infrastructure, equipment, cohesion, identity and freedom of operation and avenues for career development. Capacity development is a holistic process that is external as well as internal to an organisation.

17 New Zealand's maritime challenges and opportunities[1]

Joanna Mossop

Introduction

New Zealand is often referred to as a small country. In terms of land area and population, this is undoubtedly correct. However, when the maritime part of New Zealand's sovereign interests is considered, it becomes clear that New Zealand is, in fact, a large maritime nation. The absence of close neighbours allows New Zealand to claim an exclusive economic zone (EEZ) approximately 15 times the size of its land area. The size of this area and the distance from other states are the most significant causes of most of New Zealand's opportunities and challenges in dealing with this maritime area. However, other challenges are created by the relatively small economy and choices about priorities for managing oceans issues.

The EEZ covers more than 4 million square kilometres and is variously described as the world's fourth or fifth largest EEZ. The EEZ only meets that of another country in two places: in the north-west (Norfolk Island, Australia) and the south-west (Macquarie Island, Australia). In some places, when offshore islands are taken into account, the outer limit of the EEZ is further than 500 nm from the mainland.

New Zealand is now entitled to claim an extended continental shelf (the EEZ and extended continental shelf are shown in Figure 17.1). In September 2008, the Commission for the Limits of the Continental Shelf issued recommendations endorsing New Zealand's claim to an outer continental shelf of approximately 1.7 million square kilometres beyond the limits of the EEZ.[2] With these submissions in mind, New Zealand and Australia concluded an agreement on the boundary of their respective extended continental shelves in 2004.[3] The only maritime boundaries remaining to be agreed are in respect of the outer continental shelf boundaries with Tonga, Fiji, and possibly France in connection with New Caledonia.

The region of ocean for which New Zealand has search and rescue responsibilities is even greater: 30 million square kilometres, covering a large part of the Pacific Ocean from the Equator to the Antarctic, and from half-way to Australia to half-way to Chile (see Figure 17.2). This contributes to a sense that New Zealand's maritime interests extend well beyond its formal maritime zones. New

Zealand provides assistance to many South Pacific states on an ad hoc and ongoing basis. This includes provision of assistance with monitoring of fishing in their EEZs using Orion P3 aircraft. In 2009, New Zealand and Australia both provided navy divers to assist Tonga to locate the *Princess Ashika*, a ferry that sank with a loss of 74 lives.

It is important to keep in mind that although the maritime estate is large, in other respects New Zealand is still a small country. The per capita gross

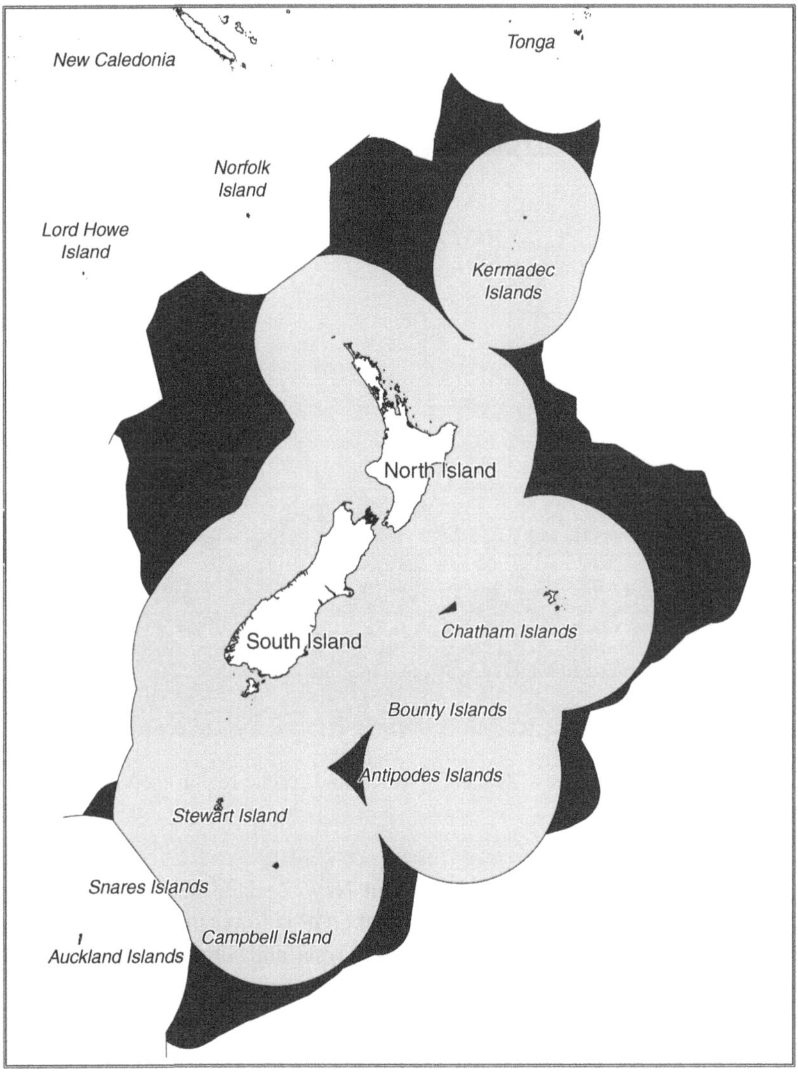

Figure 17.1 Map showing the boundaries of New Zealand's EEZ and extended continental shelf (source: Prof. Stuart Kaye, University of Western Australia).

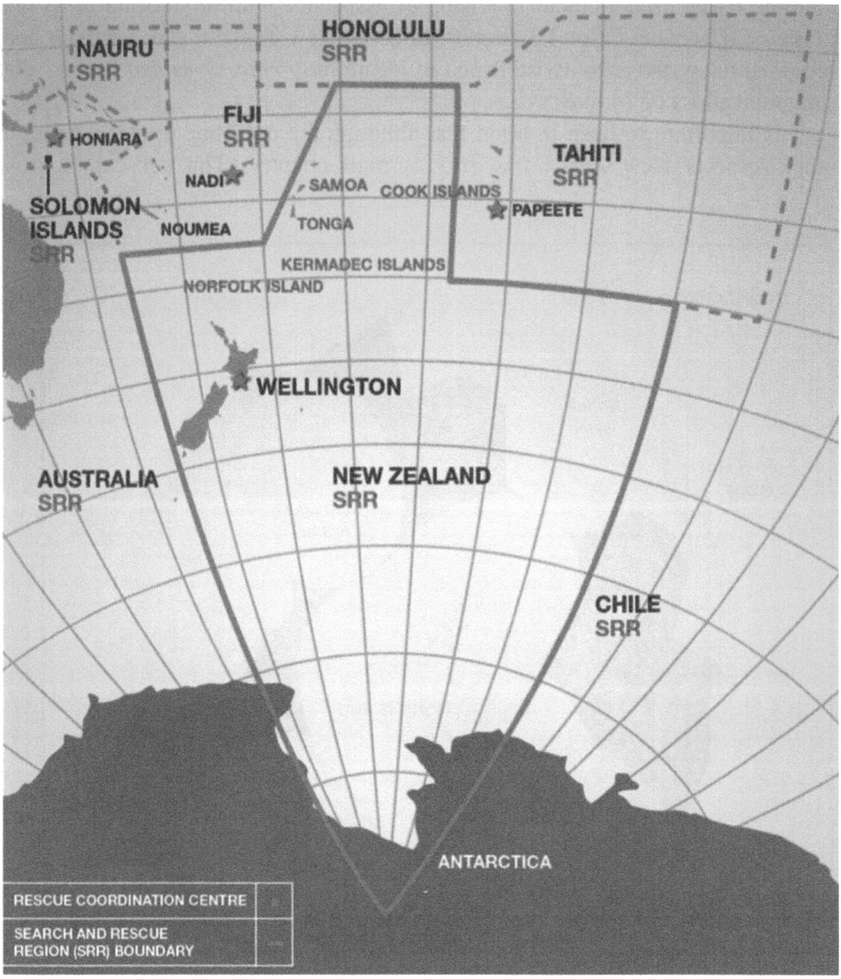

Figure 17.2 Map showing New Zealand's search and rescue region (source: Maritime New Zealand).

domestic product (GDP) is respectable,[4] but New Zealand has a population of only just over four million people and its total GDP is lower than many countries in the Asian region, including Indonesia, Malaysia and Singapore.[5] In the past, governments have not considered the oceans a high priority for spending, as will be discussed later in the chapter. This has arguably led to a situation of underfunding in relation to some maritime interests.

This chapter first provides a brief overview of many of New Zealand's interests in the maritime area, and then examines three issues that pose particular challenges for setting priorities: distance, awareness and governance.

New Zealand maritime interests[6]

Defence interests

New Zealand's large maritime zones have been described as a 'moat', implying that they convey a significant strategic benefit by dissuading hostile naval activity.[7] From a historical perspective, it is arguable that this is true. It is notable that New Zealand is among the few countries in the world never to have been directly attacked by any state.[8] Most commentators suggest that New Zealand faces no short- or medium-term direct military threat from other states.[9] This low risk and a general belief by the New Zealand public that New Zealand faces no significant defence threat has contributed to successive governments taking a relatively specialised approach to defence spending: emphasis has been placed on interoperability with the forces of other states and therefore on specialisation rather than developing a broad defence force. This is partly due to a view that New Zealand's military would be able to do little in practical terms against a military threat and that New Zealand's interests are best served by pursuing foreign policy goals.[10]

A number of states, particularly Australia, have been somewhat critical of the level of New Zealand's spending on defence, arguing that it needs to commit greater resources to its military.[11] It is true that New Zealand commits a comparatively low amount to military spending. It has been estimated that in 2005, New Zealand's spending on defence programmes was approximately 1 per cent of GDP, one of the lowest in the region (Table 17.1).

The importance of the defence force role in the maritime zones is explicitly recognised by the New Zealand Defence Force (NZDF). The NZDF mentions

Table 17.1 Comparative military expenditures by selected countries in the region as a percentage of GDP[12]

Country	*Military expenditure*
Australia	2.4
Brunei	4.5
Cambodia	3.0
China	4.3
India	2.5
Indonesia	3.0
Japan	0.8
Republic of Korea	2.7
Malaysia	2.0
Myanmar	2.1
New Zealand	1.0
Philippines	0.9
Singapore	4.9
Thailand	1.8
United States	4.1
Vietnam	2.5

the maritime domain in its mission statement, which is 'to secure New Zealand against external threat, to protect our sovereign interests, including in the exclusive economic zone (EEZ) and to be able to take action to meet likely contingencies in our strategic area of interest'.[13] More specifically, the NZDF states that it will 'secure New Zealand, including its people, and, territorial waters, exclusive economic zone, natural resources and critical infrastructure'.[14] Therefore, the protection of marine economic and environmental resources is seen as an important goal for the NZDF. It is interesting to note that neither the mission statement nor the strategic plan more generally refers to protection of New Zealand's interests on the continental shelf beyond 200 nm. Following the outcome of New Zealand's submission to the Commission on the Limits of the Continental Shelf, the protection of sovereign interests in this area is likely to become an issue for New Zealand.[15]

The branches of the NZDF most involved in maritime matters are the Royal New Zealand Navy (RNZN) and the Royal New Zealand Air Force (RNZAF).

Shipping and trade

New Zealand is dependent on shipping. Approximately 98 per cent of New Zealand's imports and exports by volume are carried by sea. Many of these shipments originate in ports such as Southampton, Panama, Tokyo, Singapore, Los Angeles or Sydney, and a large proportion travel through areas vulnerable to interruptions due to piracy or terrorism. Therefore, New Zealand has always been aware of the importance of supporting freedom of navigation and the need to suppress unlawful acts that might interfere with shipping. Because of New Zealand's long supply lines, a major interruption to shipping would be devastating to its economy.

The terror alerts of the 2000s have led to a number of states, especially the United States, in taking measures to ensure the safety of shipping containers. These measures have included increased requirements for inspections and scanning of containers and improved supply chain verification and documentation. Aware of the potential for interruption to trade, New Zealand has been ensuring that our domestic processes meet the new requirements. For example, New Zealand Customs has worked closely with the United States to develop robust procedures for screening of shipping to United States ports through a Supply Chain Security arrangement. It was one of the first in the world to develop this procedure, which involves using risk assessment and intelligence to identify high-risk shipments to receive special attention. Another innovation is a voluntary scheme called the Secure Export Partnership Scheme in which businesses undertake security measures in return for their shipments being classified as secure.[16]

Maritime resources

The fishing industry is an important contributor to the New Zealand economy. There are 1,277 commercial fishing vessels operating in New Zealand waters.

Seafood exports in 2007 were worth NZ$1.3 billion and the commercial industry directly employs over 7,000 people.[17] As well as an active capture fishery industry, New Zealand has a growing aquaculture industry in a range of species. Aquaculture exports account for NZ$223 million annually.[18] There is an interest in fish resources beyond the commercial industry: approximately 30 per cent of the New Zealand population participate in some form of recreational fishing. With these economic and social values, there is a clear need to ensure that the fish stocks are managed sustainably, and this is a high priority for the New Zealand Government. Challenges to this goal include overfishing of target stocks by New Zealanders as well as foreign vessels and the impact of fishing on the ecosystem. However, many commentators agree that New Zealand's fisheries management model has played a role in ensuring the sustainability of commercial fish species.[19]

In addition to fisheries in New Zealand's maritime zones, there are a number of New Zealand fishers who operate in the maritime zones of other countries, or on the high seas. New Zealand registered fishing vessels, or New Zealand operators of chartered foreign fishing vessels operating outside New Zealand, are required to hold a New Zealand high seas fishing permit. New Zealand nationals are forbidden from using a foreign vessel to fish on the high seas, unless they hold a permit from a state party to a regional fisheries management organisation or relevant international agreement.[20]

Oil and gas production is a significant aspect of New Zealand's economy. It is estimated that in 2008 oil production in New Zealand – the bulk of which takes place off the Taranaki coast – reached NZ$2 billion.[21] Estimates of the oil reserves in the Taranaki basin range from 79 to 1,114 million barrels of oil equivalent, but experts believe that more reserves remain to be discovered.[22] Gas production is also an important contributor to the energy market. The production of gas is estimated to be NZ$1,000 million annually.[23] In total, the oil, gas and mineral market contributed 1.1 per cent of New Zealand's GDP in 2005.[24]

Recent attention has turned to the possibility of exploiting extensive deposits of gas hydrates, many of which are located to the west and south of the North Island. The expectation is that development of this resource could reduce the need for future liquefied natural gas imports, lower the cost of gas in New Zealand and possibly lead to gas exports.[25]

There is little current information available about the extent and value of marine bioprospecting in New Zealand. There is some activity by universities, Crown Research Institutes and private companies. New Zealand has recognised that its regulatory framework governing bioprospecting is fragmented and has possible gaps, and is working to address these issues.[26]

Overall, it is clear that while the fisheries industry is arguably working to capacity at present, there is the potential for expansion of the maritime oil, gas and mineral sectors. The New Zealand Government recently announced an action plan to maximise the benefits for the country's petroleum resources.[27] There will undoubtedly be great interest in exploring the potential of other under-utilised resources located in New Zealand's maritime zones.

Terrorism, piracy and transnational crime

New Zealand has experienced one act of maritime terrorism, which was the bombing of a Greenpeace vessel, the *Rainbow Warrior*. On 10 July 1985, the *Rainbow Warrior* was damaged by two explosive devices while in port in Auckland. The ship sank, killing one crew member. Subsequent police investigations resulted in the arrest and conviction of two members of the French Armed Forces for arson and manslaughter.[28] The attack on the vessel took place in the context of the anti-nuclear protests against French nuclear testing in the Pacific. Although this incident was serious, and impacted on New Zealand's sense of security, it does not fit the profile of current concerns about maritime terrorism, which focus on the threats posed by non-state actors.

In fact, it is generally accepted that the risk of a maritime terrorism incident occurring in New Zealand is low, particularly compared to other areas of the world. However, New Zealand officials consider terrorism and piracy to be serious issues for two reasons. First, as already mentioned, any significant disruption in international shipping will potentially interrupt the flow of trade goods on which New Zealand's economy depends. New Zealand's economy could also be affected if such an incident increased the cost of shipping – possibly due to higher insurance premiums – as New Zealand exporters must compete in markets on the other side of the world. The second reason is that New Zealand is a member of international organisations that have created a number of new procedures and legal standards to improve maritime safety. For example, the International Ship and Port Facility Security Code has been implemented in all major New Zealand ports and New Zealand is in the process of evaluating building greater awareness of commercial shipping using long-range information and tracking, and automated information systems. Since 2004, New Zealand has participated in the Proliferation Security Initiative, including as an active member of the Operational Experts Group (OEG). It has hosted both a meeting of the OEG and an exercise in Auckland in September 2008 that involved 27 states.

It is arguable that commercial shipping poses a relatively insignificant threat to maritime security. Other forms of shipping, such as fishing vessels and small pleasure craft are less regulated and able to by-pass major ports if they wish. In the case of the *Rainbow Warrior*, it is believed that the convicted French agents arrived in New Zealand in a yacht from Nouméa. Gaps in information about the movement of pleasure craft throughout the Pacific have caused concern to officials.[29]

The use of ships to transport drugs, people and illegal goods is naturally a significant concern for New Zealand, and a range of agencies including police, customs and immigration are responsible for responding to these risks. Customs and police are intercepting an increasing amount of illicit drugs entering New Zealand in shipping containers.[30] Of particular recent concern have been interceptions of precursor substances in the manufacture of methamphetamine, often from the Asian region. Drugs are often hidden in shipping containers,[31] although other forms of smuggling also exist. In 2006, large packages of cocaine were discovered attached to the hulls of two vessels heading from South America to Sydney, Australia.[32] In these forms of smuggling, the crew may not even be aware of the presence of the drugs.

New Zealand is not considered to be a significant destination for human trafficking, although some evidence is that a small number of sex workers may be victims of trafficking.[33] New Zealand acknowledges the risk that illegal migrants may use vessels as a method of reaching New Zealand, and there have been occasional examples of ship jumping by crews.

Protection of the marine environment

The environmental integrity of New Zealand's oceans has importance for economic activities such as fishing, as well as social values including ecological sustainability. New Zealand has not yet suffered a catastrophic oil spill in the nature of the *Exxon Valdez* or *Prestige*.[34] However, there are a number of small spills annually. Approximately 160 oil spills are reported in New Zealand waters each year, and about 35 of these are detected through aerial monitoring.[35] The authority dealing with environmental protection, Maritime New Zealand, is rigorous about the enforcement of New Zealand's marine environmental protection rules.

The introduction of species, pests and diseases from maritime traffic is a serious risk for New Zealand, which has many unique species and is free from many pests found elsewhere. Some marine-based alien invasive species have caused considerable devastation among native species and threatened activities such as aquaculture.[36] There is also the concern that species may be introduced via cargo or baggage. New Zealand generally imposes stringent controls on the introduction of potentially harmful species at the border, and the maritime environment is one aspect of this approach. New Zealand has been active, through the International Maritime Organisation, in initiatives to reduce the risk of introduced species through ballast water and on ship's hulls.

Opportunities and challenges created by distance

The fact that New Zealand is physically isolated from its near neighbours[37] creates opportunities and challenges. The most significant opportunity is the ability to claim very large maritime zones – as already mentioned, New Zealand can claim maritime zones almost unimpeded by the claims of other countries. This allows the country to potentially have control over a significant amount of resources, although for much of the truly distant waters, not much has been done to exploit the mineral resources. Since 1977, when New Zealand claimed an EEZ, the fishing industry has undergone significant growth and change to take advantage of the sovereign rights over fisheries in the large area.

Another benefit of the distance from its neighbours is the security offered from traditional warfare, as well as piracy and many forms of transnational crime. For example, although Australia has had an influx of illegal migrants and refugee seekers by sea, New Zealand has not had the same difficulties. This is not to say that the possibility does not exist – indeed, as other destinations are closed down or made more risky by vigilant authorities, it is probable that New Zealand will become a destination for people-smuggling in the future. However, the greater practical problems in reaching New Zealand has so far dissuaded efforts to use boats to convey illegal immigrants there in any great numbers.

However, the distance from the rest of the world poses as many, if not more, challenges for New Zealand. The long supply chain imposes costs on exporters that are not faced by competitors elsewhere. New Zealand is reliant on the major shipping companies continuing to trade in New Zealand – a significant vulnerability. This reliance is exacerbated by the fact that deregulation of the shipping sector allowed foreign vessels to undertake coastal shipping in New Zealand, potentially undercutting local companies that must comply with New Zealand safety and crewing standards. The result has been that there are no New Zealand international shipping firms, and few New Zealand-owned coastal shipping operators. If, for example, international firms decided to stop servicing many of the coastal ports, which could have serious economic outcomes, the New Zealand Government may not be able to influence this decision,.

Another current concern for New Zealand exporters is the growing call, particularly in Europe, to penalise goods that have travelled long distances for their impact on the climate. The idea of 'carbon miles' is potentially devastating for New Zealand, which has no choice about the fact that its trade goods must travel a long way to their markets. In the United Kingdom, there has been a consumer movement to buy local products due to their supposedly lower carbon imprint. New Zealand has had to work quite hard to counter these ideas: the dairy industry has pointed out that although dairy products from New Zealand travel a long way, dairy products from New Zealand overall bear a lower carbon footprint because of the much less intensive methods of farming. However, this issue, and the potential impact on the economy, is likely to remain a critical one for New Zealand in the near future.

Another issue that has not yet raised much concern in New Zealand is its potential vulnerability to infrastructure failures – either deliberate or accidental. In particular, the dependence of Australia and New Zealand on submarine cables for telecommunication purposes is very high, and disruption to these cables would have severe impacts on the economy.[38] There are only three submarine cables serving New Zealand, and it is not impossible to imagine that they could be targets in the event that New Zealand became a terrorist target.

The other major obstacle is the small size of New Zealand's economy. Although the government was able to run budget surpluses until the recent economic crisis, in 2010 the government was borrowing approximately NZ$200 million a week to sustain spending at around the level before the crisis hit. There is pressure to reduce government expenditure on areas considered to be low priorities, which often include defence and oceans issues.

Improving awareness of New Zealand's maritime areas

For a country that prides itself on the extent of its maritime domain, remarkably little is known about the extended maritime areas or what happens there. In some aspects, this need for information is related to the concept of maritime domain awareness, which also focuses on the need for information in order to make an early identification of potential threats.[39] However, the need for information and awareness goes beyond the security context. A serious lack of awareness creates several challenges. It means that New Zealand is not well placed to maximise its resource interests, that poor governance decisions may be made based on incomplete information, and that the area is vulnerable to illicit exploitation such as illegal fishing.

In this section, I will focus on two aspects of awareness: surveillance and enforcement; and scientific information.

Surveillance and enforcement

New Zealand's ability to monitor and control activities in its maritime zones has undergone a significant review in the last ten years. Although civilian agencies such as police, customs and fisheries have their own dedicated vessels, these are few and primarily designed for limited in-shore surveillance and enforcement. Therefore, for tasks in more remote areas, or tasks in areas not served by a dedicated vessel, these agencies have traditionally relied on the NZDF to make military assets available. During the latter part of the twentieth century, the majority of surveillance of the EEZ was undertaken by RNZAF P3 Orion aircraft. In 1999, the NZDF sought additional funding to update the avionics of the Orion aircraft. In response, the government decided to undertake a review of the maritime surveillance capability, and the result was the 2001 Maritime Patrol Review (MPR).[40] The MPR's purpose was to assess the civilian requirements for maritime patrols and surveillance, and determine how they could best be met.

The MPR found that a very limited level of patrolling of New Zealand's EEZ was being undertaken by military or civilian agencies.[41] Although information was available about fisheries vessels through vessel monitoring systems, information about other vessels' activities was lacking. In addition there was a lack of cooperation between civilian and military agencies, and even within different branches of the NZDF.[42] The MPR found that civilian agencies were frustrated by the inability to use the NZDF assets for civilian purposes, and concluded that the allocation of those assets for civilian tasks was inadequate.[43] Very little routine surveillance of New Zealand waters was undertaken by the RNZN, but using frigates for that purpose was not considered to be an appropriate use of the resource and no other vessels were appropriately configured for the work.[44] Future areas of need were identified for fisheries, customs and marine safety and environmental protection, as well as minor requirements for conservation.[45]

The MPR made a number of recommendations to improve the efficacy of maritime patrolling in New Zealand waters.[46] First, it recommended the establishment of a Maritime Coordination Centre 'to collect information and manage tasking for all forms of military and civilian maritime surveillance to meet civilian needs' in New Zealand maritime zones, the South Pacific and the Southern Ocean. The Maritime Coordination Centre would develop means to enhance all elements of maritime patrol, including developing a ship reporting system for New Zealand waters to improve knowledge of activities in those waters. Second, the NZDF should be required to provide assets to be available for civilian purposes to a specified level, under tasking from the Maritime Coordination Centre. Third, the MPR recommended that a capacity for sea surface maritime patrol be developed. The MPR envisaged a combination of in-shore patrol vessels, vessels with mid-range offshore capabilities and a multi-role vessel with the ability to operate in the Pacific and the Southern Oceans.

The National Maritime Coordination Centre (NMCC) was established as a pilot in 2002 and its existence confirmed in December 2006.[47] The NMCC is primarily responsible for coordinating the allocation of maritime patrol assets for civilian purposes.[48] It is also expected to coordinate information about maritime activities that pose risks to New Zealand and provide that information to the relevant government agencies. Finally, it is expected to identify policy gaps and other issues regarding effective maritime patrol and surveillance. The NMCC is physically located at the NZDF Headquarters Joint Force, but administrative responsibility lies with customs, and the operation is overseen by a network of Chief Executives of New Zealand Government agencies. Currently, allocation of assets is achieved according to requests for time made by the agencies, which are discussed among the agencies involved. Ultimately, the NMCC may make the final determination on the allocation of assets in the event of disagreement.

The most significant achievement of the NMCC has been the creation of a transparent system for allocating military assets for civilian tasks. In addition, it has completed work on a risk assessment framework which informs the decision making process on priority areas to be targeted. As resourcing is improving in the NMCC, the capacity to take on policy and strategic work is expanding. However, it is important to understand the limitations of the NMCC. It did not create an integrated decision making process for all maritime security issues: rather it is a cooperative mechanism that individual agencies use to achieve their surveillance and enforcement objectives. There is also still significant work to be done on integrating sources of intelligence and information so that all government agencies have access to comprehensive information about activities in the maritime environment.

Following the MPR, a review of defence capabilities led to the emergence of two significant developments in military capability: Project Protector, which involved a significant reconfiguration of naval capability; and the upgrade of the P3 Orion communication and surveillance equipment.

Protect Protector is a NZ$500 million project designed to significantly enhance New Zealand's ability to respond to maritime threats.[49] The project is managed by the RNZN, and vessels began to enter into active service from 2007. Project Protector is delivering seven new vessels.[50] HMNZS *Canterbury* is a multi-role vessel based on a roll-on-roll-off commercial model of ship. This vessel is expected to provide a sealift capability for the transport and deployment of equipment, vehicles and personnel, and is capable of transferring cargo and personnel ashore in benign conditions when port facilities are not available. *Canterbury* can carry up to four NH90 helicopters and two 59-tonne Landing Craft Medium (LCM) capable of carrying 50 tonnes at nine knots with a range of 250 nm.[51]

In addition to the multi-role vessel, Project Protector is also delivering two offshore patrol vessels with a range of 6,000 nm, expected to be able to operate throughout New Zealand's EEZ as well as in the Pacific Islands. The offshore patrol vessels can carry a Seasprite helicopter.[52] Four in-shore patrol vessels with a range of 3,000 nm are also being delivered.[53] All the vessels in the Project Protector fleet are designed to support civilian agencies, and have dedicated space for civilian officials.

The NZDF is also undertaking an upgrade of the P3 Orion mission management, communications and navigation systems.[54] Included in the upgrade is new technology to improve the range of surveillance, as well as ensuring that the P3s can get imagery in all weather conditions and around the clock. It is expected that the upgrades will allow the P3 Orions to cover more area during their surveillance flights. New Zealand has six P3 Orions located at Whenuapai Air Base near Auckland. Currently, the P3 Orions fly 400 hours annually on dedicated civilian surveillance tasks.

It is expected that with the delivery of the new naval vessels New Zealand's ability for surface patrolling in its EEZ will dramatically increase, bringing improved enforcement and deterrence outcomes. At present, there is little capacity for coordination between New Zealand naval patrols and air surveillance, but the increased capability of Project Protector should allow better use of those assets in combination. However, it must be acknowledged that even the significant upgrade from Project Protector will only go a small way to meeting the challenge of fully responding to what is happening in New Zealand's maritime zones.

Scientific knowledge

A further concern about knowledge is related to the standard of scientific knowledge about New Zealand's marine environment. For example, only approximately 13–20 per cent of New Zealand's maritime zones have been mapped in any detail. This inhibits decision-making about maritime activities. As the uses of the oceans expand – such as increased oil and gas exploration, ocean energy production, deep-sea aquaculture and calls for protection of the marine environment – it will be even more important to understand what the shape of the marine environment is, and the potential impact of such uses on other interests and on ocean ecosystems. At present, the people with the most information tend to be the parties seeking to begin a new activity, and there is little baseline information against which applications can be assessed.

New Zealand has begun the process of addressing this knowledge imbalance. The Oceans Survey 20/20 project was announced in 2005, with the ambitious aim that by 2020 the project would produce an ocean survey that would provide New Zealand with the knowledge of its ocean territory to allow New Zealand to exercise its sovereign rights; conserve, protect, manage and sustainably utilise the ocean resources; and facilitate safe navigation.[55] The goal was to coordinate the need for information across government agencies and set priorities for the completion of research. The whole government approach is managed by Land Information New Zealand.

A number of projects were begun under Oceans Survey 20/20, and 56 projects are planned in total. It appears that two have been completed and one is currently underway,[56] a completion rate that appears unlikely to meet the goal of finishing by 2020. However, at a time when the government has to prioritise expenditure and cut a number of funding streams, it is perhaps foreseeable – although regrettable – that this promising project is struggling to attract ongoing support.

Maximising the opportunities: struggling with governance

As in many other countries, New Zealand's oceans governance framework has tended to be fragmented and poorly planned.[57] A wide range of government agencies have responsibilities directly or incidentally impacting on the use of the ocean. Agencies with significant maritime responsibilities include the Ministry of Fisheries; the Ministry of Transport (maritime security and shipping strategies); Maritime New Zealand (environmental protection and maritime safety); the Ministry of Foreign Affairs (international policy and management of foreign requests for marine scientific research); the Department of Conservation (marine protected areas); the NZDF; the Ministry for the Environment (resource management and EEZ regulation); the New Zealand Customs Service; Biosecurity New Zealand; the Ministry for Economic Development (mineral exploration and bioprospecting); and the New Zealand Police Force. This is not an exhaustive list. In addition, management of various activities is governed by a confusing array of separate pieces of legislation. Clearly, the potential for inconsistent policy development is considerable in this environment. A sectoral system of governance is likely to lead to a race for the allocation of space that, unless decision-making is well integrated, can result in winners and losers, as well as outcomes that would not have been intended if a strategic approach were taken.[58]

One of the most important weaknesses with this arrangement is that there is no strategic overview allowing prioritisation of oceanic activities or the resolution of competing uses. Contributing to the problem is the possibility that many activities (other than fisheries) may be poorly regulated, or not regulated at all. For example, interest has been expressed by foreign companies in using New Zealand maritime areas for experimental ocean fertilisation activities where large amounts of iron would be 'seeded' in the ocean to stimulate phytoplankton growth. At the time that this interest was expressed, it was not clear that New Zealand had adequate legislation in place to regulate the proposed activity.

The problems with New Zealand's legislative and administrative framework for oceans governance were highlighted when the New Zealand Government began a process to establish a national Oceans Policy in 2000. The Oceans Policy was intended to lead to a governance framework allowing integrated decision-making that reflected values shared by New Zealanders.[59] However, after a long consultation process and a large amount of work, the process was suspended in 2003. The reason given was the controversy that broke out over ownership of the foreshore and seabed following a Court of Appeal case that opened the possibility that some Maori and not the Crown might be able to claim ownership of that area. However, even after legislation was passed addressing the matter, Oceans Policy work was not resumed. It is surmised that the government decided that the process was too ambitious and preferred a simpler approach to addressing gaps in the regulatory framework.

Progress has now been made on addressing the gaps in the regulatory framework identified during the Oceans Policy process. The government is expected to introduce legislation in 2012 creating a decision-making framework in respect of activities not already regulated, a necessary and important move. Government officials are working better together at an informal level to ensure that common issues are receiving a coordinated approach. However, the failure of the Oceans Policy process is a lost opportunity to overcome the sectoral, ad hoc and sometimes inconsistent nature of oceans governance in New Zealand. It seems that oceans governance is still considered a low priority in the view of the current government.

Conclusion

All states in the region have interests in ensuring their maritime zones are managed sustainably and that peace and good order is maintained. New Zealand shares these interests but, due to the geographic situation of the country, issues caused by large maritime zones and a comparatively small economy make New Zealand's challenges and priorities unique in the region. In many respects, New Zealand is relatively well positioned, as it does not have the domestic concerns about piracy and terrorist activity that are a great concern elsewhere. Similarly, traditional security concerns and some transnational crime issues are lessened due to the distance from its neighbours. However, this does not mean that New Zealand can afford to grow complacent, or to believe that the concerns of its neighbours do not affect it. Certainly, New Zealand officials believe that issues impacting on the region also have a real impact on New Zealand. Their involvement in international initiatives aimed at addressing matters such as piracy and terrorism reflects this.

One of the serious obstacles in responding to New Zealand's maritime opportunities and challenges is a remarkable level of apathy among the public towards issues governing the use of the oceans. Because New Zealand has few high profile risks to its security and economy from the ocean, New Zealanders in general do not tend to worry too much about what is over the horizon. This contrasts with Australia, where concerns about border security have been high on the public's consciousness and it is therefore a priority for the Australian Federal Government. In a time of scarce government resources, it can be difficult to convince the government to invest heavily in oceans matters when there is little public pressure to do so.

This is not always the case. The New Zealand Government was acutely aware of the potential of the delimitation of the extended continental shelf to add to its area of sovereign interests, and provided funding to allow the best case possible to be put forward. However, outside of a small range of interested officials and non-governmental groups, the enthusiasm to create better governance structures has been lacking. Work to explore the economic value of marine resources continues to be somewhat ad hoc. If New Zealand is truly to maximise its maritime opportunities and minimise the risks, more effort can and should be put into resolving the issues outlined in this chapter.

Notes

1 This chapter is based on a presentation given at a conference, Maritime Challenges and Priorities in Asia, 20 January 2010, and is correct to that date.

2 See 'Summary of the Recommendations of the Commission on the Limits of the Continental Shelf (CLCS) in regard to the submission made by New Zealand 19 April 2006', 22 August 2008, www.un.org/Depts/los/clcs_new/submissions_files/nzl06/nzl_summary_of_recommendations.pdf.

3 *Treaty between the Government of New Zealand and the Government of Australia Establishing Certain Exclusive Economic Zone Boundaries and Continental Shelf Boundaries*, exchange of notes, 25 July 2004.

4 US$26,538 per capita in 2005. World Bank, http://siteresources.worldbank.org/ICPINT/Resources/icp-final-tables.pdf.

5 According to the World Bank World Development Indicators database, in 2008 the GDP of Indonesia was US$514 billion, Malaysia US$194 billion, Singapore US$181 billion, and New Zealand US$130 billion; www.worldbank.org.

6 This section is an extension of themes discussed in J. Mossop, 'Maritime Security in New Zealand', in N Klein, J. Mossop and D. Rothwell (eds), *Maritime Security: International Law and Policy Perspectives from Australia and New Zealand* (London: Routledge, 2009), pp. 54–75.

7 Terence O'Brien, 'Looking Out from Down Under: Diverging World Views', in Ralph Pettman (ed.), *New Zealand in a Globalising World* (Wellington: Victoria University Press, 2005), pp. 141–151, at p. 145.

8 D. McLean, *The Prickly Pair*, p. 257. As possible exceptions to this statement, McLean notes the mining of Auckland and Wellington harbours by Germany during World War Two (no loss of life ensued) and the *Rainbow Warrior* bombing in Auckland Harbour in 1985 (loss of one life). It is notable that these two incidents are both maritime.

9 Hugh White, 'New Zealand and Australia – Foreign Policy and Armed Conflict', speech to the New Zealand Institute of International Affairs, 8 October 2002, www.aspi.org.au/admin/eventFiles/publications.htm. See also *NZDF Annual Report 2006–7*, www.nzdf.mil.nz/public-documents/annual-report/default.htm, p. 16; J. Rolfe, *Cutting their Cloth: New Zealand's Defence Strategy* (Canberra: Australian Strategic Policy Institute, 2007), pp. 7–8. This view is not universally shared. See, for example, R, Smith, 'Looking at Defence Contingencies', in J. Veitch (ed.), *Strategic*

Manoeuvres: Security in the Asia-Pacific (Wellington: Centre for Strategic Studies, 2009), pp. 53–64, at p. 57.

10 Rolf, pp. 32–33.

11 Rolf, p. 35.

12 Data taken from the CIA World Fact Book, https://www.cia.gov/library/publications/the-world-factbook/index.html. Most figures are based on 2005 and 2006 data. The figures do not break spending down into maritime and terrestrial defence.

13 *New Zealand Defence Force Strategic Plan 2007–2011*, p. 2, www.nzdf.mil.nz.

14 Ibid.

15 In 2009, the Ministry of Defence undertook a Defence Review, with the aim of providing 'a fundamental assessment of New Zealand's security environment, as well as the roles and tasks the defence force is expected to fulfil and the capabilities it requires to achieve these'. For information see www.defence.govt.nz/defence-review.html. It is understood that the NZDF mission statement and other policies may be updated to rectify the current omission of the continental shelf.

16 By 2006–2007, 44 per cent of containers from New Zealand were covered by the scheme. *New Zealand Customs Annual Report 2006–7*, www.customs.govt.nz/library/Accountability+Documents/Annual+Report/Annual+Report+2006–2007.htm.

17 Ministry of Fisheries, www.fish.govt.nz. More than 90 per cent of fish landed in New Zealand are exported.

18 Ministry of Fisheries.

19 For example, see C.J. Batstone and B.M.H. Sharp, 'New Zealand's quota management system: the first ten years', *Marine Policy*, 23, 1999, p. 177.

20 Sect. 113E, Fisheries Act 1996 (NZ). See also *Draft HMS Fisheries Plan*, p. 23, www.fish.govt.nz.

21 R. Barker *The Natural Resource Potential of New Zealand* 2008, p. 4, www.minerals.co.nz/pdf/Natural_Resource_NZ_web.pdf.

22 Barker, p. 7.

23 Barker, p. 6.

24 McDouall Stuart, *Stepping Up: Options for Developing the Potential of New Zealand's Oil, Gas and Minerals Sector*, 2009, www.med.govt.nz/upload/70851/McDouall-Stuart-June-2009.pdf.

25 Centre for Advanced Engineering, *An Options Analysis for the Commercial and Economic Development of Offshore Methane Hydrates as a Future Energy Option for New Zealand* Christchurch: CAE, 2009, www.caenz.com/info/publications/books_reports/in_print/hydrates/hydrates.html.

26 Ministry of Economic Development, www.med.govt.nz.

27 Press release, Gerry Brownlie, 'Unlocking New Zealand's Petroleum Potential', 18 November 2009, www.beehive.govt.nz.

28 See M. King, *Death of the Rainbow Warrio*r (Auckland: Penguin, 1986).

29 For example, in 2006, New Zealand Customs data indicated 65 small craft departed New Zealand for Australia, but Australian Customs data indicated that number was 115. These discrepancies, among other informational gaps about the activities of small pleasure craft, are a cause for concern. See *Pacific Border Security Risks Posed by Ocean-Going Pleasure Craft* (Secretariat of the Pacific Community, 2008), p. 42.

30 *New Zealand Customs Annual Report 2006–7.*

31 For example, drugs have been discovered in shipments of bicycles, roofing material and washing powder.

32 Emily Watt, 'The Battle Against Drugs in 2006', *Dominion Post*, 6 January 2007, p. 10. In these cases, the drugs were detected on ships en route to Sydney. The parcels were removed by New Zealand Customs and replaced with other substances. The ship was then monitored on its arrival in Sydney and arrests made.

33 See www.humantrafficking.org/countries/new_zealand.

34 This statement was true at the time of writing. However, in October 2011, a cargo ship (MV *Rena*) ran aground of the coast of Tauranga, spilling up to 350 tonnes of bunker oil. This was considered New Zealand's worst maritime environmental disaster.
35 *Maritime Patrol Review*, p. 16.
36 See www.teara.govt.nz/en/marine-invaders/3.
37 New Caledonia is approximately 1,800 km from New Zealand. Australia and Fiji are more than 2,000 km from New Zealand.
38 See Stuart Kaye, 'The Protection of Platforms, Pipelines and Submarine Cables under Australian and New Zealand Law', in N. Klein, J. Mossop and D. Rothwell (eds), *Maritime Security: International Law and Policy Perspectives from Australia and New Zealand* (London: Routledge, 2009), pp. 186–201.
39 See Chris Rahman, 'Maritime Domain Awareness in Australia and New Zealand', in N. Klein, J. Mossop and D. Rothwell (eds), *Maritime Security: International Law and Policy Perspectives from Australia and New Zealand* (London: Routledge, 2009), pp. 202–223.
40 *Maritime Patrol Review*, (Wellington: Department of Prime Minister and Cabinet, 2001).
41 *Maritime Patrol Review*, p. 9. The review found that Orions undertook surveillance of local waters for just 2–3 per cent of each year, and some areas of the ocean were rarely overflown.
42 Ibid.
43 The Orion aircraft spent approximately 9 per cent of total annual hours flown on New Zealand maritime surveillance, mainly for fisheries and search and rescue tasks. This compared with 15–20 per cent of the time spend in surveillance of the South Pacific. The Ministry of Fisheries estimated that in-shore areas were receiving 5 per cent of the required level of surveillance and offshore areas less than 20 per cent. Ibid, p. 10.
44 Ibid, p. 38.
45 Ibid, pp. 10–11.
46 Ibid, p. 41.
47 Cabinet Minute (06) 47/3.
48 *National Maritime Coordination Centre Governance Framework* (Wellington: NMCC, 2006), p. 10.
49 The shape of Project Protector can be traced to the *Maritime Forces Review*, 2002, www.defence.govt.nz.
50 *Defence Long-Term Development Plan*, 2006 Update, Ministry of Defence 2006, pp. 17–20.
51 See www.navy.mil.nz. *HMNZS Canterbury* was launched on 27 October 2007.
52 HMNZS *Otago* was launched on 18 October 2006, and HMNZS *Wellington* was launched on 27 October 2007. Both ships are now in service.
53 HMNZS *Hawea* was launched on 11 December 2007 and HMNZS *Rotoiti* was due for delivery in mid-2008. Both ships are now in service.
54 Defence Long-Term Development Plan, 2006 Update, Ministry of Defence 2006, pp. 23–24.
55 Pete Hodgson, 'Ocean Survey 20/20 launch speech', 16 March 2005, www.beehive.govt.nz/speech/ocean+survey+2020+launch+speech.
56 See www.linz.govt.nz/hydro/projects-programmes/ocean-survey-2020/work-programme/index.aspx.
57 See J. Mossop, 'Achieving Effective Governance of New Zealand's Oceans', in J. Veitch (ed.), *Strategic Manoeuvres: Security in the Asia-Pacific* (Wellington: Centre for Strategic Studies, 2009).
58 R. Bess and R. Rallapudi, 'Spatial Conflicts in New Zealand Fisheries: the Rights of Fishers and Protection of the Environment', *Marine Policy* 31, 2007, pp. 719–729.

59 For further information on Oceans Policy in New Zealand, see J. Mansell, 'The Voyage Towards National Oceans Policy in New Zealand – Encountering Rocks and Shoals', *Maritime Studies*, 137, 2004, pp. 1–12; R. Peart, *Looking Out to Sea: New Zealand as a Model for Ocean Governance* (Auckland: Environmental Defence Society, 2005); J. Vince and M. Haward, 'New Zealand Oceans Governance: Calming Turbulent Waters?', *Marine Policy* 33, 2009, pp. 412–418; and P. Cozens, 'Maritime Security and Oceans Policy', in N. Klein, J. Mossop and D. Rothwell (eds), *Maritime Security: International Law and Policy Perspectives from Australia and New Zealand* (London: Routledge, 2009), pp. 155–171.

Conclusion

Identifying common maritime challenges and priorities

Sam Bateman

The chapters in this volume show the complexity of the maritime security environment in the Asia-Pacific region. Regional countries face many and varied maritime security challenges,[1] and have different priorities for dealing with them. Governments view the challenges according to their own particular national security perspective and threat perception. Some countries have a relatively benign view of the threats they face, but others, notably India, see themselves as a "threat attractor" confronted by many threats, including the unpredictable.[2] The problem is exacerbated because intelligence agencies are notoriously weak at predicting unforeseen developments that might have a major impact on security. Uncertainty is a clear theme running through many chapters, with authors identifying the possibility of new threats and challenges.

This conclusion examines the overlaps between the various challenges faced by regional countries and identifies the common maritime challenges that states try to address at an interstate level to achieve good order at sea. The four historic attributes of the sea are used as a framing device for the analysis.[3]

Defining maritime security

It is apparent from chapters in this volume that regional countries have different views on what constitutes maritime security. Some include non-traditional security threats, but others appear sensitive to going too far by including environmental threats and illegal fishing. Traditional maritime security threats, involving defence against military threats and the protection of national interests and sovereignty at sea, still figure prominently in the maritime security challenges and priorities of virtually all regional countries. However, the perspectives of individual countries vary according to their geographical circumstances, particularly whether or not they have extensive maritime zones, and their national maritime interests, such as whether they have large national shipping fleets or distant water fishing interests. For the United States, as a global sea power, a key maritime challenge is to protect the global maritime system.[4]

The two large archipelagic countries, Indonesia and the Philippines, have extensive areas of maritime jurisdiction as a consequence of the introduction in the 1982 UN Convention on the Law of the Sea of the regime of the archipelagic state. They prefer a broad definition of maritime security that takes into account their concerns for marine environmental protection; illegal, unregulated and unreported (IUU) fishing; and the safety of shipping passing through their archipelagic waters. As Hasjim Djalal discusses in his chapter, the sea plays a key role in the Indonesian Government meeting the ongoing challenge of maintaining national unity and the integrity of the Indonesia state.[5] The Philippines has major concerns for security within its archipelagic waters, especially measures to control the high incidence of trafficking in drugs, arms and people within and in and out of the Philippine archipelago, and the safety of shipping given the incidence of shipping accidents in Philippine waters.[6]

As island nations with large areas of maritime jurisdiction, both Australia and New Zealand tend towards a comprehensive view of maritime security. For New Zealand, traditional security concerns and some transnational crime issues are lessened due to the distance of its neighbours,[7] but these remain priorities for Australia, which, with its closer proximity to Asia, sees the maintenance of regional security as an important challenge.

The larger regional countries also tend to prefer a wider definition of maritime security. Japan has long had a comprehensive view of national security that recognises its critical vulnerability to the disruption of its seaborne imports of energy and other strategic commodities.[8] Concerns for the security of sea lines of communication (SLOC) have led to Japan taking a leading role in establishing cooperative measures to ensure the safety and security of shipping in the Malacca and Singapore Straits and to contribute to anti-piracy operations off the Horn of Africa.[9]

China also leans towards a broader definition of maritime security with its concept of a "harmonious ocean", which includes enhancing China's maritime security "not only in terms of naval strength but also security responses, such as environmental protection and disaster relief".[10] Non-traditional security issues, such as energy, people smuggling, maritime drug trafficking, maritime environmental protection, fishery disputes and so on, are now being incorporated into the scholarly and policy discourses of maritime security in China, although many Chinese scholars still take a hard realist view of maritime security, focussing on the military dimensions of sea power.[11]

On the other hand, countries that have relatively small maritime zones, such as Thailand, and are also distant water fishing nations are hesitant to include fishing issues within the definition of maritime security. Singapore similarly leans towards a narrow definition due to its small area of maritime jurisdiction and extensive shipping interests. Singapore has exploited its geographical location to the fullest extent possible to develop a comprehensive maritime sector encompassing entrepot trade, ship repair and maintenance, oil refining, ship building, offshore support, bunkering and so on.[12] These activities and interests dictate how Singapore views it maritime security challenges and priorities.

The sea as a resource

Many challenges related to managing the sea as a resource exist in the region. The sea has great significance as a resource for most regional countries, which have a heavy dependence on the living resources of the sea for food, and are also increasingly looking towards its non-living resources, particularly oil and gas, for their future economic prosperity. Economic development of the maritime sector is an important national challenge for most Asian countries.

Numerous chapters in this volume note the challenge faced by regional countries in maximising the economic benefits to be gained from the sea and its resources. Some countries, such as Japan and South Korea, have long recognised this challenge but others, notably China, have only begun to attach importance to the maritime sector in more recent times. In his chapter, Wilfried A. Herrmann describes the challenges faced by Thailand in developing the maritime sector, including the difficulties posed by a lack of maritime awareness in the population.[13]

At a national level, some countries have pursued comprehensive national oceans policies or maritime strategies for managing their maritime interests on an inter-sectoral basis. Australia's Oceans Policy had the ambitious objective of setting in place the framework for integrated and ecosystem-based planning and management for all of Australia's marine jurisdictions.[14] The Japanese and Chinese chapters in this volume describe how both countries are in the process of developing comprehensive maritime strategies (or oceans policies) for managing their maritime interests.

As evidenced by the chapters in this volume, competition over resources is particularly acute in the South China Sea. All of the countries bordering this sea regard access to its resources as important for their future prosperity and security. Ensuring access to the South China Sea and its resources is identified by Nguyen Hong Thao as a huge challenge for Vietnam.[15] Apart from the potential value of oil and gas reserves in the South China Sea, much of the total animal protein consumed by the Vietnamese people comes from this sea.

Cooperative arrangements for the sustainable development of the living resources of regional seas are a pressing requirement. These resources are under increasing threat from the destruction of marine habitats and increased pollution, particularly from extensive coastal developments. Without these cooperative arrangements, there are real risks of a "tragedy of the commons" where all countries eventually lose. Other emerging threats include climate change and sea level rise that are being addressed by countries with varying degrees of interest.

There is a clear lack of regimes for achieving the effective management of regional seas and oceans and their resources. Emmers has pointed out how two primary factors, nationalism and resources, can interact with each other to inhibit cooperative solutions to sovereignty disputes.[16] A nationalistic drive for sovereign control of territory and resources underlies the increasing tension that exists in the region over conflicting claims to sovereignty over offshore islands. This nationalistic fervour has been particularly evident with the dispute between

Japan and South Korea over the Takeshima/Tokdo Islands. Such fervour adds to the difficulties of finding an amicable and peaceful solution to offshore sovereignty disputes.

Controversial issues regarding the law of the sea are evident in the seas of East Asia that inhibit the exploitation of the resource potential of regional seas. The chain of seas between mainland Asia and the off-lying Japanese, Philippine and Indonesian archipelagos, and the islands and groups of islands within these seas, mean that many maritime boundaries are required, as well as a common understanding of rights and duties in the several maritime zones. These waters are virtually all subject to the jurisdiction of one state or another. However, fundamentally different views exist in the region over the rights and duties of states in the maritime zones, particularly for the exclusive economic zones (EEZs).

A balance is required between the rights and duties of a coastal state and those of other states.[17] In an EEZ, coastal states have sovereign rights over natural resources, both living and non-living, and other economic activities, such as the production of energy from the water, currents and winds.[18] They also have jurisdiction with regard to artificial islands, installations and structures; marine scientific research; and the protection and preservation of the marine environment (including the conservation of species), as well as other rights and duties, as provided for in the relevant provisions of UNCLOS.[19] However, sovereign rights to marine resources gained under the EEZ regime are not without their costs in terms of the obligations of the coastal state to preserve and protect the marine environment and conserve species in the EEZ, and to have due regard to the rights and duties of other states in its EEZ.[20]

The sea as a medium of transportation and exchange

The sea is the preferred medium for the illegal movement of goods and people. Larger quantities of cargo can be shipped at sea, generally with less risk of detection. Illicit shipments can also be transhipped at sea and brought into a country in a vessel, such as a local fishing boat, without detection by local authorities. Drug traffickers recognise that, because of the huge volume of worldwide commercial trade, it is almost impossible for custom authorities to inspect every single container or item of cargo without causing major delays and large economic losses. South-East Asia is an important hub for human smuggling from Afghanistan, Pakistan and the Middle East to elsewhere in the world. There is also evidence of human trafficking of women and children in South-East Asia for sex or forced labour purposes. Small arms and light weapons are widely available in the region and trafficking by sea is the preferred means of their movement.

The one maritime security challenge that appears to be a common concern of regional countries is the provision of security and safety for shipping and seaborne trade. This is understandable as the dependence on the seaborne carriage of intraregional trade in Asia is relatively much greater than within Europe or North America. Other than on the Malay Peninsula, and parts of the Indian subcontinent and China, the region lacks a developed road and rail infrastructure, and the vast proportion of intraregional trade must be carried by sea except for high value cargoes carried by air. Seaborne trade has been a key facilitator of regional economic growth and a large proportion of that trade (about half, even excluding the energy trade from South-West Asia) is intraregional within Asia rather than interregional to other parts of the world.[21]

The concern for the safety and security of shipping extends to a common interest in countering piracy and maritime terrorist threats, as well as a concern for search and rescue (SAR) and other marine safety services, particularly in regional choke points, such as the Malacca and Singapore Straits. The chapter by Yee Cheok Hong addresses the concern that increased shipping traffic density may pose unacceptable risks to shipping passing through these straits. However, his conclusion is that increased traffic levels are manageable for the foreseeable future in line with improved traffic management measures and technological advances.[22]

As Geoff Till argues, dependence on sea transport can be a source of both weakness and strength: weakness because of the vulnerability to disruption, and strength because it is a common interest that can provide a basis for cooperation.[23] In Asia, the dependence on sea transport is still more of a weakness. We are yet to see it emerge as a strength because, despite a lot of talk in regional forums, both Track One and Track Two, not a lot of cooperation has emerged so far, with the notable exception of the Malacca Strait with the introduction of the Malacca Strait Patrols and the Cooperative Mechanism for Safety and Environmental Protection.[24]

The security of SLOCs is cited by many regional countries as justification for expanding their navies. However, this may be a politically acceptable reason and the real explanation for naval expansion may lie in concerns about a traditional threat from a possible regional adversary. A threat to SLOCs has to come from somewhere, but countries are reluctant to share their threat perceptions in this regard.

The sea as a medium for information and the spread of ideas

This attribute should be an important one for Asia, but while it has been very evident in the past, it is less evident in contemporary circumstances. Regional approaches to the sea as a medium for information and the spread of ideas are muted at present. Some regional countries, particularly the archipelagic states, have a strong cultural affinity with the sea. While using the sea to build national solidarity, Indonesia has also developed a strong outward-looking interest in the high seas and international seabed areas,[25] and has become a world leader in maritime affairs by, for example, hosting major ocean-related international conferences, such as the World Ocean Conference (WOC) in May 2009. Other countries are more inward-looking with regard to the sea and exhibit a strong nationalistic approach to maritime affairs that limits the spread of maritime information and ideas across the region.

This is evident with the lack of success in the region in implementing Part IX of UNCLOS. This part of the convention is important for building good order in regional seas. It mandates a relatively high level of cooperation between countries bordering enclosed and semi-enclosed seas, such as the East and South China seas, but so far cooperation in these seas has failed to reach even a minimal level of effectiveness. All the seas of East Asia are "semi-enclosed seas" within the definition in Article 122 of UNCLOS.

The Regional Seas Programme (RSP) established by the United Nations Environment Programme (UNEP) provides the framework for action plans adopted by countries to implement their obligations under Part IX. Unfortunately, difficulties have been encountered with implementing these action plans. The RSPs in the Mediterranean and Caribbean seas have not achieved the desired outcomes and experience so far with the East Asian Seas Action Plan developed by the Coordinating Body on the Seas of East Asia (COBSEA) gives few grounds for optimism that successful outcomes will be achieved.[26] The lack of political will and the diversity of bordering countries underpin this pessimistic outlook.

The sea as a medium of dominion

The attribute of the sea as a medium for dominion invites consideration of the more traditional maritime security threats in the ocean. Regional countries with their growing naval budgets see such threats as possible, and the larger countries, notably China and India, are using their navies in a classical Mahanian manner to project power and influence. The capabilities being acquired by regional navies are not to deal with non-traditional threats but are rather for conventional warfare. The sinking of the South Korean corvette *Cheonan*, reportedly by the North Koreans, is a stark reminder of the extent to which traditional state-on-state rivalries still underlie naval development in the Asia-Pacific as elsewhere.[27]

There is little evidence, other than in rhetorical statements, that Asian navies are shifting towards new threats associated with the containment of international terrorism and nuclear proliferation and the maintenance of good order at sea. Most regional navies have no role in protecting and preserving the marine environment or conserving its resources. In fact, it is not navies but rather coast guards that are being developed to enforce national laws associated with these tasks, for the simple reason that these forces can cooperate more easily with each other without the sensitivities that can be associated with naval cooperation. While regional navies are still focussed on their traditional war-fighting roles, coast guards, or equivalent forces, are being increasingly used for maritime policing and, even in the case of the Japan Coast Guard, for tasks far from home waters to support foreign policy.[28]

Conventional security challenges are evident in many of the chapters in this volume. Disputed areas of maritime sovereignty and overlapping maritime boundaries between neighbouring countries are possible sources of interstate maritime conflict throughout the region. Myanmar, for example, sees a potential threat from Bangladesh to its north and to a lesser extent from Thailand in its south, and cites these threats as the reason for its projected naval build-up.[29] South Korea is another country that views the delimitation of maritime boundaries and the resolution of sovereignty disputes as major maritime priorities.[30] Other chapters have also identified the need to reach agreement on maritime boundaries and to secure maritime borders as key maritime security challenges.

The trend in the region towards higher defence spending is becoming a potential problem for maritime security. Military spending in real terms increased between 2008 and 2009 by 8.6 per cent in East Asia and 11 per cent in South Asia.[31] In February 2010, India announced a nearly 12 per cent increase in defence spending in its annual budget.[32] Almost in the same timeframe, China announced a 12.7 per cent increase in defence spending in 2011, compared with a 7.5 per cent increase in 2010.[33] Much of this increased spending is on naval capabilities. While some will argue that increased naval capabilities contribute to good order at sea and maritime security, an opposite view is that more naval activity in the region actually increases maritime insecurity and puts a premium on the importance of preventive diplomacy and confidence-building measures. It is not yet clear that regional forums are recognising the adverse consequences of naval expansion and modernisation in the region and showing any great preparedness to pursue preventive diplomacy and confidence-building measures.

It is clear from the perspectives of countries described in this volume that regional defence forces will be deploying more ships, submarines and aircraft into regional seas in the future. Submarines are of particular concern as they are likely to be deployed on covert surveillance and intelligence missions in disputed areas.[34] While there may not actually be a naval arms race, there is an arms dynamic in the region with prospects for a security dilemma as countries increase their defence spending because others are doing so.[35] Bilateral tensions are still evident in the region and the maritime domain is a source of vulnerability for most regional countries and a potential "springboard for aggressive maritime endeavour".[36]

Addressing the challenges

Intergovernmental security cooperation in the Asia-Pacific has been driven by the Association of Southeast Asian Nations (ASEAN). ASEAN has in turn spawned other forums, particularly the ASEAN Regional Forum (ARF); the East Asian Summit (EAS); ASEAN Plus Three, including China, Japan and South Korea; and the ASEAN Defence Ministers Meeting plus Eight (ADMM+8), all of which have some potential to address the challenges of maritime security.

Maritime security has been high on the agenda of both ASEAN and the ARF in recent years. After several years of talking about it, the ASEAN Maritime Forum (AMF) was eventually launched at its first meeting in Surabaya in July 2010. However, the forum will be "non-security centric" and will look at "other dimensions of maritime issues, such as the promotion of business through maritime cooperation".[37]

Focussed discussion of maritime security issues will take place at the ARF Inter-Sessional Meeting (ISM) on Maritime Security and at the Maritime Security Expert Working Group (MSEWG) established by the ADMM+8. The ISM has now had three meetings, with the last meeting in Tokyo in February 2011 agreeing a work plan for the group in which the following three priorities were identified: first, information and intelligence exchange and sharing of best practices, including transparency around naval capacity and operations; second, confidence-building measures based on international and legal frameworks, arrangements and cooperation; and third, capacity building of maritime law enforcement agencies in the region.[38] The MSEWG has not yet met. Indonesia, with its keen interest in maritime security, has said that when it takes over as ASEAN chair in 2011, it will include maritime security, particularly resolution of the South China Sea disputes, as one of the priority areas for special attention.[39]

Conclusion

The Asian region faces a range of maritime security challenges – both old and new. Unless these challenges are addressed, the region is at risk of ongoing, and even increasing, tensions at sea that could easily spiral into conflict. Although solutions to the problems may not emerge in the short term, at least by addressing the problems, the MSEWG and ARF ISM will provide some transparency and understanding. Through knowledge of each other's perspectives, countries may be better able to address the real concerns and issues behind their disagreements.

There is a temptation in regional forums to deal with the "softer" problems of maritime security, such as piracy, humanitarian assistance, disaster relief, SAR and the threat of maritime terrorism. It is relatively easy to reach consensus on what these challenges are and what needs to be done to meet them. Even so, it is sometimes still not easy to develop the necessary cooperation to deal with the challenges because even with these softer issues, nationalism and lack of political will can sometimes get in the way of effective cooperative measures.

The more difficult challenges are those associated with providing good order in regional seas in the face of conflicting maritime claims and the lack of maritime boundaries; and managing the risks of greater naval activity in the region and the possibility of interstate conflict.[40] Cooperative measures to improve the management of regional seas are an urgent requirement to ensure that the marine environment is better protected, marine living resources are sustainably developed and illegal activities more effectively countered.

The greatest maritime challenge faced by the region is the prospect of interstate conflict at sea. The risks of this challenge are increasing as navies expand their capabilities, tensions remain across the Taiwan Strait and on the Korean Peninsula, and no solution is found to the several conflicting claims to sovereignty in regional seas. There is a pressing requirement for measures of preventive diplomacy and confidence building to mitigate these risks.

Notes

1 Sam Bateman, "Managing Good Order at Sea in the Asia-Pacific", this volume, ch. 1.
2 Prabhakaran Paleri, "Maritime Challenges and Priorities in Asia: An Indian Perspective", this volume, ch. 16.

3 Geoffrey Till, "The Historic Attributes of the Sea and Maritime Developments in the Asia-Pacific", this volume, ch. 2.
4 James Kraska, "America's Maritime Challenges and Priorities: The Asian Dimension", this volume, ch. 14.
5 Hasjim Djalal, "Indonesia's Maritime Challenges and Priorities", this volume, ch. 4.
6 Mary Ann Palma, "Maintaining Good Order at Sea: Maritime Challenges and Priorities in the Philippines", this volume, ch. 7.
7 Joanna Mossop, "New Zealand's Maritime Challenges and Opportunities", this volume, ch. 17.
8 Tsuneo Akaha, "Japan's Comprehensive Security Policy: A New East Asian Environment", *Asian Survey*, 31 (4), 1991, pp. 324–340.
9 Tetsuo Kotani, "Japan's Maritime Challenges and Priorities", this volume, ch. 12.
10 Yang Minglie, "Sailing on a Harmonious Sea: A Chinese Perspective", *Global Asia*, Vol. 5 (4), Winter 2010, p. 24.
11 Wang Dong and Jiang Xin, "China's Maritime Security: Priorities and Challenges", this volume, ch. 11.
12 Joshua H. Ho, "Singapore's Maritime Interests", this volume, ch. 8.
13 Thailand, for example, as described by Wilfried A. Herrmann in "Thailand's Maritime Challenges and Priorities", this volume, ch. 9.
14 Robin Warner, "Australia's Maritime Challenges and Priorities: Recent Developments and Future Prospects", this volume, ch. 15.
15 Nguyen Hong Thao, "Good Order at Sea: Challenges and Priorities of Vietnam", this volume, ch. 10.
16 Ralf Emmers, "Japan–Korea Relations and the Tokdo/Takeshima Dispute: The Interplay of Nationalism and Natural Resources", *RSIS Working Paper*, No. 212, Singapore: S. Rajaratnam School of International Studies, 10 November 2010.
17 Robin R. Churchill and A.V. Lowe, *The Law of the Sea*, 3rd edn (Manchester: Manchester University Press, 1999), p. 175.
18 UNCLOS, Art. 56(1)(a).
19 UNCLOS, Art. 56(1)(b), (c).
20 UNCLOS, Art. 56(2).
21 UN Conference on Trade and Development (UNCTAD), *Review of Maritime Transport 2010* (United Nations: New York and Geneva, 2010), pp. 145–148 and Table 7.3.
22 Yee Cheok Hong, "Carriage Capacity of the Straits of Malacca and Singapore", this volume, ch. 3.
23 Geoffrey Till, "The Historic Attributes of the Sea".
24 Joshua H. Ho, "Singapore's Maritime Interests".
25 Hasjim Djalal, "Indonesia's Maritime Challenges and Priorities".
26 Alfred Hu Nien-Tsu, "Semi-enclosed Troubled Waters: A New Thinking on the Application of the 1982 UNCLOS Article 123 to the South China Sea", *Ocean Development and International Law* 41, No. 3 2010, pp. 281–314.
27 Geoffrey Till, "The Historic Attributes of the Sea".
28 Tetsuo Kotani, "Japan's Maritime Challenges and Priorities".
29 Maung Aung Myoe, "Myanmar's Maritime Challenges and Priorities", this volume, ch. 6.
30 Seokwoo Lee, "South Korea's Maritime Challenges and Priorities", this volume, ch. 13.
31 Stockholm International Peace Research Institute (SIPRI*), SIPRI Yearbook 2010 – Military Expenditure*, 2 June 2010, www.sipri.org/media/pressreleases/2010/pressreleasetranslations/storypackage_milex.
32 Agence France-Presse, "India Hikes Defense Spending by 12 percent", *Defense News*, 28 February 2011.
33 Robert Karniol, "Defining Beijing's defence stance", *The Straits Times*, 7 March 2011, p. A20.

34 Sam Bateman, "Perils of the Deep – The Dangers of Submarine Proliferation in the Seas of East Asia", *Asian Security* 7 (1), 2011, pp. 61–84.
35 Richard A. Bitzinger, "A New Arms Race? Explaining Recent Southeast Asian Military Acquisitions", *Contemporary Southeast Asia*, Vol. 32 (1), 2010, pp. 50–69.
36 Geoffrey Till, "The Historic Attributes of the Sea".
37 Termsak Chalermpalanupap, Director of Political and Security Directorate, ASEAN Secretariat, Jakarta, "ASEAN and Maritime Security: An Update", paper presented at Centre for International Law Workshop on International Maritime Crimes: Legal Issues and Prospects for Cooperation in ASEAN, Singapore, 17–18 January, 2011, p. 3.
38 Ibid., p. 5.
39 Evan Laksama, "Jakarta Eyes South China Sea", *The Diplomat*, 23 February 2011, http://the-diplomat.com/flashpoints-blog/2011/02/23/jakarta-eyes-south-china-sea/.
40 Sam Bateman, "Solving the 'Wicked Problems' of Maritime Security: Are Regional Forums up to the Task?", *Contemporary South East Asia*, Vol. 33 (1) (2011), pp. 1–28.

Index